HISTORY AND THEORY

Sharlene Sayegh

California State University, Long Beach

Eric Altice

California State University, Long Beach

PEARSON

Boston Columbus Indianapolis New York San Francisco Upper Saddle River
Amsterdam Cape Town Dubai London Madrid Milan Munich Paris Montréal Toronto
Delhi Mexico City São Paulo Sydney Hong Kong Seoul Singapore Taipei Tokyo

Editor in Chief: Ashley Dodge
Editorial Assistant: Amandria Guadalupe
Director of Marketing: Brandy Dawson
Executive Marketing Manager: Kelly May
Marketing Coordinator: Theresa Rotondo
Managing Editor: Denise Forlow
Program Manager: Kathy Sleys
Senior Operations Supervisor: Mary Fischer
Operations Specialist: Eileen Corallo
Art Director: Jayne Conte

Cover Designer: Suzanne Behnke
Cover Image: marekuliasz/Shutterstock
Director of Digital Media: Brian Hyland
Digital Media Editor: Learning Mate Solutions, Ltd.
Digital Media Project Manager: Tina Gagliostro
Full-Service Project Management and Composition:
 Sneha Pant/PreMediaGlobal
Printer/Binder: R.R. Donnelley
Cover Printer: R.R. Donnelley
Text Font: 11/13.5 Minion Pro Regular

Credits and acknowledgments borrowed from other sources and reproduced, with permission, in this textbook appear on appropriate page within text.

Many of the designations by manufacturers and seller to distinguish their products are claimed as trademarks. Where those designations appear in this book, and the publisher was aware of a trademark claim, the designations have been printed in initial caps or all caps.

Library of Congress Cataloging-in-Publication Data
Sayegh, Sharlene.
 History and theory / Sharlene Sayegh, California State University, Long Beach, Eric Altice, California State University, Long Beach.
  pages   cm
 Includes bibliographical references and index.
 ISBN-13: 978-0-13-615725-0
 ISBN-10: 0-13-615725-4
 1. Historiography—Textbooks.   I. Altice, Eric.   II. Title.
 D13.S3637 2013
 907.2—dc23

2013029814

ISBN 10: 0-13-615725-4
ISBN 13: 978-0-13-615725-0

CONTENTS

Preface   vii
About the Authors   ix

1   The Importance of Theory in History   1
   Empiricism or Theory: Does It Have to Be an
      "either/or"?   1
   Case Study: The History of Slavery   3
   Text Goals and Chapter Organization   5
      1.   *Introducing Historical Materialism (Chapters 3–6)*   5
      2.   *Cultural Approaches to History (Chapters 7–10)*   6
   Your Reservoir of Knowledge—Just the Tip of the
      Iceberg   6
   Endnotes   7

2   Professionalization of History: Time and
   Science in the Historical Method   8
   History from the Ancient World to the
      Enlightenment   8
   From Enlightenment to Progressive History (18th–19th
      Centuries)   11
   The Move to Objectivity, Professionalism, and Critiques
      of Progressive Histories   14
   Endnotes   16

3   Marxist History   17
   Marxist and Materialist Philosophy in Historical
      Context   19
   The Influence of Marx and Engels on Twentieth-
      Century Historical Writing   23
   Conclusion   25
   Thinking Like a Historian   26
      Primary Source: Jack Bryant, "Sunny Cal"   26
      Secondary Source: Christopher Hill, "John Bunyan and
         His Publics"   27
   Endnotes   31

4   The *Annales* School   33
   The First Generation—Bloch, Febvre, and "*Histoire
      Totale*"   34
   The Second Generation—Fernand Braudel and the
      Waves of Time   35
   The Third Generation—Le Roy Ladurie and Goubert:
      Making the *Annales* French   37
   The Fourth Generation—Roger Chartier and the
      Rediscovery of *Mentalités*   38
   Conclusion   40
   Thinking Like a Historian   40
      Primary Source: Chart: "Share of World GDP,
         1700–1890"   41
      Secondary Source: Fernand Braudel, "Towards a Serial
         History: Seville and the Atlantic, 1504–1650"   41
   Endnotes   48

5   The Transformation of Marxism—The New Left
   and Social History   50
   The British New Left   51
   The American New Left   53
   Western-European Marxism   55
   The Global New Left—Dependency Theory and
      World-Systems Theory   57
   The Impact of the New Lefts: Social History   58
   Conclusion   59
   Thinking Like a Historian   59
      Primary Source: "Mrs. Walter Pinkus": Name and Address
         of Informant Mrs Walter Pinkus, 2710-8   60
      Secondary Source: John Styles, "Time Piece: Working
         Men and Watches"   61
   Endnotes   65

6   Environmental History   68
   Natural History Through the Frontier Thesis and the
      Longue Durée: Roots of Environmental History   69

Approaching the Environment—Material or Cultural? 70

A Global Environmental History 72

Conclusion 74

Thinking Like a Historian 75

Primary Source: "Wheat" 75

Secondary Source: Richard Grove and Toyin Falola, "Chiefs, Boundaries and Sacred Woodlands: Early Nationalism and the Defeat of Colonial Conservationism in the Gold Coast and Nigeria, 1870–1916" 78

Endnotes 92

7 Post-Structuralism and Deconstruction 95

Modernism and Structuralism 96

Postmodernism 97

Post-Structuralism 98

Discourse 99

Normativity 99

The Gaze 100

Deconstruction 100

A Conclusion—Influences on the Profession 102

Thinking Like a Historian 103

Primary Source: Ordinary's Account, 19th July 1700 103

Secondary Source: David Gaimster, "Sex and Sensibility at the British Museum" 106

Endnotes 110

8 Cultural History 112

Interdisciplinary Origins 112

Early Historical Studies of Culture 114

The 'Linguistic Turn' 117

Defining the History of Culture—Some Conclusions 118

Thinking Like a Historian 119

Primary Source: "The Reconstruction Policy of Congress, as Illustrated in California" 120

Secondary Source: Robert Darnton, "The Great Cat Massacre, 1730" 121

Endnotes 127

9 Feminist and Gender History 129

Feminism—A Political Movement 130

From Women's History to Feminist History 131

Gender Theory and History 134

Queer Theory 136

Conclusion 137

Thinking Like a Historian 137

Primary Source: Revisit Chapter 5's "Mrs. Walter Pinkus" 138

Secondary Source: Tanika Sarkar, "Women in South Asia: The Raj and After" 138

Endnotes 143

10 Subaltern Studies, Postcolonial Theory, and the History of Race and Nation 145

Europe and the New Imperialism 145

Postcolonial Theory 146

Subaltern Studies 149

Theories and Histories of Race and Nation 150

Conclusion 153

Thinking Like a Historian 153

Primary Source: Arthur Horner, "Homecoming: Sour note from an Ungrateful Patrial" 154

Secondary Source: Partha Chatterjee, "Bengal: Rise and Growth of a Nationality" 154

Endnotes 163

Glossary 166

Further Reading 170

Index 174

PREFACE

To our families, with love and gratitude for their patience, and to our students,
without whose earnest desire to learn, this book would not have been written.

MAKING THE DECISION to write yet another textbook on twentieth-century historiography when there are already so many on the market may seem puzzling to some readers. This text was actually a long time in the making, emerging organically from our teaching styles and the nature of the core curriculum program at California State University, Long Beach. Our experiences in leading undergraduate seminars in Theory and History convinced us of the value of such a course. Our students consistently emerge better prepared to read secondary works more critically and to consider more complex modes of interpreting primary documents. At the same time, we were frustrated by our inability to find a text that seemed suitable to the class. Many were pitched too high, appropriate for faculty or advanced graduate students, but would lose our bright undergrads. Those tailored more for undergraduates sometimes seemed to sacrifice substance in the name of readability. We each tried several texts in our classes but none quite hit the nail on the head for us in terms of providing the kinds of interconnectivity between activism, philosophy, and the construction of meaningful stories about the past. So, after several years under our belt of teaching this course, of comparing our experiences helping students develop more sophisticated critical-reading skills, of researching different approaches to history, we had a conversation in our office and asked ourselves, "why not write our own book?" So we approached the then editor, Charles Cavaliere, about the project who very enthusiastically supported our book proposal and the beginning stages of writing. Charles has since left Pearson, but we thank him for his early support of this project. Since then, we have since been blessed with three helpful editors: Rob de George, Ashley Dodge, and Nicole Suddeth, all of whom supported this project whenever we found our energy waning.

In terms of organization, we decided simply to model the text after our own syllabi, following the trajectory of history writing in the West from professionalization in the late nineteenth century through the end of the twentieth century. We also wanted to make this book a reader and have therefore included where possible works that have had demonstrated success in our classrooms or were chosen specifically to provide a broader understanding of particular theories. Another aspect to this reader was the conscious decision to include primary as well as secondary sources. We approached the task of composing this book with the idea that we were not just teaching theory but preparing young historians for their encounters with primary documents. We knew other historiography readers did not attempt to have students role play particular theoretical positions to give them a sense of the worldview of the historians they read about in the text. This book does both.

As with all books, this one has benefited from the direct and indirect help of students, colleagues, and friends. From our graduate-school seminars in which we debated particular approaches, to our own courses, we owe debts of gratitude. Sayegh's work with scholars Jacques Derrida, Fredric Jameson, Mark Poster, Lawrence E. Klein, Kenneth Pomeranz, and Robert Moeller not only helped her to better conceptualize her own point of view, but also to think about how she might teach this material to her own students. For Altice, the list of scholars who have shaped his understanding of history and the attempt to apply theory is equally long: Joyce Appleby, Steve Aron, Barbara Loomis, Paul Longmore, Ellen Dubois, and Henry Yu all contributed, sometimes in ways they may not even realize.

We are very thankful to our friends and students who read all or parts of this manuscript. Danielle Cook,

Stefanie Lira, and John Marquez provided unique student perceptions and insight about where students might have problems with particular explanations. David Sheridan, our colleague and good friend who also teaches this class, has listened to numerous comments and explanations on approaches to the text, giving helpful advice as to direction and language. We owe a huge debt of gratitude to Laurie Chin Sayres who patiently read every single chapter of this book—some chapters more than once. Her fresh set of eyes and her own experience of teaching the history and theory seminar helped us to ensure the clarity of our discussions. Her constant support for this project, her fantastic listening skills, and her unwavering friendship have been priceless.

Sayegh would like to thank California State University, Long Beach for the Fall 2011 sabbatical that enabled her to finish a large portion of the manuscript. The Department of History, particularly the chair Nancy

Quam-Wickham, has also provided emotional and intellectual support for us over the last two years.

We would like to thank all of the blind reviewers, whose perceptions, teaching reflections, and comparative analyses were absolutely invaluable. We would also like to thank these reviwers: Todd Berryman, Hendrix College; Yung-chen Chiang, DePauw University; Robert LaFleur, Beloit College; and Anne Wohlcke, California State Polytechnic University, Pomona.

The editorial staff at Pearson and PreMedia Global has been wonderful as we moved this book into production. We thank Nicole Suddeth, Kathleen Sleys, Melissa Sacco, Sherry Sprague, Sneha Pant, and the countless others who helped transform this manuscript to a book.

Finally, we would like to thank our families: Chris, Fred, and Bridget Canada (Sayegh), and Miki, Kan, and Victoria Altice. Patient, loving support is the best support in the world.

ABOUT THE AUTHORS

A SELF-DESCRIBED (and student-acclaimed) "theory head," **Sharlene Sayegh** received her Ph.D. in history and critical theory from the University of California, Irvine. She has taught in the Department of History at California State, Long Beach for 15 years, where she also serves as the department's core curriculum coordinator. She is the University's Director of Program Review and Assessment, helping to guide the campus into best practices for student learning and engagement. A winner of the university's Distinguished Faculty Teaching Award as well as the World History Association's Teaching Prize, she remains committed to enhancing student learning and to sharing ideas about effective teaching with her colleagues. She is currently working on a microhistory of women, business and identity formation in eighteenth-century London, but still finds time to fly kites with her family, read *Harry Potter*, and watch the occasional television show.

Eric Altice received his Ph.D. in history from the University of California, Los Angeles. He taught in the Department of History at California State University, Long Beach, for nine years, and currently teaches for UCLA through the Global Classroom classroom in Nanjing, China.

A life-long traveler with earlier experience of living and teaching in China and Japan, he is currently working on a variety of essays exploring globalization, class formation, culture, and identity, while studying Chinese and maintaining a personal project of compiling a list of good, cheap, Chinese restaurants in Nanjing.

CHAPTER 1

THE IMPORTANCE OF THEORY IN HISTORY

CHAPTER OUTLINE

■ Empiricism or Theory: Does It Have to Be an "either/or"?

■ Case Study: The History of Slavery

■ Text Goals and Chapter Organization

■ Your Reservoir of Knowledge—Just the Tip of the Iceberg

"All theory is provisional. The notion of having one consistent, all-embracing theory is itself a heresy . . . I think of theory as critique, theory as polemic . . . Sometimes people talk as if you can have a methodology without a theory or as if you can keep the theory inside a locked drawer in the desk."

E.P. Thompson[1]

EMPIRICISM OR THEORY: DOES IT HAVE TO BE AN "EITHER/OR"?

As you noticed your reading list and saw this text, and as you opened its pages for the first time, you may have asked yourself, "why do I need to learn about theory? Isn't it the job of the historian to be as objective as possible and doesn't all that theory stuff just get in the way? What does this have to do with me and my education?" Certainly, historians search for meaning in the past and some "truth" that the past might convey to us. Most of us encounter histories—in books or on film—that emphasize grand narratives that, at least implicitly, focus on retention of critical information about any given topic (the French Revolution, Westward Expansion of the United States, etc.). These traditional approaches typically do not explore the **historiography** of that topic or reveal the various methods and techniques that could open up fresh ways of understanding the subject. All the debates between historians (and there are always debates on any important historical topic) and the use of theoretical frameworks for understanding the subject are submerged, often leaving the impression that the current story being presented is the only way to understand the past. As you continue through this text, it is our goal that you will not view history as a collection of facts about the past, but as a vibrant field that constructs various, sometimes competing understandings about the past, constructions that usually tell us a lot about our own society. In other words, as a profession, history seeks to uncover some truth about why the past was the way it was, and in some cases how it influences why today is the way it is.

Some practicing historians, however, are wary of such claims. According to many people, lay and professional historian alike, the business, or practice of writing history is patently untheoretical. Historians in this model claim to deal with tangible, touchable, unmediated, and raw facts that are put together like puzzle pieces. And once those pieces are placed together in the proper order, the "truth" will be clear. Theory is relegated to the sidelines, alternately scoffed at or ignored. By the time readers of history have encountered "history and theory," the theory part has been given a cold shoulder, accused of gross misdeeds against proper historical method. Who needs it, anyway?

For example, the social historian Lawrence Stone accused historians who employed **postmodern** techniques of abandoning the principles on which the historical discipline is situated. Stone argued that they contributed to the degeneration of historical method because they used sources from linguistics, cultural anthropology, or literature while neglecting "the real" facts that make up evidence. The issue of having a monopoly of what constitutes the real is a crucial aspect of historical debate in the last forty years. What exactly is real? Language? Dates? Events? Perception? Respondents to his claims argued that Stone misunderstood the way theory operates in our own discipline.[2]

Other critics have argued that that history is simply an **empirical** approach to the past. But this argument falls flat when we examine the evidence. Francis Bacon (1561–1626) put forward the concept of the scientific method in the seventeenth century in *Novum Organum*. The scientific method relies on making a hypothesis, then observing data, and finally reaching a conclusion about the viability of the hypothesis. Can history duplicate this method? Sure it can, that is why it is often considered as part of the "social sciences." Like scientists, historians generate hypotheses (or theories), observe the data, and then reach conclusions based on the observations of the data (or primary sources). Over time, this approach has shifted; rather than find "the truth" as if there were only one narrative, historians now search for "a truth" about the past. This shift has occurred as historians have increasingly recognized that they help to construct identities and meanings. In other words, historians interpret the evidence.

Interpretation is based on the ways in which we read the evidence, and we all read evidence differently. We are informed by our contexts (when and where we are in time and place) as well as by our view of the world.

For example, and we will explore this later in the text, the pioneers of working-class history embraced the evidence workers provided through a variety of sources and believed that workers' stories were just as legitimate as the stories about labor from governments and institutions. These historians were often deeply engrossed in labor movements to begin with, and thus their interpretations were based in part by their personal convictions. The same development applies for women's history and ethnic studies: as women and members of ethnic minorities pried open the previously barred doors to academia, they have brought with them perspectives rooted in their own experiences, and those perspectives have influenced their scholarly activities, creating a seismic shift in scholarship as new voices have been incorporated into old narratives.

Gender, race, ethnicity, and class are not the only factors that shape the perspective of the scholars who create, and the audiences that consume history. Ideas, or theories, also change. Beliefs that at one historical moment might have made sense to many people in society (e.g., notions of sexual or racial inferiority in the nineteenth century) may seem absurd at a later time, and thus compel historians to go back and reevaluate the work of earlier scholars writing from that erstwhile set of assumptions. This process of reevaluating both the past and the history of the past also leads to some new thorny questions: where did those original, absurd beliefs come from, and how did they become so powerful?

As E.P. Thompson stated in the quote that opens this book, these interpretations of the past are based on particular theories and those theories change. One reason they change, or are provisional, is because the context in which one writes changes. Historians, like their historical subjects, are confined by the time and place in which they write. They also learn from previous contexts. So a historian writing in 1997 can note why historians made the claims they did in 1965 and 1952. We have hindsight, history, to help us along in some ways.

However, it is not enough simply to say that historians are "products of their times." Any particular period in the life of a society is complex, and in a large, modern society, there are a variety of ways in which people relate to each other. We come from different backgrounds (class, race, sex, etc.), we are raised in different places of the world (imperial/colonized), we have different ideological standpoints (liberal versus conservative), and so on. We are not all the same, and those differences in experience lead to different questions. Because historians ask different questions, they often find new evidence. They look in places other historians had not, they find innovative ways of looking at the same material, or they read primary documents with a different eye, a new pair of lenses so to speak. The vast array of historians, studying the past from their various social and intellectual positions, and engaged in sometimes long-running debates with historians who came before them, makes the field of history far more vibrant than the standard university textbook lets on. Just beneath the tectonic plates of the seemingly stable grand narrative, historical debates run like fault lines, and historians embrace different sources, and frequently different theories, in search of new ways of understanding the past. So it is that we discover that the business of writing history is an ever-changing process. If it were not, there would be no place for newer scholars. Once we had found all the evidence, then that would be it. But history is not stagnant, and a primary reason is because of the theory embedded in all historical thought.

In fact, the study of theory provides a set of conceptual tools that you can apply in other fields, and indeed in a variety of courses throughout the social sciences and humanities. Various fields in the humanities and social sciences share a common set of conceptual categories in which scholars work. Thus, as you explore the ideas of Karl Marx on wage labor, Michel Foucault on discourse, or Benedict Anderson on nationalism, you are exploring concepts and developing a critical vocabulary that will equip you to analyze a wide variety of texts in various fields. Armed with that set of concepts, you will better understand the **monographs** you later encounter. Rather than reading simply for the historical content, you will approach a text aware of the fact that historians usually frame their historical narrative within a set of theoretical questions regarding the nature of gender, race, class development, or language.

CASE STUDY: THE HISTORY OF SLAVERY

An example from the history of slavery in the United States may better help you understand how we approach historiography in this text. In 1918, U.B. Phillips wrote a seminal history of American slavery. Relying largely on plantation records that described daily plantation life, Phillips concluded that slaves had been largely happy and loyal, and the institution of slavery

basically gentle, and at times benevolent, even going so far as to compare plantations to schools. Roughly forty years later, another eminent historian, Stanley Elkins, examined many of the same records but arrived at drastically different conclusions. What Phillips saw as peaceful, loyal, happy slaves, Elkins wrote, were individuals who suffered from such complete domination, and who had been so totally culturally uprooted, that they had developed a sycophantic identity with their oppressors. Rather than schools, Elkins explicitly compared the plantations to concentration camps, equating the slaves with prisoners, and the masters with guards. Three decades later, a new group of historians found something quite different. Again, drawing largely on the plantation records that provide the most complete information about plantation life, historians such as John Blassingame presented a more heroic, resistant picture of slave life. For Blassingame, the story of slavery was not one of complete cultural destruction, but one of cultural retention; the superficially harmonious relations between masters and slaves were a mask, a means of slaves making their way in the world of the plantation, even as they forged a separate life of their own, one that blended elements of African culture with aspects of the culture of European Americans.[3]

How is it that these three respected historians, all examining generally the same sources, arrived at such startlingly different conclusions? Do they reflect changes in the society around them? Or perhaps they are linked to theories the historians themselves bring to the documents? Identifying the changes in scholarly perspective and asking these questions about why and how perspectives change is the essence of history and theory, and indeed is the foundational argument of this text.

Historians develop their understanding of historical problems through a confluence of personal, intellectual, and social influences. Just as the events, social institutions, and individuals historians examine are the products of their environment, so too are historians and the scholarship they produce. Delving a little deeper into the brief historiography of slavery described above provides a concrete example of how this works. U.B. Phillips, author of the relatively apologetic scholarship on slavery, was himself a southerner, writing of a time and place filled with family memories. This is not to say that, in and of itself, personal connection to a subject automatically leads to a bias, especially since at times familiarity with a subject (as with the labor historians described earlier) leads to observations outsiders might miss. However, bias either for or against a particular subject must be factored into an analysis of all scholarship. Furthermore, and perhaps more significantly, Phillips wrote his work at a time when general beliefs about the link between "race" and personality and character were widespread. Phillips' assertions that blacks were essentially suited to their position as slaves and thus content with their lot both emerged from and buttressed existing racism of the early-twentieth century. Written at a time that the Jim Crow segregation laws of the south were becoming fully entrenched, and as racial violence (at least in its most extreme form of lynching) seemed to be gradually waning, the image of bucolic and tranquil race relations presented by Phillips was comforting and largely assured him a broad audience.[4]

By the time Elkins wrote his work in 1958, things had changed considerably, both sociopolitically within the United States, and intellectually in terms of thinking about race. By 1958, legal challenges to racial segregation led to the landmark *Brown v. Board of Education of Topeka, Kansas* decision that called for the desegregation of institutions of public education. Such challenges to segregation, emerging from within the black community itself, made earlier assumptions of black complaisance less believable. Furthermore, intellectuals and social critics had increasingly pointed to racism as a major problem in American society. Gunnar Myrdal, the Swedish sociologist and Nobel Prize laureate issued in 1944 his study *An American Dilemma: the Negro Problem and Democracy*, which looked to slavery for the root problem of race relations in the United States. At the same time, the Nazi policy of genocide against the Jews had horrified the world and thus undermined the common root of racism that lay at the foundation of both Adolf Hitler's "final solution" and Phillips' images of benighted but blissful slaves. Additionally, World War II provided a psychosociological model through which Elkins could provide an alternative explanation for slave subservience rather than simply relying on an assumption of racial inferiority. Using studies of concentration camp survivors that found the total oppression of the camps led to a close identity between some prisoners and their captors, Elkins used the Nazi camps as an analogy for the slave plantations of the Old South, with the slaves holding the positions of prisoners and the overseers and masters the positions of guards. For Elkins, then, the supposed happiness of the slaves was not a product of their innate nature, but of their total oppression.

Elkins' work held sway for a short period of time in the early 1960s. The work placed blame for the evils of racial segregation and discrimination squarely in the time of slavery, thus shifting the blame from African Americans. Both black and white intellectuals and political leaders found much, initially, to commend Elkins' work. However, with the emergence of the Black Power movement in the second half of the 1960s, questions that had always been quietly asked about *Slavery* came to the forefront. How, if blacks were so completely browbeaten, could they have developed a flourishing culture that contributed to such key elements of American culture as jazz and Christian spirituals? And if African Americans were so defeated, how to explain persistent acts of resistance that were present in the archives, ranging from Nat Turner's bloody rebellion of 1830 to the daily acts of resistance by less notorious slaves? And could the slave plantation have been as totally oppressive as concentration camps? With Black Power came the search for slave community, and once historians became attentive to it, the slave community appeared everywhere throughout the archive.

By the early 1970s, a number of key works, among them *The Slave Community* by John Blassingame, hit the bookshelves, detailing the resistance of slaves and their struggle to maintain a cultural identity in the face of overwhelming odds. Several key social institutions, such as the family and religion, shielded slaves against the total oppression noted by Elkins and provided a nonracist explanation for the scenes of community detailed by Phillips. Slaves no longer appeared either completely satisfied with their lot, or utterly oppressed. Rather, they were more heroic figures, struggling against long odds to preserve their community. While Elkins drew upon sociological studies of concentration camp survivors to help explain his position, Blassingame utilized the work of anthropologists such as Melville Herskovitz who examined syncretism and cultural survival to argue for the persistence of an African heritage among African Americans.

Thus we can see how scholars focusing on the same general subject, in this case the nature of master–slave relations in the United States, arrived at different positions depending on the relative acceptance or rejection of concepts such as racism, the political context of the day, and the general atmosphere that shaped the historians themselves.

Text Goals and Chapter Organization

This book proceeds from the basic premise that these shifts and turns are the essence of good historical writing. This book on the one hand is a discussion of these changes over the twentieth century, placing them in context. But on the other hand, this book very explicitly is designed as a hands-on manual to explore the practice of reading for argument and articulating themes of works encountered. In order to accomplish this task of identification, we will ask you to "dialogue with your text"—that is, ask questions of it, write in the margins, note key items from each page, or look up unfamiliar words. Demonstrating understanding of these differences enables more critical reading skills, but also, with the accompanying primary sources, the text gives the reader opportunities to practice valuable analysis of source material using the methods of particular theories in each chapter. Accordingly, readers can "mix and match" sources and theories—for example, a source we asked readers to examine as a Marxist historian can also be read through the lenses of a gender, environmental, or cultural historian. The tools of unpacking meaning and taking facts and turning them into historical evidence are central takeaways for this text, as these are crucial skill sets for demonstrating mastery of the discipline of history as a profession.

Accordingly, you will read about the theory, specifically contexts of each tradition, then move on to significant secondary sources. To further understand the significance of the perspective being argued, however, you should go through two additional processes: analyzing the way historians apply the theory, and then learning to work as an historian to apply the theory itself to primary documents. This reader addresses both phases of this method. As you thumb through these pages, always keep in mind that our categories are general categories and that historians cross these disciplinary and theoretical boundaries all the time, especially as the field continues to be shaped and reshaped by new sources and new ways to look at old sources. Finally, as you read this text, you may find that some theories and approaches are more to your liking and interests than others. For historians, recognizing the approaches that best fit their historical lenses is a key aspect to moving forward in the profession. As we encounter various histories, various approaches to the past, and various stories that have been told, we develop our own historical voice and approach that guides us as practitioners. In the end, as historians, it is not enough simply to be aware of various methods. We must always know our own method and why we make the choices we do in terms of evidence, argument, and narrative. As you leaf through these chapters, think about your own approach(es) and how those approaches complement or diverge from those discussed in this text.

We purposefully have plotted a trajectory that follows both a linear path (from the end of the late nineteenth century to the end of the twentieth century) as well as a conceptual path. We will begin our trek with an overview of the ways in which people have thought about the past in the western and western-influenced world up through the nineteenth century. This move toward "objective" history had important ramifications for our first "umbrella theory": historical materialism.

1. Introducing Historical Materialism (Chapters 3–6)

In her 1984 song "Material Girl," Madonna declared that she would only date boys who saved their money because then they could lavish her with gifts and trinkets. While this made for a great dance tune, it also makes for a great way to define history that focuses on the material. Put simply, when we talk about materialism, we are talking about the touchable, tangible, "sink-your-teeth-into" reality. For Madonna, part of this reality was economic. It did not matter if you danced well, or if you were romantic or smart, it was the cash that transformed her affections. We have all heard this in one form or another, we may even have used it, but how do we take such ideas and apply them historically?

Of course, when scholars think about the world and social relations in "materialist" ways, they do so with more complexity than Madonna's Material Girl. When we talk about the material world, we are talking about items and objects that have tangible qualities. Historical materialism is a way of thinking and writing about the past that relies on evidence that has some **ontological** basis. It looks to the world outside of the mind as the basis for knowledge and human relations. There is no one, single, homogeneous understanding of materialist history, nor is there only one approach, a "materialist" approach to thinking about the past. There are many kinds of materialism, the most obvious of which begins with the very world around us: trees, lakes, city streets, railway lines, building shapes, and geographic positions, all of these examples are *things* by which we can understand our past and ourselves. Meaning is to be found through this tangible world. Some historians focus on "material culture," artifacts created by a particular society, such as houses, clothing, household furnishings, and the like, in order to understand how a particular society is changing over time, or how various groups within a complex society have different experiences. As we will see, once historians dig into this information, their analysis may lead them into attempts to explain their evidence, and the explanations may move them beyond the material world, into an understanding of culture. But materialists emphasize the tangible over the cultural/ideological, and often hold that cultural and ideological changes are rooted in changes in the material nature of life, rather than the other way around.

In Chapters 3–6, you will read many different ways in which the world can be interpreted from a predominantly materialist framework. We will begin with a discussion of Marxist philosophy, a powerful framework for explaining how the economy and social relations define and predetermine cultural ones. Next, we will explore the first and second generations of the *Annales* School, a group of scholars whose materialism led them to ground their understanding of human societies on the foundation of economic, geological, and geographical developments that were more fundamental than national boundaries and fleeting political events. We will also briefly explore the third generation of the *Annales* school that focused on microhistory and data interpretation, specifically with **demography** or the study of population and people. We will then turn our attention to the transformation of earlier Marxist history into a new category of analysis—the New Left and social history. Still interested in social relations, but also interested in the lives of people within a class, social history is often considered to be "history from below" or the history of everyday life. Finally, we will discuss the roots and emergence of environmental history. At the end of this sequence of chapters, you should be able to define materialism as a philosophical model. But more than that, you should be able to see how historians have interpreted materialism in a variety of ways.

2. Cultural Approaches to History (Chapters 7–10)

Beginning with Chapter 7, we will detail approaches that are more **epistemological**, that is exploring identity and how meaning is constructed apart from some material exteriority. When we talk about a cultural umbrella of history, we mean those approaches that examine attitudes, values, and perceptions as primary determinants of social relations. Historians who emphasize a cultural approach examine the ways in which people create meaning even sometimes of material objects themselves.

We will begin this sequence of chapters with perhaps the most complex—and contested—ideas in the text, postmodernism and its theoretical offshoots. Next, we will explore the more general field of cultural history itself. We will then discuss women's/feminist/gender history, tracing its development from operating firmly within the realm of materialist histories to newer concepts, such as queer theory, which are highly influenced by the disruptive power of postmodernist thought. Finally, we will end the book with an exploration of postcolonial history and the concepts of race and nation.

There is, as you will discover, some overlap—many materialist theories have elements of culture and many theories we consider to be cultural have materialist roots. We also will examine the ways in which theories of history reflect the world of the time—from Marxism to the New Left, Environmental to Feminist to Postcolonial History, you will read about how peoples' views of the world inform their historical approaches. Again, these are lenses through which everyone perceives the world. We are confined by our experiences—who we are, where we are, and when we are—and those experiences shape our perspectives.

YOUR RESERVOIR OF KNOWLEDGE—JUST THE TIP OF THE ICEBERG

Our goal at all points will be threefold: first, to introduce you to the varieties of ways people have conceptualized history of the past century and to do so in an accessible way; second, to provide examples of how those ways of thinking about the past are put into practice by historians; and finally, to provide hands-on experience in reading and interpreting both primary and secondary sources using the various lenses in each chapter. This last goal is a skill you can take to any readings you encounter in the future. At this stage, when you finish this text, you should be able to recognize specific names and particular methodologies, so even if you read an article far afield from your own historical interests, you should be able to interpret its arguments and its theoretical positions quite easily.

In reading about these theories and approaches, you will build your own reservoir of knowledge about how history was written during the twentieth century. With this reservoir, you will build critical skills of reading for argument and looking for how sources are read. But this knowledge is hopefully just the tip of the iceberg, since though we will cover numerous theories, there are infinitely more we have not explored but are tremendously fascinating and useful for the historian. Chaos theory, for example, began in the sciences, but has since been applied to the humanities as a way to understand experience.[5] The works of Deleuze and Guattari have provided frameworks for those interested in visual culture and the societal gaze.[6] Slavoj Žižek, a Slovenian philosopher, also explores film theory and popular culture.[7] Nor will we explore the Hermeneutics of Hans Georg Gadamer[8] or Donna Haraway's late Feminist Cyborg theory.[9] And we do not cover newer theories, such as Poor Theory to come out of the University of California, Irvine.[10] All of these ideas have grounding in the world around us—and are ways that its practitioners have found to explain human relations and practices. It is our hope that at least one of the approaches you will explore will strike a chord and compel you to read more as you progress as an apprentice historian. At the very least, you should be thinking more critically about your own approach to history and why you hold the positions you do.

Finally, one last word: we wrote this book to provide you with a framework for your historical work. In that regard, this book serves as a place to start your journey as historians, not a place to end. As you move forward in your careers, whatever that career may be, find your own voice, your own words, and recognize that there is no single *right* way to practice history. Keep in mind, though, that there are plenty of wrong ways to write history—those that let bias interfere with appropriate reading of source material and those that disregard facts entirely. We have shown in this book that theoretical perspective and historical lenses need not undermine the historical project, and are in actuality essential to it. Theory, in fact, can provide a grounding for explaining the past and understanding ourselves along the way.

Endnotes

1. E.P. Thompson, interviewed by Mike Merrill, in *Visions of History: Interviews*, Henry Abelove, Betsy Blackmar, Peter Dimock, and Jonathan Schneer, eds. (New York: Pantheon Books, 1983), 15.

2. Lawrence Stone, "Notes: History and Postmodernism," *Past & Present*, no. 131 (May 1991): 217–218; Patrick Joyce, "History and Postmodernism, I," *Past & Present*, no. 133 (November 1991): 204–209; Lawrence Stone, "History and Postmodernism," *Past & Present*, no. 135 (May 1992): 189–208.

3. Ulrich Bonnell Phillips, *American Negro Slavery: A Survey of the Supply, Employment, and Control of Negro Labor as Determined by the Plantation Regime* (New York: D. Appleton & Co., 1918); Stanley Elkins, *Slavery: A Problem in American Institutional and Intellectual Life* (Chicago: University of Chicago Press, 1959); John Blassingame, *The Slave Community: Plantation Life in the Old South* (New York: Oxford University Press, 1979).

4. For an excellent summary of this historiography, see Carl N. Degler, "Why Historians Change Their Minds," *Pacific Historical Review*, 45/2 (May 1976): 167–184.

5. See for example, N. Katherine Hayles, *Chaos Bound: Order and Disorder in Contemporary Literature and Science* (Ithaca: Cornell University Press, 1990).

6. Gilles Deleuze and Félix Guattari, *Anti-Oedipus: Capitalism and Schizophrenia*, trans. Robert Hurley, Mark Seem, and Helen R. Lane (New York: Viking Press, 1977).

7. See for example, Slavoj Žižek, *The Art of the Ridiculous Sublime: On David Lynch's Lost Highway* (Seattle: Walter Chapin Simpson Center for the Humanities/University of Washington, 2000); also *Everything You Always Wanted to Know about Lacan (But Were Afraid to Ask Hitchcock)* (London: Verso, 1992).

8. Hans-Georg Gadamer, *Truth and Method*, 2nd revised ed., Translation revised by Joel Weinsheimer and Donald G. Marshall (New York: Continuum, 1994).

9. Donna Haraway, *Simians, Cyborgs, and Women: The Reinvention of Nature* (London: Free Association, 1991).

10. Statement of the CTI Project in Poor Theory, 2008–2012, "Poor Theory: Notes Toward a Manifesto," http://www.humanities.uci.edu/critical/poortheory.pdf, accessed 16 August 2013.

CHAPTER 2

PROFESSIONALIZATION OF HISTORY: TIME AND SCIENCE IN THE HISTORICAL METHOD

CHAPTER OUTLINE

■ History from the Ancient World
to the Enlightenment

■ From Enlightenment to Progressive
History (18th–19th Centuries)

■ The Move to Objectivity, Professionalism,
and Critiques of Progressive Histories

"Historical professionalization, then, provided the underpinning of authority which the norm of objectivity sought."

Peter Novick[1]

In the last quarter of the nineteenth century, the study of history moved from being a field dominated by talented and intelligent amateurs who had no specialized training as historians to a field shaped by the development of graduate programs specializing in the study of history (and conferring the doctorate of philosophy degree in history), refereed journals and publications (to assure professional standards of scholarly research in published works of history), and associations where scholars could participate in professional development with similarly trained historians.[2] This process, known as **professionalization**, focused on **objectivity**, that is, the removal, inasmuch as it is possible, of bias from historical writing. Historians were required to use the Baconian method if they hoped to proceed in the profession. Professionalization only occurred after a wide array of other developments in the study of history from ancient times, and tracing a brief outline of these transformations provides valuable insights into the field itself, and into debates among historians about the value and importance of theory in historical scholarship. Specifically, issues of identity, objectivity, and history's relationship to nationalism emerged as critical issues and points of debate for the profession.

HISTORY FROM THE ANCIENT WORLD TO THE ENLIGHTENMENT

Western historians often trace their roots in European scholarship back to the oral traditions of early civilizations. The Greek scholars Thucydides (460–400 BCE) and Herodotus (484–425 BCE), though, are generally perceived as the two ancient scholars most influential on the modern historical method. Herodotus, sometimes referred to as the "father" of history in the West, wrote a sweeping history of the Mediterranean people, as well as a history of the struggle between the Persians and the Greeks. Written in nine books, Herodotus' *Histories* describes the Persians, their control throughout the Mediterranean, and finally the conflict between them and the Greeks. For his part, Thucydides wrote a history of the Peloponnesian War between Sparta and Athens, which has been described as his memory of events, though tempered to be as "objective" as possible through his technique of presenting conflicting accounts of the same event and interpreting "truth" from them. In ancient Rome, the great historian and orator Marcus Tullius Cicero (106–43 BCE) advocated a study of history that took into consideration geography, context, and chronologies, all issues that are rooted in modern historical thought. Interestingly, more than 2000 years ago, Thucydides and Cicero understood the challenges faced by scholars aiming at objectivity, even as they viewed events from their own particular perspective and often ignored the role of culture in constructing truth.[3]

The medieval period has been difficult for historians to classify primarily because of the various ways historical writing was practiced.[4] Nevertheless, there were models of historical writing in the medieval period that suggest that the medieval mind viewed history in a linear fashion. Most notably, the chroniclers of the period explored events of the past or of their own day as part of larger political and social lineages that gave their age its particular characteristics. In other words, medieval chroniclers saw themselves and their worlds in a larger historical context through which they commented on human follies and espoused doctrines of faith. In addition to a linear view of history, medieval scholars also adopted many principles of ancient philosophy and translated them into **scholasticism**, a method of investigation by which the writer first sets up a problem or "difficulty" in the form of a question and then attempts to address each concern. The scholastics are a classic example of scholars using deductive reasoning, a perspective that interpreted information in the light of assumed truths. Scholastics looked to key divine texts as the sources for truth, and many thus interpreted observations about the world or society through those texts. By the thirteenth century, medieval universities emerged as centers of knowledge, and much of the scholarship generated in these institutions worked to reconcile ancient philosophers such as Aristotle to knowledge grounded in Christianity.

Perhaps the crowning achievement of the scholastic scholars was the *Summa Theologica* by Thomas Aquinas (1225–1274). Aquinas, a Dominican monk, sought to reconcile theological truth with philosophical truth and did so by asserting that all truth ultimately flowed from God; seeming contradictions reflected the limits of human understanding. Aquinas addressed the subjective nature of human knowledge in *Questiones Disputatae de Veritate* where he stated, "Nothing is in the intellect that was not first in the senses."[5] This axiom responded to "difficulties" about whether humans could actually know God. According to Aquinas in his *Summa Theologica*, knowledge of God comes to us via our senses through images (what Aquinas called "phantasms") in ways that we might understand. While we might know God imperfectly through our senses, we do get a sense of divinity. Thus, while Aquinas set out to use a logical method of inquiry to buttress the power of theology, he also raised one of the thorny questions that would challenge scholars of the social sciences in the twentieth century: the subjective nature of human knowledge. Ultimately, he resolved this issue through an assertion of faith that all knowledge ultimately emanated from God and that knowledge could be found in divine texts.

During the Renaissance Era of the fifteenth and sixteenth centuries, many educated Europeans viewed the classical past as a kind of "golden age" of European culture and scholarship. Looking to the Greeks and Romans for a glorious vision upon which to pattern themselves, Renaissance scholars found in ancient writers both cultural and intellectual predecessors to whom they could link themselves, giving them a greater prestige through their association with the "classic" historians of the past, and simultaneously challenging the intellectual and scholarly authority of the Catholic Church. This sense of "classicism" also led scholars toward the development of a **humanist** approach to the analysis of their world. That is, they moved away from late medieval scholarship such as Aquinas' that focused on issues of spirituality and the divine as the ultimate source of knowledge toward scholarship that explored the issues of civic identity, responsibility, and development of the self. This had profound implications for the study of history. Rather than looking to the past as a means of understanding God's will, Humanists examined the past as a means of understanding the nature of their own communities. For example, the Medici family of Florence—notably Cosimo de Medici (1389–1464)—scoured the Italian countryside looking for ancient documents that gave the people of the various city-states a sense of their historicity. Under his patronage, Florence witnessed the Renaissance artistically, socially, and politically. Petrarch (1304–1374), one of the earliest of the Renaissance historicists, praised the past for its virtuous superiority to his own time, but many others, such as Vasari in his *Lives of the Artists* or even Niccolo Machiavelli (1469–1527), reflected on their own period as the end product of a long lineage dating from the ancients. This historical mindset was very much connected to the earlier frameworks provided by their ancient mentors—Thucydides and Cicero. Machiavelli, for example, often receives very cynical attention, but one of his lessons in *The Prince* was that the study of history was essential to prevent the mistakes of the past.

The development of this new historical consciousness rested on changes in the perception of time that privileged linear time versus cyclical time that likewise emerged during the Renaissance and continued to develop all the way into the nineteenth century. This is a deep, and in some ways inconsistent shift that is a vital part of the cultural armature that led to the dominance of narrative history as an element of Western perceptions of the world, and a Western understanding of history. This change both buttressed, and relied on, intellectual developments in the sciences as well. Together, the shifting sense of time challenged older perceptions rooted either in the Bible as a religious and historical text, or other perceptions linked to rhythms of nature.

Prior to the Renaissance, much human life in agricultural societies took its structure from cyclical patterns associated with planting, such as the rising and setting of the sun, the changing of the seasons, and times for planting and harvesting. Such grounding in nature provided a powerful foundation for human existence in general. This cyclical perception of time and human experience coexisted with a sense of time that was both more linear and more religious. Christianity, with its focus on the return of Christ at the millennium, sacralized time in two ways: it presented the Bible as both a religious and historical text (reflected in the deductive reasoning of the scholastic scholars such as Aquinas); and it generated a **teleological** sense that events occurring in the world led in some way toward the second coming of Christ and the end of historical development as we know it.

Gradually, between the Renaissance and the Enlightenment, these senses of cyclical and religious-linear time were eclipsed by a perception of time that was linear and secular. Developments in the sciences, such as the heliocentrism of Copernicus (ca. 1514) and Galileo (ca. 1600) as well as the discovery of the New World, which was filled with peoples, plants, and animals unaccounted for in religious works, threw into question the centrality of the Bible as a historical text, and the rediscovery of antiquity during the Renaissance, mentioned earlier, provoked a new appreciation of historical development. As is so often the case in cultural transitions, the transformation of the understanding of time did not occur in one fell swoop; as late as the mid-1600s, Archbishop James Ussher worked from the Bible to argue that the earth had been created exactly in 4004 BCE. Rather, different conceptions of time coexisted with one another (and, some might argue, continue to do so to this day; certain preconceptions of impending apocalypse common with some evangelical Christian groups in our own society contain strong strains of the teleological-religious sense of time of earlier eras).

The shifting nature of time coincided with the development of new modes of perceiving and understanding the natural world. In roughly the same age, Galileo argued for a sun-centered universe, Francis Bacon (1561–1626) developed a scientific method that privileged a certain type of thought, **inductive reasoning**, which works from observed data to generate ideas, over **deductive reasoning**, in which a person begins with a set of assumptions and uses these to understand whatever he or she is observing. Over the centuries, scholars have weighed in on these seeming polarizations and applied them not only to phenomena observable in nature, but in society as well. Ideally, for Bacon, the scientific observer freed himself of all such preconceptions and saw the world **objectively**. Unlike Aquinas with his belief that human knowledge was mediated through "phantasms," for Bacon the position of the observer was relatively unproblematic: he assumed that observers could achieve an unbiased and objective position. Discovery of the truth was possible only with a new method of creating knowledge that privileged observation over time as opposed to immediate acceptance of authority.[6] The influence of Bacon's philosophy and the spread of scientific ideas throughout the sixteenth century marked what historians term the Scientific Revolution, a period of unyielding intellectual growth in all realms of science as the political power of the Catholic Church waned.

During the Enlightenment, historical scholarship rooted in the scientific perspective championed earlier by Bacon was applied by scientists such as Sir Isaac Newton and others such as John Locke or Voltaire. Such thinkers believed that this perspective would lead to a more rational understanding of the world and thus erode the power of traditional forms of intellectual authority such as religion and monarchical government (both of which they considered to be institutions enshrouded in superstitious "darkness"). Critical of what they saw as the anachronistic vestiges of a benighted past that remained in their own societies, philosophers such as Voltaire (1694–1778) launched attacks on monarchical authority, censorship, religious intolerance, and other aspects of traditional society. While Voltaire was successful as a writer and philosopher, his political positions often brought him into conflict with those he challenged, and he sometimes found himself exiled or imprisoned. Nevertheless, his work is characteristic of a larger shift in Europe during the Scientific Revolution and the Enlightenment that privileged investigation, inquiry, and inductive logic. The seeming superiority of the scientific and rational method gained greater authority with the development of new technologies and methods of organizing work that made economic production more efficient. The wealth produced by this industrial revolution led to broader acceptance of various forms of inquiry and scholarship linked to it.

However, we should be cautious about seeing Voltaire and the other Enlightenment Era philosophers as immediately victorious over their intellectual rivals. Rather, the challenge of Enlightenment Era scholarship triggered a long transitional period during which many suppositions of traditional learning (such as the power of divine forces in the life of individuals and societies) continued to exert great influence, sometimes blending with new historical investigative techniques.

FROM ENLIGHTENMENT TO PROGRESSIVE HISTORY (18TH–19TH CENTURIES)

Developments in the late eighteenth and early nineteenth centuries were critical not only to the development of economic wealth and scientific knowledge, but also to the emergence of linear-secular time noted earlier in the chapter. The work of geologists such as Sir Charles Lyell extended the age of the earth backward, making the planet a much older place than it was imagined to be by people such as Archbishop Ussher. The new dating of the age of the planet allowed for the development of concepts such as the slow evolution of nature developed by Charles Darwin. The transformative impact of industrialization, which catapulted Western societies into economic dynamos (and also helped to transform the perception of time through the development of time clocks as a way of managing and segmenting time), all provided foundations for reimagining the very nature of time. Time became, at the individual level, a commodity, something that could be segmented, bought, and sold. At the grander level, the dominant perception of history came to imagine it as secularized and linear, an account of unfolding human events, interconnected in links of cause and effect, but often without any divine, guiding hand. Rapid change and the expansion of powerful nations in Western Europe and the United States supported the idea of progress, with the industrialized nations of the world sitting at the cutting edge of human development, and the nonindustrialized nations trailing along at various levels of underdevelopment.

As a result of this twofold transformation of science and economy, many nineteenth-century intellectuals saw a world in which progress seemed to reign, and where the vestiges of feudalism could be cast off in a move toward perfection. This general paradigm emerged in the late eighteenth century and early nineteenth century in the works of key scholars in various fields. The German philosopher Georg W.F. Hegel held that historical development pointed toward greater freedom in the civic sphere; the Scottish economist and philosopher Adam Smith argued that economic liberation and the "invisible hand" of the market would result in greater income all around; even the sociologist and political scientist Karl Marx, the great critic of capitalism, held onto the notion that free market capitalism was a necessary phase as human societies progressed toward communism.

Auguste Comte (1798–1857) was a particularly influential thinker who thought along similar lines of historical development. Comte held that all human societies obeyed laws of development that took them through stages, all of which could be identified by closely observing human communities. Comte's theories, which came to be known as **positivism**, also argued that all human knowledge is possible only through experience, thus falling along the general ideas of science put forth by Bacon. The term positivism, though, actually has two distinct, but related meanings. The first is the idea noted above—that human societies follow specific patterns (much as Newton and Bacon asserted that the physical universe followed identifiable laws) that could be revealed through close observation. The other meaning had to do with the techniques of the scientific method: historians and sociologists should observe societies closely, compile their data, and then allow the data to dictate to the scholar its meaning. Through this process of objective reflection, the laws of both the physical universe and human societies would reveal themselves to the thoughtful observer.

These ideas of progress occurred simultaneously with the rise of science and scientific outlooks and cannot be extricated from them easily. If, as the visionaries of human improvement asserted, the general pattern of human development pointed toward progress (a Eurocentric idea that understood "western" societies to be the model for *all* human societies), then why did some societies seem to be lagging behind? The triumph of science has been linked to the theories of "social Darwinism," made popular by Herbert Spencer's application of Darwin's theory of evolution to society. But Charles Darwin himself made connections between his theories about the animal kingdom and the way human cultures develop. In any case, social Darwinism provided a scientific explanation for the discrepancies in social, political, and economic development across the globe. Most important, science helped Europeans explain to themselves their special provenance: that there were different species of humanity and of those species some were more evolved than others, such as whites over blacks or men over women. The less evolved groups needed Western men to come in and help them. In this way, ideas of progress were tightly linked to ideas of imperialism, what Rudyard Kipling famously described as "the white man's burden." What this meant was that science "explained" social difference and encouraged those with "modern technology" (i.e., Europeans and Americans) to colonize others based on the notion that theirs was a "civilizing mission." A man who became closely associated with biological supremacy, Karl Pearson—pioneer **eugenicist**—succinctly summarized the way in which Social Darwinism could serve as a justification for imperialism when he asserted

> this struggle of tribe with tribe, and nation with nation, may have its mournful side, but we see as a result of it the gradual progress of mankind to higher intellectual and physical efficiency. It is idle to condemn it; we can only see that it exists and recognise what we have gained by it—civilization and social sympathy.[7]

Most important for Pearson was the potentially destructive organization of modern European society that undermined the birth rates of the "superior stocks"—those people who brought the light of civilization to the rest of the world. In this way, the vision of history as progressive not only reflected and supported particular national identities, but also ethnic and racial, and gender identities as well.

The people who held the monopoly on historical production in the nineteenth century built on this emergent theory of knowledge and wrote about history as a forward movement, a **teleology**. This idea of history is both specifically western and quite linear. However, while this vision of progress emanated from Europe and the West, and was thus closely linked with western self-perception of Europe and the United States as the most developed and progressive regions of the globe, scholars in various locations adopted key elements of the story, finding it useful as a means of locating and understanding the development of their own nations in the general stream of history. History, again, emerged as a powerful means of both explaining the world, and a way of defining social and civic identity. By examining the national histories penned by four different scholars in four distinct locations around the globe in the 1800s, we can get a glimpse of the power of this ideology of progress in shaping the perception of history.

In the United States, no other historian better represented the faith in progress, and linked progress to the nation, than George Bancroft. Bancroft wrote the magisterial *History of the United States, from the discovery of the American continent* between 1854 and 1878. Trained at Harvard and in Europe, Bancroft embraced many of the methods that would define a good scholarly history today. Bancroft scoured state archives as well as collections of materials in Europe for information to be included in his history. Thus, he drew from primary sources in an attempt to incorporate the voices of historical actors into his tale of the formation of the United States. However, at the same time, Bancroft clearly begins his project with a particular perspective that merged his religious values with his strident nationalism, a perspective that was a legacy of his early training as a Unitarian minister during the intensely patriotic postrevolutionary era. For Bancroft, the formation of the United States was not merely fortuitous, but providential. The formation of the new nation marked a watershed of human development, and the United States itself seemed to be both a product and an instrument of God's will. This notion may well have been drawn as well from the intellectual tradition of Jonathan Edwards, the noted eighteenth-century

New England clergyman who saw the American colonies as a New Jerusalem, and divinely charged with the project of challenging Catholicism and heathenism in the New World. Simultaneously, however, in much of Bancroft's history of the United States, the divine nature of the history of the nation is submerged beneath a narrative grounded in historical documents and containing the voices of prominent historical actors. Thus, we might take Bancroft as an example of a scholar who embraced many of the modern techniques of scholarship while retaining a decidedly religious and nationalistic worldview regarding the forces that shape history. Most significantly, Bancroft links the history of the United States to a story of human progress and improvement.[8]

Similar attitudes about progress flourished among European history makers in the nineteenth century. In Great Britain, Lord Thomas Macaulay (1800–1859), a reformer, philanthropist, and career politician penned the *History of England*, a book that focused on the Revolution of 1688 and its consequent effects on the democratization of British society. The *History* is a discussion of the consolidation of the Revolution in which the partisans of parliamentary control (ultimately known as "Whigs") emerged victorious over the partisans of monarchical control ("Tories") to oust the Catholic James II and install his Protestant daughter Mary and her husband, William of Orange as queen and king. At this point, according to Macaulay, the abusive tendencies of the monarchy were finally tempered after centuries of conflict with Parliament. Though the revolution, he argued, was "imperfect" in its activities, it ultimately paved the way for freedom—and any "right minded" person would recognize that fact.[9] In other words, in Macaulay's view of events, 1688 was a watershed moment inaugurating freedom from despotism and opening political, economic, and social possibilities for Britons. In any case, after the revolution, Whigs and Tories maintained their political and social grievances against each other and emerged as political parties in England. As the son of a reformer, and as a supporter of reforming legislation himself, Macaulay inherited this tradition of privileging parliamentary authority, and as such, wrote with deep-seated Whig political sympathies. Macauley saw these political developments as markers of English *progress*, as clear-cut manifestations of Britain's transformation to the great industrial and imperial power it was during his lifetime.

As the **New Europes** moved toward independence throughout the nineteenth century, they retained not only their European attitudes toward race and nation,

but also toward history. Domingo Faustino Sarmiento (1811–1888), the educator-president of Argentina, articulated an approach to the past mediated by a vision for the future. During the presidency of Juan Manuel de Rosas, one of many **caudillos** who controlled Argentinian politics from the 1820s, Sarmiento found himself in exile in Chile, writing against caudillismo and promoting educational reform. He was active as a political journalist and helped in the 1852 overthrow of Rosas and the reinstitution of democratic politics. He ruled as president of Argentina from 1868 to 1874, continuing to promote educational reform along models he encountered on visits to the United States and Europe. During his time in exile, Sarmiento wrote a book condemning the concept of *caudillismo* translated as *Life in the Argentine Republic in the Days of the Tyrants*. While the book is meant ostensibly to critique the caudillo Facundo Quiroga and his ally Juan Manuel de Rosas, it actually critiques an entire political system and the culture that promoted it. Specifically, Sarmiento critiqued a system dominated by **mestizos**. This system, predominantly rural with a significant indigenous and mixed-race population, could never understand or be capable of progress. The non-European population of Argentina had, according to Sarmiento, a muddled sense of religion, culture, and politics, and everything related to progress, development, and democracy, was confined to urban areas. In this way, Sarmiento not only critiqued Quiroga and Rosas, both of whom were mestizos who commanded personal loyalty from rural masses, but also critiqued a way of life and approach to history. Contemporaneous with Macauley, then, Sarmiento devised a program of political and social progress for Argentina partly predicated on political, geographic, and racial exclusion. Such exclusion was warranted objectively according to Sarmiento; while cultures might have their own unique and positive attributes, not all were conducive to modernity. Specifically, he disdained tribal cultures that laid no claim to private property or industry—what Sarmiento called "permanent possession of the soil." This line of thinking is very much in keeping with a linear notion of history and one that very clearly rests on ideas of science as determinants of cultural development.[10]

Finally, in Japan, intellectuals sometimes adopted this linear approach to history as a way of competing with the West, which suggests that this move toward progressive histories was global in scope. While intellectuals in South Asia and China adopted some elements of this new intellectual approach to the past, Japan's preeminent scholar and founder of Keio University, Fukuzawa Yukichi (1835–1901) most clearly reflects the transition to a history rooted in a science of progress and objectivity and a linear notion of time. Born into a poor samurai family and following in his brother's footsteps after the untimely death of their father, Fukuzawa traveled through Japan for linguistic training. Educated first as a Dutch language expert, Fukuzawa turned to the study of English, even traveling to the United States for a brief period to learn about American education which, he argued, held the key to Japan's material and cultural development. Fukuzawa returned to Japan as it faced political revolution and an overthrow of the traditional shogunate. After the revolution that transformed Japanese political and economic life, Fukuzawa had the option of continuing government service, but he refused, preferring instead to continue educating students at his university. Here, Fukuzawa wrote the great tomes for which he is known: *The Encouragement of Learning and An Outline of a Theory of Civilization*. In both of these works, Fukuzawa clearly articulated the necessity for education in science and mathematics instead of the more traditional Confucian philosophy that dominated historical production. Specifically, he desired to educate the masses of Japan and to work within the framework of the Anglo-American vision of the past. In other words, Fukuzawa articulated a linear philosophy of history, one in which the path to "civilization" and empowerment was progressive, technological, and scientific. In fact, Fukuzawa's vision of Japanese history paralleled the progressive visions articulated by Bancroft and Macauley, and his later works articulate a view of Japanese civilization as one of salvation for East Asia. A decaying China, committed to retrograde Confucian ideals had little in common with modernity, argued Fukuzawa, and so would fall behind other nations' development. In Fukuzawa's view of Japan's historical development, only Japan possessed the right mix of educational and social reform manifested in progress and conquest.[11]

The Move to Objectivity, Professionalism, and Critiques of Progressive Histories

While the end of the nineteenth century saw historical production removed from the hands of writers who held a personal stake in the outcome of their story

such as Macauley, Bancroft, Sarmiento, or Fukuzawa, this across-the-board acceptance of science continued to affect the way that stories of the past and present were told. A primary goal was to place the field of history in the hands of people trained in standardized methods. A crucial component of this standardization was the quest for **objectivity**. Many seized on the work of noted German philosopher Leopold von Ranke (1795–1886), particularly his phrase that we should study history *wie es eigentlich gewesen*—as it actually happened—to claim that Ranke challenged earlier historical traditions in his quest for **historicism**. Following this vein, historians who supported this interpretation of von Ranke's work argued that the historian's craft should rely wholly on empirical methods of reading archival sources to write about the past and recognize the differences between knowledge gained *a priori* and that gained *a posteriori*. As might be gleaned from the Latin, knowledge gained *a posteriori*, or after the fact, held more weight than that riddled with *a priori* ideas—that is, ideas held before, or prior to, encounters with artifacts and archives. Consequently, historians came to believe that they could ultimately find the past "as it actually happened." Facts were single elements of the "truth" of the past, and as such were incontrovertible. As a result, historians equipped with the tools of science long in development, and amply armed with the standards of a profession, claimed a monopoly on knowledge. The "truth was out there," to borrow from a popular 1990s science-fiction show, and people needed only the skills to properly unearth it. The unmediated and raw form of the "fact" was the ultimate expression of the past and where society had moved. Facts required no interpretation; Bacon, Comte, and Ranke showed historians the possibilities of seeing the world purely objectively through observation; Darwin, Spencer, and Pearson provided vehicles for explaining those observations historically; and standardized methods assured that all scholarly historical production conformed to the new search for fact-based, objective history.

There is a debate over this notion of the historian as the dispassionate, objective observer, and his or her contributions to the expansion of western and male power. Was this really just an innocent search for knowledge, or were the connections between imperialism, male dominance, and the social sciences a product of power relations? To what degree was the observer not objective but **subjective**, and if subjective what are the implications of that subjectivity? This debate centers around the recognition that approaching the evidence of the past from a purely **ontological** standpoint is in itself a theoretical decision buttressed on the one hand by the methods codified at the end of the nineteenth century and on the other a sense of the ability to intellectually master the universe, and the world. Contemporaneous with the movement at the end of the nineteenth century to create history as a profession—a craft—was the movement that imported science into the history of human development and that lay at the heart of the social sciences—sociology, anthropology, psychology, and history. Europeans, secure with their objective evidence from the past, could claim with complete conviction their superiority over others—both within their societies and around the globe—and their rights to rule over them. The language of the sciences—medicine, anthropology, and so on—suggested that the legacy of the Baconian method carried an insidious component: justification of the right of one group of people to subjugate another.

Future historians thought little of the supposed connections between a revolution that retained a privileged crown and aristocracy and supposed economic progress. Consequently, they appropriated Macaulay's political affiliation (Whig) to critique what they perceived as facile and problematic approaches to thinking and writing about the past. In 1931, a young historian named Herbert Butterfield wrote *The Whig Interpretation of History* not only against approaches common in the nineteenth century, but also against some of the more famous historians of his own time. Butterfield railed against assumptions of the past based on knowledge of the present—**presentism**—and how such presentism affected reconstruction of past events. As we explained in our discussion of Macaulay and Bancroft, their own histories were inflected with a presentist view of history.[12]

Butterfield found this type of attitude disturbing, as it implies a direct progression to a better world and emphasizes a congratulatory account of the past. Indeed, the historian Peter Novick recounts Butterfield's description of whiggism as "the tendency in many historians . . . to emphasize certain principles of progress in the past and to produce a story which is the ratification if not the glorification of the present."[13] In other words, historians' accounts that emphasize progress and minimize the more complicated story (Macaulay's "imperfect" revolution) are whiggish.

Writing at almost the same exact moment as Butterfield, Carl Becker also challenged the assumed objectivity of historians, as well as the connections to scientific modes of inquiry described by Von Ranke. In his 1932 speech "Everyman His Own Historian," delivered upon his acceptance of the office of President of the American Historical Association, Becker argued that the process by which historians conducted research could not help but be subjective, as historians picked among the fragmentary shards of evidence remaining from a complex past and attempted to construct comprehensive stories. Inevitably, for Becker, historians created histories that reflected the vital interests of their own era, rather than a timeless, objective appraisal of the past. In this way, historians created meaningful stories (Becker provocatively termed them "myths") that helped people understand themselves and their place in the world. In making his arguments, Becker directly challenged the authority of "scientific historians," while opening up the possibility, even the inevitability, of each generation rewriting history to suit its own needs. While some historians seemed threatened by Becker's assertion of the relativism of historical thought, Becker himself argued for the vitality of the field as a whole. For purposes of this book, it is important to see the way in which both Butterfield and Becker, writing in the early twentieth century, challenged the theoretical foundations of the discipline.[14]

This critique of historical knowledge, and of the whole notion of objectivity, became most pronounced in the last third of the twentieth century with the emergence of scholarship generally lumped under the heading of **postmodernism**, which we will address in Chapter 7. However, other theoretical perspectives not quite so trenchant as postmodernism also raised questions of objectivity earlier in the century, and much of this book addresses these concerns at some level. Whether the critique emanated from **Marxist** scholars who focused on links between class interest and ideology, or *Annales* **School** historians who explore the distinct *mentalités* of societies, or **cultural historians** who likewise looked at the mental frameworks that informed people about their world and themselves throughout history, many of the theoretical frameworks adopted by historians have either implicitly or explicitly challenged the dominant framework of the objective social science upon which the field of History, and all of the social sciences, were grounded in the late nineteenth century. Gradually, historians have come to acknowledge that the histories they write are products of a particular time, and a particular perspective, and by paying attention to such issues we can learn a great deal about not just the historical subject they are studying, but about the context in which that work of history was written. This shifting perspective is illustrated by the increasing frequency with which historians introduce their work with a section of personal reflection in which they attempt to lay out what they understand to be the factors that influence their particular perspective. But, at the same time that this decentering of the historian has taken place, as historians have come to understand that they must account for their *perspective*, they have continued to hold onto the *techniques* pioneered in the nineteenth century: careful analysis of primary documents that define and limit the particular work of history. Thus, a certain tension has crept into much historical literature: historians recognize their own subjective nature, and try to acknowledge it, yet continue on with a method that positions them as a powerful observer of documents of the past. In the body of historical literature, the self-referential aspect of the introduction usually disappears, and the historian also becomes concealed by the omniscient third person voice.

It may, in fact, be this tension within the field of history that has led a growing number of history departments to incorporate some elements of theory into their undergraduate programs. The tension is certainly a key part of the intellectual context in which we are writing this book. We believe that one of the benefits of instructing students in theory is the way in which such study challenges young scholars to consider carefully their own role in the construction of history. History no longer appears as simply the process of finding some primary sources and relaying their contents. Rather, those who study history come away with a greater self-consciousness of the assumptions they themselves are bringing to those documents, even as they are considering the context in which the document was originally produced.

Endnotes

1. Peter Novick, *That Noble Dream: The "Objectivity Question" and the American Historical Profession* (Cambridge: Cambridge University Press, 1988), 53.

2. *Ibid.*, chapters 1–2.

3. A useful discussion of historical interpretation in the ancient world is found in Marshall Sahlins, *Apologies to Thucydides: Understanding History as Culture and Vice Versa* (Chicago: University of Chicago Press, 2004).

4. Gabrielle Spiegel, "Historical Thought in Medieval Europe," in *A Companion to Western Historical Thought*, Lloyd Kramer and Sara Maza, eds. (Malden, MA: Blackwell Publishers, 2002), 78–79.

5. Thomas Aquinas, *The Disputed Questions on Truth*, Question 2, Article 3, Answers to Difficulties #19, translated from the definitive Leonine Text by Robert W. Mulligan, Questions I–X, Volume 1 (Chicago: Henry Regnery Company, 1952), 76.

6. Francis Bacon, *Novum Organum: With Other Parts of the Great Instauration*, Book 1: Aphorisms 70, 84, translated and edited by Peter Urbach and John Gibson (Chicago, IL: Open Court Publishing Company, 1994), 78–80, 92–93.

7. Karl Pearson, *National Life from the Standpoint of Science* (London: A & C Black, 1905), 61.

8. George Bancroft, *History of the United States of America from the Discovery of the Continent* (New York: D. Appleton and Company, 1886).

9. Thomas Babington Macaulay, *History of England* (New York: Penguin Books, 1979), 553.

10. Domingo Faustino Sarmiento, *Life in the Argentine Republic in the Days of the Tyrants, or Civilization and Barbarism* (New York: Collier Books, 1961).

11. Yukichi Fukuzawa, *An Outline of a Theory of Civilization* (Tokyo: Sophia University, 1973).

12. Herbert Butterfield, "The Underlying Assumption," in *The Whig Interpretation of History* (London: G. Bell and Sons, 1959).

13. Novick, *That Noble Dream: The "Objectivity Question" and the American Historical Profession*, 13.

14. Carl Becker, "Everyman His Own Historian," *American Historical Review* 37/2 (1932): 221–236.

CHAPTER 3

MARXIST HISTORY

CHAPTER OUTLINE

■ Marxist and Materialist Philosophy
  in Historical Context

■ The Influence of Marx and Engels on
  Twentieth-Century Historical Writing

■ Conclusion

■ Thinking Like a Historian

"Every historian has his or her lifetime, a private perch from which to survey the world. My own perch is constructed, among other materials, of a childhood in the Vienna of the 1920s, the years of Hitler's rise in Berlin, which determined my politics and my interest in history, and the England, and especially the Cambridge, of the 1930s, which confirmed both."

Eric Hobsbawm[1]

When we hear the names Karl Marx and Friedrich Engels, our minds may jump to the major revolutionary upheavals of the twentieth century, such as the Russian Revolution of 1917, or the Chinese Revolution of 1949. Some may even protest that "communist guy" does not warrant our attention since communism as a major economic institution is said to have "lost" the Cold War struggle with free market capitalism. Sometimes, we find that we like to blame Marx for the sins of his followers, but this merely ignores the complex and important role Marxist philosophy still holds in modern economic thought, and of course historical studies. To understand Marx's relationship with history, we need first to explore his own context and understand him as a nineteenth-century scholar, one who died long before revolutionaries defined their efforts by invoking his name.

Karl Marx was born in Trier in what is now Germany in 1818. He studied law and philosophy in the 1830s, hoping to earn a professorial position. Disenchanted with what he described as the reactionary politics of the Prussian university system, he moved to Cologne and worked as a journalist, becoming editor-in-chief for the *Rheinische Zeitung* in 1842. After only a year, the government first censored and then banned the paper, as it had increasingly argued for radical political change. By 1844, Marx moved to Paris, where he met Friedrich Engels and the two formed a lifelong friendship and intellectual partnership. Marx and Engels collaborated as journalists in Paris and also worked on the *Neue Rheinische Zeitung* in Cologne.

Both Marx and Engels wrote in a revolutionary milieu that had deep-seated roots in the previous century. Europe still reeled from the effects of the French Revolution of 1789 and the subsequent Napoleonic Wars as well as the growing pangs of the early industrial revolution. As recent as 1830, workers in Paris had fought unsuccessfully for their own liberty against the reactionary state. The nineteenth-century movement was in part a result of growing class inequalities stemming from the Industrial Revolution. Industrial development, while making production more efficient and reducing costs for consumers, also exacerbated the already downward mobility, or **proletarianization**, of workers. Although the 1830 revolution coincided with a rise in socialist theory, it was hardly socialist. In fact, it primarily consolidated the power of the middle class. The new king Charles X sought to get rid of the Constitutional Charter adopted by Louis XVIII at the end of the Napoleonic Wars and the exile of Napoleon. The Constitutional Charter ensured "Public Rights of the French" such as equality before the law, liberty of religious choice, limited freedom of speech, and the abolition of conscription. When Charles X tried to curtail these rights, he was forced from power. The revolution showed that France would no longer tolerate ultraroyalism, but neither would it willingly accept power sharing with workers.

While the struggle was not socialist in nature, many workers fought not only for political rights but also for basic working rights. And they were not the first workers to do so. The first attempts at unionization, known as combination, were by English woollen spinners and weavers at the end of the eighteenth century. The spinners argued that "feelings of humanity will lead those who have it in their power to prevent the use of those machines, to give every discouragement they can to what has a tendency so prejudicial to their fellow-creatures." But these organizations were met with laws that banned their right to exist and that jailed those who fought to improve their lives (e.g., Combination Acts). Throughout the early 1800s, workers known as **Luddites** broke machines throughout England, hoping to forestall the mechanization of labor and the downward slope of wages. Machines simplified labor. Simplified labor meant **deskilling**—or workers needed only for labor power, not for skill. Over time, knowledge about how to create a product, which had been central to the authority and economic position of skilled artisans, and which had traditionally been passed on from master craftsmen to apprentices (who themselves would eventually ascend

to the status of master), was lost. Deskilling led to lower wages since there was no longer a need for a worker with a specialized skill set. Master artisans and craftsmen were replaced with unskilled factory workers, capable of mass producing a product for a much lower price. To think of this in our own times, consider prefabricated furniture that comes with assembly required: relatively inexpensive and of acceptable quality, but certainly not requiring any highly specialized labor by trained craftsmen during the machine-dominated mass-production process. Followers of the mythical Ned Ludd hoped to secure their positions by breaking machines that destroyed their livelihoods. It didn't work.

In a continuation of this struggle, in 1819, workers marched on Saint Peter's Fields in Manchester, England to petition their government for better working conditions and to agitate for political enfranchisement. The government's response was to open fire on the people—men, women, children—killing nearly 20 and injuring 600, earning the day the moniker "Peterloo Massacre" in reference to Napoleon's historic defeat at Waterloo just four years earlier. Despite the tragedy at St. Peter's Fields, workers and intellectuals continued lobbying for greater rights. For example, in England, a group of people called **Chartists** hoped to pass a petition through Parliament (known as the Peoples' Charter) that would provide universal manhood suffrage and the secret ballot, ideas that we might take for granted today but were nonexistent before the twentieth century. After more than a decade of meetings, marches, and appeals to Parliament for greater enfranchisement (voting rights), Chartism as a political movement collapsed just prior to the 1848 revolutions.

As stated earlier, the revolution of 1830 in France was a continuation of these social struggles and did not mark the end of workers' struggle in Europe. The year 1848 witnessed cataclysmic events with revolutions taking place throughout the European continent. The thirty-year-old Karl Marx and nearly thirty Friedrich Engels participated in the revolution by coediting the *Neue Rheinische Zeitung*. Just previous to the outbreak of the revolutions, Marx and Engels, who were already well known for their revolutionary publishing, began working with the German Communist League, a group of radical German workers living in Paris. The League was formed in 1836, and by 1847, it held congresses for its members to debate policy and constitutional issues. In that year, the League commissioned Marx and Engels to write a platform for their meeting, stating the general beliefs and aims of the organization. This statement became Marx and Engels's most famous (though not their most intellectually important) work, *The Manifesto of the Communist Party* (more commonly known as *The Communist Manifesto*). We will discuss the content of *The Manifesto* later in the chapter.

In France, the revolution began when the new king Louis Philippe announced that there would be no electoral reform. The subsequent revolt in Paris led to the creation of a provisional government comprised of **liberals** and socialists, but unsurprisingly, they could not agree on basic tenets for the new government. Moreover, there remained a fear of socialism. Nineteenth-century liberalism is not to be conflated with twenty-first-century ideas of politics. The liberal tradition in this period was essentially a child of the Enlightenment, as it built around the idea that at its core, humanity was rational. Further, drawing from authors such as Locke and Paine, liberals believed that people had natural (or inalienable) rights, and it was the responsibility of those with political power to ensure the implementation of these rights. The tension, and the attempt to exclude workers, led to a violent Paris uprising known as the **June Days**. The revolution ended with the rise of Louis Napoleon, an elected leader who sided with the middle classes and effectively stifled rebellion.

MARXIST AND MATERIALIST PHILOSOPHY IN HISTORICAL CONTEXT

Marx and Engels were part of a large lineage of materialist thinkers, and their immediate intellectual forebear, G.W.F Hegel (1770–1831) interacted with this tradition in his philosophy. Hegel's philosophy is part of the period we call German idealism. Working in dialogue with the theories of Immanuel Kant, Hegel sought to develop a rational idea of the progress of history and so, like others we have discussed in Chapter 2, wrote of history as teleology.

What has come to be known as Hegel's **dialectic** is actually a triadic model of history that deals with struggle, or conflict, between opposing forces that result in a more developed, nuanced version of the original. For Hegel, this struggle continues and is the progressive force of history, propelling it ever-forward. Hegel refers to the sum total of our reality as the Absolute Spirit. His philosophy is, by consequence, historical, because

history simply manifested this struggle of conflicting ideas. For Hegel, there is no escaping the framework of struggle and synthesis. In diagram form, the dialectical framework looks something like this:

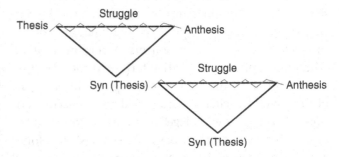

Those who followed Hegel, either his direct students, or those who shared a philosophical affinity with his ideas, broke off into two radically different directions. A right-wing group, known as the Old Hegelians, emerged that tried to reconcile Hegel's phenomenology with a more spiritual and religious framework. A left-wing group, known ultimately as the Young Hegelians, was revolutionary and approached Hegel's philosophy increasingly from an atheistic position. Specifically, the young Hegelians, such as Ludwig Feuerbach, argued that Hegel's philosophy was most useful in reverse. In other words, the real world could be used to explain the ideal. Feuerbach felt that Hegel was most interested in proving the existence of the Absolute Spirit by tracing its progress in the world. So Feuerbach, in *The Essence of Christianity*, argued that religion makes sense only as a human-oriented philosophy. Feuerbach suggested that despite Hegel's claims to a **phenomenology**, or the "study of things shown," his main concern was in providing meaning for something nonhuman—God, the Absolute Spirit, what have you. If a phenomenology in the Platonic sense seeks to explore the distinction between that which is seen/experienced (ontology) and that which is intelligible (epistemology), then Hegel's gradual move in the nineteenth century to exploring consciousness moved away from his original conception of dialectical struggle. On the contrary, Feuerbach stated that religion was not before humans, but actually human constructed to satisfy their psychological needs. In other words, Feuerbach critiqued Hegel's move toward the mind as being too dismissive of experience.

Marx, too, was a Young Hegelian, powerfully influenced by Hegel's philosophy. He took his philosophical interests to the political realm, however. Marx fits into this debate because of the ways in which he critiqued both Hegel's seeming "spiritual" side as well as Feuerbach's seeming unwillingness to completely invert the Hegelian model. If, according to Feuerbach, Hegel failed to emphasize the real experiences of real people in his articulation of the Spirit, then according to Marx, Feuerbach's primary fault was in not emphasizing human **praxis** (or the process of putting ideas into practice), the application of this model to revolutionary movements. According to Marx, "the philosophers have only interpreted the world, in various ways; but the point is to change it."[2] Initially part of the Young Hegelians, Marx honed his intellectual critique of both groups of Hegelians by articulating that the basis of life lay in essential physical needs—shelter, food/ raiment, and reproduction of the species. These physical needs reflect Marx's idea of the role of life and are intricately bound with his economic theories. For Marx, the material defined everything—it was the base on which everything in society was built.

Marx's materialist philosophy occupied most of his career. And, as we have discovered, Hegel's philosophy was a "direct theoretical premise" for it.[3] Marx and Engels took the premise of struggle and contention as the basis of historical development and focused on the economy. In this way, they developed what they called the "the materialist conception of history." This derives from the first premise of history that "men must be in a position to live in order to be able to 'make history.' That requires food, drink, housing, and clothes as mentioned earlier. Thus, the 'production of material life itself' was the first historical act."[4] The way in which a society produced life's necessities was called the **mode of production** that included all elements that contribute to that production such as tools, labor, or raw materials such as cotton, wood, or brick.

Marx and Engels developed this philosophy on the basis of observation. Living in a world of the triumph of science as a means for explaining human societies, they, as social commentators, believed they could apply the scientific method of observation to the past. For Marx and Engels, the world was divided between the "haves" and the "have nots." In other words, humans, as social animals, had a fundamentally exploitative relationship with each other. There may be equitable relations within a class, but the basic struggle of society was built around those who own the **means of production** and those who own only their own labor. In their observations, they saw economic inequality as the basis of human societies and in all human communities, one found subordinate groups struggling against a dominant group

for supremacy. In this way, societies moved from tribal, communal, feudal, and finally industrial capitalist ways of organization. All were economic systems or modes of production, in which the ruling class was usurped as a consequence of historic struggles with another group. This marks, in part, the influence of Hegelianism on their conception of history. In the penultimate stage of economic development, industrial capitalism, class structure had been reduced to the relationship between two groups, which Marx and Engels could see, living and breathing all around them—the **bourgeoisie**, or capitalist class controlling property and the means of production; and the **proletariat** or working class, barely able to subsist on its wages, and possessing only its own labor power—that aspect of their labor which they sold piecemeal for wages.

While the roots of Marx's sense of the development of human societies can be found in Hegel's theory of the dialectic, the sense of progress that both philosophers saw (and even though Marx's understanding of capitalism was in many ways quite bleak, he did ultimately see it as a necessary, and thus progressive, step toward the final stage of human development, communism) is a hallmark of Enlightenment thought generally. A variety of social philosophers, economists, and political theorists, such as Adam Smith, Thomas Jefferson, Thomas Paine, David Ricardo, and August Comte all, in varying ways, understood the nineteenth century as the age when humanity had finally shaken off the chains of superstition and political and economic oppression that marked so much of history. Rationality, science, and the nascent social sciences promised even greater progress and emancipation for the human race. While Marx sharply criticized much of this thought, particularly the economic rhetoric and theories around capitalism that overlooked the reality of economics from the perspective of the proletariat, he nonetheless had an overall understanding of social development and progress. In both his faith in the "scientific" (i.e., objective) nature of his own findings, and in his belief in human progress, some have noted Marx was a quintessential Enlightenment figure.

Marx and Engels began to explore these interlocking theories of economics, historical development, and society, in their journals and honed the philosophy throughout the 1840s in *The German Ideology* (1845–1846), *Wage-Labour and Capital* (1847, and the seed for their major tome *Capital*), and by 1848 *The Manifesto of the Communist Party*. But the intellectual strength of the philosophy was only seen in later work, the most important of which is *Capital*. Nevertheless, it is *The Manifesto* that often receives the most attention even though it is not really a well-developed articulation of their philosophy. As mentioned earlier, the men were commissioned to write a political platform for a possible party, much in the same way people might be commissioned to develop a platform for the Democratic or Republican parties during a presidential election cycle in the United States. It is often referred to as the direct connection of twentieth-century revolutions, that Marx and Engels provided the blueprint of how to conduct a revolution. However, this assumption is imprecise at best and ideologically biased at worst. *The Manifesto* did conclude with the following: "The proletarians have nothing to lose but their chains. They have a world to win. Working men of all countries, unite!" This was more a statement of philosophy than a rallying cry, however, since in Marx and Engels' Hegelian view of the world, revolution and overthrow of the bourgeoisie was an inevitable conclusion to the age of industrial capitalism.

As followers of Hegelianism, Marx and Engels argued that the revolution to come merely represented the flow of history. It was dialectical as it was about struggle, and teleological because there was a natural end to history. Unlike Hegel, who saw complete rationality (or the Absolute Spirit) at the end of history, Marx and Engels saw a classless world free of exploitation ("from each according to his abilities, to each according to his needs").[5]

But the theories developed by Marx and Engels extended far beyond simply an understanding of the progressive stages through which human history moved. They also explored the connections between interests (particularly class interests) and ideas or **ideologies**, and the relationship between the particular economic means of production, the **base** of society, and the institutions and culture such as government, laws, and the structure of work and family life that emerge from the economy, what has come to be called the **superstructure** built atop the economic base.

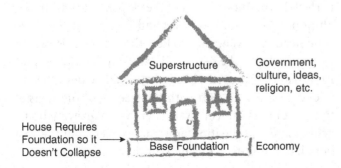

At one point in his career, Marx famously declared that "religion is the opium of the people."[6] Given his belief that human society—and hence social relations—is dictated by the economic base, anything outside of economic relations (what we could call culture) simply worked to support the economic hierarchy. Therefore religion as well as value systems, education, social characteristics, and so on, simply rest on that base. Just as a house is considerably weakened if not resting on a solid foundation, so the superstructure of society cannot adequately stand without the economic base. Religion, then, was simply a mechanism for the powers that be to assert control—your lot in life is horrible, but the "meek" (or poor) shall inherit the earth. Do not worry too much about your position in this life, which is fleeting; good behavior in this life can help you secure eternal happiness in the next. For Marx and Engels, religion was a form of social control that very often lay in the hands of political elites.

An example of this base/superstructure framework drawn from US history points to other connections between the economic "base" and the cultural/religious "superstructure." In the 1830s, as the United States was just entering the early phases of industrialization, the nation witnessed a wave of religious revivals known as the Second Great Awakening. The most prominent revivalist of this era was a man named Charles Grandison Finney, a former lawyer who turned to evangelism. Finney, working primarily in the American Northeastern and Midwestern states, where the descendants of Puritan founders had settled, famously argued that the old ideas of predestination so strongly argued in Calvinist Orthodoxy were mistaken. Borrowing a term from the economics of the market economy that was transforming the lived experience of so many Americans, Finney argued that human beings were in fact "moral free agents," responsible for making their own decisions in religion, and thus responsible for choosing their own salvation. This example of how a concept and language associated originally with market economics (the base) can shape the language of religion and salvation (the religious element of the superstructure) in a society making a dramatic economic change.

Marx and Engels also explored the concept of **alienation**, the way in which human beings in capitalist society become separated from the direct product of their labor, which they perceive as merely a commodity. As we will see, in the twentieth century, scholars have often found these areas of Marxist theory that touch on the relationships among the economy, society, the individual, and ideology, to be some of the most thought-provoking, and it is in these areas that Marxist thought has often exerted a great influence, even among scholars who would not claim to be Marxist.

In 1848, however, the rhetoric of revolution and class struggle dominated the public perception of the ideas of Marx and Engels. Fear of communism, they argued, is a result of a "spectre" or ghost, haunting peoples' consciousness as a result of political ignorance. The bourgeoisie throw ideas out to spook the populace: "They're going to take away your property! They're going to do away with marriage!" Their response to the first scare is that 90% of the population has no property anyway, so the claim is false. Even those who may say they own something have probably mortgaged that property in some way. To the second fear, they argued that women are kept in subjection because their productive capacity consists in creating more bourgeoisie. In supporting this farce by buying into the bourgeois notion of the family, working families themselves are undermined as the proletarian family is ripped apart to provide labor for the industrial capitalist system.[7]

Karl Marx died in 1883, Engels twelve years later. Neither lived to see a successful Communist revolution nor the fulfillment of their idea of the inevitability of revolution. Indeed, by 1899, philosophers, accepting the basic ideas of class struggle and inequality proffered by Marx and Engels, began to hypothesize a different outcome. For example, German economist Edouard Bernstein, influenced by socialism as well as prevailing ideas of evolution brought about through Charles Darwin's work at the middle of the century, wrote a tract called **Evolutionary Socialism**. In his conceptualization, the bourgeoisie was not decreasing, but increasing and consolidating its power. Given this situation, how were workers ever to improve their lot? The answer, argued Bernstein, was not to continue waiting for the so-called inevitable revolution, the answer was to actively incorporate workers into the political system to develop mechanisms for workers to improve their economic security within the already existing system.

This is also not to say that Marxian socialism was the only socialist model previous to Bernstein. Neither Marx nor Engels was the founder of socialism or communism. There have been variants of socialism throughout history. Various attempts at land redistribution during the Roman Republic or in Han China, for example, show ancient roots to the awareness of economic inequalities and

the idea of leveling of society. But the nineteenth century in Europe, at the intersection of the Enlightenment, the French Revolution, and industrialization, was a defining moment in history. Radical ideas popped up throughout Europe in the forms of liberalism, utopian socialism, and yes, Marxian socialism. Political liberalism's basic tenets focused on representative government, but it was primarily an ideology designed for and by the middle classes to the increasing exclusion of workers. In France, a variety of socialist ideologies emerged, including utopian socialism. The goal of utopian socialism was to ensure economic equality in a perfectly harmonious society. Utopian socialists included Charles Fourier, Claude Henri de St.-Simon, Louis Blanc, and Robert Owen. Robert Owen's community of New Harmony, Indiana probably was the furthest developed and imagined of the socialist communities of the nineteenth century. There were variations among these writers and social thinkers, but despite their differences, socialists all displayed hostility toward the privileges that seemed to flow to the bourgeoisie by embracing laissez-faire economics as described by Adam Smith.

The first successful revolution in Marx's name was the Bolsehevik Revolution of 1917/1918 in Russia. But the revolution and its ideas, led by Vladimir Lenin, hardly looked like anything Marx and Engels envisioned. First, Lenin created an idea called the **vanguard** of the proletariat. For Lenin, workers were really never going to develop an appropriately revolutionary consciousness. They would be mollified too easily by small efforts by the capitalist class, such as granting better wages or providing some kind of health insurance. For the revolution in their name to succeed, a group of intellectuals—dedicated revolutionaries—was needed to ensure the revolution would actually happen. Moreover, the historical circumstances were different between the Soviet revolution and Marx's dialectic. The revolution was possible, according to Marx and Engels, because industrial capitalism, the most developed historical phase, was crumbling and therefore society was moving toward the perfect, harmonious world of the classless society. If revolution is inevitable, as Marx and Engels argued, there is no need for a vanguard to help things along. Russia in 1917 could hardly be described as fully industrial capitalist. It had only moved out of what could be described as a feudal society in 1861 with the freeing of the **serfs** at the end of the Crimean War. There was a growing bourgeoisie and a population of urban workers, but the vast population of Russia during World War I was peasant.

Nevertheless, by 1921, when the Civil War in Russia ended and Lenin established the Union of Soviet Socialist Republics (USSR, or Soviet Union) with other provinces once part of the Russian Empire, to the outside world, this seemed like a success. Over the next ten years, the Soviet Union surpassed most industrial countries in steel production, had a visible and viable claim of the equality of women, and was arguably a fully formed industrial capitalist country. To many in the world outside the Soviet Union, communism seemed to be working.

THE INFLUENCE OF MARX AND ENGELS ON TWENTIETH-CENTURY HISTORICAL WRITING

Now that we have explored the nineteenth-century context, the philosophy of Marx and Engels, and briefly discussed the revolution we often refer to as the first successful Marxist Revolution (a misnomer at best as we have discussed), it is essential that we explore the ways in which Marx and Engels' theories influenced historians of the twentieth century. In this regard, Marx and Engels as revolutionaries and Marx and Engels as political economists are both important to the story, because the historians calling themselves "Marxists" were influenced by their own political milieu—one that coexisted with the Soviet Union.

Marx and Engels left a lasting legacy for politicians, philosophers, and historians. They conceptualized human societies and thought in a way that not only accepted but prioritized the material world. They rethought the framework of **capital**, dialoguing with some of the greatest financial minds of the modern period (such as Adam Smith or Thomas Malthus). But more than economic thinkers, they explored the economy from a historical perspective. It is in and through historical processes that humans vie for change, that humans engage in social relations built on the economy, and through which meaning for ourselves is to be found. This legacy, far more than the revolutions of the twentieth century, earns Marx and Engels such pivotal roles in modern economic and historic thought.

Early Marxist historians in Britain were intrigued by the seeming success of the Soviet project. In the lean years of global depression in the 1930s, with high unemployment, horrible repercussions for trades union members lobbying for better wages and conditions, and low agricultural and industrial productivity, many left-leaning scholars saw the Soviet Union as a successful model. The Soviet project still looked good—it had increased productivity, workers seemed happy, and for the most part it avoided the perilous financial plunge of the early 1930s. It is easy to dismiss these ideas in the twenty-first century, but in the context of the 1930s, the Soviets were a success story. Scholars in the West were not privy to the fact that the USSR kept a very tight lid on internal problems associated with industrial development; they also kept the repression of the Soviet citizens and the purges of the middle of the 1930s well under wraps so that to the outside observer, it seemed a utopian society. Many left-leaning scholars not only admired the Soviet system but also were members of their own country's Communist parties. Many fought against ultraconservative, fascist governments both in the twenties and thirties, such as against Benito Mussolini's corporatism and against Franco's quest for power in the Spanish Civil War, not to mention Hitler's consolidation of power in Germany.

While many scholars maintained a Marxist perspective in their writings, matching their political commitments on the global world stage, some both in the West and in the Soviet Union adopted what is known as a "vulgar Marxist" position. A **vulgar Marxist** position essentially states that great events have great causes, and that political changes catch up to economic changes. In other words, vulgar Marxists follow the teleology very specifically—capitalism is the final stage of historical development before the inevitable revolution. Sometimes referred to as **economism**, vulgar Marxism sees the economic base as the determinant of all social action. So all historical processes are economically determined. Consequently, Soviet historians commissioned as part of the Stalin regime wrote about the inevitability of the Soviet Revolution and the necessary overthrow of the bourgeois world of the Tsar and his family. In the west itself, historians and economists who subscribed to this view of history saw various parts of history solely in terms of phases established in Marxist theory. In other words, vulgar Marxists were unwilling to challenge some of the theoretical inadequacies of this portion of Marx's philosophy: all societies are class societies; revolution is necessary and inevitable; economic determinism; class consciousness is necessary for revolution.

Not all, or even most, historians using a Marxist perspective were "vulgar Marxists," however. In fact, in the early 1950s, a variety of work emerged that focused on the agency of the working class and its fight against capitalist oppression. Using Marxist economic models of the wage minimum, class struggle, and consciousness, these historians, including the historian assigned at the end of the section, raised the lives of workers out of obscurity and gave working-class struggle an important role in the history of the Industrial Revolution. These new, or **neo-Marxists** were more sophisticated in their understanding of the ways in which Marxist theory connects to historical practice (and to lived experience of the past). A better definition—Neo-Marxist historians focus on the nature of exploitation in society; they explore causes behind existing exploitation, very often resulting from unequal economic relations that are reaffirmed through the power elite of a society. But the outcomes are not always the same. The important point for Marxist historians is the use of a particular method to test the validity of a historical truth. In other words, these historians considered themselves materialists and used sources that emphasized that touchable, tangible, "sink your teeth into" reality. They focused on the ontological framework of the past (what we often state is "lived experience"). Borrowing the Marxist conception of materialism, they emphasized economic relations. So the theoretical framework established in Marxist theory was successfully applied in the ways in which scholars influenced by this theory interpreted primary sources and crafted stories about the past.

In Great Britain, three men most clearly embody the new Marxist historiography of the 1940s to early 1960s: Christopher Hill, Eric Hobsbawm, and Edward Thompson (we will address Hill and Hobsbawm in this chapter, and look at Thompson in Chapter 5). Christopher Hill (1912–2003) was the son of a York solicitor. Though sources are unclear as to when Hill became a Marxist, we do know that he joined the Communist Party in 1935 and spent a year in the USSR. In 1940, he joined the British Army and eventually served in the British Foreign Office. That same year, he published his first analysis of the English Civil War. His work on the English Revolution of 1640 and again of 1688 is a classic argument of class struggle in the emergent capitalist economy. Characterizing the revolution as a "Bourgeois Revolution," Hill argued that the revolution represented the new world of capitalism defined in Marx and Engels' articulations of the periods of history. By the end of the war, Hill's work was largely discussed by younger English historians who established a Communist historians'

group. Hill remained influential throughout his life, even among historians who critiqued his approach to the seventeenth century. Like many of his generation, he broke his commitment to a political Marxism after 1956.

Christopher Hill's work in the 1950s focused on the ways in which the revolutionary upheaval of seventeenth-century England that culminated with the "Glorious Revolution" of 1688 represented in some ways the prototypical "bourgeois revolution" that would ultimately usher in the phase of industrial capitalism as explained by Marx. In early incarnations of his work on Britain's seventeenth-century social conflicts, Hill characterized the transfer of power from monarch to Parliament as a Bourgeois revolution. In other words, he read the economic and political sources surrounding a century of conflict through the lens of Marxist theory. He saw a new class emerge in power politics to displace the aristocracy, and this new class, comprised of merchants, landowners, and industrialists, would form the core of the Bourgeois world of industrial capitalism.[8] While Hill eventually abandoned this supposition by the 1970s as new evidence was found, his original argument reveals how powerfully theoretical premises can inform scholarship. While later in his career, Hill clarified points and softened his position (as you may detect in our reading for this chapter), this early work clearly represents Marxist philosophy and demonstrates the ways in which Hill viewed the world in materialist terms.

Eric Hobsbawm (1917–2012) was an immigrant from Egypt via Austria and Germany. At the outbreak of World War II, he, like Hill, joined the army and served with the Royal Engineers and the Educational Corps. Hobsbawm's work is more varied than Hill's, writing on such topics as machine breakers during early industrialization, the connections between industry and the rise of empire, and traditions and mythology (most notably, *The Invention of Tradition* and *Captain Swing*). He was also more unashamedly and unapologetically a Marxist historian throughout his life. Hobsbawm was orphaned in his early teens, and living with his uncle in Berlin he joined the Communist Party. Though frustrated with Soviet politics, Hobsbawm, like many others, retained a commitment to Marxism. He reflected later in life that being a first-hand witness to Hitler's Germany indelibly affected his outlook. As the statement opening this chapter suggests, Hobsbawm was a product of his time. His obituaries were both staunchly supportive of his intellectual prowess and simultaneously sneering of his Marxist "attachments," especially his decision to remain in the Communist Party after 1956 when failure of the Soviet project became so clear to so many.

Nor were Hobsbawm and Hill alone in their intellectual work. There was quite a bit of sophisticated economic history to emerge from the classical period of Marxist history. Indeed, the highly esteemed journal *Past and Present* was established in 1952 as a venue for scholars, such as Hobsbawm, to articulate their histories of working-class struggle. In France, for example, some of the most exciting work emphasizing history of the lower orders during the French Revolution came from a Marxist perspective. Marxism remained particularly strong in French history because of the struggles with Fascism during the 1930s and World War II. The historian Georges Lefebvre, for example, introduced the peasant as a class into the historiography of the French Revolution. His article "Les Paysans et La Révolution française" intimated the significant role peasants played in the revolution, and it is also in this article that Lefebvre articulated phases of the revolution representative of the bourgeois and workers' revolutions. While this article (and his earlier work on rural class history) faced numerous critiques, especially from his own students, it remains the standard bearer for understanding the French Revolution from below.[9] Nevertheless, those same students, such as Albert Soboul, maintained the Marxist perspective of class struggle as the basis of the revolution throughout their works. Soboul (1914–1982) was the third generation of Marxist scholars to hold a prestigious chair in History at the Sorbonne in Paris. Born in Algeria and raised in France after the death of his parents, Soboul joined the French Communist Party and worked for the French Resistance against the collaborationist Vichy regime during World War II. His dissertation on the sans-culottes of the French Revolution was infused with an incisive class analysis, viewing the period of 1793–1794, much like Christopher Hill viewed the English Revolution of 1688, as a bourgeois revolution. While he continued to write about the class struggle inherent in the centralization of power in the first years of the French Republic, he also began to examine the French peasantry as well as the role of religion during the Republic, focusing on the ways in which the masses contributed to historical change.

There are other committed Marxist historians who hail from and work on areas outside Europe. Irfan Habib (b. 1931), for example, is an Indian historian, self-described as a Marxist, who has explored the agrarian systems of premodern India. His major work *The Agrarian System of Mughal India, 1526–1707* was the first to explore exhaustively the relationships between trade and agriculture, and between rural aristocracy, working poor, and Mughal elite. Like Soboul, Brazilian historian Jacob Gorender (b. 1923) has focused on the agrarian elite and class relations. His seminal work *Colonial Slavery*,[10] published in 1978, puts forth an argument that colonial slavery became a new mode of production, one that certainly was not capitalist. This argument runs counter to many works that see plantation labor as serving the interests of capitalism even as the unfree labor used for those ends does not quite fit a traditional Marxist model of capitalism, but also introduces plantation slavery as a form of exploitation that differed from other unfree labor (feudalism for example).

In the United States, Howard Zinn published a "radical" history of the country from a Marxist perspective. In *A Peoples' History of the United States*, Zinn argues that the history of the United States has been built on subjugation of the vast majority of people, from the indigenous population sent into exile to the immigrant workers of the twentieth century. More recently, the urban historian Mike Davis has explored the urban landscape from California to Caracas, examining the combined effects of urban growth with growing inequality, an effect that has exacerbated class tensions and the plight of the poor.[11] As an editor and frequent contributor to the *New Left Review*, Davis has continued the tradition of polemical writing prominent among the British scholars who coined the "New Left" with his focus on history from below (to be discussed in Chapter 5).

CONCLUSION

The Marxist tradition has undergone tremendous evolution since the 1930s. In 1953, Josef Stalin died, and his successor, Nikita Khrushchev, began a program of "de-Stalinization" designed to recoup the intellectual and political losses of the Stalinist period. British Leftists were shocked, but hoped that this new period would show the USSR as the utopia it was once perceived as. Such hopes were shattered, when in 1956, Khrushchev delivered a speech to the Politburo (Soviet government) stating that the USSR was open to negotiations with its satellite states and would welcome open dialogue and more independence from them. In the same breath, Soviet tanks plowed into Hungary, arresting intellectuals and undermining any attempts at democratic discourse. The Left in Britain and elsewhere turned away from the

Soviet Union with its model of aggression and saw its political commitments unravel. It remained committed though to the use of Marxist models as vehicles for historical investigation, even as it abandoned political connections and alignments. We will discuss more thoroughly this transformation in Chapter 5.

Marxist historians continue to focus on class struggle, and emphasize the haves versus the have-nots, but they have long neglected the thornier points of Marxist philosophy—namely the possibility of revolution (or even the desirability of it) in favor of more nuanced approaches to understanding how people have fought for their best interests even while accommodating to and advocating for the existence of capitalism. In later chapters, we will see how this historiography has branched out both in direct argument against Soviet politics as well as in more organic philosophical traditions.

THINKING LIKE A HISTORIAN

An American worker and folksong writer wrote the primary source for this chapter in 1940 while living in a Farm Security Administration Migrant Camp in California. This period in US history was the time of the Dust Bowl, the New Deal, and numerous Federal projects to get people back to work. Like the more famous folk singer Woody Guthrie (1912–1967), this writer characterizes the nature of capitalism, particularly the gross inequalities of wealth during the period of the Great Depression. Folk music is an excellent source for scholars interested in the past, because the songs often relate in some way to national culture. In particular, it often lamented the lack of empathy in American society at a time when so many people were suffering from the consequences of poor investments, agricultural decline, and global depression. Because of their rich stories of common people, folk lyrics have been useful for historians of popular culture, economics, and society to tease out the lives of everyday folk. For this exercise, use your understanding of Marxist theory to read this source as a Marxist might. Ask yourself the following questions:

- What is the basic historical context you can pull from the song? Does it reference places? people? systems?
- What does the experience of this migrant's story signify? Is there a perception versus reality at work? If so, describe this juxtaposition.
- Is the writer happy living in his cabin? What were the circumstances leading him to his new home? Explain

how this secondary migration ties into the writer's larger social comment—in other words, what is the writer trying to say with this song?

- Finally, once you have answered these background questions, put forth a preliminary argument. If you were a Marxist historian, how could this source help you explain 1930s' US history? How could you provide meaning for this period?

The secondary source you are reading, Christopher Hill's "John Bunyan and His Publics," examines the writings of the early-modern English radical (1628–1688) and author of the now classic *The Pilgrim's Progress*. As you read the article, ask yourself the following questions:

- What was Bunyan's personal history? According to Hill, what were his two "schools" and then his "university," and how did that "education" shape his outlook?
- On the surface, this article (and Bunyan's life) might read as a piece of religious history, but Hill argues that class was central to Bunyan's worldview. Explain how religion and class coincided in seventeenth-century Britain.
- Describe how *The Pilgrim's Progress* can be read as a work of class struggle. How did Bunyan's contemporaries perceive this work? Was there a difference between Anglican (Church of England) and Nonconformist (those Protestants who did not follow Anglicanism)? Between the gentry and the artisans? How did future generations perceive this work?
- How does this piece reflect materialist theory? Marxist? How are materialism and Marxism different, if at all?

Sunny Cal (Sunny Cal 4147 60B1)

Jack Bryant, Firebaugh Camp, 1940[12]

You've all heard the story of sunny little Cal,
The place where it never rains; they say it don't know how,
You can sleep out on that ground at night, you can hear the
    people say,
And the moon is always shining almost as bright as day.

They'll say "'Come on, you Okies, work is easy found,
Bring along your cotton sack, you can pick the whole year
    round.
Get your money every night and spread your blankets
    down,
It's always bright and warm; you can sleep out on the ground."

But listen to me, Okies, I came out here one day,
Spent all my money getting here, now I can't get away.
The night that I landed, it almost came a flood
I spread the tent out on the ground and laid down in
the mud.

It rained here all nightlong, boys, I thought we all would
drown.
We all got the flu from sleeping on the ground.
I finally found a cabin so I guess I'll have to stay,
'Cause I haven't got the money and I cannot get away.

Now listen to me Okies, I'll hand it to you straight,
I came out here a week ago and I haven't worked a day,
But now I'm on relief, boys, I guess I done my best.
If it wasn't for old Uncle Sam I guess we'd starve to death. ◼

Full Lyrics are heard here: http://memory.loc.gov/afc/afcts
/audio/414/4147b1.mp3 LOC text version does not have the full lyrics
(see: http://memory.loc.gov/cgi-bin/query/r?ammem/todd:@field
(DOCID+st106)

John Bunyan And His Publics

*Christopher Hill[13] marks the 300th anniversary of
Bunyan's death with a portrait of a self-educated
radical seen as a subversive by Restoration England's
Establishment.*

BERNARD SHAW THOUGHT THAT JOHN Bunyan was Britain's greatest prose writer. *The Pilgrim's Progress*, long a
popular favourite, is now a secure English literary classic, included in university syllabuses. This would have astonished
Bunyan's contemporaries. For most of them he was a tinker,
that emblem of vulgarity and drunkenness. Bunyan's father
was illiterate, and he himself had little formal education. He
probably did not attend a grammar school, certainly not a
university. Academically-trained divines sneered at the presumption of a man who did not know how to form a syl-
logism daring to preach, let alone to publish.

The tercentenary of Bunyan's death fell on August
31st this year. He owed much to the fact that he lived
through the greatest crisis of English history. He was born
in 1628, the year of the Petition of Rights, the first great concession Charles I made to his Parliament. Bunyan died just
before William of Orange came over from the Netherlands
to consolidate Parliamentary sovereignty in the 'Glorious
Revolution'. In 1642 civil war broke out between King and
Parliament. Bunyan was sixteen when he joined (or was
conscripted into) the Parliamentarian army two years
later. The army was his first school. Bunyan saw little active

fighting, for the war ended when he had been in the army
only six months. In the next two years the troops had not
much to do except sit and talk. As in 1918–19 and 1945–46,
their talk became very radical.

Before 1640 England had been under strict controls. But
then the censorship broke down completely, and there
was a fantastic outpouring of books and pamphlets on
every subject under the sun, which were greedily read by
a news-starved public. The monopoly of the Church collapsed too, and congregations sprang up everywhere. They
were in effect discussion groups in which ordinary people
argued about religion, politics, economics, morality. In
Cromwell's army free discussion was positively encouraged.

Bunyan, a poor boy from a Bedfordshire village, can
never have heard anything like it. The range of subjects
discussed was astonishing. At the height of what used to
be called 'the Puritan Revolution' all religion was called in
question. Bunyan tells us how men asked whether heaven
and hell existed,' whether there would be a day of judgment, whether the Bible was really the word of God and
'not rather a fable and cunning story', 'devised by cunning men' to hold 'poor ignorant people' in subjection.
Bunyan himself was bewildered by these speculations.
'Everyone doth think his own religion rightest', Jews and
Moslems and pagans. How could you know that the Bible
was true and the Koran not? 'And how if all our faith, and
Christ, and Scriptures, should be but a think-so? Bunyan
tells us that he had many even worse thoughts 'which
at this time I may not, nor dare not, utter'. One wonders
what they could be.

Bunyan's account of the goings-on in his garrison of
Newport Pagnell is confirmed by its commanding officer,
Sir Samuel Luke, later immortalised by Samuel Butler as
Hudibras. Luke was appalled by what he saw and heard.
'Men and women', he moaned, 'lie together and insist it
not to be adultery'. Bunyan later recorded hearing a man
who was trying to seduce a girl tell her to say 'that you are
with child by the Holy Ghost' if she became pregnant.

When Bunyan returned to his village at the age of nine-
teen the country yokel had become a wide-boy. He took
the lead in a group of sceptical, irreverent young men who
continued such discussions. He was 'a brisk talker', he tells
us, and a great swearer, who 'infected all the youths of the
town where I was born with all manner of youthful vani-
ties'. The idea that sin existed only in the imagination, and
so you could do what you liked Bunyan found seductive,
'I being but a young man, and my nature in its prime'. But
he assures us that he was chaste *after* his marriage, which
probably took place in 1649. Bunyan went on arguing with

those whom he called Ranters for the rest of his life. They figure in *The Pilgrim's Progress* and *The Life and Death of Mr Badman*. A treatise on which Bunyan was working when he died was still concerned to refute the Ranter idea that matter was eternal and so that God had not created the world.

In the late 1640s 'all sorts of people dreamed of an Utopia and infinite liberty', a disgruntled person tells us. Levellers called for a democratic republic, Diggers for a communist society, Ranters for sexual freedom. When the army took over effective political power in the summer of 1647, just after Bunyan was demobilised, anything seemed possible. Charles I was tried and executed as a traitor to the people of England, the republic was proclaimed; but the radical phase of the Revolution had passed its peak. The generals set resolutely about restoring social hierarchy and discipline. Levellers, Diggers and Ranters were suppressed. There is no reason to suppose Bunyan had ever shared their democratic aspirations; but he had participated in discussions of all sorts, in the army and in his own village. As the intellectual climate gradually changed, he went through a prolonged religious crisis, which ended with his acceptance in 1653 into the Bedford congregation with which he was to be associated for the rest of his life.

This was Bunyan's second school. It was egalitarian and democratic. Like most congregations during the Revolution, that in Bedford was composed of shopkeepers and artisans, hatters, cobblers, wheelmakers and their womenfolk. 'When you are met as a church', said its founder, 'there's neither rich nor poor, bond nor free in Christ Jesus'. Like most congregations, it was deeply involved in politics on the radical side. In 1653 it welcomed Oliver Cromwell's dissolution of the Long Parliament. In 1657 several members of the congregation protested in the name of the Good Old Cause (the republican cause) against a proposal to make Cromwell king. The congregation set a day apart 'to seek God about . . . the affairs of the nation, and the work of God in the world'. When Oliver rejected the crown, the congregation held a day of praise to God for his goodness. As the restoration of Charles II loomed, many days were given up 'to seek the Lord upon the account of the distractions of the nation'. Just before the restoration they prayed for the nation and God's work; just after it they prayed God to direct their governors. Then they lapsed into silence over the political matters which had hitherto so much concerned them.

One object of the restoration was indeed to prevent common people presuming to interfere in politics. Another object was to stop tinkers and other craftsmen preaching. By this time Bunyan had become a very successful preacher in Bedford and its neighbourhood. He was given the option of promising to stop preaching or going to gaol. He believed that preaching was his God-given vocation, and chose gaol. The JPs drawn from the Bedfordshire gentry thought that tinkers should stick to their pots and pans. Bunyan remained in prison for twelve years. That was longer than the sentence imposed on anyone but regicides or notorious leaders of revolutionary groups. Bunyan had to be extremely tough to survive so long a period in the overcrowded, insanitary prisons of the day, privatised and therefore naturally corrupt. Why was Bunyan so severely treated? He and his church had opposed monarchy, but he was not a political leader.

It was seditious for an unordained tinker to preach. But there were more specific reasons for the Bedfordshire gentry regarding Bunyan as 'a pestilential fellow', the worst in the county. His preaching was fiercely class-conscious. The parable of Dives and Lazarus was used to denounce 'the sad condition of those that are for the most part rich men'. God's own are 'most commonly of the poorer sort'. 'The great ones of the world will go strutting up and down the streets . . . hunting and whoring', whilst they eject their godly tenants or 'pull down the house on their heads'. 'More servants than masters, . . . more tenants than landlords, will inherit the kingdom of heaven'. But 'there is a time coming . . . that . . . the righteous shall wash his feet in the blood of the wicked'. The Bedfordshire gentry cannot have liked that. So Bunyan was silenced.

If the army and the Bedford congregation had been Bunyan's schools, the different comradeship of prison was his university. In gaol he met a murderer and an alleged witch, as well as fellow-sufferers for religion's sake. With some of these he discussed the future organisation of nonconformist congregations in Bedfordshire. Bunyan had previously fiercely attacked Quakers, whom he barely distinguished from Ranters. Getting to know large numbers of them in prison modified his attitude. Despite having to work to earn money for his family, Bunyan found time for reading and writing. *The Pilgrim's Progress* was written in Bedford gaol.

The Pilgrim's Progress is as class-conscious as the sermon on Dives and Lazarus. Wicked characters are invariably labelled as gentlemen and gentlewomen, lords and ladies. *The Pilgrim's Progress* is unique in that both the narrator and the hero are poor men. The appeal is to a very different public from that which read traditional epics. *The Life and Death of Mr Badman*, published in 1680, two years after *The Pilgrim's Progress*, was intended as a companion piece. The latter was the story of a poor man who was a predestined saint. Mr Badman on the other hand starts with enough money to make him want more. His rich father set him up in business, and marriage brought him a handsome dowry. There is much sarcasm at the expense of 'great men's funerals, those badges and escutcheons of their honour'. There are anecdotes of 'a great man' who was 'a very unclean person', of a lady from 'a stately house' who murdered her new-born bastard by 'a brave young gentleman'. 'The poor', Bunyan insisted, 'because they are poor, are not capable of sinning against God as the rich man does.'

Mr Badman is an allegory about the life and death of a sinner; but it also contains a good deal of what Bunyan intended as useful practical advice. Mrs Badman should not have trusted 'her own, poor, raw, womanish judgment' when she married Mr Badman; she should have sought advice from her elders. Mr Badman's career contains many lessons on conduct in business for shopkeepers and small traders, of whom Bunyan's congregation mainly consisted. Their traditional standards were being upset by the perplexing advance of the capitalist economy. Sharp economic practice by one member of the congregation reflected badly on the whole, and so on God's cause. Fraudulent bankruptcy, deceitful weights and measures, pawn-broking and usury—the godly seem to have been tempted by all these methods of making profits. *Mr Badman* is a tract for the times as well as a precursor of Defoe's realistic novels.

Mr Badman continues Bunyan's controversy with his past self. Mr Badman was an atheist. The Scriptures, he thought, are 'as a nose of wax, and a man may turn them whithersoever he lists'. They were 'the cause of all dissensions and discords that are in the land'. Mr Badman made Ranter jokes about marriage: 'Who would keep a cow of their own, that can have a quart of milk for a penny?' When Mr Badman was ill and showed signs of repenting of his wicked ways, his doctor laughed him out of it with the Ranter argument that 'sick-bed fears' 'did arise from the height of his distemper'. Badman had a good sleep, got well, and 'never minded religion more'.

The restoration brought back strict censorship as well as ending freedom of assembly for congregations which did not accept the state church. We must never forget this censorship when reading Bunyan's post-1660 writings. He was a marked man, a 'turbulent spirit' who spent a third of his adult life in prison. One printer, when asked why he had not complied with the 1662 Licensing Act by applying for a licence to print a book by Bunyan, laughed and said everybody knew that he wouldn't have got a licence for a book by *him*. It was not worth applying. The Puritan Richard Baxter confirmed that censorship was applied to authors rather than to the contents of their books. More than fifty of Bunyan's sixty-odd publications appeared illegally, without a licence. In all of them he had to express himself carefully.

He could not, for instance, say in so many words that he deplored the acceptance of the restoration of king and bishops by many former Puritans. Instead he wrote in a poem of 1663:

The politicans that professed*
For base and worldly ends
Do now appear to us at best
But Machiavellian friends . . .
Here we see also who turns round
Like weathercocks with wind

———————
*ie proclaimed themselves Puritans

In *The Pilgrim's Progress* Faithful referred to 'one Temporary', whom he had known 'about ten years ago' and was 'a forward man in religion *then*' (my italics: Bunyan presumably wrote *circa* 1670). 'He was resolved to go on pilgrimage, . . . but all of a sudden he grew acquainted with one Save-self, and then he became a stranger to me'. The pilgrim Faithful was sentenced to be burnt in Vanity Fair because he said that the town's 'religion was naught and such by which a man could by no means please God', as Bunyan had been charged with thinking Anglicanism 'naught'. Like Bunyan, Faithful was described as 'a very pestilent fellow'. More free to speak his mind than Bunyan, Faithful declared that 'the prince of this town' was 'more fit for a being in hell than this town and country'. Faithful railed against 'all the rest of our nobility' and 'most of the gentry of our town'—again just like Bunyan. In a later pamphlet called *Advice to Sufferers* Bunyan said:

> . . . tis a sad sight to see a man that has been suffering for
> righteousness restored to his former estate, while the
> righteousness for which he suffered remains under
> locks and irons.

To evade the censorship Bunyan relied, among other devices, on Biblical code language. 'Cain's brood' are landlords and persecutors; Abel's seed 'have their necks under oppression'. Cain is a symbol for all persecutors, Nimrod for all tyrants. Mountains signify the upper classes. A boar in a vineyard can refer to persecutors. Bunyan always very carefully insisted that whatever his adversaries say, 'the church ... moveth no sedition'. At the most it may defend itself against attack. Yet in one unguarded (and unpublished) passage, Bunyan asked:

> ... and suppose they were the truly godly that made the first
> assault, can they be blamed? For who can endure a boar in a
> vineyard? ... Who bid the boar come there? What had he to do
> in God's house?

Careful comparison of Bunyan's published works with the many treatises he prepared for the press but did not publish throws a great deal of light on what he was really thinking; just as Milton's unpublishable *Of Christian Doctrine* illuminates *Paradise Lost* and *Samson Agonistes*.

A special virtue of Bunyan's style is its simplicity. This derives from Puritan sermons, designed to appeal to ordinary people rather than to university-educated intellectuals; and from the propaganda pamphlets of the civil war which spoke directly to those normally excluded from political affairs. For Bunyan, who was always on the side of the poor against the rich, this was a matter of deliberate choice. 'Words easy to be understood', he insisted, 'do often hit the mark when high and learned ones do only pierce the air.' He drew his metaphor from the popular sport of archery, with which the least educated of his readers would be well acquainted.

Grace Abounding, Bunyan's spiritual autobiography, aims to lead such people to the true faith. Here Bunyan carefully emphasises the banal normality of his experiences:

> One day, as I was travelling in the country ... At another time, as
> I sat by the fire in my house, and musing on my wretchedness ...
> Once as I was walking to and fro in a good man's shop ... One
> day, as I was in a meeting of God's people, full of sadness and
> terror ...

It was when the young Bunyan was playing tipcat, 'just as I was about to strike it the second time, a voice did suddenly dart from heaven into my soul'.

His literary realism, his calculatedly plain style, extended to his poetry as well as his prose. It used to be thought that Bunyan wrote very simple verse because he could do no better: that he was a failed Herbert, Crashawe or Vaughan. Since Graham Midgley's edition of Bunyan's *Poems* (1980), this is no longer plausible. Midgley has shown that Bunyan was writing consciously in a popular tradition of verse which goes back to the ballads, to the immensely popular metrical translation of the Psalms by Sternhold and Hopkins, to countless broadsides and chapbooks. The ballad quatrain had been used by Raleigh and was to be used by Rochester: then it fell out of fashion until the romantic revival. Bunyan used it with a sophisticated wit which reminds us that he was a contemporary of Sedley and Rochester. I quote from a dialogue between Christ and the Sinner, though I cite only the latter:

> Thy mercy, Lord, I do accept as mine.
> Thy grace is free, and that thy Word doth say:
> And I will turn to thee another time,
> Hereafter, Lord, when 'tis my dying day.
>
> . . .
>
> I fear not but thy love I shall obtain,
> Though I with Sin be still in hearty love:
> I need not yet forsake my worldly gain,
> 'Tis grace, not works, that brings to Heaven above.
>
> . . .
>
> I have a mind to Heaven, I must confess,
> I fear to feel the sore revenging smart;
> Yet Sin give me, though Heaven I have the less;
> Take thou my mouth, but let Sin have my heart.
>
> . . .
>
> This world 1 present, that world is to come,
> And I for my part am for present pay:
> Take thou all that, give me of this but some,
> I will not for thy wages make delay.
>
> . . .
>
> My work is great, my time is short also,
> My children's portions I have still to get:
> The world must be my friend and not my foe;
> I'll come hereafter, though I cannot come yet.

That is a much wittier satire of complacent Puritan hypocrisy than any in anti-Puritan literature, because Bunyan knew exactly what he was talking about: the parody of Puritan phrase-mongering hits home. Much of his later writing was taken up with criticisms of the godly who were too ready to accept the standards of this world.

Bunyan was not primarily interested in politics. But politics were forced on him by the conditions of the world in which he lived. If he and his co-religionists were to worship God in the way in which they believed God wished, they had to be prepared to break the law, to go to prison, to face death or exile, as Bunyan did when he transferred all his property to his wife in 1685, in the aftermath of Monmouth's rebellion. When James II offered toleration at the price of co-operation in reestablishing Catholicism and perhaps monarchical absolutism, political decisions were forced on Bunyan and his congregation. Some members cooperated with James. Bunyan himself, we are told, was offered 'a place of public trust'. He is said to have refused, but the story comes after Bunyan's death and the expulsion of James. My point is that a nonconformist could not avoid political decisions. *The Holy War* (1682) is an epic about the history of humanity since the Fall, combined with an allegory about the process of conversion within the human soul. But it is also about the politics of Bedford Corporation, the purges and counter-purges which took place between 1650 and 1682. The spiritual and secular spheres were not separated in reality, and they were not separated in Bunyan's imaginative writings. *The Pilgrim's Progress* records a spiritual pilgrimage, but the pilgrims pass from a City of Destruction which is much like London, through recognisable Bedfordshire countryside to a Celestial City in which they have houses of their own.

Bunyan's upper-class contemporaries saw him as an uneducated agitator, a gaolbird, a regular breaker of the law. A contemporary Bedfordshire parson, himself a former Puritan who had conformed at the restoration, spoke of Bunyan's 'ignorant fanatic zeal'. He was a 'firebrand and most impudent malicious schismatic', who should not be tolerated. The writer was a spokesman for the 'moderate divines', and a future bishop. The Reverend Thomas Cox, who wrote about Bedfordshire in 1720, did not conceal his contempt:

> John Bunyan, author of *The Pilgrim's Progress*, and several other little books of an antinomian spirit, too frequently to be met with in the hands of the common people, was, if we mistake not, a brazier of Bedford.

Bunyan's reputation with the literary establishment was low throughout the eighteenth century, though Swift, Sterne and Cowper are notable exceptions. Hume thought that to compare Bunyan with Addison would be like maintaining 'a molehill to be as high as Tenerife or a pond as extensive as the ocean'. Bunyan was despised

for his social inferiority and disliked for his open hostility towards the gentry and the clergy of the established church. Yet *The Pilgrim's Progress* was a best-seller from its first publication, translated into most of the languages of the world. Johnson roundly declared that 'the general and continued approbation of mankind' was 'the best evidence of its merit'. But *The Pilgrim's Progress'* initial popularity was with the lower and middling sort, and in the American colonies, where gentry and Anglican parsons were thin on the ground. A Chartist prisoner after 1848 claimed Bunyan as a kindred 'rebel'. The message which such people took from *The Pilgrim's Progress* was to hold fast and keep the faith, to maintain solidarity, in poverty, oppression and persecution. 'Be ye watchful, and cast away fear; be sober, and hope to the end'. 'There is a time coming . . .'

Bunyan's reputation in polite circles came only as the middling sort and evangelical religion gained respectability in nineteenth-century England. Then missionaries carried *The Pilgrim's Progress* all over Africa and Asia, where its readers may have appreciated Bunyan's appeal to the downtrodden and the persecuted better than those who had it translated. Bunyan might have preferred his earlier popular audience to the earnest academic attention which he now receives. 'God's little ones', he said in a splendidly dismissive phrase, 'are not gentlemen'. They 'cannot, with Pontius Pilate, speak Hebrew, Greek and Latin'. They suffered, Bunyan implies, with Christ. ∎

Endnotes

1. Eric Hobsbawm, *On History* (New York: New Press, 1997), 229.

2. Karl Marx and Friedrich Engels, "Theses on Feurbach," in *The Marx-Engels Reader*, 2nd ed., Robert C. Tucker, ed. (New York: W.W. Norton, 1978), 145.

3. Robert C. Tucker, "Introduction," in *The Marx-Engels Reader*, Robert C. Tucker, ed., xxii.

4. Karl Marx, "The German Ideology," in *The Marx-Engels Reader* (New York: W.W. Norton, 1978), 155–156.

5. Karl Marx, "Critique of the Gotha Program," in *The Marx-Engels Reader*, Robert C. Tucker, ed. (New York: W.W. Norton, 1978), 531.

6. Karl Marx, "Contribution to the Critique of Hegel's *Philosophy of Right*: Introduction," in *The Marx-Engels Reader*, Robert C. Tucker, ed. (New York: W.W. Norton, 1978), 54.

7. Karl Marx and Friedrich Engels, "The Manifesto of the Communist Party," in *The Marx-Engels Reader*, 2nd ed.,

Robert C. Tucker, ed. (New York: W.W. Norton, 1978), 486–488.

8. Christopher Hill, *The English Revolution, 1640: An Essay* (London: Lawrence & Wishart, Ltd., 1955).

9. Peter M. Jones, "Georges Lefebvre and the Peasant Revolution: Fifty Years On," *French Historical Studies* 16/3 (Spring 1990): 645–663.

10. Jacob Gorender, *Colonial Slavery* (Atica: Sao Paolo, 1978).

11. See for example, Mike Davis, *City of Quartz: Excavating the Future in Los Angeles* (London: Vintage, 1990) and *Planet of Slums* (London: Verso, 2006).

12. Jack Bryant, "Sunny Cal," Sound Recording and Text, Firebaugh FSA Camp, CA, 1940, Library of Congress American Memory Project, *Voices from the Dust Bowl: The Charles L. Todd and Robert Sonkin Migrant Worker Collection, 1940–1941,*.mp3, http://memory.loc.gov/afc/afcts/audio/414/4147b1.mp3 (sound recording) and http://memory.loc.gov/cgi-bin/query/r?ammem/todd:@field (DOCID+st106) (shortened text lyrics), accessed 16 August 2013.

13. Christopher Hill, "John Bunyan and His Publics," *History Today* 38/10 (1988): 13–19.

CHAPTER 4

THE *ANNALES* SCHOOL

CHAPTER OUTLINE

■ The First Generation—Bloch, Febvre, and "*Histoire Totale*"

■ The Second Generation—Fernand Braudel and the Waves of Time

■ The Third Generation—Le Roy Ladurie and Goubert: Making the *Annales* French

■ The Fourth Generation—Roger Chartier and the Rediscovery of *Mentalités*

■ Conclusion

■ Thinking Like a Historian

"In truth, the historian can never get away from the question of time in history: time sticks to his thinking like soil to a gardener's spade."
Fernand Braudel, 1958[1]

One of the most influential schools of historical study in the twentieth century was the *Annales*, a loosely knit group of scholars united by their common connection with the historical journal the *Annales d'histoire Economique et Sociale*. From the founding of the journal in 1929 to the 1970s, successive generations of **Annalistes** blazed new pathways, opening up fresh modes of incorporating the insights of disciplines such as anthropology, sociology, and geography into the broader study of history. The eclectic nature of *Annales* scholarship defies easy categorization, but one thing successive generations of *Annales* School scholars share is an unwavering interest in recharacterizing the role of time in scholarship. As the opening quote by second-generation scholar Fernand Braudel attests, historians by necessity deal with time. However, how we approach those dates is a matter of debate.

The early *Annales* School practitioners believed, as did Marxists of the time, in a materialist conception of history, and that culture rested on society that rested on the economy. To truly understand this relationship, *Annalistes* wanted to take a snapshot of a society and explore all of its components. Think about a picture you may have on your wall (perhaps a family picture). There is an obvious subject (the family in the foreground). But there are other elements that inform the picture. The choice of background for example (a building, trees, or ocean), and other elements of background "noise" (someone walking in the background, a boat on the sea) and background context (was there an argument before the picture? What was the occasion for the photo?). All of these items "fill" a photograph and give it its unique character in time and place—so the same is with history according to the early *Annalistes*. They argued that we cannot simply focus on the foreground of history, but sought what is called a "total history," what Traian Stojanovich described as emphasizing "social, functional, structural approaches to understanding society as a total integrated organism."[2]

While the *Annales* pioneered a wide variety of new approaches to history, four general approaches are considered to comprise the movement. First the *Annales* journal, and especially Marc Bloch and Lucien Febvre, developed new methods in sociological history. This new history shifted the gaze of historians away from the "great man" history, with its interest in political leaders, warfare, diplomacy and, often, nationalism to an emphasis on social development with its focus on economics, demographics, and community development. The second major aspect of the *Annales* School is the reframing of time to focus on large-scale periodizations, further removing history from the study of "the moment." This approach, primarily associated with the work of Fernand Braudel (though used by most *Annaliste* scholars), explored the relationship between the long and short time spans. The third approach—or generation as the developments of the *Annales* are known—swung the pendulum from large-scale, global geographic time introduced by Bloch and realized by Braudel, back to smaller, particularly French frameworks. The third generation popularized the intensive examination of statistical and quantitative models of historical explanation as well was **microhistorical** approaches through detailed studies of one region, sometimes one town over time. The fourth major thrust of the *Annales* historians has been the exploration of popular **mentalités**, or the structure of thought of a given society, at both the popular and elite level, but with a clear emphasis on understanding the worldview of the common folk. During the course of the twentieth century, these research agendas sparked the development of two of the most popular fields of history: social history, with a focus on the lived experience of the masses of a society, and cultural history, with its focus on the meanings people impart to their world. In addition, a number of important subfields of history sprouted from the main thrusts of *Annales* scholarship: environmental history, world-systems theories about the development of capitalism, a major influence on world history proper, and recent literature on family history, the history of emotions, and studies on the impact of literacy and others, all can be traced to the work of various generations of *Annales* historians. We will talk about these developments in later chapters. This chapter will introduce you to the four generations of the *Annales* School and explore their relations to each other and influences on historical study.

THE FIRST GENERATION— BLOCH, FEBVRE, AND "*HISTOIRE TOTALE*"

The *Annales* emerged in the late 1920s under the leadership of two French historians who worked at the University of Strasbourg: Marc Bloch and Lucien Febvre. Marc Bloch lived from 1886 to 1944 when he was executed before a firing squad for his role in the French Resistance to Nazi occupation during World War II.[3] His partner, Lucien Febvre (1878–1956) helped lead the *Annales* School into the mainstream of historical scholarship through his leadership of a department at the *Collège de France*. The name *Annales* School is derived from the journal founded by the two in 1929, the *Annales d'histoire économique et sociale*. This journal was designed to combat what they perceived as the increasing sequestration and isolated research of disciplines and subdisciplines by scholars both in history and throughout the social sciences. In the opening issue of the journal, Febvre declared that these isolationist tendencies were "serious schisms . . . by which we intend to rise. Not by means of articles about method, not by means of theoretical disquisitions, but by means of examples, by means of achieved results! The example of workers of different backgrounds and specializations . . . who will show the results of their research on subjects within their competence and of their choice."[4] By the middle of the 1930s, the *Annales* had moved to Paris, a more central location both geographically and intellectually. This journal became a site where historians interested in exploring innovative research agendas could find a welcoming environment.[5]

This period witnessed a powerful challenge for history from other academic disciplines, particularly sociology, which questioned whether history as a field should even be considered a science. Sociologists such as Emile Durkheim openly asserted that history relied too much on the simple narration of stories to have the hard, analytical edge necessary to qualify as a science. Furthermore, history was always limited in its access to sources about the past, which undermined all historical works' claims to comprehensive understanding of the past. A variety of historians, not only the *Annales*, responded in attempts to defend the nature of their discipline. As we discussed in Chapter 2, for example, Carl Becker responded to these assertions by accepting that history might not meet the qualifications of science, but that historians engaged with a different, but equally important, form of knowledge, much more akin to bards and significant storytellers of past ages.[6]

The *Annales* School, however, took a different tact. Embracing elements of their sociological critics, the *Annales* began to shift their focus away from the emphasis on narratives of important political leaders and events and toward the *structure* of society and examinations of how societies change over time. More important than any particular king or any particular battle for the *Annales* were things such as the prices of agricultural goods and increases and decreases in the population level. Rather than focusing on the marriages that united European royal families, Bloch and Febvre looked at the family structure and nativity patterns for *average* members of those European societies. Accessing this information required the plumbing of whole new sets of sources that had gone largely unexamined by earlier historians: birth and death records, marriage and baptismal sources in church archives. The *Annalistes* also began to piece together the economic life of communities by exploring the records of merchants, tax collectors, and customs agents.

The most comprehensive example of this sociological history is Marc Bloch's *Feudal Society* (*La Société Féodale*), originally published in two volumes in 1940 and 1941, and translated into English twenty years later. Here, Bloch mapped out in detail both the material development of the society of medieval Europe (with France as his primary test case) and the ideological framework that justified the hierarchical system of the age. The traditional history of monarchs, dignitaries, and dramatic military conflict disappeared, submerged in a sea of information focused on the lives and relationships of people situated below the seats of power. Patterns of trade, land holding, explorations of hygiene and health, and relations between nobles and serfs, are just a few of the areas explored by Bloch that had been essentially untouched by earlier scholars of the era. Liberated from an overweening attachment to monarchs, Bloch's history dealt with the vast expanses of time and space necessary to understand patterns of development that took place at the lower levels of society. While individuals often disappeared into the mass in *Feudal Society*, the peasant as a significant *type* emerged as never before in a work of history. Bloch evoked a sense of the texture of peasant life, and in doing so opened up a space for exploring the lives of ordinary people.

In noting the importance of Bloch's *Feudal Society*, we should not give the impression that, suddenly, sociologically informed scholarship ruled the day in historical studies. In fact, the traditional history focused on elites and the development of the state continued (and continues to this day) to hold great sway in the field. But if we see *Feudal Society* as a response to the intellectual and disciplinary challenges of its era, we begin to capture the immediate significance of the work. Some have argued that by responding to the critics of scholars such as Emile Durkheim by embracing a new brand of sociologically informed history, Bloch, Febvre, and the rest of the *Annalistes* hoped to move the field of history back to a central place among the social sciences.[7] Whether such an agenda was successful or not is impossible to determine. But, in retrospect, we can clearly see one important long-term consequence of Bloch's scholarship: the development through the course of the twentieth century of the field of social history, which focuses on the lives of ordinary people (to be discussed in Chapter 5).

While Bloch's sociological approach to medieval Europe has received the lion's share of historians' attention when they examine *Feudal Society*, Bloch also explored other, more intimate and less material aspects of society in his work. Sections of *Feudal Society* titled "Conditions of Life and Mental Climate" and "Modes of Feeling and Thought" point to ways in which Bloch attempted to link the mental and emotional world of the peasants with the material world of land holding and economic life. In this way, Bloch was working to forge an understanding of what *Annalistes* would dub the *mentalités* of the average person.[8] While the concept of *mentalités* certainly existed in the early works of Febvre and Bloch, it would emerge in more substantively defined form in the fourth generation, which we will discuss later in the chapter.

THE SECOND GENERATION— FERNAND BRAUDEL AND THE WAVES OF TIME

While historiographers typically hold up Bloch and Febvre as the founders of the *Annales* School, the name most commonly linked to the intellectual movement is that of Febvre's student, Fernand Braudel (1902–1985). Braudel ambitiously sought to expand on the work of his predecessors to create a **total history (*histoire totale*)**. Braudel sought to link the sociological history of Bloch with a more fully developed sense of history rooted in geology and geography. Furthermore, Braudel aimed more explicitly to rethink periodization (how historians define time periods to limit their research) and geographical boundaries in his innovative works, *The Mediterranean and the Mediterranean World in the Age of Phillip II* and *The Wheels of Commerce*.

Braudel's education was truly global and his subsequent approach to history reflected his experiences. Born in Lorraine, France, he spent about a decade (1922–1933) teaching in Algerian schools. Beginning in 1935, he spent three years at the University of São Paolo in Brazil where he managed to continue his research by photographing records and shipping the film to Brazil (i.e., microfilm). Like many of his colleagues, he joined the fight in World War II. Caught by the Nazis and imprisoned, Braudel managed to write a draft of his masterwork, *The Mediterranean and the Mediterranean World in the Age of Phillip II*, while imprisoned in a Nazi prisoner of war camp, sending notebook after notebook to his mentor Lucien Febvre.[9]

Braudel's work sought an even broader history than practiced by Bloch and Febvre, one that transcended national boundaries and the conventional limits of chronology that most fields of history imposed upon themselves. Drawing deeply on the fields of geology and geography, Braudel conceived of human social development taking place simultaneously along three different temporal levels, which he famously compared to different portions of a wave in the ocean. At the base of this wave, the **longue durée**, are deep currents that are essentially invisible but are in fact the most powerful force moving water around the globe. This time span, often referred to a geologic time by historians, suggests that human society cannot be divorced from the shifts of the earth and the deep influence of specific types of geological features in shaping social development: the power of mountains to isolate some groups; the proximity of other societies to major bodies of water that served as trading routes. In a 1958 essay, he wrote, "For centuries, man has been a prisoner of climate, of vegetation, of the animal population, of a particular agriculture, of a whole slowly established balance from which he cannot escape without everything's being upset."[10] For better or worse, humans are inextricably tied to their geography.

Carrying on with the wave analogy, the middle section of the wave (dubbed **conjoncture** by Braudel), what we might call the body of the wave, is more readily visible than the deep current; this is the gradually rising and falling mass of water that we might identify as the full wave itself. In Braudel's analogy to human history, this section of the wave corresponds with long-term developments in human societies: economic revolutions such as industrialization, population increase or decline, urbanization, and so on. Like geological time, these transformations extend beyond the boundaries of particular nations and often transcend the temporal boundaries of a particular, politically defined era, such as the "Elizabethan Era" or the "Age of Jackson." While it is in the space of the conjoncture that Braudel also located the changes in consciousness or *mentalités* explored by the earlier *Annalistes*, he clearly gave it less significance than other, more material aspects of historical time. Braudel was interested in transformations that took place over decades, or even centuries, and that were not governed by the political transitions of the day. These more ephemeral developments, such as the rise of a particular state or the prosecution of a particular war, took place in Braudel's conceptualization at the most superficial part of the wave (the **événementielle**), the froth or foam that appeared at the crest of the powerful wave below. For Braudel, traditional history spent far too much time focused on the froth, those events that might, on the surface, appear spectacularly, as foam that shimmers in the moonlight and washes up on the beach on chilly evenings. But ultimately these frothy events lacked staying power and, more to the point, were only the superficial manifestation of much deeper developments occurring below. An example of such an event might be the assassination of the Archduke Franz Ferdinand by Gavrilo Princep in Sarajevo. This moment in the summer of 1914 was the spark that ignited the flames of World War I, but there were deep-seated processes already at work in the political, social, and geographic framework of Europe generally and the Balkans specifically that led to the spark—in other words, the waves created the foam.

Further, Braudel explored the nature of the movement of time, contrasting the seeming nonmovement of large-scale practices—the **synchronic**—with patterns of change over time that truly characterize history—the **diachronic**.[11] Arguing that historical time "lends itself easily to the supple double action of synchrony and diachrony," Braudel concluded that history "cannot envisage life as a mechanism that can be stopped at leisure in order to reveal a frozen image."[12] Here, like his *Annales* forefathers, Braudel drew a line in the sand between history and sociology and their conceptions of time and human societies. Braudel argued that the very nature of the historian's craft—time—set itself apart from other fields and necessitated its existence in the larger realm of the social sciences.

By creating an awareness of the depth of human social developments, Braudel hoped to be able to create a "total history" of human societies that simultaneously brought into focus the relationship of man to his geological environment with its almost glacial rate of change, the somewhat more rapid but still gradual change in the middle range, as well as the more visible, but ultimately superficial and less powerful transformations of the moment on the surface. Braudel attempted to carry his project through in his study *The Mediterranean and the Mediterranean World in the Age of Phillip II*. Braudel's interest in long-term developments of human societies led him in time to develop the concept of the *longue durée* or periods of history that are measured in the hundreds of years and that sync up with various processes and developments, such as the development of industrial society or urbanization. Furthermore, Braudel's expanded sense of geography allowed him to conceive of the "Mediterranean World" as including areas of Northern Europe and Central Asia, regions linked to the Mediterranean through commerce. He accomplished this through his conception of **structures** and **models**. On the surface, structures appear synonymous with the *longue durée*, but Braudel connects structures to mental processes (in part a concept borrowed from his colleagues in other fields, as we will discuss in Chapter 8). According to Braudel, structures are constructs that appear synchronous (never changing) because of their long duration. Humans have a difficult time conceiving of something in any other way. Such a structure might be capitalism or imperialism. But, as Braudel argued, while structures seem ever present and unchanging, they, like the geographic *longue durée*, are simply slow-moving frameworks. To define and limit structures, Braudel established his notion of the model, described as a ship in his framework. Braudel stated that the limits of structures are determined by how long the theoretical ship floats along the currents of time. You try out your ship on the waves waiting for the moment when it will take to the sea and not sink, then you track the ship's movements until it sinks again. The duration of the floating ship marks the moment of periodization. In this way, Braudel could look at a particular Mediterranean world during the long reign of Philip II of Spain (1556–1598) or a particular moment of the emergence of capitalism (the fifteenth through the eighteenth centuries).

Febvre described Braudel's scholarship as "a revolutionary new way of looking at history . . . a historic mutation of the first magnitude."[13] But in many ways,

Braudel was not blazing new theoretical paths for historians so much as he was pushing the first-generation *Annales* scholarship to its furthest points and giving them specific articulation. He continued Bloch's interest in commerce, prices, and demographic shifts, while adding a more thorough discussion of geography and pursuing the links of commerce ever farther abroad from his nominal subject. And, much like Bloch and Febvre, Braudel directed his gaze away from prominent leaders, warfare, and diplomacy (the froth on the crest of Braudel's wave), and toward the lower, for Braudel more significant levels of social development. While Bloch had been critiqued for focusing too much on the collective and not enough on the individual, Braudel did him one better, incorporating the nonhuman into his scholarship as significant actors. Mountain ranges, rivers, and the Mediterranean Sea itself play a prominent role in Braudel's work.[14] Braudel's focus on the *longue durée* has led some critics to assert that his work becomes essentially static and thus, in a sense, nonhistorical despite his emphasis on the diachronic.

Despite the criticism, the impact of the *Annales* School on the profession of history soared in the years following World War II when Braudel became most associated with the movement. The *Annales* found a new institutional home in the Sixth Section for Economic and Social Sciences of the *École Pratique des Hautes Études*. Braudel's work on the emergence of capitalism may have had particular political resonance in the Cold War environment of the second half of the twentieth century as an alternative to the Marxist explanation for the rise of the free market.

THE THIRD GENERATION—LE ROY LADURIE AND GOUBERT: MAKING THE *ANNALES* FRENCH

While Braudel expanded his work into areas of geology, and spent less time on *mentalités*, a new generation of *Annalistes*, sometimes referred to as the Third Generation, returned to, and expanded the study of the mental structures of human societies. Braudel's work was so reaching in scope that younger scholars felt a tug back to national history was necessary. Braudel, the leader of the second generation of the *Annales*, editor of its journal from 1956 to 1967 (under whose tenure the journal fashioned its third and most longstanding name, *Annales: Economies, sociétés, civilizations*) found his positions questioned, much in the same way he questioned his own mentors. What we characterize in this book as the third generation is often rolled into the Braudel years because of his profound influence and the third generation's continuation of studying patterns of the *longue durée*. However, it is clear that there truly was a methodological break between Braudel and scholars who wrote their theses in the 1950s and 1960s. Specifically, the third generation of the *Annales* School, led by historians such as Pierre Goubert and Emmanuel Le Roy Ladurie strove to make the *Annales* School more French. Focusing on demographic and other quantitative records to create intricate microhistories of particular regions, the third generation bore little resemblance to its predecessors, at least on the surface.

Pierre Goubert (1915–2012) decided to become an historian after his encounters in the 1930s with Marc Bloch. Studying under Ernest Labrousse and Meuvret, and therefore well-versed in quantitative approaches to the study of the past, he completed his thesis *Beauvais and the Beauvaisis 1600 to 1730* in 1960. He was eventually appointed to the Sorbonne in 1969. Like Braudel before him, Goubert's approach to history was influenced by his experiences. His mother's side of the family took "300 years to move the ten miles from their village to Saumur,"[15] and he projected this personal history into his approach to writing about French peasant culture. An early modern historian, he wrote The *French Peasantry in the Seventeenth Century* intricately exploring the social lives of peasants through an examination of court records, church records, and other sources. His relationship with the two previous *Annales* generations is obvious: a connection to economic and demographic study as well as a *longue durée* approach to his regional study. His work contains extensive statistical information that provides a unique window into peasant society in the seventeenth century, and this emphasis on the quantitative kept Goubert's work firmly grounded in the materialist tradition of his *Annales* forebears. In so doing, he pioneered a generation of **demographic** history. He differed in his focus on the micro—one region in France—and on his insertion of statistical methods of analysis to understand the peasant communities of the past.

For his part, Emmanuel Le Roy Ladurie (1929–) contested the insistence on the diachronic nature of all structures when he introduced the concept of an *histoire immobile* (immobile, or "motionless" history) that juxtaposed economic stagnation to political development. His historical perception was influenced by his father's

political work, first as an agricultural minister under Pétain's collaborationist Vichy France, then as a fighter in the French Resistance after 1943. He was educated at the University of Paris and secured a position at the *École Pratique des Haute Études*, where he took over editorship of *Annales* from Braudel in 1967.

His monograph *The Peasants of Languedoc* (originally published in 1966) is perhaps the most well-known example of this third generation. Le Roy Ladurie also built off of the work of his predecessors, linking shifts in public consciousness (or *mentalités*) to specific demographic shifts. Le Roy Ladurie sought to blend the demographic/statistical with the cognitive/ideological in important ways, but often for him the *mentalités* of the peasants served as a block to innovation, leaving one with a sense of peasants always resisting any type of change.[16] Further, the state was an imposing structure, and while the several centuries represented a socioeconomic immobility, there was nevertheless tremendous development in cultural and state institutions, so much that Le Roy Ladurie could describe this period not as a period of preindustrial transition, as Marxist scholars might argue, but as a working society in and of itself.[17] Through the exploration of centuries of church tithe records, price and wage records, and land tax records among others, Le Roy Ladurie found a society that remained stagnant despite a brief interlude in which peasants cleared new land and grew new crops. Higher prices for food, ecological problems of the mini ice age of the sixteenth through seventeenth centuries, the shocks of the Protestant Reformation, and the demands of a highly intrusive bureaucratic state all served to immobilize the peasant community of Languedoc. Thus, like Goubert, Le Roy Ladurie maintained crucial methodological elements that we can describe as *Annaliste*, but added the regional component as well as the suffocating structure of immobility to his analysis.

THE FOURTH GENERATION— ROGER CHARTIER AND THE REDISCOVERY OF *MENTALITÉS*

The third generation led very quickly to a fourth generation of the *Annales*—one focused more intensely on the previously discussed *mentalités*. When we talk about a history of *mentalités*, we mean in effect the history of the attitudes, values, taboos, and other "unconscious" thoughts held by a society at a given moment. While the fourth generation is characterized by the general acceptance of *mentalités* and use of less tangible source material, we need to remember that the first inklings of thinking about the worldview of regular, ordinary folk began with the work of Febvre and Bloch. Much as the sociological approach to history shifted the historians' focus from political leaders to the masses of society, the history of *mentalités* directs our attention away from elite philosophers and theologians to the nature of popular thought. Most often in Bloch's *Feudal Society*, an understanding of popular *mentalités* is derived from the broad statistical patterns revealed in the demographic data. Shrinking family size, for example, may provide evidence of changing attitudes toward children and the family itself; social attitudes regarding death will shift with changing mortality rates. In this sense, the early strain of *Annales* scholarship remained firmly materialist, assuming that *mentalités* follows the actual life experience. By the time Bloch published *Feudal Society*, the goal of exploring and understanding the mental world of average folk had long been part of the *Annales* agenda. Bloch himself made a major contribution to the study of *mentalités* in his work *The Royal Touch: Monarchy and Miracles in France and England*. In this work, Bloch examined the ritualistic healing touch of the king and contextualized the act by examining common understanding of magic and spirituality in the medieval era. Bloch also noted the way in which the public display of such healing acts also played into the image of the king and the projection of royal power, but in tracing the development of the history of *mentalités* the more critical innovation is the reading of the mental world of the era.

But the most influential exploration of *mentalités* by the early *Annalistes* was not Bloch's *Royal Touch* but Lucien Febvre's *The Problem of Unbelief in the Sixteenth Century: The Religion of Rabelais* (1942). In this work, Febvre examines the mental and spiritual world of Europe in the 1500s, emphasizing the near impossibility of atheism in the age. Febvre's exploration of religious belief revolutionized the field, looking as he did beyond the particular church doctrine that had occupied most works of religious history up to this point, and instead exploring spirituality at the grassroots level, and through the thought of religious outsiders.

Just as earlier generations of *Annales* scholars were influenced by their predecessors, the fourth generation was greatly influenced by the work of Febvre, Bloch, and Braudel, but found their point of interest in *mentalités*.

Led by Roger Chartier (1945-), the prolific author of works on print culture and the French Revolution, the fourth generation builds from the microhistory of the third generation by using local records and transcripts not merely to gain an understanding of property-holding patterns, birth rates, and the working of the court system, but also to explore the worldview, the *mentalités* of the peoples of the past. His works, including *The Cultural Origins of the French Revolution*, *A History of Private Life*, and *A History of Reading* all remain firmly within the *Annaliste* tradition. In a sense, the fourth-generation *Annalistes* questioned whether the social structure does not derive from the values and perceptions of the members of society, rather than the other way around as Bloch and Febvre articulated. This debate about the meeting point of consciousness and lived experience remains a critical point of debate among social theorists.

This relationship of the *mentalités* of the people to their surrounding context as articulated by this generation of the *Annales* influenced scholars such as Natalie Zemon Davis in her work *The Return of Martin Guerre*, which on the surface is a retelling of a sixteenth-century legal case of an imposter but is more deeply a story about sexual relations and the changing attitudes and value systems produced by the upheavals of the Protestant Reformation. Fourth-generation *Annales* influence is seen also in Carlo Ginzburg's study of the cosmology of a medieval miller, *The Cheese and the Worms* again about a legal case and the worldview of those during the period of the Inquisition. Even more radically, historians such as Ginzburg and Davis go even further into the peasant experience by looking at particular individuals in addition to regions. Such microhistories aim to reveal the experience of life for common folk (again, using public records such as Inquisition transcripts and court/church records) to reconstruct as much as possible the lives of individual people. Along the way, Ginzburg and Davis both reveal the communities in which these individuals lived, but there are always the questions about whether these individual case studies are too idiosyncratic to truly cast light on the general experience of being a peasant in early modern Europe.

With all work of the fourth generation and work inspired by it, the social world remained important, but it no longer held the primary role in conceiving the reality of peoples' lived experiences. Indeed, as Chartier argued, no longer did culture rest on society that rested on the economy, but the economy itself was a cultural formation. For Chartier, "it is on this reduced scale, and possibly only on this scale, that we can avoid deterministic reduction in grasping the relation between systems of belief, values and representations and social affiliations."[18] This in itself was a radical turnaround in the *Annales* methodology.

CONCLUSION

As you can see, the divisions of the various generations of the *Annales* School oftentimes overlap. For the most part, the first three generations of the *Annales* School remained firmly planted in a materialist tradition, exploring geography, demography, and economy to such a degree that there are debates about how substantive their differences truly are. Even while recognizing the world of the ordinary, the material world often dominated. Only with the fourth generation, and with the later works of Le Roy Ladurie did the *Annales* School explore less tangible aspects of history. One of the major critiques of Le Roy Ladurie's groundbreaking work was his imposition of possible dialogue for his early modern peasants. For many scholars, reading the memories, beliefs, actions, and voices into the documents goes against the grain of historical scholarship. But as we will see in later chapters, reading "against the grain" sometimes became a necessity.

The impact of the *Annales* was enhanced as their work was published in English in the early 1960s. Suddenly scholars outside of France had far greater access to the work of Bloch, Febvre, Braudel, and others. The impact on scholarship internationally was profound. Social historians in the United States found towns, especially New England towns, provided ample records with which to take up the same questions of demography and economic development that Bloch had explored in the *Feudal Society*. Kenneth Lockridge published *A New England Town: the First Hundred Years*, addressing a single community over the span of a century (a classic *longue durée*), and addressing demographic shifts, literacy rates, and social attitudes. Phillip Greven looked at four generations of families in Andover, Massachusetts, to see what could be discerned about land holding patterns and family relationships over a similarly *longue durée*. Meanwhile, scholars working in a different vein of Braudel's work, his interest in the global functions of capitalism, established the Fernand Braudel Center for the Study of Economies, Historical Systems, and Civilizations at the State University of New York in Binghamton.[19]

These multiple swings of the *Annales* School mark the transition from an interdisciplinary theory in which the material world was emphasized to one in which the intangible aspects of the world become the "primary determinant of historical reality."[20] As we will see in the following chapters, many historical theories have borrowed or built from the multifaceted work of the *Annales* School, so much so that despite its seeming lack of cohesion, it remained one of the most influential schools of historical thought in the twentieth century.

THINKING LIKE A HISTORIAN

The following primary source consists of a chart noting global economic development in the long nineteenth century.

- How do charts serve as primary sources for the historian?

- What does this chart say specifically about global relationships? What is the information provided?

- Now, read this chart like an *Annales* historian. How might a second-generation scholar differ from a third- or fourth-generation *Annaliste* in interpreting the data?

- Choose one of the generations of the *Annales* School and put forth a working argument about what the information tells us, and how we as historians can derive meaning from these numbers.

The secondary source we have provided for this chapter, a 1963 book review by Fernand Braudel of Pierre Chaunu's history of Seville and the Atlantic, is a rather nontraditional source for a reader, and at first glance you might ask yourself why we chose this reading.[21] Generally speaking, book reviews analyze published works and speak to the success of the arguments put forth by the author. This book review, however, moves beyond the regular form for this genre to operate on two levels. On the first level, it is in dialogue specifically with Chaunu's work. On the second and more profound level (and more relevant for this chapter), the article puts forth its own working argument about Atlantic history tied to the major theoretical positions of the second generation of the *Annales* School. As you read, ask yourself the following questions:

- What is the guiding focus or thesis beyond whether Chaunu's work is successful?

- How does Braudel define "series" here and how might you fit the term into his larger *Annaliste* vocabulary (such as structures or models) for understanding the past?

- In his critique of Chaunu's monograph, Braudel brings in his own vast knowledge of early modern history, particularly the history of the Atlantic and of trade and economic systems. In articulating this history, Braudel inches toward constructing a counterargument to Chaunu's about the nature of Atlantic trade and social relations. Pinpoint the paragraphs where Braudel creates his own *longue durée* of the Atlantic that is more global than Chaunu's (hint: some of it is in the section "The Structuring of the Median Atlantic").

- Why is the sixteenth century particularly important for Braudel (discussed throughout, but particularly in "The Triumph of the Serial.") and what evidence does he use to substantiate his claims?

- Where is the *longue durée* in this excerpt? How does Braudel provide a structure for his analysis?

- How might a book review serve as a historical work in its own right? How does the *critique* in this article, rather than the *secondary argument* serve as a classic second-generation historical approach (hint: refer to the section in the chapter on the second generation and see how Braudel applies his own concepts to Chaunu's work).

Chart: "Shares of World GDP, 1700–1952"[22]

	1700	1820	1890	1952
China	23.1	32.4	13.2	5.2
India	22.6	15.7	11.0	3.8
Europe	23.3	26.6	40.3	29.7

Source: Angus Maddison, *Chinese Economic Performance in the Long Run*, Paris 1998, p. 40.

Toward a Serial History: Seville and the Atlantic, 1504–1650

Fernand Braudel[23]

In order to describe Pierre Chaunu's monumental work,[1] one needs an expression that will define both his enterprise and the novelty, deliberately both powerful and restrained, of the kind of history which he is putting forward. Let us call it *serial history*, since that is what Pierre Chaunu himself has recently called it,[2] and since it points up the main perspective of a work in which the reader as he goes along is in danger of letting himself be distracted by the variety of paths offered, and so of losing the thread and getting well and truly lost.

Having read the book a first time and closely, pen in hand, I must admit that I understood the accumulation of approaches and unexpected, deliberate silences better on a second reading. Within the framework of a serial history, this book can find its unity, its justification, and its previously accepted limits.

A work even of such magnificent dimensions must be a question of choices. Serial history, to which Pierre Chaunu confines himself, makes its own demands. It is "less interested in the individual event . . . than in the repeated element, . . . which can be integrated into a homogeneous series capable of then supporting the classic mathematical procedures of series analysis." It has in consequence a language of its own—and an extremely abstract, disembodied language.

This sort of history calls for and absolutely requires the use of *series*, and it is that which gives it its name and its raison d'être. By series is meant a coherent succession, or a succession which has been rendered coherent, of measurements linked one to another, as, say, a function of historical time whose progress has to be patiently established and then its meaning deduced, the more so since its track is sometimes hard to follow and the calculations involved at the beginning never can be sure of determining it automatically in advance.

Function and explanation of historical time? These images and formulas are perhaps not really clear enough. Such a series of figures denoting valid interrelated measurements is like a highway built across our uncertain knowledge, allowing us to travel only along a particular route, but that one a favored one.

The traffic which existed between Seville and the Americas from 1504 to 1650, reconstituted as to its original volume and value, such is the historically prestigious series offered to our understanding as a "continuous body of quantified facts." In order to establish it, between 1955 and 1957 Huguette and Pierre Chaunu published seven great columns of harbor accounts.[3] At one and the same time they have both constructed the series and *invented* it. The crucial thing in their eyes was to establish, long before the beginnings of the eighteenth century and its easily accessible statistics, that solid highway of figures, "to push back in some degree, no matter how small," as Pierre Chaunu has written, "the frontier between measurable economies and those which must be left to a purely qualitative appraisal."

We have known since Earl J. Hamilton that Spanish greatness in the sixteenth century can be measured. We know it even better now. And given the wealth of the

Peninsular archives, further progress is yet to be made along the favored approach of the series.

Thus it was only at the end of an enormous labor of innovation that Pierre Chaunu built, single-handedly this time, this huge thesis running to over 3,000 pages. He offers us but a single aspect of Spanish greatness, a single aspect of the world economy, but the axis he chooses is crucial, dominant, bringing an irresistible order to a whole area of thousands of acquired ideas and fragments of knowledge. All historians and economists interested in the beginnings of modernity in the world will find when they read this book that they are called upon to verify and sometimes to throw out the old explanations. When one is enamored of history, there can surely be no finer sight than such a book, so long as one puts it properly in its context and does not ask more of it than it can and, more especially, than it is prepared to deliver.

Structure and Conjuncture

Despite the obvious resemblance and connections which Pierre Chaunu, with his customary and overgenerous kindness, is good enough to note, I do not believe that the Sevillian Atlantic which he offers us is in any way a repetition or an extension of *The Mediterranean and the Mediterranean World in the Age of Philip II*, a book which came out ten years before his, in 1949. For a start, the Atlantic which he depicts is not considered in its entirety, but is an arbitrary expanse, from the Antilles to the mouth of the Guadalquivir, as the author constantly points out: he is, in his own words, dealing with a "median Atlantic," "the early Atlantic, enclosure of the Iberias," "the Atlantic exclusive to Seville."

It is more a question of a constructed human reality than of an unmodified geographic whole, a question of a system of trade routes ending in Seville "where everything comes together . . . in a bottleneck," and from where it all starts off again.

There is another fundamental difference which Pierre Chaunu perceived immediately and which does indeed spring to the eye: the difference between the oldest stretch of sea ever dominated by man—the Mediterranean—with a whole past behind it, and at that time (the sixteenth century) coming to the end of its greatness, and a sea (the Atlantic) with nothing but a borrowed and hastily constructed past.

Doubtless, when he draws a distinction between structure and conjuncture, between stillness and movement, Pierre Chaunu is for a moment following the example

which I had set earlier and which seems to have influenced a number of recent theses. So Pierre Chaunu too has let himself be seduced by the useful dialectic between the *longue durée* and the short. But, for all that, his purpose is not at all the same as mine was. In *the Mediterranean* I sought to envisage as best I could a global history, ranging from stillness to the liveliest movements of men. Pierre Chaunu neither claims nor desires to do this. In his book, the descriptions of the main immobile masses (the first part), and then the narrative of the particular conjuncture (the second part) are intended to reconstruct only a certain economic reality, separate from a global history through which it travels but which overwhelms it on all sides. I even suspect that Pierre Chaunu consciously preferred the conjunctural narrative, closer as it is to history as it is lived, and easier to grasp, more scientific if it is enclosed in curves, than structural history, which can be observed only in the abstraction of the *longue durée*.

There were not yet any real structures existing in the Atlantic considered from 1504, the year when the Sevillian primacy took effect and a dozen years after Columbus's voyage. So they had to be imported, to be constructed, in short. Because of this did not Pierre Chaunu see, in the separation of the *longue durée* from the fluctuating, a wonderful opportunity of ridding his conjunctural study from the start—and it is the conjuncture which is the aim of the book and the crux of the undertaking—of anything which got in the way of his ordering of his subject, or which hindered the flow of his commentary? The mathematician does the same in grouping together or casting all his constant terms in one element of an equation.

To put things more clearly, the first volume of Pierre Chaunu's thesis, however rich it may be, is nothing but a preamble to the serial construction which will follow it. If we consider it on its own, we will see in it weakness, lacunas, surprising omissions, but these disappear and justify themselves in the general perspective of his work, which corresponds to the architect's intention or rather to the obligation which he has chosen.

The Structuring of the Median Atlantic

Doubtless I tended too much in my initial reaction to Pierre Chaunu's work to think of his first volume as being a book in its own right, which should have then made its own particular demands and above all had its own unity. That the book should go by the ambiguous title of *Les structures géographiques* did not help. This first book is concerned with more than the timeless, and for Pierre Chaunu, as for all historians who have come into contact with Lucien Febvre, geography, however particular its point of view, entails a consideration of the whole lived experience of man, today's as well as yesterday's. In fact, geography is not restrictive here, but on the contrary indicative. It advises and justifies a regional scheme based on proximity in space. An easy scheme, but terribly monotonous and not at all concerned with grouping problems together or with introducing, for the sake of organizing the material, the notion of historical time, though that is here the constructor of structures. From page 164 on, we proceed steadily from one stage to the next according to a program of numbering which could hardly be seriously defended. We will be told that it makes for a pretty impressive array of index cards. True. But what a book might not Pierre Chaunu have written, as the beginning of his oeuvre and in tune with his particular temperament, if he had paid attention to the slow transformation of structures, for they do in fact move and develop. A slow motion film would have been far preferable to the fixity of these magic lantern slides. Besides, on several occasions Pierre Chaunu has multiplied individual histories and, what is more, subordinated them to a typological geography which of itself transcends purely local truths and regroups them, but then he unfortunately proceeds to abandon it on the following page.

The journey, for this first part, consists in a detailed and slow-moving journey, moving from the Old World to the New. In what conditions, historically and geographically speaking, did the Sevillian monopoly on American trade become established, what were its limits and above all its weak points? How, in the shelter of its commanding primacy, did the Iberian world conduct itself, as glimpsed for a moment in its depths and along its coastal fringes? These are the first questions, to which we are given excellent answers. Then Chaunu considers the "islands of Europe," the Canaries (which are extensively studied), Madeira, and the Azores. From these islands, he passes on naturally to those of the New World, Santo Domingo, Puerto Rico, Jamaica, the Bermudas, and the Floridian peninsula. When dealing with the geographical entities offered us by the New World, it was tempting to distinguish between lightweight entities (the "continental islands") and heavyweight entities (the "continents": New Spain and Peru), without forgetting the isthmuses, especially the Panamanian isthmus, which our author not unreasonably claims to be a "Sevillian isthmus."

On all these questions, whether far-ranging or restricted, this book frequently manages to cast fresh light. Pierre Chaunu has been lavish with a whole wealth of learning, and whenever his series of trade figures allowed to do so

in advance, he increased his notation of important factors, fixed the exchanges, marked the success of major products: leather, gold, silver, sugar, tobacco. And the result is a whole map of production forces and areas of production, a whole dictionary stuffed with facts ready to be consulted. So what are we complaining about?

I say it again, about all that this first book does not go into. More specifically, about the fact that it falls short of a history of the whole body of structures, despite all the materials available which it would have been necessary to use and coordinate. Pierre Chaunu was well enough aware of this himself in the first hundred or so pages of *Structures* (pp. 40–163), which curiously are given over to a narrative frequently and above all concerned with superficial events, in which Columbus occupies a large place, followed by the stages of the conquest, and concluding with important and original thoughts about the "*conquista*" in terms of place and of men (pp. 143–59). But this narrative, however useful, is not the large-scale vista which I seek and which, it seems to me, ought to have shed light on the slow establishment of the Atlantic structures and the difficulties involved in laying them down.

The Atlantic and its European and American coasts, the islands in midocean and along the continental seaboards, the maritime routes linking all together were empty spaces at the time of the discoveries. Man was absent from them, or at most rarely and ineffectively present. What construction there was, here and there, depended on a concentration of men, whether black, white, or Indian. It meant the transfer and repeated implantation of cultural imports: boats, cultivated plants, domestic animals. Frequently, too, variation in prices was an important factor: "the low American prices dominated the market," to repeat a remark made by Ernest Labrousse. The whole was based on particular favored centers, and founded in the framework of existing structures: religions, political institutions, administrations, urban organization, and over and above all of this, an ancient, insidious, supple mercantile capitalism, already capable of bridging the ocean and subduing it to its will.

Many years ago, André E. Sayous,[4] in his investigations of the notarial archives in Seville (*Archive de Protocolos*), concerned himself with these great ventures, emphasizing in particular the innovatory and hazardous undertakings of the Genoese merchants. Since then, a good many studies of details of these undertakings have appeared. Even now we are awaiting a definitive work on the subject by Guillermo Lohmann Villena.[5] But we already have Enrique Otte's original studies,[6] and the letters of the merchant

Simón Ruiz[7] (for the second half of the sixteenth century) which are begging to be used,[8] or the priceless papers of Florentine merchants published by Federigo Melis.[9]

So one cannot help being surprised that this long prologue should tell us nothing, except incidentally, about the merchants, the prime movers of Sevillian trade. Nor is there a word about the Iberian cities, matrices for the cities of the New World, or about urban typology on one side of the Atlantic and the other. Nor, in conclusion, is there a word about the very city of Seville itself, truly a "neck" for several different: bottles. It led not only to the Indies, but also to the Mediterranean, to the Spanish heartland (as Pierre Chaunu does demonstrate splendidly), and to the northern countries, to Flanders, England, the Baltic, which he does not show at all. It can even be said that it was the coastal navigation around Spain, from Gibraltar to London and Bruges, which prepared the way and finally made possible the great discoveries. It is international capitalist concentration in Seville which goes a long way toward explaining early America.

So Seville *belongs* to other maritime areas, to other routes of shipping, trade, and money than the Seville–Vera Cruz axis alone, and insofar as the "Iberian ocean" was a "dominant" area (in the sense in which François Perroux uses the term in "dominant pole," and "dominant economy"), was it not important to note the forms of "asymmetry," of imbalance, all the visible inferiority complexes which the superiority of the Sevillian ocean brought about in other spheres of oceanic traffic? Yet Pierre Chaunu tells us, when speaking of the Pacific of the distant Philippines,[10] that the Atlantic Ocean annexed it to its own "voracious" existence: so why, when considering geographic structures, did he not turn his gaze toward the North Sea, or toward the Mediterranean of Alicante, of Genoa, and soon to be significant Leghorn? Obviously, in order to clarify these problems he would have needed to widen his archival researches, consulting in Seville the extremely rich *Protocolos*, in Simancas the innumerable papers there on Seville and Flanders. But Pierre Chaunu has chosen of his own free will to remain within the boundaries of his own serial history, without taking any account of other series which might exist.

Seville at any rate had the right to be represented in all its living totality, and not just as a port, below the bridge of boats linking it to the suburb of Triana; to be represented not only in its institutions like the glorious *Casa de la Contratación*, but also in its economic, social, and urban realities, in its hordes of merchants, retailers, money changers, seamen, and insurers—and indeed in all

the characteristic jerky rhythm of its life, regulated by the fleets which by turns enriched it and drained it, alternately bringing to the financial markets of the plaza what contemporary documents call the "easiness" and the "tightness" of money. Going through, at Simancas, the *padrón* of Seville, that exhaustive census made of its dwellings and inhabitants in 1561, I was struck by all that Pierre Chaunu denied himself, and denied us.

The Triumph of the Serial

The two volumes on the conjuncture (volumes 2 and 3 of the work) alarm us at once by their insolent use of the singular. Over and above their concern with the registration of Sevillian traffic, they are in fact concerned with *the* international, universal conjuncture, with the rhythms of a *Weltwirtschaft* extending over all the great civilizations and economies of the world and which Pierre Chaunu sees (though with a good deal of caution, vol. 2, p. 43), as I do myself, as being *one*. Perhaps it was a unity already, long before the close of the fifteenth century, as far as the Old World was concerned, that world apart, with its centuries-long coherence, from Europe to China, India, and Black Africa, thanks to the long-standing dominance of Moslem navigation and caravans. Something which more than one noneconomic historian will have already said many years ago.

All the more reason why there should be a conjuncture in the sixteenth century, when the circles were widening to such a degree and the pace of life quickening at such a rate; and so we read that "the universality of fluctuations . . . seems really to come into being, somewhere between Seville and Vera Cruz." Of course, this worldwide conjuncture does not disrupt everything: "A world economy, in depth, would not be possible until much later, not before the technical and demographic explosion of the nineteenth and twentieth centuries." But in the end, and Pierre Chaunu has said as much in his own defense, the choice of the Atlantic "is a daring choice, it means trying to explain the world." I like this rash pronouncement—it appeals to me.

It is at any rate to this level, that of the world conjuncture, that any criticism of this book should either return or attempt to elevate itself. Pierre Chaunu may say a thousand things (as he already did in his first volume) on the Spanish Empire, but it is not in this context, on which we have a host of other and often more complete information, that we should regard his work. The thing is to move outside the Hispanic universe, and grasp the world conjuncture.

So it was interesting and useful, having dispatched these important but nonetheless secondary explanations, to leave space squarely behind and turn to time, and then to devote himself exclusively to a leisurely account of all its phases, periods, rhythms, and even moments, according to the clock of the arrivals and departures of the Sevillian fleets. We are given an estimate of both the size and the value of cargoes; journeys out and home are examined either separately or cumulatively, and raw curves treated in several different ways (quinquennial averages, the mean over seven or thirteen years).

The record is finally presented as a maze of curves. That these curves have had to be reconstructed, sometimes invented, and often corrected is an indication of the preliminary work necessary to the arrangement of all the serial material. The most difficult obstacle to overcome was the (variable) estimate of the *tonelada*; that alone shows the dangers and risks which had to be accepted, reconnoitered, and in one way or another overcome.

But these considerations on the construction of the book will be of interest only to specialists (are there many of them?). The historian will not be risking much in accepting the author's numerical decisions and conclusions. So he may proceed to join without qualms in the prolonged certainly tedious, and equally certainly necessary concerns to which Pierre Chaunu calmly devotes himself for at least 2,000 pages. Henri Lapeyre has written recently that our author might have abridged and condensed what he has written.[11] True, but would it have been so easy? And besides, do we actually have to read all these pages with our customary close attention? The most hard pressed among us can simply refer to the atlas accompanying the book, while those with particular concerns need only choose the discussions relevant to them.

Anyway, thank God, the conclusions of the whole thing are both clear and solid.

The *trend* of the centuries describes two great movements: an ascent, which can be called phase A, from 1506 to 1608, and a descent, phase B, from 1608 to 1650.

All the same, Pierre Chaunu prefers to bring his chronology and his observations to a halt at shorter measurements and movements, at periods of from twenty to fifty years at most (though one of them is a good deal shorter than that) and which he calls, in a misleading or at least an ambiguous way, "intercycles," although they are more appropriately half-Kondratievs. But the term hardly matters. It is much easier to forgive Pierre Chaunu his use of "intercycle" than that of "decade," which he persistently employs instead of *decennium*.[12]

So there is a succession of contradictory intercycles, five in all: first, a rise from 1504 to 1550; second, a downward trend from 1550 to 1559–62 (could this be, as I think, a Labroussian intercycle?); third, a rise from 1559–62 to 1592; fourth, a leveling-off from 1592 to 1622; and fifth, a frank decline from 1622 to 1650.

Within these intercycles, analysis owing nothing to chiromancy can find, once again, a succession of cycles lasting a decade. It is even possible to make even shorter fluctuations, "Kitchins."

I do not believe for a moment that the dates and periods thus encapsulated are selected in any way subjectively. On the contrary, they are valid measures with which to gauge the passing of time and its material existence. They do not tell us more about this passage of time than the taking of a temperature tells us about a patient's illness, but that much at least they do tell us, and that is no small help.

So the immense effort which goes to the creation of a serial history results in the fixing of a chronological scale, with all its multiples and submultiples. The main dividing point of this scale comes as no surprise to us. World prosperity splits in two on either side of the watershed of 1608, when the whirlpool of the trend of the century changes direction, though in fact it must be said that the change did not take place in a day, or in a year, but over a long indecisive period of time strewn with illusions and underlying catastrophes. In our necessary periodization (without which there could be no comprehensible general history), some would prefer to choose the preceding years, that is to say the 1590s, and others the concluding years (thus, for Carlo M. Cipolla 1619 or 1620, or for R. Romano 1619–23, or recently for myself 1620).

It is obvious that the debate is by no means closed, and that we are hardly accustomed as yet (even given Earl J. Hamilton's recent work) to discussing the exceptional events which the changes in direction of a secular trend must be. Such an event, of greater intrinsic importance, is much more difficult to explain within the present logic of our profession than the Invincible Armada (about which, as about English piracy, Pierre Chaunu confirms what we already know), or than the beginnings of the so-called Thirty Years' War. It is incontrovertible that the secular trend is by no means a classic subject for discussion yet. At Aix, at the Congress in September of 1962, despite the presence of the author, none of the theses of Mme. J. Griziotti-Kretschmann[13] was discussed, since none of the historians present, with the exception of Ruggiero Romano, Frank Spooner, and myself, had read her extremely rare book.

It is undeniable that a great change did take place between 1590 and 1630, and our imagination if not our reason can let itself go in trying to see to what it can be attributed. It could be the diminishing returns from the American mines (as Ernest Labrousse would readily claim), or the rapid decline of the Indian population in New Spain and doubtless in Peru as well. The old explanations have been abandoned: the absorption of white metal by the growing Hispano-Portuguese economy, or its diversion toward the Philippines and China, or its capture by the increased smuggling toward the Rio de la Plata . . . Smuggling, stealing have as we know been caught up in the same conjuncture as more normal routes. I would happily suggest, though I am not sure about it, that the crisis of a certain sort of capitalism, rather more financial and speculative than mercantile, had its part to play in the affair. The end of the sixteenth century saw a decline in profits, just as the eighteenth century did toward its end. Whether it is a cause or a consequence, it is nonetheless so!

But the state of our research is still insufficient and the problematic is too desperately meager in these areas for the problem, however well posed, to be properly resolved. Economic thinking, even the most advanced, has not yet furnished us with the necessary explanatory framework.

The problem is too huge, the wise will say. But more restricted problems are not always any clearer to us. This is the case, for instance, to give a good example, with a short intercycle dating from 1550 to 1562 in Seville, which Pierre Chaunu's inquiries have brought to light.

Much more than a warning shot, the transition, fairly dramatic in our eyes, from the age of Charles the Fifth which appears so radiant, to the sad, difficult, and gloomy age of Philip II was a great lurch in the whole "dominant" economy of Seville. In France, the transition from the years of François I to the somber seasons of Henri II . . . Perhaps tomorrow a historian will tell us that Labrousse's intercycle on the eve of the French Revolution has its equivalent in this "crisis" on the eve of the wars of religion, which like the French Revolution involved the whole of Europe.

This is all the more reason to regret the fact that, on this subject, Pierre Chaunu never ventured outside his Sevillian curves to offer a history of Europe and the world on the scale of the series, or even a descriptive history which would at least have the value of a preliminary sounding: thus the abrupt halt of the movement of English shipping toward the Mediterranean, thus the assured success (even, perhaps, as early as 1530) of Dutch shipping from the North Sea down as far as Seville. Why not seek to find whether the Sevillian cycle was shaped by the American

demand or by the potential of the European economy, and how (then and at other times) it projected itself toward the European markets?

At Stake: The History of Production

It would take pages and pages to give any idea of the riches contained in this endless conjunctural narrative, or to formulate any criticisms or doubts which one might have about it. They are not lacking, but they are all questions of detail. And they are not the crucial concern of Pierre Chaunu's book. So let us proceed to these crucial concerns, to the last great debate which his book opens up, and which I am amazed not to have seen remarked on by any critics previously.

A curve of the harbor traffic bears witness to the circulation of merchandise and money—but this circulation which has been the prey of a mathematical approach to history for many a long year, doubtless because it lay within our reach, Pierre Chaunu maintains can also give us information about production in Spain and, beyond that, in Europe. Circulation, as the old writers tell us, completes production and follows its momentum. During some recent reading, in particular Gaston Imbert's book,[14] I have been struck by the intrinsic dissimilarity between movements of price and of production. As far as the sixteenth century is concerned, we are familiar with only a few curves of textile production (Hondschoote, Leyden, Venice). They all have the classic appearance of the parabolic curve, meaning in brief that they go up quickly, almost vertically, and then go almost vertically down. The long rise in prices seems to release their swift ascent, but always one step behind prices; when the prices begin to go down slowly, then production drops off sharply, always one step ahead of prices.

Now, it is just the case that there is no exact correlation between Pierre Chaunu's (Sevillian traffic) curves and Hamilton's price curves either. On the whole there is a positive correlation, but there are important differences. "The secular price curve," writes Pierre Chaunu, "has in its entirety from 1504 to 1608 and from 1608 to 1650 . . . a similar orientation, but with three or four times less of a declivity. For the ascendant period, prices multiply themselves by five! trade multiplies by fifteen or twenty. For the descendant phase, on the other hand, trade must be cut by more than two to one, while the prices/metals curve drops by 20% to 30%." All of which, for me, goes some way toward proving, or at least toward beginning to prove, that the Sevillian curves behave like production curves. The demonstration is not complete, but its outlines can be seen.

Am I wrong in thinking that much is at stake here, and that a history of different overlapping cycles within a new dialectic is being mapped out in close accordance with the theoretical and current researches of, say, Geoffrey Moore, for example? And that it would be rewarding not to limit cyclic oscillation to the movement of prices alone, which tends to dominate the thinking of French economic historians? The research done by Felipe Ruiz Martín, our colleague from Bilbao, which is as yet unpublished, though nearing publication, on textile production in Segovia, Cordoba, Toledo, and Cuenca in the sixteenth century will reinforce Pierre Chaunu's work. Broadly speaking, they indicate a characteristic mutation of international capitalism with regard to Spain during the 1580s, at just the time when, a victim as much as an instigator, Spanish imperialism was about to attempt some spectacular undertakings. Let us also note the forthcoming publication in *Annales* of the curve of *asientos* (loans) to the Castillian monarchy, by our colleague from Valencia, Alvaro Castillo.[15] All these series must be put together and coordinated if one wishes to get any overall picture of world history. In short, we must get away from price curves in order to reach other forms of recording, and then perhaps we may be able to measure that production which heretofore has always escaped us because we have had far too many a priori explanations.

To Write Long or to Write Well?

The great labors of Pierre and, we must not forget, of Huguette Chaunu have been crowned with great success. There can be no question but that that is so. And yet is not this oceanic book too long, too discursive, in sum too hastily written? Pierre Chaunu writes as he speaks; if he had submitted his text to me what arguments we would have had. But every fault has its advantages. By dint of speaking and writing freely, Pierre Chaunu often succeeds in finding some excellent and illuminating formulation.

His text is studded with lucky finds. Here we have (outside Las Palmas) the open unprotected lanes of Grand Canary Island, "only accessible," writes Chaunu, "to boats prepared to go in for microcaboting." Here we are, in the vast continent of New Spain, looking for silver mines at the meeting point of the two Mexicos, the arid and the humid. They are logically sited along the eastern edge of the Sierra Madre: "The mine needs men, but fears water. Flooding is the danger one fears most (as soon as one goes any distance below the surface), since the technical problem of getting rid of the water will not be properly solved before the generalized use of steam pumps in the nineteenth century. Miners found the best safeguard against flooding to be to operate in a subarid climate. They would have gone even farther into the desert if they had not run into other problems: lack of water, food for the men." What could one possibly wish to alter in such a text, or in many others which one could quote from the first volume, in which geography has so often inspired our author to such good effect? "As a recent area of colonization," he writes, "Andalusia (in the sixteenth century) continued to absorb the wealth of northern Spain, and to feed and flourish on it" (1:29). He adds further on, following the same line of thought: "Spain from 1500 to 1600, completing its internal colonization, is a Spain whose weight is shifting toward the south" (1:246). Or yet again, speaking this time of the colonization of the New World: "The first Spanish colonization imported wheat, which necessitated unwieldy and madly expensive communications lines. The second colonization ceased to rely to anything like the same extent on the import of supplies, because between 1520 and 1530, in going from the Greater Antilles toward the continental plateaus, the center of gravity of the Indies had moved from a manioc-producing area to a maize-producing area" (1:518–19). Mediocrity of manioc as support for a culture, magnificence of maize as support for a civilization! Has anyone else ever put it so well? There are particular phrases which I like too, such as "sailing, fossilized in its Mediterranean past." Or this bold phrase: "The deep ground swell of demographic growth since the end of the eleventh century had forced the Christian West toward intelligence and the finding of new solutions." Or this forceful and simple remark: "The great price revolution of the sixteenth century must be placed in its context, and one must not lose sight of the fact that the first phase, running from 1500 to 1550, did no more than fill in the trough of the long and dramatic wave which covered the second half of the fourteenth and all of the fifteenth centuries" (2:51).

If these finds were not buried in a welter of words, if Pierre Chaunu could force himself to write more briefly—which means performing afresh, on the first draft, that labor of elimination and choice which is more than just a question of form—then he would in fact be able to occupy the position in the forefront of young historians to which the force of his work and his passion for history already give him an obvious right. ∎

Reading Notes

1. *Séville et l'Atlantique, 1550–1650* (Paris: S.E.V.P.E.N., 1959).

2. "Dynamique conjoncturelle et histoire sérielle," *Industrie*, 6 June 1960.

3. Huguette and Pierre Chaunu, *Séville et l'Atlantique,* first part: Statistical Section (1504–1650), 6 vols. (Paris: S.E.V.P.E.N., 1955–56), plus an atlas. *Construction graphique* (1957). Pierre Chaunu's thesis is contained in the second, so-called interpretative section of *Séville et l'Atlantique,* whence the initially rather confusing numbering of his volumes: VIII1, VIII2, VIII2 *bis.*

4. "La Genèse du système capitaliste: La pratique des affaires et leur mentalité dans l'Espagne au XVIe siècle," *Annales d'histoire économique et sociale* (1936), pp. 334–54.

5. *Les Espinosa* (Paris: S.E.V.P.E.N., 1968).

6. "La Rochelle et l'Espagne: L'Expédition de Diego Ingenios à l'Île des Perles en 1528," *Revue d'histoire économique et sociale* vol. 37, no. 1 (1959).

7. Especially those made use of by H. Lapeyre in his thesis *Une Famille de marchands: Les Ruiz,* "Affaires et gens d'affaires" (Paris: S.E.V.P.E.N., 1955).

8. Used by Bennassar, "Facteurs et Sévillans au XVIe siècle," *Annales E.S.C.,* no. 1 (1957), p. 60; and by F. Braudel, "Réalités économiques et prises de conscience: Quelques témoignages sur le XVIe siècle," ibid., no. 4 (1959), p. 732.

9. *Il Commercio transatlantico di una compagnia fiorentina stabilita a Siviglia,* 1954.

10. Pierre Chaunu, *Les Philippines et le Pacifique des îles iberiques, XVIe–XVIIIe siècles* (Paris: S.E.V.P.E.N., 1960).

11. *Revue historique* (1962), p. 327.

12. *Decade* = ten days (ed.).

13. *Il problema del trend secolare nelle fluttuazioni dei prezzi* (Pavia, 1935).

14. *Des Mouvements de longue durée Kondratieff* (Aix-en-Provence, 1959).

15. "Dette flottante et dette consolidée en Espagne de 1557 à 1600," *Annales E.S.C.* (1963), pp. 745–59. ∎

Endnotes

1. Fernand Braudel, "History and the Social Sciences: The *Longue Durée,*" in *On History,* trans. Sarah Matthews (Chicago: University of Chicago Press, 1980), 47.

2. Quoted in Lynn Hunt, "Introduction: History, Culture, and Text," in *The New Cultural History,* ed. Lynn Hunt (Berkeley: University of California Press, 1989), 2.

3. A poignant account of Bloch's execution is recounted in "History Heroes: Marc Bloch," Past Imperfect Blog, *The Smithsonian* November 10, 2011 http://blogs.smithsonianmag.com/history/2011/11/history-heroes-marc-bloch/.

4. Quoted in Fernand Braudel, "Personal Testimony," *The Journal of Modern History* 44/4 (December 1972), 262.

5. Lynn Hunt, "French History in the Last Twenty Years: The Rise and Fall of the *Annales* Paradigm," *Journal of Contemporary History* 21 (1986), 209.

6. Carl Becker, "Everyman His Own Historian," *The American Historical Review* 37/2 (January 1932): 221–236.

7. André Burguière, "The Fate of the History of *Mentalités* in the *Annales,*" *Comparative Studies in Society and History* 24/3 (July 1982), 425.

8. *Ibid.,* 432–433.

9. Braudel, "Personal Testimony," 453. Braudel and Bloch were each imprisoned by the Nazis during World War II, with Bloch eventually being executed for his role in the French Resistance as described in the text. Not only did Braudel pen the original drafts of *The Mediterranean World* while imprisoned, but Bloch wrote one of the most influential statements of the nature of historical studies while being held, *The Historian's Craft,* which was published posthumously. The role of the massive destruction and loss of life entailed by the two world wars is often seen as a turning point in western nations' confidence in their own progressive improvement, a tone that permeates Bloch's writing in *The Historian's Craft,* where he begins his text with the rhetorical question, "What is the use of History?"

10. Fernand Braudel, "History and the Social Sciences: The *Longue Durée,*" 31.

11. In Chapter 7, we will discuss synchronic and diachronic in a linguistic, rather than historical context.

12. Braudel, "History and the Social Sciences: The *Longue Durée,*" 48.

13. Quoted in Hunt, "French History in the Last Twenty Years," 210.

14. Though in all fairness to Bloch, we should note that in *The Historian's Craft* he recounts the story of Bruges, a great commercial town that receded in importance as the current of the gulf of Zwin brought sand, making it more difficult to access commercial waterways. But unlike Braudel, Bloch asked the question, "Does the physical ever affect the social, unless its operations have been prepared, abetted, and given scope by other factors which themselves have already derived from man?" Quoted in *The Historian's Craft* (Manchester: Manchester University Press, 1963), 20–21.

15. James B. Collins, "Pierre Goubert," in *French Historians, 1900–2000: New Historical Writing in Twentieth-Century France,* eds. Philip Daileader and Philip Whalen (Oxford [UK]: Blackwell Publishing, 2010), 317–318.

16. Michael A. Gismondi, "'The Gift of Theory': A Critique of the *histoire des mentalités*," *Social History* 10/2 (May 1985): 211–230.

17. André Burguière, *The Annales School: An Intellectual History*, trans. Jane Marie Todd (Ithaca, NY: Cornell University Press, 2009).

18. Roger Chartier, "Intellectual History and the History of *Mentalités*: A Dual Re-evaluation," in *The Annales School: Critical Assessments*, ed. Stuart Clark (London: Routledge, 1999), 473.

19. Hunt, "French History in the Last Twenty Years," 210.

20. Hunt, "Introduction," *The New Cultural History*, 7.

21. It is difficult to find short studies representative of the second-generation *Annales* School. However, an excellent alternate reading for instructors and students can be found in Braudel's "Production: Or Capitalism Away from Home," *Civilization and Capitalism, 15th–18th Century: Volume 2, The Wheels of Commerce*, trans. Siân Reynolds (New York: Harper & Row, 1981), 265–282. A very short excerpt from a long volume of a three-volume history of early-modern capitalism, "Production" draws connections between seemingly disparate areas of the world. One question to ask if you read this short excerpt is the following: How do the second serfdom in Eastern Europe and plantation economies in the Caribbean and South America contribute to a history of capitalism?

22. "Share of World GDP, 1700–1890," in Mike Davis, *Late Victorian Holocausts* (London: Verso, 2001), 293.

23. Fernand Braudel, "Towards A Serial History: Seville and the Atlantic," in *On History*, trans. Sarah Matthews (Chicago: University of Chicago Press, 1980): 91–104.

CHAPTER 5

THE TRANSFORMATION OF MARXISM—THE NEW LEFT AND SOCIAL HISTORY

CHAPTER OUTLINE

■ The British New Left

■ The American New Left

■ Western-European Marxism

■ The Global New Left—Dependency Theory and World-Systems Theory

■ The Impact of the New Lefts: Social History

■ Conclusion

■ Thinking Like a Historian

"I don't think that historical consciousness is disabling at all . . . Historical consciousness ought to assist one to understand the possibilities of transformation and the possibilities within people."

E.P. Thompson[1]

When we think of the New Left, we are often taught to think in terms of 1960s political activism. A recent edition of a well-known Western civilization textbook defines the New Left as "a movement of students in the West who advocated simpler, purer societies based on an updated, romanticized version of Marxism."[2] As such, the New Left could then be tied to a series of student uprisings in 1968 throughout the globe: Paris (aligned with a workers' strike to demand education reform and an end to the government of Charles de Gaulle); the United States (antiwar protests and outrage over the assassination of Martin Luther King, Jr.); Mexico City (demands for political reform); Warsaw (censorship); Prague (the "Prague Spring," a movement mostly by students to reform communism in Czechoslovakia and replace it with a "human face"); Madrid (protesting the Fascist Franco government's commissioning of a mass for Adolf Hitler); and finally Tokyo (protesting American military presence in Japan as a stepping ground to Vietnam).[3] But this story is only partially correct. The surge in grassroots political activism also developed from several critical perspectives in the West that were themselves a response to global developments of the mid-twentieth century: the rise and decline of Fascism, global and Cold War conflict, and the tensions within societies in Western Europe and the United States marked by greater levels of affluence, but simultaneously greater levels of alienation.

Further, the New Left has a distinctly academic trajectory as well. Many historians were guided by their own political activism during the period and found an outlet through their academic, scholarly work. These historians worked around the globe, just as the student activists fought around the globe. The activists and academics who made up these New Lefts shared certain general positions: Many were linked to Marxist and Socialist political ideologies, or at least found a class analysis to be critical to understanding modern society. The interest in class divisions led many New Left scholars to look at politics and society "from the bottom up," and sparked a surge in scholarship that focused on the lived experience of "average" folk, whether defined as workers, women, or racial or ethnic minorities. Many New Left scholars, working in the repressive political atmosphere of the Cold War, had grown dissatisfied with scholarship that seemed simply to reinforce the status quo, and sought to bring their political activism into a sharply critical focus on the structures of society that legitimized inequalities of power.

While these similarities are important, it is equally important to note that the specific national peculiarities of each movement cannot be lumped under a single rubric. Instead, it is better to explore multiple "New Lefts" that developed in distinct ways, were drawn from specific scholarly and intellectual trajectories, and that merged and overlapped in the mid-twentieth century. To understand the theoretical and historiographical developments of the mid-twentieth century as related to earlier parts of this text, we examine only four different scholarly movements: the British, Continental European, Latin American, and US American and then discuss the academic inheritance of the New Left—social history.

THE BRITISH NEW LEFT

In Great Britain, when we last left the world of Marxist history, scholars were thrown into disarray as a consequence of the Soviet invasion of Hungary in 1956. Many of these intellectuals permanently broke their connection with Marxism as a political philosophy—that is, they no longer saw any promise of Marxist philosophy coming to fruition in the real world and very materially manifested that by renouncing their Communist Party memberships. E.P. Thompson (1924–1993) was the son of British Methodist missionaries. Like many of his contemporaries, including Hill and Hobsbawm discussed in Chapter 3, he joined the army during World War II and fought in Italy. Educated at Cambridge both before and after the war, he was an active member of the Communist Party of Britain up through 1956, at which time he renounced all commitments to communism and in fact organized politics generally. From then until his death in 1993, he was committed to **pacifism** and to nuclear nonproliferation, referring to nuclear politics in the early years of the New Left's engagement with the

Cold War as the "Natopolitan nuclear alliance."[4] For a large part of his early career, he taught adult education at the University of Warwick.

Even during his tenure in the Communist Party, Thompson had doubts about the possibility of truly achieving the goals of helping the disenfranchised and the down and out. Reflecting on his brother's work in the Party before his death in World War II, Thompson states that "his commitment was to people and above all to the astonishing heroism of the partisan movements of southern Europe. In a sense that insurgent, popular-front-type political moment reached its peak between '43 and '46. It was destroyed by both British and American reaction and inwardly destroyed by Stalinism."[5]

Over the next several years, the Left reconfigured itself. For scholars who still found value in Marx's analysis of capitalism, even as they soured on the application of these ideals in the real world, the problem was clear—how to write a history that drew on Marxian ideas of class struggle or economic exploitation without reverting to a teleology? By 1960, the question had in part been answered. The "New Left" as it was to be called, reestablished itself, forming a journal *New Left Review* (NLR) in the same year, and focusing on relations between and within classes. The NLR represented a merger between two journals—*The Universities and Left Review and The New Reasoner* (founded by Thompson). From its inception, the NLR moved beyond the emphasis on the economic base of society that characterized more traditional Marxist theory and history. In the inaugural essay to the journal, editor Stuart Hall stated, "the humanist strengths of socialism which are the foundations for a genuinely popular socialist movement—must be developed in cultural and social terms, as well as in economic and political." Further, Hall claimed that "at some point, the distant wariness between intellectual and industrial workers *must* be broken down . . . Our hope is that NLR will begin to knit together this broken conversation."[6]

Thus, the Left as rearticulated in NLR sought to forge a bond between producers of knowledge and producers of commodities. As the opening quote in this chapter suggests, one's experiences of historical moments and one's interpretations of them can be quite powerful. Many of the leading figures in the New Left had, indeed, worked in factories or were labor or social activists. Many engaged in outreach with the working population, many of whom were autodidacts in relation to leftist theory. They not only talked about the trenches, they lived in the trenches, and these experiences and commitments did not wane after 1956. E.P. Thompson taught night school to workers in Warwick, Stuart Hall was a Caribbean migrant, and Richard Hoggart and Raymond Williams both came from working-class backgrounds.[7]

Moving away from the teleology of Marx, they accepted certain elements of Marxist theory, such as class struggle, but not as an ahistorical concept. In the second issue of NLR, E.P. Thompson wrote, "there is no iron law of history, discovered by Marx or by Trotsky, which establishes the priority for 'industrial struggle' over all other forms of political or intellectual conflict."[8] Thompson and scholars like him realized they could develop a working theory that drew on Marx's strengths while rejecting his theoretical inadequacies. Like the *Annales* before them, the New Left scholars' creation of the journal provided a venue in which they could share their ideas about the role of Marxist theory in modern historical thought. Within a decade, two more journals had been founded, *The Journal of Social History* (1967) and *Radical History Review* (1972), both designed to encourage scholars to explore the radical tradition in the past as well as the everyday lives of average people. According to Eric Hobsbawm, "the effect of '56 on us—and I am talking about the Marxist historians in Britain—was chiefly to set us free to do more history because before '56 we'd spent an enormous amount of our time on political activity. If you look at somebody like Christopher Hill and compare what he published between 1940 and 1956 with what he's published since, you can see the difference that can make."[9]

As you read in Chapter 4, this interest in exploring the common lives of the "average Joe" was hardly new. At the turn of the twentieth century, for example, the **Fabian** couple Sidney and Beatrice Webb worked to ensure the end to such discriminatory features of British society as the Poor Laws while at the same time writing histories of working-class activism, writing such seminal books as *The History of Trade Unionism* (1894) and *Industrial Democracy* (1897). In addition to the Webbs, other writers were concerned with activism and the historical treatment of workers in the world of industrial capitalism. However, during the first half of the twentieth century, much historical work neglected workers in favor of histories of large institutions or of great men. The Marxist scholars of the 1930s and 1940s such as Christopher Hill (discussed in Chapter 3) and the *Annales* scholars such as Marc Bloch (discussed in Chapter 4) began a shift toward exploring

the nonelites of society, but even then often focused on larger structures and institutions.

So, the Left of the 1960s brought a change to the historical field, and one which would have profound, far-reaching consequences on the ways in which we look at the practice of history today. The New Left was still materialist, in that its practitioners believed that the economic framework of society defined social relations, but its practitioners put more emphasis on the ways in which people interacted with each other in their everyday lives. As a consequence, the New Left history to emerge after 1960 has several names—"history from below," "history of everyday life," or often in the German "*Alltagsgeschichte*." E.P. Thompson, discussing his reasoning for writing his seminal *The Making of the English Working Class* stated, "I was polemicizing against this notion in order to show the existing plebeian consciousness refracted by new experiences in social being, which experiences were handled in cultural ways by the people, thus giving rise to a transformed consciousness."[10] In other words, culture could be just as important as economics to understanding societies past.

When E.P. Thompson was commissioned to write *The Making of the English Working Class*, no one knew that it would become the bedrock of the New Left. As he later admitted, he accepted the job because he needed money. But at the same time, he wanted to write a book about a formative moment for workers, one in which they moved from what he described as a "transitory period" of the eighteenth century—not quite industrial capitalist in which workers received the bare minimum to subsist and return to work the next day, not quite a period of perquisites in which favors like a holiday goose defined superior/subordinate relations—to one in which they had firmly defined interests vis-à-vis the bourgeoisie. In this way, the working class did not simply emerge as a consequence of becoming proletarianized. According to Thompson, it is important to understand the political and social traditions surrounding and defined by workers, which enabled them to construct themselves as a class.

Thompson looked at later correspondence between Marx and Engels that showed their discussion of class and revolution, among other things, to show that class development does not simply happen. It is a process—a historical process to be precise. *The Making of the English Working Class* is, in part, an attempt to explore that process. How do workers, who at the end of the eighteenth century shared some economic but certainly very few social connections, get over their craft divisions to unite as a class? This process, according to Thompson, began near the start of the French Revolution and was only completed in 1832. His periodization is important here. In 1832, Great Britain passed what is referred to as "The Great Reform Act." This Act, however, did little for the workers of Britain. Instead it solidified the political power of the already economically strong bourgeoisie. Thompson explores this first half of the nineteenth century by examining the radical tradition in Britain and how that radical tradition was infused in the craft tradition, particularly that of the weavers who saw the most downward economic mobility as a consequence of the mechanization of cloth making.[11]

The Making of the English Working Class influenced an entire generation of scholars interested in the everyday lives of nonelites. Thompson's work provided an opportunity for historians to explore the theoretical strengths of Marxist thought while rejecting some of its more problematic concepts. In other words, Marx and Engels' works could serve as models for historians to use and explain events in the past without relying on the concepts of the ultimate revolution. Sometimes, as Thompson once profoundly evoked, you can have "class struggle without class" and you can have economic exploitation without the possibility of revolution.[12] Perhaps even more important, Thompson laid the groundwork for historians to explore the lower echelons of society *on their own terms.* It was perfectly possible to explore workers, slaves, or women, as a group with its own dynamism without necessary reference to class/race/gender struggle.

As stated earlier, Thompson, along with a number of contemporaries including Raymond Williams and Richard Hoggart, infused the New Left with not just materialist qualities of economic relations, but increasingly with ideas of culture. In *The Making of the English Working Class,* one of the crucial aspects of worker consciousness lay in the cultural framework of the time. What did workers read, if they read anything? How did the radical traditions of "The Liberty Tree" and the French Revolution permeate working-class mentalities? Why did workers want to define themselves in a particular way, and why did they have such disagreements with each other? To answer these kinds of questions, one has to look beyond economic and material questions and explore questions of culture. More than anyone else of the New Left, E.P. Thompson showed young historians influenced by Marx that it was OK to think

in terms of culture. With his colleagues, he worked to form the Centre for Contemporary Cultural Studies in Birmingham in 1964, a center that put forth what would be known as the "Birmingham School," an approach to history we will discuss in Chapter 8.

THE AMERICAN NEW LEFT

The American New Left differed in origins from the British New Left led by Thompson, Hobsbawm, and the editors of the NLR. Whereas the British New Left took root in the aftershocks of 1956, the American New Left emerged in the context of McCarthyism. Many American scholars of the 1940s and 1950s, responding to the tensions inherent in an American society marked by both unprecedented abundance and the pressures linked to the Cold War and McCarthyism, focused on explaining what seemed to be the exceptional nature of the United States: an expanding economy, improving levels of personal wealth, the weak nature of class tensions in America, and what appeared to be a general consensus on values.[13] This marks the emergence of what is known as the Consensus School. For example, as a young man, the Consensus historian Richard Hofstadter (1916–1970) briefly joined the Communist Party and was outspokenly critical of capitalism. But he turned away from political connections to Communism after the Nazi-Soviet Non-Aggression Treaty of 1939, much earlier than British Marxists, who saw the Communist state as a bulwark against Fascism against which they had more direct experience fighting. While still vehemently anti-capitalist, by the mid-1940s Hofstadter had moved away from a focus on class conflict in American society and focused instead on the values he believed even political opponents shared in the United States.

Even earlier than Hofstadter, other historians' interests in class and social inequality included Charles and Mary Beard and Vernon Parrington. Writing during the Progressive Era of the early twentieth century, the Beards and Parrington focused on the rise of corporate power that had taken place in the late 1880s. Rather than a full-blown Marxist critique of class formation and oppression, they saw American politics reflecting business versus agrarian interests, and the eventual emergence of corporate power as a dominant and corrupting influence on the American political system.[14] Beard's work identifies conflict between agrarian and commercial interests in the debates during the Constitutional Convention, and Parrington's work saw conflict between Hamiltonian business interests and Jeffersonian agriculturalists. While class is an important aspect of both scholars' works, their critiques are not fully Marxist.

During the interwar period, historical work focused on labor and the working class had been dominated by the work of John R. Commons (1862–1945), Selig Perlman (1888–1959), and their students, who focused almost exclusively on the development of unions in the United States. While at the University of Wisconsin, Commons amassed an enormous archive of documents related to labor organizations and published the four-volume *History of Labor in the United States* and argued that unions in the United States were not institutions of class conflict so much as organizations aimed purely at improvement of workers' wages.[15] The Wisconsin School, as it was most often called, examined the institutional history of the American Federation of Labor, the early efforts to limit hours and improve wages, and the struggle of unions to establish themselves in the face of an often hostile set of governments.

By the late 1950s and early 1960s then, a variety of social and political critics implicitly challenged the assumptions of these Consensus historians. The Civil Rights movement, creeping into the American political discourse through the late 1940s and early 1950s, burst onto the American consciousness with the Supreme Court's *Brown v. Board of Education of Topeka, Kansas* decision in 1954. In general, the Civil Rights movement pointed out the limits of political and economic empowerment in the nation. Critics of McCarthyism pointed out that consensus might emerge not only through shared values, but also through intimidation and fear. America's assumption of the mantle of French power in Vietnam in the 1950s and 1960s prompted some to question whether America had betrayed its opposition to imperial power, or even if that dedication to freedom and liberty was anything more than mere ideology masking economic interests. Outside the halls of academia, social critics such as the **Beatniks** critiqued the value of material abundance that defined mainstream American society in the 1950s. To people like Allen Ginsberg and Jack Kerouac, the comfortable life of suburban America was a conformist trap, eroding the very values of individuality that the Consensus historians found to be so important in American culture. Scholarly works such as John Kenneth Galbraith's *The Affluent Society* (1958), while acknowledging the general increase of wealth in the United States, questioned how the wealth was being distributed and, perhaps most importantly for the New

Left of the early 1960s, pointed out the role of economic interests in creating consumers and particular consumptive appetites through advertising.[16]

By the 1960s, in the context of the work of British historians such as Thompson and Hobsbawm, several key historians began to develop new ways of looking at the experiences of working Americans, and in doing so created what became known in the United States as the New Labor History. The New Labor History is closely tied to British trends in history from below with its rejection of older, institutional analyses of labor and its emphasis on working-class lives on their own terms. Like their British colleagues, American New Left scholars were deeply tied to political activism, had personal experiences in the labor movement, or both. David Brody, for example, grew up in a working-class immigrant household and worked odd jobs to pay his way through college. Brody's interest in labor history stemmed from personal experience:

> I grew up in the working-class neighborhoods of a small industrial city, and I worked my way through college (with the aid of scholarships) in dining rooms, shoe stores, and factories. Studying history after World War II, I was both excited by the new scholarship in American social history and bothered that so little of it explored the experience of workers. But in the end, what turned me to labor history was the discovery in graduate school of how interesting the problems and how rich the materials were for that subject.[17]

Brody's academic work focused on workers, their lives, and their quest for unionization. Fifteen years after his pathbreaking New Labor book on the unionization efforts in the meatpacking industry in the early twentieth century, Brody wrote an influential retrospective on the New Labor History—differentiating between the "old" labor history that focused too much on the institutional history of unions and the "new" which, beginning in the early 1960s, attempted to bring workers and their stories to the forefront of history. Brody argued that the radical politics of the 1960s facilitated a change in approach to finally push back the hegemony of the Wisconsin School and create the kind of worker-centered history prevalent in Great Britain.[18]

In addition, David Montgomery (1927–2011) worked as a machinist and was a member of the International Association of Machinists, the United Electrical, Radio, and Machine Union, and the Teamsters' Unions. He entered academia when he found himself blacklisted as a union activist. Montgomery argued that the proliferation of the Keynesian formula of economics "became a point of departure for most of the New Left that came along in the sixties."[19] Coming from this labor background, Montgomery firmly believed that labor and academics go hand-in-hand, arguing that intellectual work should penetrate the lives of workers and hold some meaning for them since, he maintained, history is crucial for workers' self-identity. Montgomery's *Beyond Equality* (1967) examined the relationships between labor organizers and the struggle to secure political rights for African Americans during the Civil War and Reconstruction Era, a focus that reflected the civil rights struggles of Montgomery's own time.[20]

Finally, Herbert Gutman (1928–1985) was a child of immigrants and raised in a politically active household. He worked under Richard Hofstadter and Selig Perlman at different points in his graduate studies and focused on labor history. E.P. Thompson's first visit to the United States was to visit Gutman, and Gutman was influenced by Thompson's view of culture and class. Eventually, he left academia to teach the history of labor to union members and ended his career teaching at Historically Black Colleges and Universities.[21] Two key works of Gutman's closely examine the experiences of rank-and-file workers in the United States and the blending of class interest and culture in ways that mirror the work of E.P. Thompson. In *Work, Culture, and Society in Industrializing America*, Gutman collected essays published throughout the 1960s that explored the varieties of working-class experience in the United States, examining waves of immigration as well as diverse working-class experiences, arguing that we cannot look at one single, defined class in Marxian terms as the working class in the United States continually transformed socially, ethnically, and culturally. *Work, Culture, and Society*, much like *Making of the English Working Class*, views class formation through the lens of working-class culture. But in the American experience of class formation according to Gutman, you did not have only one working class with one class-based culture, but multiple working classes, each entering the United States in successive waves of immigration.[22]

Gutman's second major work, however, focuses not on the working class adapting to the industrial environment of America. Rather, he looks at African-American history and specifically the history of the black family. In *The Black Family in Slavery and Freedom, 1750–1925*,

Gutman delved into social and race history and directly into a debate about the nature of African-American families that flared up after the publication of the Moynihan Report. Released in 1965, the report was an examination of the roots of black poverty in America and concluded that economic conditions profoundly affect social conditions. Gutman was, in fact, both an influential voice calling for a focus on class relations in American history and an early leader in the move to develop the field of African-American history. This focus on African Americans and on slavery points to the unique historical experiences of labor in the United States that necessarily led to new explorations in scholarship. In the United States, class divisions had been articulated through race in unique ways, and until 1865, slavery had shaped the experience of American laborers, both black and white. And even as Gutman broke new ground by focusing on the intersection of labor, race, politics, and culture, the field of Labor History became even more diverse as a number of historians, their attention drawn to the topic by the women's movement of the 1960s, blended a feminist analysis into their research on the experience of the working class (to be discussed in Chapter 9).

WESTERN-EUROPEAN MARXISM

In Western Europe, New Left activism was closely tied to early twentieth-century critiques of modern society as a consequence of the devastation of World War I. The Institute for Social Research was founded in Frankfurt, Germany in 1923 with a conventional Marxist approach to scholarship. After 1930, Max Horkheimer, the new director of the Institute, gathered scholars from a variety of disciplines to begin blending Marxism with fields such as psychology, art, literary criticism, and philosophy to develop a multidisciplinary perspective that became known simply as critical theory. Developing during an era of global economic depression and rising Fascism in Europe, the **Frankfurt School** had a utopian objective. By 1934, as the National Socialists rose to power in Germany, the Institute closed its doors and its members fled first to Switzerland and eventually to Columbia University in New York. From a more general focus on class relations in modern, industrialized society, the Institute's membership embarked for a time on projects designed to explain the rise of Fascism in the twentieth century.[23]

In 1944, Horkheimer and Theodore Adorno, perhaps the best known of the Frankfurt School scholars, published the *Dialectic of the Enlightenment*, a collection of essays that focused less on specific class relations emerging from the dialectical development of capitalism and instead pointed to what they considered to be a tension central to the Enlightenment itself: the alienation of man from the world around him due to the development of rationality and science that gave man seeming mastery over nature. While science helped mankind escape the vagaries of nature's power, lessening the terrors of flood, famine, and disease that had marked so much of human history, the conquest of nature required man to restructure his own mind, to subjugate all impulses that inhibited rationality, thus leading mankind to lose touch with the emotions and thereby alienating man from key aspects of himself. This then led to the development of increasingly deadly methods of warfare and self-destruction. While Enlightenment thinkers held rationality to be the lever by which mankind could achieve greater levels of freedom, Adorno pointed out that by the 1960s, the story of progress was as much about moving "from the slingshot to the atom bomb" as it was about freedom.[24]

While Adorno launched his challenges to the Enlightenment, Herbert Marcuse, another member of the Frankfurt School, leveled his attention on modern society, questioning the impact of affluence, consumerism, and bureaucracy on human character. Marcuse's *Eros and Civilization* sought to fuse the ideas of Marx and Freud into a critique of repressive modern society. One of the first of his works to be translated into English, *Eros and Civilization* proposed a rebellion against repression that focused less on class struggle so much as sexual revolution and the struggle to create a more open society, ideas that reinforced the challenges to conventional sexuality already making their way through western societies and later championed by the New Left. Marcuse's other critical work, *One Dimensional Man*, became a touchstone of the student movements in the United States and Europe discussed at the beginning of this chapter. In this work, Marcuse analyzed the nature of modern societies, both capitalist and Marxist, and found them both to be repressive. Zeroing in on education, advertising, consumerism, and ideology, Marcuse argued that modern societies created conditions that made true revolutionary action and thought nearly impossible. Rather than waiting for a revolutionary proletariat to overthrow the capitalist system, Marcuse found greater hope in the possibility of mobilizing those groups that were systematically marginalized and silenced in society: minorities, women, and the poor.[25]

While Marcuse provided one guiding theoretical light for the New Left, academics across the globe found another useful lens through which to understand modern society in the work of the Italian Marxist Antonio Gramsci (1891–1937). Unlike Adorno, who was still actively lecturing and publishing in the 1960s and 1970s, Gramsci's work covers two distinct periods—both before World War II. The first period encompasses his early life and education, his political transformation, and his marriage. The second period is known simply as his prison period and lasted from 1926 until his death. Gramsci was a socialist before World War I and began working with the Italian Communist Party (PCI) after 1915. After the Russian Revolution in 1917, Gramsci spent some time in Soviet Russia, working for the Communist International (Comintern). At the same time, Fascist movements arose in several areas of Europe, particularly in his own country of Italy. In Moscow, he met his wife, with whom he had two children, and shuttled back-and-forth between Russia, France, and Italy in his work for the Comintern. In 1926, his work intensified, as the Italian Communist Party became disenchanted with the schism within the party in Moscow and attempted to voice their discontent. In addition, Gramsci continued to write and express support for various workers' movements, including the short-lived British miners' strike. Later that year, the Italian Fascist state began arresting left-leaning journalists, writers, and activists after an assassination attempt against dictator Benito Mussolini. In November, Gramsci was detained by police in Rome, arrested, put on trial, and sentenced in 1928 to over twenty years in prison for supposed crimes against the Fascist state. He spent the remainder of his life in prison and during these years, he drafted several notebooks of critical analysis. These notebooks were published posthumously as *The Prison Notebooks*.

Gramsci began to consider the nature of power and control in modern, capitalist nations, in the process rethinking the teleological element of Marx while retaining those elements in which Marx's insights still proved useful. One of his most lasting ideas, his reevaluation of the concept of **hegemony**, focused precisely on the enduring aspects of capitalism. Writing against the theoretical framework of other Marxist scholars who envisioned the working classes as able to deal one major blow to the capitalist state, Gramsci argued that revolution was not immediate but a process, one that required the working class to establish its own hegemony vis-à-vis the bourgeoisie. Hegemony is not simply ideology, nor is it dominance. It is not only power exerted by one group against another ensuring submission. Hegemony is quite literally the union of base and superstructure and the all-encompassing control that entails over socioeconomic life.

In Marxist terms, Gramsci focused more on the "superstructure" of society (education, media, ideology) than the economic base (the mode of production) to understand how power works and how potentially revolutionary elements in society find themselves limited and ultimately co-opted into society. To summarize a very complex idea, Gramsci argued that capitalism was far more flexible than Marx had understood; that in the face of potentially revolutionary movements the cultural elements that supported the class structure adjusted, giving small victories to potential revolutionaries (think: minimum-wage laws, workers' compensation, workplace safety, etc.) while securing the general class structure of society. Ideologically, the education system, the media, and the law all could shift their message to stabilize society (e.g., demonizing revolutionaries but embracing reformers who work within the system) or generating counterrevolutionary ideologies like Fascism. For Gramsci then, in terms that synthesize to some degree with the Frankfurt School, while class remains a vital aspect of modern society, class struggle might take place not simply in the streets or the industrial workplaces, but in the schools, the media, the churches, and the courts.

THE GLOBAL NEW LEFT— DEPENDENCY THEORY AND WORLD-SYSTEMS THEORY

Marxian influence on scholars and activists, as alluded to at the beginning of the chapter, was quite global. Among Latin American historians, **dependency theory** emerged as a major analytical framework of New Left historiography. Historians of dependency theory maintain a materialist explanation of history informed both by Gramsci's work and the Western thinkers discussed earlier. Dependency theory examines the ways in which world economies create economic inequality for nonindustrialized nations. Despite "investment" from Western countries, Latin American nations (among others) cannot rise out of poverty because they feed the demands of the few wealthy nations. In short, dependency theory is a macrostudy of the exploitive nature of global

capitalism. Developing nations cannot break out of their subordinate status, because they are subject to the economic power of industrial nations through sanctions (nominally because of particular revolutionary activity) or some other economic relationship. The key to dependency theory is that these nations are forced to remain in the capitalist system even when they push against it.

Perhaps the most well-known practitioner of dependency theory was Andre Gunder Frank (1929–2005) who examined a global system that moved beyond a facile "modernization" framework to put forth a radical explanation of the global relationship of poverty to wealth. In *Capitalism and Underdevelopment in Latin America*, Frank explored dependency by arguing that as long as a state services the needs of the métropole (political center) before its own economic and social needs, it will remain in a state of underdevelopment, subject to the demands of a monopolistic capitalist system. Moving beyond traditional Marxism, Frank and his work articulate a perspective of global economics very much informed by the politics and critiques of the New Left. One of his last monographs, *ReOrient: Global Economy in the Asian Age*, argues that a global analysis is required to truly understand Western control of the global economy over the last two centuries. By examining Western dominance through the prism of global economics and politics, Frank makes the case that previous to the nineteenth century, the real global leader was Asia. Europe pushed itself out of its provincialism and into global markets only through an onslaught of exports and engaging in what is known as import substitution.[26] In other words, Europe simply engaged in an already existing global marketplace and was simply part of a temporary global shift in economic dominance, a shift that is showing signs of reversing itself in the twentieth century.

Closely connected to dependency theory is world-systems analysis. Immanuel Wallerstein (1930–), the first major proponent of world-systems analysis, was trained as a sociologist, and has held both sociological and historical positions, including serving as the director of the Fernand Braudel Center for the Study of Economies, Historical Systems, and Civilizations at SUNY Binghampton. He drew for his influences not only from dependency theory, but also the traditions of Marxism and the *Annales* School, particularly its second generation. Influenced by, but moving beyond all three, world-systems theory suggests that the modernization theory prevalent during the 1950s and 1960s simply was not analytically sophisticated enough to explain global affairs.

In addition, while dependency theory was a particularly strong category of analysis for Latin Americanists, world-systems analysis argued for a global reach. As described earlier, dependency theory could have global consequences, but it was focused on specific periphery/métropole frameworks. The connection to all three foundational influences is clear: From Marxism, Wallerstein drew on the nature of capitalism and capitalist exploitation as well as the dialectical paradigm of struggle and historical change; from the *Annales* School (particularly from Braudel), he explored the *longue durée* of capitalist structures binding the modern world together; and from dependency theory, he established the core/periphery exploitative relationship.[27] As a result of this global approach to explaining the world, world-systems analysis served as a bedrock for two generations of world historians and scholars. Curiously, Gunder Frank's monograph *Re-Orient*, discussed earlier, critiqued Wallerstein's work (and Braudel's of half a century earlier) for enabling a distinct Eurocentric understanding of global economics of the last half millennium. Regardless of their intellectual differences, both Wallerstein's and Gunder Frank's works reflect the transformation of Marxian thought prevalent in New Left history.

THE IMPACT OF THE NEW LEFTS: SOCIAL HISTORY

Considered broadly, the New Left marks a significant shift in the course of scholarship. Bringing in elements of Western Marxism (the Frankfurt School, Gramsci, the British New Left) and a commitment to political activism in scholarship, the New Left drew on the energy and activism of the 1960s to help make scholarship itself more activist and political. This has had a variety of ramifications, making scholarship more relevant for many, but also opening it up for charges of partisanship and bias from opponents who held other viewpoints. But this is perfectly appropriate for many scholars. According to David Montgomery for example, labor and academics go hand-in-hand: "when you come right down to it, history is the only teacher the workers have. A central task that all of us face today is going back to square one in our own revolutionary experience."[28]

Social history is the universal term for the variety of New Lefts that emerged in the academic sphere during this period. Influences on social history include not only the New Left political movements and the variants

of Marxist theory discussed in this chapter, but also other theories and traditions we have covered in earlier chapters. Both Marxist and *Annaliste* historians were concerned with the people who were not part of the elite of society. In fact, the third generation of the *Annales* School both had profound influence on and was a representative feature of the New Social History—de-emphasis of politics and institutions and focus on history from below, of people with average lives through the use of the "background" of history—demographic and quantitative records. Described rather vaguely by Robert Gallman, past president of the Society for Economic History, as "amorphous around the edges"[29] social history has certain characteristics such as emphasis on quantitative evidence and interest in groups of people rather than individuals. But even self-named social historians admit that there is a generality to its study. Harold Perkin, the "first university teacher in Britain to be paid specifically to teach" the field, places its connections back to 1952 with the emergence of *Past and Present* and to the founding by E.P. Thompson of the Centre for Social History at the University of Warwick, and therefore has deep connections with labor history.[30] It is also described as a methodology intent on smoothing over some of the disciplinary differences with sociology—concern about relationships within and between groups is paramount.[31] One of the most famous and polarizing social histories of the United States is Howard Zinn's *Peoples' History of the United States*, which examined American history from the perspectives of the working class, African Americans, Native Americans, and women. Howard Zinn (1922–2010) grew up in an immigrant, working-class household in Brooklyn and became an advisor to the Student Nonviolent Coordinating Committee, proclaimed by Staughton Lynd in 1969 to be the first New Left organizing campaign in the United States.[32] Staughton Lynd and Jesse Lemisch each focused on "history from the bottom up," a phrase that, by itself, implies distinctions of class and status in the United States that many of the Consensus school historians had slighted. It is also a phrase that connects with the larger European tradition of "history from below" so well articulated in the British New Left.

In addition, certain key American social histories in the 1960s and 1970s explicitly embraced Gramsci's concept of hegemony, applying it in ways that might have surprised Gramsci himself. Two key works examined aspects of slavery. David Brion Davis' *The Problem of Slavery in the Age of Revolution* applied the concept of hegemony to show the flexibility of the ideologies of capitalism that direct attention at one heinous form of labor exploitation and call for its abolition (slavery) while at the same time, and as part of the ideology, justify and rationalize another form of exploitation (the wage system and industrialization). For Davis, ideologies associated with capitalism ultimately served the interests of class, though they could have simultaneously positive (abolition of slavery) and negative (the development of unregulated wage-labor exploitation) consequences.[33]

Another important work regarding slavery that applied the idea of hegemony was Eugene Genovese's *Roll, Jordan, Roll: The World the Slaves Made*. Examining the relationship between masters and slaves, Genovese asserted that the slaveholders developed an ideology of paternalism to justify their holding of other human beings in bondage. And while this ideology clearly served their interests, it could also be used by slaves themselves, appealing to their masters as father figures to gain very limited levels of influence in the slave system (seen in acts such as appealing to masters to remove sadistic overseers). Genovese argued that ultimately the slave owners' desire to see themselves as benevolent fathers, in other words, their embracing of paternalistic ideology, served to soften somewhat the hard edges of the slave system, and the slaves' acceptance of their position gave them an avenue through which they could attempt to make the system more bearable. Genovese writes extensively about the difference between the version of Christianity espoused by slaveholders, emphasizing obedience and reward in the next world, and the Christianity embraced by slaves that focused on the story of Moses and on themes of liberation and justice. It should be noted that Genovese was roundly criticized at the time and since for accepting too easily the self-serving platitudes of American slaveholders and thus essentially accepting the justifications of slavery. But as an application of Gramscian ideas of hegemony, and how hegemonic ideologies can shape elements of society as varied as the legal system, religious belief, and the direct social relations between classes, few works are as ambitious as *Roll, Jordan, Roll*.[34]

Conclusion

The New Left, especially in its very early years, was as much a political activism as an intellectual movement. Indeed, the leaders of the movement globally saw the two necessarily interwoven, complicit in each others'

successes and failures. The strength of the New Left was its willingness to recognize not only the profound strength of Marxist theory, but also its practical limits. For those intellectuals who most define the movement, the so-called "theoretical irrelevancies"[35] helped to maintain a distinct identity for the movement, a new form of socialism, political organization, and discourse. For many, the New Left offered an opportunity to explore their own experiences in an historical framework. What was the role of Mexican women workers in California? How did Irish immigrants forge a new politics in Wyoming? How did the African-American community create a material culture in the alleys of Washington, D.C.? These and many more topics show that scholars, energized both by their personal histories and a particular historical moment, drew on the diversity of their experiences to create vibrant histories of everyday life told from the workers' and others' perspectives.

Thinking Like a Historian

The primary source you are reading is an interview with a woman taken during the Great Depression as part of the Federal Writers' Project. Mrs. Walter Pinkus provided information to the interviewer about her life in the United States.

- If New Left historians are interested in the "history from below," what aspects of this interview provide historians with this kind of evidence? How would you use this evidence to explain life in Poland or the United States, or the history of immigration?

- Mrs. Pinkus talks about going out to work. How would you integrate this story into a New Left history?

The secondary source you are assigned focuses specifically on the culture of workers. Ask yourself the following questions:

- How does this history of workers differ from the history of workers explored in Chapter 3?

- Why is the autobiography of William Hutton atypical for the eighteenth century?

- What are probate inventories and why are they not helpful in determining whether Hutton's account of watch owning is typical for his station? How do records of the criminal courts provide information not able to be gleaned from probate inventories and how do they help us to learn about the lives of working people?

- How does Styles dialogue with the work of E.P. Thompson and what does this dialogue suggest to you about the general historical approach of the article?

- When were watches and timepieces generally stolen? Were watches ever stolen while people were working? What, argues Styles, does the manner in which timepieces were stolen tell the historian about the working and personal lives of workers in the eighteenth century?

- Explain how this story of watches and their wearers serves as a history from below.

"Mrs. Walter Pinkus"[36]

The farm, that my parents lived on was a small one, consisting of 4 or 5 acres – about 20 acres in the American way of measurement. The farms on the average were larger than that, but the folks didn't try to see how much land they could acquire, they worked and saved and enjoyed themselves, while raising their family of 5.

On this little farm, I was born. We didn't go to school on account of the great distance from home to school, besides everyone had their particular work to do. The people, at that time didn't think that education was of great importance. The main thing was to learn how to work and earn a living, because someday there would be a family of their own to feed. So education, was not considered of that importance, where would one use it in the rural area. The thought of going to the city and being a business man, or a teacher in the higher places of learning did not enter the mind. The young people were contented where they were.

About the first thing in the line of work, that I was required to do was to herd geese. This seemed to me to be a great responsibility, and later grew to be quite tiresome. Of course there was no use of complaining, because if one did, more often than not, a licking was dealt out and the work being done anyway. So, it didn't take long and there was no complaining. However, sometimes other children would come to play and the worker forgot his and surely something went wrong, a licking was given the child for his not paying attention to his work. Licking[s] were dealt out often, even to the larger children for this.

A licking was easy to be had there, the people all used this form of thought for, as they put it, the education of the children. This was not only a punishment for children,

the grownups were whipped for different misdemeanors when sentenced by the court.

When I was older I went to work for the lord of the district. My job was in the stable. Here I had to arise very early and wash the cows from head to foot, not only wash but scrub as well. They had to be spotlessly clean. After which they were fed and milked. The milk was taken to the city and sold. Woe to the person that washed a cow and found to be dirty somewhere by the boss. Without question he would administer a severe licking or whipping.

The lord, having a large establishment and the work, being done mostly by hand, had many bosses and workers. There was a boss for the horses, one for the cattle, one for the gardens, one for the farm-work, one for the forest, one for the orchard and etc. Wherever there was a certain kind of work, there was a certain boss for that particular work.

The lord himself did little or none of the actual bossing. If he had any special orders he would have the head foreman give the orders to the bosses. The lord and his family lived a life of ease and visiting. On rare occasions, the lord would go around and look over the different parts of his land or the barns and horses and his cattle and the like. I would watch for him and when he came close to me I would tie him with a ribbon kept handy for that purpose. On these occasions he would give me a dollar as a present. My boss didn't like this but as it was alright with the lord he didn't say much. He did tell us not to do this but there was surely a dollar in it for me and I tied the lord with this ribbon every chance I had.

I had to help out here and there where they were short of workers, but the main work was to take care of the cows. These had to be milked three times a day. So the work was from early morn to dark, seven days a week. For this work I received about $40 per year.

I stayed here and worked for a period of about three years. I had already met a handsome young man by the name of Stanislaus Wilcynski, who wanted to marry me. I liked this young man and finally married him in November of 1886.

My husband received the farm from the lord, to do this he had to put in his application. It was granted and as pay for this land (about 6 acres) my husband agreed to work for the lord three days per week for so many years. In this time the land would be paid for.

If the owner of such a farm had a lot of work of his own, and couldn't go himself, he would have to hire someone to go in his place. If he couldn't hire anyone, he had to leave his work go and go to the lord and fulfill his part of the agreement. What would happen if he didn't go? He would be brought in court, charged with the misdemeanor. The sentence would probably be, so many strikes with a whip.

Many times I took my little baby into the field with me and kept working, taking care of it as best I could. This did not seem unusual because everyone had to do the same, but now as one looks back, it seems almost impossible.

My mother often related stories about the Polish revolution. At that time she was working for one of the lords in the community being only about eighteen years old.

This revolution was to be against the Emperor but in a very short time turned to be a revolution against the lords. Most of the men took whatever they could grab and went wherever they thought they could find a lord. Most of the time he was killed and many times so badly beaten that he died in a short time. Mother says that they carried scythes, pitch-forks, whips, hoes and what have you/

This revolution only lasted a few days. And after the commotion most of the rich were killed off. Mother says that the dead were gathered and hauled to the different cemeteries in wagons. The most awful sight that one could imagine.

The owner of the estate where she worked ran away to the forest. In just a little while the men came inquiring about the lord.

While the lord was running away, his wife had not the time to go with him. Mother hid her in the stable, covering her with manure, and when the men came to inquire about the lord and finding him gone, the inquired about the where-abouts of the lady of the house. To this the young girl replied, "that she didn't know where either had gone"/ The leader suspected that she wasn't telling the truth, and ordered the men to give her so many stripes with a whip. Some of the men however, persuaded the leader to leave mother alone.

After the men had gone, the lady of the house came out of her hiding place but with a great fear for the safety of her husband. In several days he came back home.

By this time the anger of the mob had subsided and when the revolutionists learned of the return of this lord, they immediately came with a wagon and took him in it. Among the men was my father who pleaded that the life of this lord be spared, which was done. He was taken to Tarnov and forced to sign papers, giving the common people more rights than they had before.

After this commotion the [p]roperties were restored to the rightful owners or their heirs and the [u]prising came to an end.

After farming our little farm in Poland for a period of about seven years, we decided to sell our property and come to the United States of America. The land of promise. We had many friends that had come here and word came back that most of them became wealthy.

After selling our holdings we set out for the new world. Taking two of our children with us we were on our way. We arrived in Columbus, Nebraska, in the spring of 1893. By this time our funds had depleted to the grand sum of $100.

Here we were and no place to go. We stayed with friends for about a year, deciding to buy a small property in town and making our home.

This we did by purchasing a lot in the city of Columbus and building a frame structure, consisting of two rooms and not even having any plaster or siding. In this we lived for five years.

By this time we, build a better and larger home. This home was plastered and had siding. We lived in this for five years. Then we built the third home, which was the best one. In this home, Mr. Wiłcynski passed to his reward on Oct. 22, 1923.

Things weren't easy for me here in this country. I did washing for different people her[e] in town. To do this I had to go to their home, and the pay was around $1 per day. Now it is so much per pound.

At that time the washing was done on a scrub-board, all by hand. There were no electric washing machines as there are today. But I stayed right with it and complained not, glad to get the work.

My husband stayed at home and took care of the children, thus leaving me free to go and do this work. His health prevented him from doing very heavy work. Anyway all the work that there was for a foreigner around here was on the railroad and away from home. After paying his board and room he wouldn't have much left. I thought that I could make more at washing while he took care of the little folks. ■

Time Piece, Working Men and Watches

John Styles[37]

John Styles considers whether the fashion for wearing pocket-watches flourished among working men in the eighteenth century because it was stylish, because they needed to know the time accurately, or for some other reason.

In 1747, William Hutton, a twenty-four-year old journeyman framework knitter at Nottingham, bought a silver watch for 35 shillings. It had been the pride of my life, ever since pride commenced, to wear a watch', he later remembered in his autobiography. The watch turned out badly.

> It went ill. I kept it four years, then gave that and a guinea for another, which went as ill. I afterwards exchanged this for a brass one, which, going not better. I sold it for five shillings, and, to close the watch farce, gave the five shillings away and went without for thirty years.

Hutton's reminiscences tell us three important things about watches and those who wore them in eighteenth-century England. First, although Hutton was only a humble framework knitter, he was able to acquire two expensive silver watches in the course of four years, and also to realize some of their value when he disposed of them. Second, wanting to own a watch was an expression of sartorial aspiration for young working men like Hutton, and owning one was in large part about display. Third, the watches Hutton bought were disappointments as timepieces, although it was many years before frustration at their functional shortcomings finally conquered his desire to own one.

Few autobiographies survive from the eighteenth century like William Hutton's, written by someone who began life as a working man. So unusual is their survival that they provide little help in establishing whether Hutton's experience with his watches was typical of the generality of working people, or whether it was altogether exceptional, evidence of the aspirational cast of mind that propelled him later in life to a successful career as a Birmingham book dealer. Probate inventories—lists of possessions drawn up after the owner's death for inheritance purposes—have been the main source used by historians to provide evidence of what people owned. They are of little assistance here. They deal mainly with the wealthier half of the population and survive infrequently after 1740. There is, however, one other, less familiar means of finding out what working people owned—the lists of things stolen from them that survive in the records of the criminal courts. They show that William Hutton was not exceptional. By the later years of the eighteenth century, ordinary men comprised a majority of victims of watch theft whose cases came to court, drawn from among the small farmers, day labourers, artisans and petty tradesmen who comprised the bulk of the male population.

The records of prosecutions for theft have a tendency to over-represent valuable items that were more attractive to steal. Nevertheless, there were thousands of prosecutions for thefts of things worth considerably less than William Hutton's five shilling brass watch. Watches were consistently the most valuable item of a apparel stolen from working men in the eighteenth century—more valuable than other expensive items of clothing such as coats and waistcoats, cloaks and gowns. This was because the cases which housed the watch mechanisms were made overwhelmingly from silver, despite the availability of cheaper alternatives. The silver watch that William Hutton was so proud to acquire in 1747 cost him a hard-earned 35 shillings. Yet it was probably only a second-hand one. Moreover, the expense of a watch did not end with its purchase. Watches regularly needed professional cleaning and oiling, and parts like springs wore out and had to be replaced.

How did such an expensive item come to be widely owned among that portion of the population least able to afford it? William Hutton, exasperated at the unreliability of his silver watches, may have been driven to make do with a cheap brass-cased watch, but few men of his class were prepared to follow his example. Forty-two out of forty-seven watches stolen from plebeian owners, and identified by material in the records of criminal courts in the north of England, had silver cases. The same pattern emerges from the pledge book of a York pawnbroker George Fettes over an eighteen month period in 1777 and 1778. Of 176 watches taken in pawn where the case material is named, 168 were silver, four were gold and four were cheap alloy.

In the first half of the century, few working men in provincial England achieved their ambition to own a watch, however. This is evident from the surviving depositions of the Assizes (the criminal court which dealt with more serious offences), where, outside London, cases of watch theft were usually tried. Of 117 cases of this kind from the Assizes for Yorkshire, Northumberland. Cumberland and Westmorland between 1640 and 1800, only seven date from before 1750, and only one of the victims of theft was a working man—in this case a sailor whose watch was stolen in 1749. The other owners, as far as they are identified, were gentlemen. By contrast, a far greater number of watches were stolen after 1770, and of these more than half the owners were working men, such as small farmers, day labourers, artisans and petty tradesmen. This pattern was not confined to the north of England. In Worcestershire and Oxfordshire too, prosecutions for watch theft were much more common after 1750, although it is rarely possible to identify the occupations of their owners.

In London the picture was different. Numerous watch thefts are recorded earlier in the century, suggesting watches were widespread in the capital sooner than elsewhere. The proportion of Old Bailey trials involving watches rose continuously each decade from the 1700s to the 1770s; by 1756, working men accounted for over half the victims (excluding watchmakers) of watch theft. They remained a small majority in 1785.

Watches achieved reasonable accuracy as timekeepers only during the second half of the seventeenth century when improvements were introduced, for example, to the balance spring, which together with the balance wheel, acts as the oscillator that controls the motion of the watch mechanism. In London the number of watches owned by working men increased during the half-century immediately following these improvements. The delay in diffusion to the provinces may be explained by the greater purchasing power among sections of the common people of the capital compared with their country cousins. It may also have been due to the proximity of London consumers to the workshops of the capital, where the finishing stages of the watch-making industry were concentrated. Over two-thirds of the watches recorded in the northern Assize records carried the names of London makers. The same was true of the watches entered in George Fettes' pledge hook.

Our understanding of the history of the diffusion of timepieces has been dominated by E.P. Thompson's claim that changes in people's inward notion of time are linked to the transformation in work disciplines caused by the Industrial Revolution. Natural time associated with task-orientated labour in field or workshop was replaced, Thompson proposed, by the tyranny of the clock, associated with time-orientated labour at the machine. Widespread ownership of clocks and watches was, for Thompson, evidence of this profound cultural shift, as well as one of its driving forces. He insisted that a general diffusion of clocks and watches occurred only at the moment when the Industrial Revolution demanded greater synchronization of labour. Thompson's critics argue that he failed to appreciate just how widely clocks were available in both public and domestic settings before the Industrial Revolution, indeed well before the eighteenth century. From the late Middle Ages, clocks had proliferated in churches and other public buildings, and subsequently in the halls, kitchens and parlours of the well-to-do. By the early eighteenth century, few English men and women were out of earshot of their chimes.

Thompson argued that the take-up of watches by working people did not occur before the close of the eighteenth century. Nevertheless, he acknowledged that the imperatives of industrialization alone cannot explain why they became prized consumer items. He proposed that watches had three main attractions for their plebeian wearers. First, they were utilitarian tools for measuring time, evidence that working people had internalized the new time disciplines demanded by industrial capitalism. Second, they were sources of prestige. Third, they were realizable assets, the poor man's bank. But if, as we have seen, working people came to own watches earlier than Thompson believed, which of these attractions was most powerful in encouraging their acquisition?

Watches were certainly used by eighteenth-century working people to raise money. In 1734, a woman who lodged in a single room in London worried about the watch hung up by her chimney being stolen. She explained: 'if I or my Husband should be taken ill, we had nothing else that we could make a little Money of.'

According to Fettes' pledge book, watches accounted for half the objects against which he lent the largest sums of money, more than any other type of possession. The pawnbroker lent an average 15 shillings for a silver watch, which represented a far better store of value than the brass watch an exasperated William Hutton got rid of for five shillings. Nevertheless, the fact that silver watches were readily pawned does not, in itself, explain why working people acquired them in the first place.

Did the attraction of owning a watch rest for working people on the need for time discipline? To answer this question, we need to know whether watches were actually used for timekeeping at work. More than half the fifty-three plebeian owners of stolen watches in the northern Assize depositions between 1749 and 1799 were involved in working trades, some of them as employees, others working on their own account on a small scale. The largest single group among them was seamen (nine), followed by textile workers (five), and then a diversity of trades, from coal miner and gardener to tailor and shoemaker. Other occupations included servant, labourer, husbandman and soldier.

None of these watch owners worked in one of the new cotton or worsted mills that proliferated in the north after 1780, despite the fact that workers in these factories appear in the criminal records as victims of other kinds of theft. Most of the workers in the early factories were women and children. Only one of the fifty-three watch owners highlighted above was a woman, an unmarried servant. Ownership of goods by women is often concealed in eighteenth-century criminal records by rules which vested legal ownership in their husbands and fathers—even so, the proportion of females among plebeian owners of stolen watches in the northern depositions is tiny by comparison with other stolen goods. Fettes' records also bear this out. Of 197 people who pawned watches with him for the period of his pledge book, only eleven were women, yet women accounted for more than three-quarters of the total pledges he received in those years. Generally, the most valuable items pawned by women were gowns, but these didn't command anything like the sums Fettes lent against men's watches. This suggests that women could rarely afford to acquire watches or own them in their own right.

The small numbers of women, labourers and husband-men among owners of stolen watches in the northern depositions and the large numbers of seamen and textile workers—especially those, like William Hutton, who worked at home or in small workshops, rather than in the new factories—demonstrate that ownership of silver watches was greatest among men in the higher-earning manual occupations that were prospering as manufacturing and mining expanded in the north of England in the course of the eighteenth century. Younger men employed in weaving, coal mining, and shipping could command substantial wages during periods of full employment, especially towards the end of the century. Yet it is difficult to imagine that most of these men needed a watch for timekeeping at their work. Sailors toiled at sea to the rhythm of four-hourly watches set by the ship's master, weavers laboured at the loom to the weekly rhythms of the putting-out system, pitmen hewed coal in shifts measured by set output quotas, and even those urban journeymen whose working hours were fixed according to the different amounts of daylight available in summer and winter would have known the time of day by the chimes of their parish church clock.

Very few watches were stolen from their owners as they worked. In part this was because other circumstances were more propitious for theft, especially night-time bedrooms, busy inn parlours, drunken sexual assignations, unsupervised storage chests and lonely highways. Nevertheless, it is clear from the evidence in a number of the Assize cases that watches did not usually accompany their owners to work. The silver watch belonging to William Brooke, a collier from West Ardsley in Yorkshire, was stolen from his house after he had left for work early on a Friday morning in June 1789. James Groves, servant to Matthew Ridley of Heaton House, near Newcastle, lost his silver watch while working in December 1751, when it was hung on a nail at the foot of his bed. James Stockdale, a sailor in the whale fishery, acquired a silver watch in South Shields after returning in August 1787 from the long and dangerous, but lucrative, summer voyage to the David Straits between Greenland and Baffin Island.

One group of workers was the exception, however. Men who worked in transport depended on accurate time-keeping—and they were sometimes the victims of watch theft at work, especially if they were coach or carriage drivers. Drivers worked unsupervised and were expected to keep to timetables. Indeed, under the new mail coach system instituted in 1784, the Post Office guards who rode the mail coaches were provided with watches calibrated to London time. They were required to keep a record of arrival and departure times along the journey. The victims of watch theft in the northern Assize depositions included a mail coach driver from Shap on the road from Kendal to Carlisle and a chaise driver employed by an innkeeper at Glenwhelt on the road from Newcastle to Carlisle.

For the majority of working class owners who did not need their watches for work, the timepieces hanging from their bedsteads or chimney breasts may have woken them for the start of the working day, serving perhaps as substitutes for domestic clocks. Nevertheless, watches were designed first and foremost to be carried. Most watches were stolen from the pockets of their owners, especially when they were at leisure. Relieving a drunken, befuddled victim of his watch may have been easy work for a thief and, as a consequence, prosecutions for watch theft may tend to over-represent watches stolen under such circumstances. Nevertheless, watches were stolen far more often when their owners were out enjoying themselves at an inn or at the races than when they were at work. These were evidently occasions when it was considered appropriate for watches to be worn and displayed. A silver watch with a china face was picked from the pocket of a tailor. James Hargreaves, as he stood near the starting post at the races at Thornton in Craven in Yorkshire in September 1765. A silver watch with a blue and white striped ribbon 'fastened to it in order to pull it out by', was stolen from the pocket of James Harrison, servant to a Swaledale yeoman, during a fight at an inn in Richmond, Yorkshire, one evening in August 1774. The next year a silver watch with 'a china face with a steel single linked chain, a brass key, two seals', belonging to William Jennison a saddletree plater, was taken from his 'watch pocket in his breeches' at a public house in Ripon on a Tuesday evening in February.

Although the watch itself tended to be concealed in a breeches' fob pocket, the decorative ribbon or chain used to pull it out was usually worn hanging below the waistcoat for all to see, often with seals and a watch key attached to it. Watch chains, made mostly from bright steel, were attached to twenty of the stolen watches in the northern depositions. Three more watches were stolen with coloured silk ribbons. Fifteen of the chains and ribbons had seals fastened to them when stolen. Most were cheap steel seals, valued at one or two pennies, but a few are described as set in silver or copper, and were probably made from semi-precious stones such as cornelian or crystal.

James Stockdale of South Shields had a seal with an angel and an anchor on one side and a head on the other; another seaman's seal was embossed with a flaming heart. The anchor might have been simply nautical in its associations, but it could also represent hope, an allegorical symbol common in late eighteenth-century jewellery, just as the flaming heart could represent passion. Nautical imagery was not confined to sailors. William Jennison, the Ripon saddletree plater, had two seals, one of which was 'half brass half steel having the impression of a ship on one side thereof and on the other side a man's head'. His other seal was a steel one 'with an impression of a cock heading a hen'. The Yorkshire servant Elizabeth Rose's seal simply had the letter E engraved on it. Such motifs were not confined to seals worn by plebeian owners. They probably bought them ready-made, but exactly the same sorts of devices were found on seals engraved to order for much richer men and women.

How often these seals had a practical use for their plebeian owners is hard to ascertain. Only four of the fifteen owners of watch seals in the group from the Assize depositions were unable to sign their names, suggesting cheap seals were not substitutes for a signature employed by the illiterate. Undoubtedly, watch seals and the chains from which they hung offered plebeian men an important vehicle for sartorial display, just as they did for the rich, the fashionable, and the famous. Chains and seals did not have to be worn hanging out of the fob pocket, but it was normal for them to be displayed in this way. When a silver watch with a steel chain and a small silver seal set with a red stone was stolen in 1778 from Benjamin Proctor, a peddler living at Old Malton in Yorkshire, he followed the thief to Newcastle, over sixty miles away. Suspicion was aroused there when the thief, having had the chain and seal hanging out of his pocket, was seen to 'put the said chain and seal into his pocket and draw the flap of his waistcoat over it'.

Watches were decorative items as well as sophisticated pieces of technology. Their compact size, elegant cases in shining silver, reflective watch glasses, and enamelled or china dials combined many of the elements of eighteenth-century jewellery. Despite normally being concealed, showing off one's timepiece required a certain flourish as the watch was removed from the pocket, the performance adding to the sense that this was an object to be displayed. When a London labourer, James Johnson, first tried on an expensive new suit of clothes in 1789, he 'insisted on having his watch, and a looking glass; says he, I am a fine gentleman'.

Of E.P. Thompson's three reasons to explain the attraction of watches to working men, we should not underestimate their importance as practical tools for measuring time, despite their unreliability. Nevertheless, for all but a few who worked in road transport, watches were not indispensable necessities when it came to timekeeping. What they did offer those workers who could afford them was reasonably accurate, general-purpose timekeeping in a conveniently portable form.

In addition, as Thompson argues, they were both a quickly realizable store of value and a prestigious form of male jewellery.

The particular importance of display is emphasized by the aesthetics of watch design and the ways in which watches were personalized by means of cheap, expressive accessories. Silver watches signalled enviable affluence combined with a suitably masculine command of technology, of the kind richer men manifested through purchases of scientific instruments and the like. Not that richer men were immune to the decorative allure of watches. 'A fool cannot withstand the charms of a toy-shop,' the Earl of Chesterfield warned his son in 1749, 'snuff boxes, watches, heads of canes, etc. are his destruction'. It is no wonder that for William Hutton, a clothes-conscious young journeyman, to wear a watch, even a second-hand one, was the pride of his life. ■

Endnotes

1. E.P. Thompson, interviewed by Mike Merrill, in *Visions of History: Interviews*, eds. Henry Abelove, Betsy Blackmar, Peter Dimock, and Jonathan Schneer (New York: Pantheon Books, 1983), 16.

2. John P. McKay, et. al., *A History of Western Society*, 10th ed. (New York: Bedford/St. Martin's, 2011), 963.

3. *Ibid.*, 967–968.

4. E.P. Thompson, "The Point of Production," *New Left Review* 1/2 (1960), 68.

5. E.P. Thompson, *Visions of History*, 12.

6. Stuart Hall, "Introducing NLR," *New Left Review* 1 (1960), 1.

7. "Working-Class Attitudes: A Conversation between Richard Hoggart and Raymond Williams," *New Left Review* (1960), 26. Revised transcript of a recorded conversation between Richard Hoggart and Raymond Williams – August Bank Holiday, 1959.

8. E.P. Thompson, "The Point of Production," *New Left Review* 1/2 (1960), 68.

9. Eric Hobsbawm, interviewed by Pat Thane, in *Visions of History: Interviews*, eds. Henry Abelove, Betsy Blackmar, Peter Dimock, and Jonathan Schneer (New York: Pantheon Books, 1983), 33.

10. E.P. Thompson, *Visions of History*, 7.

11. E.P. Thompson, *The Making of the English Working Class* (New York: Vintage Books, 1966).

12. E.P. Thompson, "Eighteenth-Century English Society: Class Struggle without Class?" *Social History* 3/2 (May 1978): 133–165.

13. Key texts of the Consensus School include Louis Hartz, *The Liberal Tradition in America: An Interpretation of American Political Thought Since the Revolution* (New York: Harcourt, Brace, Jovanovich, 1955); David M. Potter, *People of Plenty: Economic Abundance and the American Character* (Chicago: University of Chicago Press, 1954); Richard Hofstadter, *The American Political Tradition and the Men Who Made It* (New York: A.A. Knopf, 1948).

14. Charles Beard, *An Economic Interpretation of the Constitution of the United States* (New York: The Macmillan Company, 1913); Vernon Parrington, *Main Currents in American Thought* (New York: Harcourt Brace & Company, 1927).

15. John R. Commons, *History of Labour in the United States* (New York: The Macmillan Company, 1926); Selig Perlman, *A Theory of the Labor Movement* (New York: A.M. Kelley, 1928).

16. John Kenneth Galbraith, *The Affluent Society* (Boston: Houghton Mifflin, 1958); Allen Ginsberg, *Howl and Other Poems*, Introduction by William Carlos Williams (San Francisco: City Lights Books, 2001).

17. David Brody, "Why Become a Historian," *American Historical Association*, accessed March 17, 2013, http://www.historians.org/pubs/Free/why/brody.htm.

18. David Brody, *The Butcher Workmen: A Study of Unionization* (Cambridge [MA]: Harvard University Press, 1964). See also his "The Old Labor History and the New: In Search of an American Working Class," *Labor History* 20/1 (1979): 111–126.

19. David Montgomery, interviewed by Mark Naison and Paul Buhle in *Visions of History: Interviews*, eds. Henry Abelove, Betsy Blackmar, Peter Dimock, and Jonathan Schneer, eds. (New York: Pantheon Books, 1983), 175.

20. David Montgomery, 180.

21. Gregory S. Kealy, "Herbert G. Gutman, 1928–1985, and the Writing of Working-Class History," *Monthly Review: An Independent Socialist Magazine* 38 (1986): 22–30.

22. Herbert Gutman, *Work, Culture, and Society in Industrializing America: Essays in American Working-Class and Social History* (New York: Vintage Books, 1976).

23. Stephen Eric Bronner and Douglas MacKay Kellner, "Introduction," in *Critical Theory and Society: A Reader*, eds. Stephen Eric Bronner and Douglas MacKay Kellner (New York: Routledge, 1989).

24. Theodore Adorno and Rolf Tiederman, *History and Freedom: Lectures, 1964–1965* (New York: Polity Press, 2006), 12.

25. Herbert Marcuse, *Eros and Civilization* (New York: Vintage Books, 1955) and *One Dimensional Man* (London: Sphere Books, 1964).

26. Andre Gunder Frank, *Latin America: Underdevelopment or Revolution: Essays on the Development of Underdevelopment and the Immediate Enemy* (New York: Monthly Review Press, 1969). Also *ReOrient: Global Economy in the Asian Age* (Berkeley: University of California Press, 1998).

27. Immanuel Wallerstein, *The Modern World-System: Capitalist Agriculture and the Origins of the European World Economy in the Sixteenth Century* (New York: Academic Press, 1974). There are subsequent volumes to this work, including the fourth volume which focuses on the long nineteenth century from the French Revolution to World War I.

28. David Montgomery, *Visions of History*, 180.

29. Robert Gallman, "Notes on the New Social History," *Journal of Economic History* 37/1 (1977): 5.

30. Harold Perkin, "Social History in Britain," *Journal of Social History* 10/2 (1976): 129, 133.

31. Werner Conze and Charles A. Wright, "Social History," *Journal of Social History* 1/1 (1967): 7–16.

32. David Montgomery, *Visions of History*, 175; Staughton Lynd, "The New Left," *Annals of the American Academy of Political and Social Science* 382, Protest in the Sixties (March 1969): 66.

33. David Brion Davis, *The Problem of Slavery in the Age of Revolution* (Ithaca [NY]: Cornell University Press, 1975).

34. Eugene Genovese, *Roll, Jordan, Roll: The World the Slaves Made* (New York: Vintage Press, 1974).

35. Staughton Lynd, 67.

36. "Mrs. Walter Pinkus," Transcript of an Interview Conducted through the Federal Writer's Project, 1936–1940, Library of Congress, http://www.loc.gov/resource/wpalh1.17010109/#seq-1.

37. John Styles, "Time Piece: Working Men and Watches," *History Today* 58/1 (2008): 44–50.

CHAPTER 6

ENVIRONMENTAL HISTORY

CHAPTER OUTLINE

■ Natural History Through the Frontier Thesis and the *Longue Durée*: Roots of Environmental History

■ Approaching the Environment— Material or Cultural?

■ A Global Environmental History

■ Conclusion

■ Thinking Like a Historian

"There cannot be people outside of nature; there can only be people thinking they are outside nature."

William Cronon[1]

If you recall our discussion of Fernand Braudel and the second generation of the *Annales* School, you will remember that his examination of global processes was critiqued for focusing too much on the nonhuman. How could the earth's shifts and groans possibly affect human society? While Braudel and other scholars certainly spoke to those connections, it would take another generation for the history of humans as intricately and inextricably linked to the world around them—environmental history—to take root.

Environmental history is often seen as merely a methodology, a way of doing history. However, it is also a way of looking at the world, a lens through which people construct stories and make meaning about their past. While one need not be an environmentalist to study environmental history, many environmental historians have a concern for the world around them. Environmental history is, quite simply, history that takes the role of the environment in human history seriously. As such, environmental history, by its very nature, is a materialist philosophy. Its emphasis on human interaction with and connection to the environment as well as its emphasis on the "real," make it one of the most materialist philosophies out there, certainly more than other theories already discussed in this text. In fact, environmental historians have been known to complain that Marx and Marxist philosophy simply were not materialist enough to be of any use.[2] It is also by its nature a multidisciplinary history. Environmental historians rely on geography, geology, epidemiology, literature, and history (among other fields) for their source material.

This connection to the material world has given rise to critics to deride environmental history as too deterministic. Critics claim that historians are wedded to environmental determinism and are therefore limited in the scope of their research. Environmental determinism suggests that the characteristics of the geography of a region create the societal manifestations, thereby removing human agency from the historical equation. Fernand Braudel was accused of environmental determinism when he spoke in *The Mediterranean and the Mediterranean World in the Age of Philip II* of the mountain villages of Italy giving rise to particular qualities of surrounding villages, for example. More recently, the work of geographer Jared Diamond has received both praise and criticism. While on the one hand it represents a sweeping history of the world over 14,000 years and brings Oceania and Australasia into the center of world history, on the other hand, it relies too readily on using the environment to make claims about empire and the spread of human civilization.[3] Regardless, Diamond's discussion of the biodiversity of the world's land masses thousands of years ago as the geographic accident that contributed to some populations' ability to dominate others is an excellent example of the ways in which human life is tied to the earth.

Environmental historians, however, while recognizing this kind of fatalism, are far more sophisticated in their approaches than critics suggest. As we have seen with other theoretical traditions, the impetus for thinking historically about a topic was tied to real-world experiences. Environmental history's emergence as a fully fledged field of study was no different. According to Alfred Crosby, the events of the 1960s, most specifically the publication of Rachel Carson's *Silent Spring* and the 1969 moon landing finally put humanity's smallness in perspective. The universe is larger than us, and the Earth, this globe to which we are confined, is not healthy. Consequently, we are bound to it as much as it is to us. It was a defining moment and people were finally ready to take seriously Braudel's statement we have already encountered: We are inextricably bound to the environment and cannot separate without undermining the delicate balance between it and us.[4] As the opening quote of this chapter suggests, humans are inextricably tied to nature and "to live as human beings is to change the world around us."[5] That is the central focus of the historian of the environment, that humans have as much an effect on the environment as the environment does on human life. Consequently, we must pay attention to this relationship as we write histories of our own past.

As a theoretical perspective, then, environmental history postulates a materialist conception of history, one in which the crucial primary source is the physical world itself. From its building blocks with natural history to Braudel's oceans and mountains, environmental

scholars explore ways in which the environment was used as a vehicle for social, economic, and political decision making. But there is disagreement among environmental historians about how material that history really is. In many ways, it is also a cultural approach, as increasing numbers of scholars in the field believe that "environment" itself, despite the ontological reality of the globe, is constructed by societies and people. This chapter explores the tension and dialogue between these seemingly competing lenses and perspectives, beginning with the intellectual lineage of the field.

So what, then, is environmental history? On the one hand, environmental history is a discipline of history, like regional or intellectual specialties. On the other, as a discipline, it recognizes the environment itself as a historical actor. The natural world itself creates certain changes over time, and environmental historians explore the relationships between humanity and the world.

NATURAL HISTORY THROUGH THE FRONTIER THESIS AND THE *LONGUE DURÉE*: ROOTS OF ENVIRONMENTAL HISTORY

While currently considered a completely different field housed in the natural sciences, the natural history of the world—which has existed in some form since ancient times—is an important piece of the lineage of environmental history. Natural history focuses on observable nature—how humans collect artifacts and make sense of the world around them. As such, natural history is fairly interdisciplinary, as it is a system of classification and interpretation of the entire natural world. In the first century CE, the scholar Pliny the Elder wrote an encyclopedia of natural history focusing on everything from botany to zoology to pharmacology. Also included in his encyclopedia is a discussion of anthropology and mineralogy. Though fairly wide-ranging, Pliny the Elder's work nicely represents the breadth of natural history and its uses for particular cultures. Fast forwarding to the early modern period, natural history was at the forefront of scientific endeavors. Carl Linnaeus (c. 1707–1778), for example, the Swedish natural scientist, pioneered the field of botany and is considered to be one of the founders of modern ecology as well as taxonomy (the science of classification). Linnaeus toured various places in Europe to search for and catalogue new plants and other natural resources. Linnaeus' discoveries and methods provided a "modern," "scientific" way of cataloguing the world's flora and fauna, and therefore influenced other fields that developed during the age of professionalization over the next century. So, while natural history today continues to be its own field—and there are natural history museums in almost every major metropolis around the world—new disciplines such as physiology, zoology, or paleontology were formed between the eighteenth and twentieth centuries, reflecting an expansion of fields as a result of natural history's developments.

Within the field of history itself are three influential authors for contemporary environmental history—Frederick Jackson Turner, Walter Prescott Webb, and Fernand Braudel. Nearly all American environmental historians recognize the genesis of their field in late nineteenth-century ideas about conservation, particularly the work of Frederick Jackson Turner. Turner's work on the American Frontier with his 1893 argument that the frontier had closed and therefore Americans ought to conserve and preserve their land, serves as the foundational framework for thinking about the relationship between humans and their world. The US Census Bureau declared the frontier line closed in 1890, meaning that for Turner, that form of Americanization one gained through triumph over the perils of the savage land also disappeared. In many ways, the Turner thesis sets up the framework for the history of the American West as well as the history of the environment.

Another early scholar to influence the field was Walter Prescott Webb, particularly his 1931 book *The Great Plains*. This monograph takes a *longue durée* approach to the history of the Western Plains, exploring the relationship between the land and various peoples who inhabited the area, from the Plains Indians to the ranchers and farmers of the twentieth century. Prescott Webb asserted that the goal of his book was to show how the Plains "affected the various peoples, nations as well as individuals who came to take and occupy it and was affected by them."[6] Two decades later, his book *The Great Frontier* (published in 1951) postulated the *idea* of a frontier as a guiding force of Western (i.e., Western civilization) history and a way for all peoples (not just Americans) to think of their relationship to the world around them.

While we discussed the work of Fernand Braudel in Chapter 4, we should discuss his relationship to environmental history more fully here. Braudel's concept of the *longue durée*, as you recall, relies on a way of privileging geographic time over the history of the event. The slow fits and spurts of the Earth's movement, the boundaries of geographic borders such as mountains or the seas, impacted human lives, in some ways dictating the direction of human relations. This privileging of the role of the environment in human history served as a distinctive historiographic model for future environmental historians. In fact, the very concept of a *longue durée* takes seriously geologic time, and therefore the role of the environment in human history.

APPROACHING THE ENVIRONMENT—MATERIAL OR CULTURAL?

In 2003, the eminent world historian J.R. McNeill dissected the subtheories within environmental history, arguing that there are three basic frameworks: cultural/intellectual, material, and political. Political environmental history is that history informed by and interested in policy decisions, a history that is connected to activism and a desire to change the direction of human engagement with the land. Material environmental history focuses on the processes of the land itself and the relationship of humans to that environment, and finally, cultural/intellectual environmental history examines the shifting perceptions and attitudes humans had over time to the world around them. McNeill's framework is an excellent place to start. Douglas Weiner has very recently discussed the unavoidable slippage of post-structuralism into the framework of the environment. Rather than some ontological "out there" for which historians must discover some "truth," many scholars recognize the environment as being a product of human construction. In this regard then, environmental history reflects a kaleidoscope of historical lenses—at once ontological and epistemological—that is, both material and cultural. Those who approach the history of the environment from this position are content seeing environmental history as an indefinable domain.[7]

Early, path-breaking historians such as Roderick Nash, Donald Worster, and William Cronon tended to blur these lines as well, complicating McNeill's narrative. Environmental history as a unit of analysis (and a legitimate historical field) was said to have been first articulated by the American wilderness historian Roderick Nash. At the same time, it was also Nash who claimed that wilderness is not an ontological "out there" to be discerned as described above, but rather that "civilization created wilderness."[8] He devoted much time to discussing the ways in which, for example, there is no "wilderness" without human construction of the "idea" of wilderness. Just a few years after the publication of this book, Nash instituted a new course entitled "American Environmental History," which quite unexpectedly registered over 400 students. In that class, Nash worked to shift the perceptions of nature and wilderness, at one point playing a recording of howling wolves and asking students to insert themselves into the world of those in the past who experienced this wilderness. In his reminiscence of that class, Nash also outlined a working theory of environmental history, stating that it would, "refer to the past contact of man with his total environment."[9]

Another early environmental historian to blur these divisions is Donald Worster (b. 1941), who began his education at the University of Kansas, earned his Ph.D. in 1971 from Yale University and eventually returned to teach at the University of Kansas. His first book, *Nature's Economy: A History of Ecological Ideas* (1977) argued that humans have had profoundly different relationships with nature over the past three centuries. Specifically, he explores various attitudes toward nature that assumed human superiority over nature, and how those attitudes led to ecological disasters of the twentieth century. But it was his second book, *Dust Bowl: The Southern Plains in the 1930s* that propelled him to leadership in the field. Winner of the Bancroft Prize in US history from the American Historical Association, it, like Nash's book, was also nominated for a Pulitzer Prize. Combining a policy and material approach to the environment, the monograph drew connections between the Dust Bowl and the Depression, suggesting that the ecological and economic catastrophes were the result of American economic and geographic policies. The twin calamities provided immediate opportunities for reform, but also provided a rare moment for Americans to reflect on their use and abuse of nature. Worster's most recent monograph is a highly praised biography of the environmentalist John Muir, taking yet another, a more cultural approach to studying our environmental past.[10] Worster remains a public intellectual, providing commentary about the social impact of the Dust Bowl.

Since environmental history was so closely linked to concerns for the environment, many environmental historians began to define their audience more carefully, linking the three elements described by McNeill. For example, William Cronon articulated five distinct audiences, each with different needs and outlooks: fellow historians, policy makers, fellow environmentalists, the "general public," and finally, the earth itself. While there is some overlap with each of these groups (e.g., you may find historians concerned with policy), Cronon argued that environmental historians needed to clearly define *usefulness* of the project to address the multifaceted layers of engagement from each of these groups. For example, in setting itself in place vis-à-vis other historical fields, environmental history "erodes the boundaries among traditional historical subfields, be they national or thematic, and suggests valuable new ways of building bridges among them."[11] Cronon (b. 1954) is currently the Frederick Jackson Turner Professor of History, Geography, and Environmental Studies at the University of Wisconsin, Madison and remains one of the most preeminent scholars of the environment and a dedicated social activist. His first major work, *Changes in the Land: Indians, Colonists, and the Ecology of New England* (1983) was a pioneering work that traced the ways in which the landscape of New England was radically altered as a consequence of European takeover of the land.

Policy approaches to environmental history most clearly reside in activism (think of the influence of Rachel Carson's *Silent Spring* discussed earlier), consequently, environmentalism—that is, concern for protecting the delicate balance of the environment. Far from being a twentieth-century phenomenon, environmentalism stems back at least to the eighteenth century according to Richard Grove: "from the late eighteenth century onwards, we find that the leading pioneers of environmentalism all had a deep sense of historical perspective on environmental change and very often a wide and very scholarly appreciation of the historical evidence for rapid environmental change over time."[12] Himself a conservation historian, Grove's works focus on the global early modern period (1500–1800), but particularly the emergence of conservation in imperial settings. Grove's claim about the origins of European environmental history is subject to some debate, however, as others in his field suggest an eastward trajectory from the American West to Europe and the globe.[13] Nevertheless, it is clear that the role of natural history in Western Europe discussed earlier played some part in shaping the intellectual and cultural outlook of those concerned with the environment, and in turn, those concerned with the history of the environment.

The more intellectual approaches to the history of the environment draw from the ideas of *mentalités* and changing human perceptions. In addition, many cultural/intellectual approaches to the environment are influenced by postcolonial theory and are concerned with relationships between peoples mediated through "frontiers" or "borderlands." In these environmental histories, race becomes a central focus of analysis. To be sure, race had always had an implicit, if not explicit, role in environmental history, especially with scholars such as Nash or White talking about cultural frontiers. As Colin Fisher argues in "Race and US Environmental History," race had always been a central focus of the field as the impact of the westward movement profoundly affected Native Americans.[14] An example of recent scholarship weaving race into environmental history, Carolyn Merchant's "Shades of Darkness" examines the problematic role race has played in the construction of environmental problems such as the westward movement and urban growth.[15] Carolyn Merchant has also discussed the concept of gender in the writing of world environmental history. In particular, Merchant suggests that the analysis of reproduction is a central category for exploring production offering what she describes as a more "balanced and complete view of past interactions with nature."[16]

A GLOBAL ENVIRONMENTAL HISTORY

While many leaders of environmental history were historians of the United States, specifically of the American West, environmental history also has global reach. According to Donald Worster, "environmental history is not an exclusively American invention; it has emerged under different names and sometimes well in advance of our own efforts in other countries, too."[17] While we discussed Le Roy Ladurie's *Montaillou* as a third-generation *Annales* work in Chapter 4, Worster sees this discussion of a fourteenth-century peasant community as smack in the middle of environmental history as it deals with ecological shifts in the town's move to modernity. But there is more to environmental history in Europe and the world than the *Annales* School, no matter how influential it may have been on historical studies.

There are at least two basic threads running through global environmental history. The first thread explores the environment as a component of empire or as a transnational phenomenon that "demanded categories of analysis other than the nation."[18] For example, works such as Crosby's *Columbian Exchange* or Mike Davis' *Late Victorian Holocausts: El Niño Famines and the Making of the Third World* (2000) tie imperial administration to environmental problems in colonized (or semi-colonial) regions.[19] Moreover, there are a variety of histories that deal with colonial administration and environmental history. Richard Grove's work, for example, examines colonial conservation. His *Green Imperialism: Colonial Expansion, Tropical Island Edens and the Origins of Environmentalism, 1600–1860* examines how "discoveries" of edenic islands lent themselves to transforming colonial attitudes to the environment, specifically by propelling a conservation movement within the imperial government to prevent waste of the land. And often, this imperial desire to maintain the beauty of these islands negatively impacted indigenous use of the soil.[20]

Alfred Crosby (b. 1931), Professor Emeritus of American Studies at University of Texas, Austin, has also pushed this transregional discussion of environmental history. Crosby's early work in the 1960s explored hemp as a global commodity, but his more radical contribution to the emergent field of environmental history was his work on what he called "The Columbian Exchange," the network of exchange between Old World and New of disease, commodities, and people that fundamentally shifted the global balance of power. Moreover, he changed the debate about Montezuma and the Aztecs. Previous histories glorified Hernan Cortes and his Spanish conquistadores, attributing Aztec fear of the horses and the Spaniards to their defeat. Crosby's significant work on blood and disease, however, stated that on the contrary it was pestilence—disease—that undermined Aztec ability to push back the Spaniards. We now casually accept this argument since we know so much more now about the spread of disease, but Crosby's article was radical for its time and an example of the varieties of environmental history.[21]

Another way to approach a transregional environmental history is through the lens of world history. As with environmental history, some scholars have difficulty defining world history precisely because it operates on such a large scale. To complicate matters, recent trends in referring to global, transnational, or world history have created dilemmas for many. The World History Association explicitly posits a difference between global history and world history—which emphasizes comparison.[22] A recent monograph edited by the esteemed world historians Kenneth Pomeranz and Edmund Burke III entitled *The Environment and World History* attempts to broach the incredible overlap between the two fields. The monograph specifically approaches environmental history through a comparative framework, moving beyond the regional studies of environmental processes. Divided into three sections explaining first the theoretical connections between world and environmental history, then explaining specific regional stories and frontier histories, and then finally looking at the intellectual approaches to the environment and the ways in which knowledge about it is controlled and dispersed, this monograph represents the varieties of approaches within the field. More than simply a method then, this book shows environmental history as a fundamentally distinct worldview.[23]

One example is J.R. McNeill's own work as a world environmental historian. *Something New Under the Sun* is a global environmental history of the twentieth century. His argument for focusing solely on one century, but in a global context, centers around his analysis of the enormous environmental transformations the globe has faced in those hundred years compared to the four million or so years of human activity preceding it. As such, the century needs to be studied on its own terms.[24]

Another example is Kenneth Pomeranz's individual work, *The Great Divergence*, a comparative political, economic and environmental analysis of China and England at the end of the eighteenth century. Referring to Britain as a "fortunate freak," Pomeranz makes the case for British exceptionalism not through political or intellectual ingenuity, but through a combination of environmental factors and imperial policy. In the monograph, Pomeranz also examines borderland (or hinterland) policy and how regional environmental policies reflected back to (or didn't) the métropole. Whereas Beijing developed policy for rural farming and sustainable agriculture in far-removed provinces, Britain's policies toward its provinces (i.e., the Americas) operated within a larger mercantilist framework—and as such, worked for the betterment of the center (i.e., London and England).[25]

Another thread of global environmental history explores environments and nations through a subregional or even nationalist framework, and these, too, have several layers and subsets. These histories tend to examine the ways in which environmental policy or particular uses of the environment both constructed and were constructed by specific identities. Years before *Something New Under the Sun or The Great Divergence*, a rich tradition of subregional environmental history emerged, particularly in South Asian historiography. One major work of this thread is Madhav Gadgil's and Ramachandra Guha's *This Fissured Land*, which examines the ecological history of South Asia. Critiqued by some for its heavy reliance on biological studies, *This Fissured Land* nevertheless offers a stunning glimpse at deforestation on the subcontinent and the effects of deforestation on the populace. Specifically, the book examines how local, traditional use of the land (stemming back thousands of years) flew in the face of governmental policies, both imperial and national, to control and parcel out resources.[26]

These regional environmental histories exist for every continent, including Antarctica, and scholars approach these regional histories from various perspectives. Some scholars believe that the earth's processes, natural (or man-made) phenomenon, and the flora and fauna of the globe deserve particular attention in helping understand the world as larger than humanity yet also tied inextricably with it. Here, the environment operates as a historical actor. Stephen Pyne's enormous study of *The Ice*, for example, examines peoples' relationship with the continent of Antarctica, particularly as a result of increased environmentalism. A professor of Life Sciences at Arizona State University, Pyne has shifted his academic attention to the history of fire and has written about its effects on a global scale, from the Canadian borderlands to the Australian outback.[27] More recently, scholars have been examining the environmental impact of fishing on the Southern Ocean and the surrounding area. Other scholars, such as Tom Standage, explore the ways in which drinks (culled and refined from natural resources) have shaped human pathways; Mark Kurlansky's popular history *Salt: A World History* examines in a macrohistorical way how salt has influenced the directions of human history and his *Cod: A Biography of the Fish that Changed the World* argues that fishing for the North Atlantic white fish with tender flesh dramatically transformed the lives of Northern Europeans as Europeans fished them to near-extinction.[28]

Latin America drew some of the early environmental histories, as we have already discussed. Alfred Crosby's narrative of the Columbian Exchange has fundamentally transformed our understanding of the environment, of world history, and of the general narrative of discovery. There are other heavy-hitting works including Warren

Dean's final monograph, *With Broadax and Firebrand: The Destruction of the Brazilian Atlantic Forest*, a work that explores the Amazon from prehistory through the twentieth century. According to Lise Sedrez, the environmental history of Latin America over the last twenty years focuses on tragic stories of the degradation of the land and consequent social effects because of the rapid destruction of the natural world. At the same time, however, the literature has provided new questions as to what constitutes regional Latin American environmental history, particularly in terms of thinking beyond the nation state.[29]

African environmental history is just as diverse, with subjects on everything from mining to land use to colonial struggle to perceptions of the land. In addition to exploring traditional themes, African environmental historiography also has been a rich domain for ecofeminism as well as analyses of rural poverty and land use.[30] In addition, African environmental historians are interested in perceptions of resources, production, and conservation. For example, James C. McCann published *Green Land, Brown Land, Black Land*, which challenged previous attitudes about the African landscape by suggesting that human interaction with the land transformed it.[31] McCann has also written about the introduction of maize (corn) to Africa and the ways in which one crop changed the landscape to become one of the most prolific crops in many African countries.[32] One of the major scholars of Equatorial Africa, Tamara Giles-Vernick has written numerous works regarding the region and perceptions of environmental policy and has earned her the esteemed Aldo Leopold Prize in Environmental History. Her book, *Cutting the Vines of the Past* juxtaposes perceptions of the indigenous people with those of governance, suggesting that conservation efforts were often seen as foreign intrusion—or, after colonialism, as remnants of empire.[33]

Europe, too, has seen development of regional environmental histories. Britain has had a long tradition of environmental history as well as landscape history—that history linking the ideal of the land to historical and political realities. Ann Bermingham's *Landscape and Ideology*, for example, linked class-based division of agricultural lands to rural fantasies of the idyllic countryside. Landscape histories such as Bermingham's (or more recently Simon Schama's) have been critiqued by some historians as not adequately linked to the environment; it has nevertheless opened the door. Very recently, Peter Thorsheim has explored the human consequences of industrialization in Britain, looking at the ways in which the move to coke from coal was supposed to be a "greener" alternative, but instead negatively impacted peoples' health.[34] Combining history of environmental changes in industrial Britain with perceptions of Britons, Thorsheim's work provides a provocative analysis of health, hygiene, and pollution.

While Great Britain from the eighteenth century seems a logical place for historians to examine human interaction with the environment given its long industrial history, other European countries also lend themselves very easily to environmental discussion. For example, the Netherlands, sitting below sea level, provided some of the technological education to Britain to drain the fens for new industries and farm work. Environmental historians have probed even earlier into Europe's environmental past to examine ancient Greek and Roman history, medieval towns, Middle Eastern history up to the Ottomans, or frontiers and borderlands in the early modern period. Because of the dense forests in their countries, German and Nordic scholars have long examined forestry history. Beyond forestry history, however, each has regionally specific concerns—industrial pollution in the case of Germany and technology and the conceptualization of the natural world for Nordic scholars.[35]

Conclusion

In this chapter, you have read about some of the ideas and scholars who have propelled environmental history into the mainstream, and our discussion has suggested both broad and deep world-historical and theoretical connections for those who study the environment. What began as a field looking at the long cycles of the earth's geological temperament grew to include histories of public policy as well as particular products of the environment, and even peoples' perceptions of the world around them. No matter the direction, environmental history has in some ways retained a fundamentally materialist approach—that is, a recognition that the material world has a profound relationship to human activity. At the same time, however, as historians and scholars from other disciplines strove to better understand the environment, they complicated their own stories, arguing that the very concept of "environment" was bound to perceptions of the world around us and to a connection of the epistemological to the ontological. In other words, scholars increasingly found evidence that the environment—in policy, in culture, on its own terms—is a site of power in which control over knowledge and access can be (and has been) asserted. Environmental history, in Harriet Ritvo's term, is more like a "blob" that haphazardly covers different regions, time periods, and approaches, which in itself can be a good thing, because it enables scholars to look beyond their own constructed geographic and biological borders.[36]

Perhaps the natural direction for environmental history is to swing the pendulum back to histories reminiscent of the *longue durée*. In world history, this has taken the form of Big History most closely associated with the work of David Christian. In *Maps of Time: An Introduction to Big History*, Christian begins his history of the world with the big bang—or rather, the origins of the universe—moving slowly toward human history, which really is only a fraction of geologic time.[37] From concern about the vanishing frontier to an examination of "this fleeting world,"[38] histories that incorporate the environment have made important contributions to our understanding of the past, our relationship to it, and the living, breathing world around us.

Thinking Like a Historian

The primary source you are reading in this chapter is a US government publication from 1930 about the status of wheat production and prices. This publication was produced just prior to the emergence of the Dust Bowl, that moment in US history when overuse of soil in the Great Plains combined with years of drought eroded and desiccated the soil. In reading this source, keep that context in mind and address the following questions:

- Does the US Department of Agriculture provide any clue that there are problems with agricultural production? If so, where?

- Why is the comparison with global wheat output significant?

- How could you read this source with different environmental approaches? Discuss the varieties of ways different generations of environmental historians might approach explaining the source material.

The secondary source you are reading is coauthored by Richard Grove (discussed in the chapter) and Toyin Falola and examines the tension between European colonizers and the indigenous population of West Africa over land-use rights.

- How does their discussion of "conservationism" resonate with different approaches raised in this chapter?

- How was conservation in West Africa affected by "conditions of indirect rule and local autonomy"?

- How do religion, tribal politics, and traditional land use tie into conservationist politics?

- What arguments did local chiefs make regarding the need to protect forests in West Africa?

- How does this environmental history complicate the history of colonialism? You may want to return to this question after you read Chapter 10.

Wheat[39]

The present very low level of wheat prices has brought into operation forces tending to cause an improvement, but despite this, another year of low wheat prices is in prospect for 1931. For several years, world production has increased more rapidly than consumption and burdensome stocks have accumulated. The world carry-over on July 1, 1931, will again be abnormally large. At present there is no indication that there will be any material change in the world acreage of wheat to be harvested in 1931, and thus far weather conditions have been generally favorable for the fall-sown crop. It is too early to forecast yields, but if yields approach the average, the new crop, plus the very large carry-over, would again result in burdensome supplies. Prices in the United States now average in the vicinity of 30 to 35 cents per bushel above an export parity. If prices in the United States are on a normal export basis next summer, it would mean that world prices would have to rise about 30 to 35 cents per bushel in order for United States prices to remain at their present levels. Looking further ahead, substantial adjustments may be expected through forced contraction of high-cost acreage, through checking the expansion in low-cost acreage, through increased purchasing power, and through modification of import and milling restrictions which are now tending to reduce consumption. A better balance between production and consumption is likely eventually to be reached at price levels that will average above those now prevailing in world markets, but will be lower than have prevailed during most of the last 10 years. Any surplus of wheat that the United States may have for export will continue to face severe competition from other low-cost producing countries.

The general downward trend in wheat prices during the last four years and the recent extremely low prices are the result of factors which have been affecting the situation for several years, reinforced by additional factors which have more recently come into operation. The most important factor has been the expansion of world wheat acreage and production, notably in exporting countries, at a rate more rapid than the rate" of increase in world consumption. This has resulted in an increase of world stocks and carry-overs to burdensome proportions.

World wheat acreage has been expanding rapidly since 1924. In that year the total wheat acreage, outside of Russia and China, is estimated to have been 224,000,000 acres; by 1930 it had reached 250,000,000 acres, an increase of about 12 per cent. In addition, Russia's acreage has been increasing rapidly, having risen from 52,700,000 acres in 1924 to 84,100,000 acres in 1930, the present area being nearly 10,000,000 acres in excess of the pre-war average for the years 1909-1913. The increase of nearly 60 per cent, or more than 31,000,000 acres since 1924, was over 5,000,000 acres more than the Increase In the rest of the world combined during this period. Furthermore, average yields per acre in the world, outside of Russia and China, especially during 1927 and 1928, were considerably higher than during the early years after the World War. Although yields were low in 1929, consumption was reduced, so that the world carry-over remained considerably above normal levels on July 1, 1930.

The increased acreage of recent years has apparently been due in part to the encouragement of high prices received for the crops of 1924 and 1925 and in part to the lowering of costs of production and the increasing of acreages that can be grown by farmers in the subhumid areas through the use of improved machinery. The extent to which lower production costs and the lower general price level may result in a more-or-less permanently lower level of wheat prices is uncertain. Only to the extent that there is a long-run tendency for wheat production costs to be reduced more rapidly than the cost of producing other commodities can wheat be expected permanently to fall in price as compared with other commodities. Declines in wheat prices in line with declines in the general price level, however, affect the wheat grower in so far as he may have incurred fixed expenses, such as debts and interest charges, at higher price levels.

Another important factor which affected the situation last year was the raising of tariffs in several of the continental European countries and the promulgation of milling restrictions. These measures have tended not only to reduce the imports into these countries, but to prevent an accumulation of stocks and to encourage increased acreage. During 1930 Germany, France, and Italy greatly increased their tariffs on wheat and some countries are fixing the quantities of foreign wheats which can be used for mixing. So long as these barriers are maintained they will tend to restrict the outlet for wheat from other countries.

More recent declines in world wheat prices have been accentuated by several factors, such as material increases in later estimates of the 1930 crop in a number of countries and the pressing of Russian wheat upon an export market already abundantly supplied. These factors have overbalanced the influence of greatly increased use of wheat in the United States for feed and the restriction of United States exports by price support here. As a result world wheat prices are now at extremely low levels. It is doubtful if wheat has ever been so cheap in terms of commodities in general as it has been during recent months. Although it can not be confidently predicted that the bottom has been reached, it seems improbable that world wheat prices can go much lower; for prices at Liverpool, Winnipeg, Buenos Aires, and other important markets are now so low as to return to growers in many wheat-producing regions little more than threshing and shipping costs.

The world carry-over (accounted for as of July 1, 1930, of 537,000,000 bushels, the 1930 world wheat crop, excluding Russia and China, of about 3,777,000,000 bushels, and about 100,000,000 bushels estimated as the probable total of shipments from Russia, amount to 4,414,000,000. bushels. This is an increase of 320,000,000 bushels over the preceding year. World consumption during 1930-31 will be larger than in 1929-30. The greatest part of this increase will be due to increased feeding of wheat in the United States, but in addition, wheat feeding has probably increased slightly in Canada and a few other countries, and some increase in the use of wheat for food by non-European importers is also probable. These point to an increase in the disappearance of wheat in the world outside Russia and China about equal to the increase of supplies.

Supplies available for export and carry-over as of January 1, 1931, in the four principal exporting countries were from 90,000,000 to 140,000,0000 bushels larger than they were a year earlier. In addition, it is likely that there will be material shipments from Russia during the next six months, so that supplies available to fill importers' requirements will exceed those of the corresponding period last year by about 150,000,000 bushels or more. Altogether, indications are that the world carry-over, outside Russia and China, as of July 1, 1931, will again be abnormally large and perhaps not materially different from that of July 1, 1930.

There is at present no reason to expect that total world production for 1931 will be greatly different from that of 1930. Although the increased acreage for the world as a whole, outside Russia and China, may have been checked, there is no indication of an appreciable decrease. Moreover, there may be some further increase in the Russian acreage for 1931. On an acreage about as large as that of 1930, average yields would result in a world crop for 1931 about equal to that of 1930, and total supplies available for 1931-32 would be about the same as those for 1930-31.

On the demand side, some improvement may be expected through improving world business conditions, and growth in population, but this will probably be counterbalanced, in part at least, by a decrease in the quantity of wheat used for feed. It is not to be expected that the United States will have another short corn crop In 1931, with its resulting heavy feeding of wheat Consequently, no marked increase in wheat consumption is in prospect for next season. Under the present circumstances no prediction as to the precise level of prices during the coming year can be safely ventured, but present indications are that it will again be low.

Wheat prices in the United States since November have been maintained well above export parity, largely through operations of the Grain Stabilization Corporation. As a result, exports of wheat and flour are being restricted but this is being more than offset by the heavy feeding of wheat which can be exacted to continue into next fall. The carry-over on July 1 in the United States is likely to be somewhat lower than last year, but yet abnormally heavy, and it will be more heavily concentrated In visible positions. As the crop of the United States usually provides a surplus for export it is to be expected that, unless yields should be exceptionally low, the new crop, added to the heavy carry-over, will result in a large exportable surplus next summer. Since prices in the United States now average in the vicinity of 30 to 35 cents per bushel above an export parity, placing them upon an export basis would mean that world prices would have to rise about 30 to 35 cents per bushel if our prices are not to fall below their present levels. As indications point to a continuation of burdensome world supplies, wheat prices in the United States next summer may be below the levels which prevailed last summer.

The area seeded to winter wheat in the United States is estimated at 42,042,000 acres, a decrease of 1.1 per cent from that seeded in the fall of 1929. Unusually favorable conditions for fall sowings, the need of wheat for pasture, the cheapness of seed wheat, and low prices for alternative crops, prevented the greater reduction which low wheat prices tended to bring about. Reductions of 12 per cent in Nebraska and Colorado, 6 per cent in Oklahoma, and 1 per cent in Kansas, brought about a 3.7 per cent reduction in the hard winter wheat States in spite of a 3 per cent increase in Texas. There was a slight increase from the low levels of 1929 in the group of States producing chiefly soft red winter wheat, owing in part to increased needs for pasture and for wheat to feed next summer. The principal increase in sowings took place in the State of Washington where spring plantings seem likely to be correspondingly reduced.

Conditions for winter wheat to date have been generally favorable, except that deficiencies of subsoil moisture in large sections affected by the drought may make for reduced yields per acre sown. Unless adverse conditions develop between now and harvest time, another large crop of winter wheat will be produced in 1931. If yields and abandonment are equal to the average of those of the last 10 years, the acreage seeded would result in a production of approximately 542,000,000 bushels. Of this total, hard red winter wheat would comprise about 329,000,000 bushels, soft red winter about 172,000,000 bushels, and white wheat 41,000,000 bushels. This production would keep us on a level far above the domestic consumption of soft winter wheat during most recent years. In 1930 the production of hard red winter amounted to about 366,000,000 bushels and that of soft red winter to about 194,000,000 bushels.

The total area sown to spring wheat (including durum) in 1930 was nearly 1,000,000 acres less than in 1929. Much of this acreage was replaced by flax. Higher yields of wheat per acre, however, led to a production of 14,000,000 bushels more than in 1929.

The area of hard red spring wheat remained about constant and at a level which, with average yields, appears to be ample to supply our normal domestic consumption and to leave a small surplus for export from the Pacific Northwest. Because of yields slightly below average, 1930 production amounted to about 152,000,000 bushels or about 5,000,000 bushels less than would have resulted with average yields.

Most of the net decrease of the 1930 spring-wheat area was in durum, the decrease in the four principal States amounting to nearly 1,000,000 acres. This was accomplished in part by substitution of flax for durum and in part by shifting from durum to new varieties of rust-resistant hard red spring wheat. Thus far during the current season prices of durum have not been enough below those of spring bread wheats to give much Incentive for further shifting, but some further shift may be made to the rust-resistant bread wheats which would still further reduce the durum acreage. The 1930 durum acreage was sufficient to produce about a 60,000,000-bushel crop if yields were average. Such a crop is large enough to place durum prices on an export basis in ordinary years and to make the level of durum prices, as compared with other wheat prices, largely dependent upon the world durum situation.

We may expect competition from overseas durum production to be as keen next year as this year, or keener. Italy, an important market for our surplus, has increased total winter wheat acreage, and thus has probably increased durum acreage also. The chances are that yields in Italy will be as large or larger than in 1930, when they were below the average of recent years. Russia is a potential source of competition which must be watched closely. Russia sent a little durum to Italy in 1929-30 and is known to be sending some there this year. North African prospects are still uncertain, but durum production from this region appears to have little influence upon the foreign demand for durum wheat from this country. Indicated exports from the United States since July 1 have been heavier this year than last, and disappearance from sight in Minneapolis, where durum is used largely for semolina and durum flour manufacture, is slightly larger than last year. Elsewhere in the United States disappearance has been slow, leaving the balance on hand nearly equal to that of a year ago. ■

Chiefs, Boundaries, and Sacred Woodlands: Early Nationalism and the Defeat of Colonial Conservationism in the Gold Coast and Nigeria, 1870–1916[1]

Richard Grove, University of Cambridge and
Toyin Falola, The University of Texas at Austin[40]

I. Introduction

The main aim of this essay is to make a tentative assessment of some of the attempts made by the British colonial authorities to introduce forest conservation programs into Anglophone West Africa, and to sketch out the nature of some of the more elitist indigenous responses to those attempts. In the course of the essay we also aim to characterize the changing emphases and fashions of conservationism in West Africa and make some brief comparative remarks about contemporary developments in other parts of the British Empire.

The story of colonial conservation in West Africa was inextricably bound up with the developing tension between two entirely different agendas of power, one indigenous and the other governmental, within which the state attempted to assert its own notions of environmental control and land-use planning, reflecting both international changes in conservation thinking as well as an empirical and institutional learning process on the part of the local colonial apparatus. Simultaneously the indigenous populations, or at least their leaders, learnt increasingly to adjust to the weaknesses of the colonial state as specifically manifested in an environmental policy, seeking eventually to manipulate the agendas and mechanisms of colonial conservation to their advantage, often with some success. This essay, then, sets out quite deliberately to question the assumption engendered in some quarters that colonial conservation was, throughout the imperial context, a vigorous and militarized instrument of colonial oppression.[2] Certainly, in British West Africa this was far from the case. On the contrary, the evidence indicates that, in the context of Western economic penetration, the general pattern of land use change and forest survival was dictated far less by the colonial state than by indigenous political interest groups in close alliance with the interests of metropolitan capital. This analysis actually corresponds with existing and highly insightful research by economic anthropologists.[3]

To a greater extent than in other parts of the colonial world, conservation in West Africa was affected by the distinctive conditions of indirect rule and local autonomy. Far from succeeding in establishing an environmental hegemony, the conservation propagandists of the colonial state found themselves, from the outset, in an extremely weak position and one in which any "success" in their programs was entirely contingent on the support or acquiescence of the indigenous rulers and elites. Indeed, in the Lagos Colony Forest Ordinance of 1902, this principle of acquiescence was actually enshrined in law. As a result, when more broad-based popular resistance developed to the very real commoditization and sub-division of the landscape by the state and its collaborators, it was manifested less in terms of direct clashes with the colonial state and more in terms of conflicts between indigenous groups, communities and classes and, not least, between men and women. In other words,

African Economic History 24 (1996): 1–23

colonial conservation helped to intensify and internalize economic and political struggles in terms both of gender and of class.

The fundamental weakness of the colonial state in West Africa in its conservationist guise was closely associated with the limitations of the colonial state in general, particularly with regard to the lack of control over land. This meant that the opportunities for social and resource control which developed in some other colonies did not develop very far in the Gold Coast and Nigeria. Instead, especially in the Gold Coast, the struggle between the rulers and ruled quickly developed into an open arena for the testing of relative political strengths and the creation of political identities. Partly as a consequence of this, the economic ambitions of the colonial state were diverted far more quickly than elsewhere into a discourse about "development," as ambitions for straightforward control slowly foundered. This discourse had very early origins in the policies of Alfred Moloney, a visionary and conservationist colonial official.[4] In both Ghana and Nigeria, these ambivalent tendencies were intensified by the close proximity of the biologically wealthy wet forest zones to the coastal trade routes and towns, the nature of preexisting trade patterns and the rapidly escalating commercial demands for tree and plantation crops. In this setting, the fight for indigenous control over land was fired by the desire to retain control over commercial potential and incoming capital. As we shall see, this led to a considerable contradiction, and one in which the colonial state found itself hopelessly enmeshed.

The dynamics of external economic penetration as well as the externally derived antecedents of colonial environmental attitudes dictated the environmental history of the region. In particular, the environmental histories of the Gold Coast and Nigeria were closely intertwined. While they often diverged (especially in Nigeria where there were important regional differences in the development of forest policy), the inter-colonial (even international) nature of colonial scientific expertise meant that important cross-connections were retained in the development of colonial environmental policy. More importantly, the political networks of "ecological resistance" became increasingly closely connected, particularly between the Gold Coast and the Lagos Colony.

II. The Mankesim Incident

The conflict between colonial European and indigenous African views of nature had deep roots in West Africa.

Moreover, as time went by it became a steadily more complex social clash, complicated primarily by the varying incentives offered by capitalist penetration and the lure of profits to trading elites, both African and European. Indeed, the identities and motivations of these interest-groups were often deeply intertwined and united in opposition to colonial conservation policy.

To begin with, however, the story was a simpler one, and had more to do with clashes between different religious interpretations of the environment rather than conflicts between different economic groups. A series of incidents that took place at Mankesim, near Cape Coast, helps to illustrate this point.[5] Both the initial cause of the conflict and the nature of the indigenous response to the problem were greatly constrained by the influence of Christian missionary education. One of the major centres for this activity was at Cape Coast, where both Basel missionaries and the Wesleyan church were active.[6] An early Wesleyan school was founded during the 1840s at Asafa, a village near Mankesim, well inland from Cape Coast. The foundation was thus very close to the shrine of the great Brafo cult at Mankesim. This shrine was, effectively, one of the most sacred religious sites of the Fante people.[7] The Brafo was believed to dwell in a sacred hollow in the forest adjacent to Mankesim, and was consulted both by the local people and by pilgrims, some of whom came from a great distance. Any movement of Christians to a point near the shrine would therefore be unwelcome. Local communal politics therefore came to a crisis in late 1849, when Christian converts from Asafa felt the need to abuse and ridicule the Brafo's worshippers. Finally, they even went so far as to clear the bush in the immediate neighborhood of the sacred grove, in order to make their farms and take advantage of the rich unworked soil which was to be found there. This was much more than the priests were prepared to stand for and they called upon the chiefs and people to defend the honor of their god. They did not, however, take more direct action, being convinced that the Brafo would avenge himself without human aid. It was not until they had been disappointed in this and had seen unusually good crops growing in the Christian farms (and seen one of the invaders actually shoot a deer within the woodland), that it was felt incumbent on the priests to do something more active. A council was then held and it was agreed that the Fante chiefs should combine to defend the honor of the god.

Adu, King of Mankesim, was appointed the immediate guardian of the shrine, and proceeded to rally the support of neighboring chiefs. Soon after this arrangement was made, one of the priests, of a lesser grade, decided to join the Christians and, with others, entered the sacred grove and cut several poles there for building purposes. Hearing of this, the priests went to Adu and called on him to punish the miscreants. Adu then collected his people, invaded the Christian village at night, burnt it to the ground, and carried away ten Christian villagers to Mankesim. Very soon afterwards, the Governor at Cape Coast came to hear of the incident and summoned Adu to his office.

A neighboring chief, Amoku, King of Anomabu, was also summoned by the Judicial Assessor at the Castle and asked to intervene and prevail on Adu to comply with the Governor's summons, which Adu had initially chosen not to do. By now, however, the Fante chiefs from further afield were gathering and, to the Governor, all the makings of a very troublesome rebellion appeared to be present. Moreover, a massacre of Christians was threatened, while Adu threatened to have the turncoat priest drowned. Suddenly, however, as quickly as the rebellion had threatened, the chaos started to die down. This was because a sufficiently large number of the chiefs summoned by Adu, many of whom had initially supported him, became far more concerned about the interruption to trade and the increasingly disturbed state of the country. They preferred to persuade Adu to come to Cape Coast and, eventually, to reach an amicable settlement with the Governor. The Christians, meanwhile, were discouraged, apparently, from further violations of the sacred woodlands of Brafo.[8]

The Mankesim incident highlighted, in a microcosm, some of the apparently contradictory factors that were to shape and constrain the struggle between the Gold Coast chiefs and the inroads of Christian culture, more especially when the contest involved European claims over forest land long endowed with indigenous religious and customary meaning. Already, though, at Mankesim, the increasingly attractive priorities of trade had already made themselves felt. Two important shifts were to take place in this dynamic. First of all the prosyletisers of Christianity and the products of the Cape Coast Christian establishment were to change sides, ending up as redoubtable defenders of indigenous sacred sites and indigenous control of forests and lands. Anomabu had already, at Mankesim, indicated that an undisturbed hinterland for trade took precedence over the moral economy of sacred woodlands. While apparently contradictory, these two developments, the advocacy of local land rights by the Christian educated elite and the growth of African capitalism, together sowed the seeds for an incipient nationalist movement in the Gold Coast and, within that, the basis for an increasingly strong movement against colonial conservation.

Without doubt, a marriage of convenience took place between the defence of ancestral land rights on the one hand and the advocacy of unrestricted African capitalism on the other. The contemporary strength of the latter should not be under-estimated, as it formed, for example, the formative force behind the dynamic growth of the indigenous cocoa industry in the early twentieth century.[9]

While the seeds of hostility to colonial environmental and land policy were already in existence at the time of the Mankesim incident, the beginnings of a real movement did not appear to take root for a further forty years. By that time, the indigenous movement had to face a conflict with a forest conservation ideology that was both complex in its origins and comprehensive in its ambitions for control of land. The multi-faceted roots of colonial conservation ideology are now beginning to be better understood, and had oriental as well as western roots. The motivations behind conservation ideology were far more than simply economic, and, arguably, it was the "scientific" moral economy behind much of colonial conservation that gave it strength, and made it such a useful ally of colonial control agendas in India and other parts of Africa.[10] In West Africa, however, this ideology encountered an equally complex and resourceful indigenous adversary.

III. Alfred Moloney and the Elements of British West African Conservation Ideology

The origins of the kind of forest conservation that colonial governments attempted to apply in West Africa can be found in conservation strategies first worked out in Mauritius, India, Burma and the Cape Colony.[11] How were these strategies adapted to the purposes of the late-developing colonial state in West Africa? Essential to the early development of conservationism was the involvement of a cadre of professional botanists nurtured in the medical schools of the Scottish Universities and the botanic gardens of Paris and Edinburgh and, more latterly, at the Royal Botanic Gardens, Kew. One of the central figures propagandizing state forest conservation in India and South Africa had been Joseph Dalton Hooker, Director of Kew for several decades.[12] In his view the application of the kind of state forestry that had developed in India was far too long delayed in other parts of the colonial empire. In 1868, at the Paris Exhibition, he decried the fact that it was only in France, Germany and India that forest management and training was firmly established. "Wherever English rule extends," he wrote,

> with the single exception of India, the same apathy, or at least inaction prevails. In South Africa, according to colonial botanists' reports, millions of acres have been made desert, and more are being made desert annually, through the destruction of indigenous forests[13]

It was this account of the danger of widespread desiccation, with its implied threat to the economic basis of colonial rule, (lent further credibility by Hooker's position as Director of Kew), that first encouraged the Colonial Office to contemplate some kind of unified environmental policy in the colonies. As we shall see, Hooker and his successor at Kew, Arthur Thistleton-Dyer, continued to act as a *de facto* conservation lobby, continually exhorting the Colonial Office and individual colonial governors to pursue forest protection policies and to develop official biological expertise, generally by founding botanic gardens. Unlike much of India and Southern Africa, the manifestly rich West African coastal forests were, in the 1870s, as yet little affected by deforestation. Desiccation would both remove their commercial potential and threaten more drastic climatic consequences. Hooker's Paris warning was reprinted in the *Journal of Applied Science* in 1872, thus reaching a wide audience.[14]

Within two years, the Colonial Office had taken the decision to issue a Circular Despatch (along with a copy of representations made to it, on the basis of Hooker's paper, by the English Commissioner of Woods and Forests), to all the "Officers Administering the Governments of Her Majesty's Colonies". A similar endeavor was made in June 1874 by the Foreign Office, "through Her Majesty's representative abroad, towards the collection of information on the production and consumption of timber in foreign countries."[15] The Circular required answers to a long list of questions, drawing particular attention to rates of deforestation and the threat of climatic change, as well as the commercial potential of forests. Particularly significant was the question; "Are the forests . . . owned by the Government, or private persons?"[16]

Fairly rapid [responses] were made to these circulars by the Cape Colony and Natal, and by the African island colonies, above all St Helena and Mauritius. On the West African mainland, however, the only official response was one received from the Gambia. A fuller response from the rest of West Africa had to await the appearance of a book written by Alfred Moloney, a Roman Catholic colonial official (later Governor of Lagos Colony), and an enthusiastic advocate of forest conservation. His book, first published in 1887 and entitled *Sketch of the Forestry of West Africa*, formed the basis and the main stimulant for official conservation policy in the region, and also seems to have influenced the attitudes of the Colonial Office itself.[17] Its constituent ideology is therefore worthy of some attention.

More than most contemporary colonial administrators, Moloney had had the opportunity to travel widely throughout West Africa, and he was especially familiar with conditions in the Gambia, Sierra Leone, the Gold Coast and Lagos Colony. Two main influences seem to have moved Moloney to write his conservationist tract, a work which might be compared with earlier, and more widely influential, pieces by Hugh Cleghorn and George Perkins Marsh.[18] Firstly, Moloney had long been a keen advocate of the development of the rubber industry in West Africa. Equally, he had become increasingly aware of its destructive effects, particularly in French West Africa and on the coast of Mozambique. "In Gaboon," he wrote,

> it is well known that there has been almost an extermination of the tree that produced this valuable article of commerce . . . which has now caused it, I am told, to be excluded among the exports from that part of West Africa - how different it would have been had there been some system of forest conservancy or re forestation or even had timely advice been tendered and advantageously followed as to the treatment of the trees and the collection of the rubber. This was a regular case of killing the goose for the golden eggs and adds another instance . . . of the result brought about by the reckless destruction of trees . . . blind adherence to one industry is not to be advocated, as was proved though somewhat late, to the cost of many, in some of our colonies; but when we have a good thing we should treat it kindly and tenderly.[19]

There was no reason, he thought, why such destruction should take place in "Her Majesty's possessions on the Gambia, on the Gold Coast, and at Lagos". "Let the sad experience here recorded", he added, "be a lesson both to buyers and collectors in Colonies named, that we may not have . . . to listen to a tale of woe and to the cry of 'spilt milk,' in consequence of the destruction of the rubber trees." Furthermore, he believed that large scale re-afforestation might be advisable, and suggested the use of *Casuarina* trees.[20]

Moloney was most concerned, however, with the likelihood, as he saw it, that deforestation might cause rapid climatic change. The dry and treeless reaches of the Accra plains were early evidence of this, he believed. During the early 1880s he had actively propagandized this view, writing frequent letters on the subject to the *Lagos Times*, ironically at a time when he was also actively supporting expansion of the rubber-collection industry, one of the chief agents of deforestation in Lagos Colony and the phenomenon that eventually provoked the first forest legislation in the colony. He quoted Alexander von Humboldt (who had said "by felling trees which are adapted to the soil of the sides and summits of mountains, men, in every climate, prepare for future generations two calamities at once, want of firewood and scarcity of water") on deforestation, and also repeated the pessimistic dictum of Schleiden that, "forests precede a population, and deserts follow it."[21]

With respect to the threat of desiccation and desertification the field evidence which Moloney found most convincing consisted in the formal replies, published in 1878, that had been made to the Colonial and Foreign Office Circulars of 1874. He recorded approvingly that, at the Cape Colony, "the immunity which British Kaffraria enjoys from the droughts so common in South Africa is believed to be due to the influence of the forests."[22] At St Helena and Mauritius, despite pioneering attempts at state conservation, early uncontrolled deforestation had brought years of disastrous and alternate floods and droughts. The lessons of this experience, he said, needed to be learnt in West Africa before it was too late. "Let landlords," he exhorted, "be influenced by the suggestions briefly given in this chapter, and let them specially conserve, at least, such belts of wooded land as cover for mountains or hills and the flanks of rivers and streams." He spoke out against "shortsighted greed for a yard or two more ground for the production of sugar cane or some other plant when the price of sugar . . . stood temporarily high – sheer selfish greed for immediate gain." Sugar cane plantations had, of course, nearly destroyed the forests of Mauritius at an earlier period and the crop was not yet important in West Africa. Nevertheless, the commoditization of agricultural output and the penetration of European market demand was, as Moloney hinted he knew, largely responsible for what he admitted was a very recent increase in rates of deforestation, as local farmers and rubber collectors (rather than plantation owners) responded to the growing market, especially, at this stage, in Lagos Colony, and to the financial impositions of the colonial state.[23] The main message of Moloney's book

was that uncontrolled deforestation would lead to uncontrollable declines in rainfall, and he quoted what appeared to be convincing figures from the far more deforested colony of Sierra Leone. Such rainfall declines would lead to famine, he said, and "it would be well to take warning from our Eastern allies, profiting by their experience, and put a stop to this unlimited practice of shaving the forest of timber."[24] Moloney remained unspecific as to the methods by which forest conservation might be introduced into West Africa. This was partly because he was clearly aware of the problems of adapting traditional land-holding arrangements to the threat posed by the new economic situation. Selling of concessions by Gold Coast and Yoruba chiefs to timber cutters was already widespread by the 1880s. One solution, he thought, might be to impose conditions of replanting on the concession holder. Moloney was, perhaps surprisingly, very well informed about the environmentally stabilizing impact of the religious importance attached to certain trees and woodlands in Yorubaland, a region which he had already come to know well. "I may mention," he said,

> that I am aware of the superstitious respect that attaches in the Yoruba country to the *Oroko, Afon, Araba, Ashori,* and other large trees, and to the consequent immunity they enjoy from the axe, as also the understanding that palm trees on allotted sites are preserved and remain the property of the landlord.[25]

But more than this was now necessary, he considered, and it would be to the landholder's commercial advantage to adopt conservation methods, "notwithstanding he will surely be ready to increase the value of his recognised vested interest by the adoption of my suggestions as they stand, or in some modified, yet advantageous form."

To sum up, Moloney's conservation message, as outlined in his book, exhibited some unusually sophisticated views about the social realities involved in controlling environmental change, particularly in a book intentionally published in 1887 to celebrate such an obviously "imperialist" event as Queen Victoria's Golden Jubilee. Much of the book was consciously development-oriented, particularly in its prescriptions for the establishment of Model Farms and Botanic Gardens, and for the introduction of new crops, specifically for local production on small-holdings. It was also, however, intended to panic colonial administrators, with its constant references to the dangers of climatic change, into declaring new forest laws. There was "no time to be lost," he cajoled. "Let us take time by the forelock," he suggested:

in the older colonies, such as the Cape of Good Hope, Ceylon, Mauritius, Canada, New Zealand, South Australia, laws and regulations now exist for the conservation of their forests. There it was not that "necessity had no law," but rather law became an absolute necessity, and legal restraints had to be exercised. It was in some instances almost a case of shutting the stable door after the horse had got out.[26]

Traditional land-use practices would have to be over-ridden, he implied, for the greater good. Furthermore, Moloney recommended the revolutionary idea that African people should be fully trained for service as technicians and forest conservation experts. He quickly put this into practice, and in 1889 Thomas Dawodu and George Leigh proceeded to training at Hope Gardens, Jamaica and the Royal Botanical Gardens at Kew. They later took control of the Ebute Metta horticultural station and in the 1890s toured many parts of Yorubaland promoting agricultural extension policies and providing expertise.[27] In 1897 Dawodu and Leigh wrote a critical joint paper highlighting the serious deforestation in Ijebu and Ibadan close to Lagos.[28] They also made constant pleas, significantly emulating Moloney's colourful imagery, that indigenous rubber tappers should not 'kill the goose that lays the golden eggs'. Their expertise was useful ammunition for the government and was quickly utilized.[29]

As we shall see, once Moloney's notions and his staffing policies were taken up by alarmed (or opportunist) colonial governments, the scene was set for complex conflict.

IV. The Politics of Conservation in the Gold Coast 1887-1902

To some extent, the conflict between indigenous landholders and colonial restrictions on land-use had already emerged in the Gold Coast well before Moloney's book was published in 1887.[30] Initial protests were provoked by the conditions of the Public Lands Ordinance enacted in 1876. By 1886, King Tackie, a chief of Usshertown, Accra, objected to new boundaries drawn by the government under the Act for construction purposes on the edge of Accra. His protests were successful and, when the government sought to strengthen the Act, the request was turned down by the Secretary of State for the Colonies in London.

By 1889 Moloney's views had become well known and were clearly reaching official ears in Accra. In that year the Governor, Sir Brandford Griffith, proposed a remedy to all the gathering arguments on state versus chiefly land control, by proposing that the whole colony should be taken over as "Crown land" and administered to "greater advantage than the inhabitants could do it for themselves." This was not, of course, quite what Moloney had in mind. Conservation arguments were often, in this way, twisted to the advantage of a colonial executive. The Colonial Office itself remained more cautious and asked for more detailed proposals. However, the hidden agenda of the government in Accra was now on open display as far as the chiefs were concerned. Already apparent, too, was the clearly different view taken in London. These differences soon became even more apparent.

During 1891 the Chief Justice of the Gold Coast, J. T. Hutchinson, was asked to consider a proposal for taking over all "waste lands" as government "property." He immediately warned that "the importance of the chiefs and heads of families would be reduced and a sense of injustice and consequent hostility to government would be created in the minds of the people." This was a prophetic statement, and made by a lawyer who already realized the very weak legal position of the government. Instead, Hutchinson suggested, the Crown might take control of minerals and "unused or unoccupied forest land." Brandford-Griffiths was not satisfied with this, however, and, at the suggestion of his son, (significantly a colonial administrator in Jamaica), proposed the introduction of a land tax which, if not paid, would render lands forfeit to the Crown. In response to this, Hutchinson pointed out that there were two very practical obstacles to such a policy. Firstly, the country had never been surveyed (as, by contrast, the whole of India had been by this period) and lacked any fences or boundary marks. Secondly the chiefs, who had never accepted the principle of trusteeship, were already selling land to speculators and to each other, often utilising English property law; such transactions could not, retrospectively, be undone. By late 1893, the Governor was forced to try another tack and announce that "the rapid expansion of the timber trade would make legislation necessary at no distant date; in order to ensure fair play [sic] to landowners and to prevent the loss of valuable resources." At this stage the Secretary of State for the Colonies, Lord Ripon, was now seriously worried about the apparently high rate of loss of the timber resource, almost certainly alerted (as Brandford-Griffith had been) by Moloney's warnings, as well as by what he was learning about plans for a timber railway, to be constructed between Elmina and Cape Coast.

Pressure from London during 1894 then resulted in the drafting, in Accra, of a Lands Bill designed, contrary to

Hutchinson's consistent advice, "to vest waste lands, for-est lands and minerals in the Queen." By this measure, an end would be put to the system whereby rural chiefs could conclude mining or timber rights over vast and ill-defined areas of country. Receiving the draft bill in London, the Colonial Office agreed that the government should be able to prevent the lands of the colony falling into the hands of [European] concession mongers for a bottle of rum or a case of gin." This patronizing attitude (in fact large sums of money were involved in concession sales!) foreshadowed a severe under-estimation of the reaction of the population to the 1894 Lands Bill. Almost immediately after the first reading of the Bill in the Legislative Council, protests began to coalesce and gather strength, initially around Accra itself. Soon newspapers such as the *Gold Coast Methodist Times* took up the issue, foreshadowing both the later involve-ment of the Cape Coast Methodist lawyers in the forest is-sue and the critical part played by African newspapers in popularizing it among the educated classes. The first peti-tions to the Legislative Council argued that the Public Lands Ordinance of 1876 was already quite powerful enough for the government's purposes. The real intention of the Governor, they feared, was to deprive the chiefs of their "lands, their gold mines, their gum trees, their rubber trees, their kola trees and everything that is worth having and which descended to them from their remote ancestors." There was, the petitioners argued, no such thing as "waste land" as all land was "owned by Kings, chiefs or private indi-viduals." This assertion was, in fact, far from the truth.

In late 1894 the Attorney-General and Colonial Secretary both returned to the Colony after an absence to find the issue well ablaze. Though having somewhat differ-ent views of the matter, both men were highly critical of the concept of the Lands Bill, which had been introduced while they had been on leave. Hodgson, the Colonial Secretary, was especially concerned about casual and ille-gal annulment of all existing ownerships of vast tracts of so-called "unoccupied" forest land. He believed, too, that such heavy-handed interventions were quite unnecessary. The government would profit itself far more, he wrote with perspicacity, by safeguarding "the interests of the in-habitants and the capitalists."

At this point Brandford-Griffith, the originator of the Lands Bill, left the Gold Coast for good. Meanwhile, the agitations which he had first provoked continued to grow, having now spread as far away from Accra as Tarkwa and Anomabu, towards the South-West. Europeans sympa-thetic to the native view, such as James Drew, now pointed out that the 1876 Ordinance had, as the chiefs had realized,

already securely confirmed and legitimized their land rights. The Gold Coast, Drew asserted, was in quite a different po-sition from other colonial protectorates, since it had not been acquired by conquest, cession or treaty. John Maxwell, the Governor succeeding Brandford-Griffith, does not ap-pear to have accepted this critical difference. Instead, in the first of many appeals to "legal" precedents established in other colonies, he argued for the adoption in the Gold Coast of the system applied on the Malay States, whereby land sales concessions by chiefs would only be valid if coun-tersigned by British authorities. This too proved unwork-able under the terms of the 1876 Ordinance.

By 1895 there was an additional factor in the situation, in the form of a new Colonial Secretary, Joseph Chamberlain, an arch-advocate of non-intervention and of business in-terests. It was this latter preference, as well as his desire to maintain good relations with the chiefs of the Gold Coast and Yorubaland, that set the scene for the subsequent epi-sodes of resistance against forest policy in both regions. The issues in the two areas continued to be seen as intercon-nected, particularly as far as Chamberlain was concerned. He felt, however, that some legislation was necessary in or-der to prevent indiscriminate felling, but refused to be hur-ried into a decision that could prove politically damaging, in direct contrast to the local governments in Accra and Lagos. In October, 1895, therefore, Governor Maxwell de-cided to drop the Lands Bill and focus on a newer and nar-rower Bill. The chiefs, with the effective aid of Chamberlain, had therefore achieved an extraordinary initial victory.

The protesters' complaint was not only about the dis-ruption of traditional land-use claims and family identity. It also concerned a more basic racial theme. The implication of the Governor's Bill was, essentially, that African claims were not as valid as imposed European legal principles. The English-language newspapers recognized this as an un-acceptably racial matter. One journal, *Truth*, commented with heavy irony that "the native's untutored mind does not grasp the idea that the colour of his skin justifies the confiscation of his property." This was the issue in a nut-shell. On the other hand, the efficacy of opposition to the Lands Bill was related, above all, to the close involvement of African lawyers from both Accra, and, more particularly, from Cape Coast, where the early institution of secondary schooling by Wesleyan missionaries had produced, by the mid-1890s, a considerable crop of London-trained lawyers and potential campaigners, many of whom were thinking in increasingly nationalist terms. Indeed, in 1895 an exas-perated Maxwell was led to complain that opposition to the Lands Bill was "fostered and fed on every conceivable occasion by African lawyers." The lively Gold Coast newspapers added their literate voice, sometimes with increasingly Shakespearean hyperbole. The *Gold Coast Methodist Times* commented, for instance, that the Lands Bill was "pregnant with fell and butcherly stratagems . . . .by an erroneous, mutinous and unnatural hypothesis, land of economic importance" was being "diplomatically enveloped in the term "waste" so that it could be wrested from its owners," a procedure which the newspapers termed "unusual robbery and British Brigandism!"

The more restricted Lands Bill of 1897 sought only to "administer waste and forest lands and not to vest them in the Queen." However it met with equally determined resistance, as the mechanisms it proposed for concessions threatened the wholesale conversion of traditional rights to rights sanctioned by European law. The arrival back in the Gold Coast of J. E. Casely-Hayford, later a prolific writer and nationalist, also served to encourage the protesters, who had, to some extent, already tasted success. Resistance to the 1897 Bill, after it had been put to the Legislative Council, now gave rise to a new movement. This was based on the Fante association known as Mfantsi Amanbuhu Fekuw, an established grouping at Cape Coast. In April 1897 this was now re-named The Gold Coast Aborigines' Rights Protection Society (or ARPS).[31] The ARPS was, of course, led by an elite group closely allied, especially at Cape Coast and Axim, with more militant members of the Wesleyan Church. However the relations with the church could be quickly used as a network to convene meetings and "educate" the Chiefs of many districts as to the state of play on the forest issue. From hindsight it can be argued, quite correctly, that the ARPS was supporting the interests of incipient indigenous land speculators and capitalists, many of them in league with European capitalists and traders. However, this does not detract from the sincerity of the movement, which was quickly finding that it had powerful and perhaps unexpected allies abroad. Already, the Liverpool and Manchester Chambers of Commerce had expressed their dislike of the Gold Coast land bills and other proposals to restrict forest use.

Joseph Chamberlain, himself a highly successful Birmingham businessman, as well as radical politician, clearly took the same kind of view. A decisive moment came in June 1897, when a Dispatch was drafted to the Governor in Accra, warning him that "alarm and uncertainty amongst capitalists in Britain might discourage enterprise in the Gold Coast." The ARPS was also finding useful ammunition from other official sources. In 1895 Governor Maxwell had commissioned a study of Gold Coast land tenure systems.[32]

He had hoped that this would strengthen the hand of government (as similar studies had done in India). However the report was inconclusive and unhelpful as far as the government was concerned. The ARPS, however, found that it could be used to support their case. The report confirmed that "every piece of land in the Gold Coast" had an owner. Only on the failure of successors, it pointed out, did it fall back into the common land of the village, subject to control of chiefs and elders. "Not only are the bonds of society to be snapped, but family ties are to be broken and family relationships destroyed," wrote Mensah Sarbah, a lawyer of the ARPS. The report, he said, showed that the Bill "refers to the whole land of this country, depriving the aborigines of their right in the soil of their native land." [33]

Chamberlain's June 1898 draft Despatch to the Governor indicated how the tide had turned in favor of the ARPS. Thus, although Casely-Hayford, in 1898, led a deputation of lawyers and chiefs to London to protest against the 1897 Bill, the Colonial Office had already itself conceded to the opposition and determined to have the Accra government drop the Bill. Instead a "Concessions Ordinance" was brought forward and passed through the Legislature in 1900. To avoid unnecessary argument, this Bill was actually drawn up in consultation with the solicitors of the ARPS in London. It merely restricted the size of concessions and made no claims to public lands or interference in African ownership. Finally, all clauses relating to forest protection had been removed.

Ultimately, then, the colonial government, pursuing an agenda which combined conservation aims with a desire for greater control over land (as well as political control over chiefs, one may surmise), was defeated by what was eventually a very multi-faceted alliance of chiefs, lawyers, British business interests and radical politicians, personified by Joseph Chamberlain, Casely-Hayford and Mensah Sarbah. A somewhat concealed element in the story relates to the political instability on the borders of Yorubaland, caused by apprehension about French territorial ambitions. This was a matter that was actually uppermost in Chamberlain's mind in 1897, and from which the Gold Coast anti-Land Bill movement clearly benefited. Chamberlain was in fact now even more determined not to upset the political economy of Yorubaland and the Lagos Colony.

V. Opposition to Forest Conservation Proposals in the Lagos Colony

The progress and success of the opposition to the 1897 Lands Bill in the Gold Coast had an immediate impact in the Lagos Colony where, in November 1897, a Bill had been introduced that was aimed primarily at controlling the wave of forest destruction being caused by the kind of uncontrolled rubber-tapping which Moloney had previously warned against.[34] This bill, intended to become law on January 1 1898, would have made it unlawful for any person to cut or remove trees or timber (except for firewood or building) or to collect fibre, gum or rubber, without a licence from a District Commissioner, Travelling Commissioner or Chief Magistrate. Although the bill aimed, on the basis of the Gold Coast experience, to avoid land tenure matters, it still evoked an immediate tide of opposition, encouraged by local newspapers which were, as in the Gold Coast, very prominent in raising issues and binding opposition forces together. "The forests of Yoruba," the *Lagos Standard* trumpeted, "are not government property, nor are they subject to any alienation to any foreign power [sic]. It is to be presumed, therefore, that considering local considerations and feeling, the proposed Ordinance will be withdrawn and nullified."[35] The *Lagos Times* was more geographically ambitious, and added:

forest lands in Africa compose lands allowed to be fallowed and every forest has its owner. To demand that an owner should first obtain a licence and pay a royalty before he can collect the products of his own land is arbitrary to say the least; while it will be more arbitrary still to declare that no ownership attached to such forest lands and thereby deprive the native of his legitimate rights. Nor would it be less arbitrary and objectionable for the governor to be vested with power to determine by proclamation when a man could collect the produce of his own land, and when he could not . . . the bill overshoots the mark and is calculated to cause trouble and vexation rather than to confer benefits.[36]

The Bill had, in fact, been framed on the basis of a Indian forest conservation model, after Sir Ralph Moor, the High Commissioner, had proposed to the Colonial Office that the Indian forest system was ideal for the Lagos colony. This marked one of the first of many attempts to impose Indian land-use models on the region, a concept finally discredited only as late as 1938, with the publication of the Leverhulme Commission on West African Agriculture.

By November 1897, the campaign against the 1897 Lands Bill in the Gold Coast was reaching a climax, and this caused Sir Henry McCallum, the Lagos Governor, to withdraw the Lagos Forest Bill from the legislature in 1898 with unusual speed, almost before local opposition had got off the ground. The Colonial Office acted with even more haste, demanding that the Bill should be withdrawn

completely. Not only had the extent of the Gold Coast opposition become apparent in the critical six months between March 1897 (the date of the Gold Coast Lands Bill) and November 1897, but the threat from the French had also grown greater.

VI. The Trouble at Ijebu-Ode

The apparent willingness on the part of government to placate opposition by the Lagos Colony chiefs to the bill was further supplemented in early 1898 by the explosive political impact of a clash between guardians of a traditional religious site and Christian converts, very much on the lines of the Mankesim incident in the Gold Coast fifty years before. Considerable local unrest had been caused at Ijebu-Ode, (north of Lagos), when Christians had violated a sacred *Oro* woodland and carried away a pig. The matter came to a head when the Police Inspector-General, Mitchell, arrived at Ijebu-Ode to investigate the matter, and ordered the Awujale, the local king, to be sent for. When the Awujale did not respond, Hausa soldiers were sent to fetch him. Fighting broke out, and some chiefs were wounded.

The matter was only finally resolved when the Governor appointed a Commissioner to deal with the situation. The Commissioner appreciated the harm that had been done and the Awujale received an official apology. George Denton, the Acting Governor, also authorized the King to collect a heavy duty on all rubber collected in the area. This effectively drove a coach and horses through the provisions of the 1897 Bill. Denton minuted that

At the present juncture I am desirous that the great unrest which has just been tided over, should not again be resuscitated at a time when foreign politics are so much more important than domestic politics, especially as the government is in such matters dependent upon the active assistance of the natives . . .[37]

Chamberlain reinforced this argument, writing that, "the bill should be dropped notwithstanding the fact that the destruction of rubber trees is so serious as to call for prompt measures to stop it." [38]

One immediate result of these political concessions to the Yoruba chiefs was that deforestation continued unabated. A copy of a report on the level of destruction eventually reached Thistleton-Dyer, Joseph Hooker's successor as Director of Kew. It was, of course, Thistleton-Dyer who had encouraged Moloney's enthusiasm for the rubber trade. Now he was seriously alarmed at the consequences of the trade and put the Lagos government in an embarrassing position by calling for immediate action to stop timber-cutting. Chamberlain reluctantly agreed to support some measures and, in January 1899, draft Forest Rules were circulated. On this occasion, the Director of Kew made the innovative suggestion that the chiefs and local authorities should be made responsible for forest management.

This suggestion was immediately taken up by Chamberlain as a way out of his dilemma. MacGregor, the new Governor, was vehemently opposed to this notion, and horror-struck at the degree of power that would thereby be conferred on the chiefs. Nevertheless, eventually even he agreed that there was no alternative way out of the problem. Essentially, by July 1899, the onus of responsibility had been handed over to the chiefs, leaving the government in only an advisory capacity. Although this situation did not persist without alteration for long, an important principle had been conceded, largely at the behest of Thistleton-Dyer and Joseph Chamberlain. It amounted to the beginnings of a far more conciliatory policy than that which was to prevail in the Gold Coast, where the power of the chiefs in terms of forest management was retained largely through (albeit successful) prolonged resistance and confrontation. In Lagos Colony, the principle of local management was to develop into the formalized system of Native Administration Forest Reserves, a device designed by Sir Frederick Lugard to recognize the *de facto* submission of the colonial government to the ecological, land tenure and religious claims of the Yoruba chiefs.

The concessions to the Lagos chiefs in 1899 did not mean, of course, that the majority of the rural population was happy with the arrangement. On the contrary, they now had to pay fees to the chiefs for produce that had, until now, been freely available. The compromise was thus one that benefited the (senior) chiefs and also benefited the colonial government, which could remove itself from unnecessary confrontation. On the other hand, this policy now displaced serious conflicts about changing mechanisms of resource allocation into a series of disputes between those privileged by the colonial state and those who had been, effectively, restricted or impoverished as a result. In fact, in this context, and for the next sixty years, disputes over forest use in Nigeria often involved, (through this process of social distortion), the making of appeals to officers of the colonial state against the chiefs. Such appeals were, characteristically, made by shifting cultivators, migrants, and, not least, deputations of women, the latter protesting against agreements made between the indigenous patriarchy and the Forest Department. In the Gold

Coast, where land was generally passed down through the female line, such disputes were less common. It was only in the late 1920s and 1930s that the government again found itself in conflict with the higher echelon of chiefs, as a direct consequence of changes in conservation policy.

In 1899 a report written by Dr Cyril Punch for Thistleton-Dyer on the forests of Lagos colony had indicated that the rubber industry was continuing to cause serious damage. On receiving his copy of the report in May 1899, Chamberlain expressed a further apparently unorthodox view: he thought that it "might be practicable to educate the indigenous population to act more wisely in future" with respect to forest resources. This was a logical further step to supplement the principle of control being handed over to the chiefs. Unfortunately, the development of such interesting notions was disrupted by Denton, the Governor, who declared an arbitrary ban on rubber collection, thereby destroying any obvious economic incentive the chiefs might have for preventing deforestation, through fee income. In fact, Denton's measure actually served to re-awaken opposition and, moreover, to bring in the Liverpool and Manchester Chambers of Commerce on the side of the chiefs, just as had happened in the Gold Coast.

Once more, under pressure from Kew, a new Forest Ordinance was brought forward by Governor Denton in October 1900. He found himself supported by Kew. Thistleton-Dyer had by this time changed his mind and decided to opt for a system of direct government control.[39] The new Bill led to mass meetings in Lagos on September 19th 1901, and to unrest in Egbaland a week later. The Alake and his chiefs then visited Sir Gilbert Carter, the new Governor. At the meeting, the Egba pointed out that the bill transgressed all the premises of the 1893 Egba treaty with the British. Once more, as with the 1876 Gold Coast Ordinance, the British were hoist by their own legal petard. Subsequently, opposition developed among a whole variety of elite groups. Moreover, the level of opposition to the Forest Bill in the Lagos colony was faithfully reported in the *Gold Coast Globe and Ashanti Argus* and in *West Africa*.

Eventually, Chamberlain was once again forced to intervene to accept the local protesters' view that the proposed legislation transgressed traditional land rights. The Colonial Office therefore forced an amendment to the Forest Bill, by stipulating that the Governor might apply forest regulations subject only to the consent of any African rulers in the districts affected. This was, of course, a major concession, and marked the effectiveness of the popular and business pressures that had been exerted against the Lagos Government. Furthermore, by requiring chiefly consent to forest regulations, the Colonial Office effectively defused opposition to the Forest Bill, which was passed in an amended form on March 11th 1902. It also ended most organized opposition to state forest conservation, at least in South-West Nigeria, and laid the basis for Lugard's special treatment of the Yoruba chiefs, formally notified in the Nigerian Forest Ordinance of 1916.

The Native Administration Forest Reserves, a concept designed by Lugard (and at first unique to Nigeria), were a belated recognition of the extent to which real power over forests had been conceded to the Yoruba chiefs. However, the success of the resistance movement affected a much wider area than Yorubaland and even ensured that in some areas, particularly in the Delta and Calabar regions of Southern Nigeria, no government forest reserves were declared at all, for fear of arousing uncontrollable political turmoil.

By 1916 the extent of structural adaptation of a colonial forest conservation system to the realities of Lugardian indirect rule, to the religious and political significance of the Southern Nigerian forests, and to successful pressure-group tactics, was being tacitly admitted by government. This became especially apparent in Lugard's own *Memos on Forestry in Nigeria*, published as part of a more general treatise on colonial government in 1918:

> The conditions which prevail in the Oyo and Abeokuta provinces are to some extent different from those obtaining elsewhere in Nigeria. These progressive Yoruba-speaking Provinces formerly asserted a quasi-independence by treaty. They are exceedingly tenacious of the tribal or family ownership of the land (including forests), and their proximity to the Colony of Lagos, and the influence of native lawyers who have become imbued with European ideas of land tenure, have combined to introduce among them the beginnings of a conception of individual ownership—though this conception is fiercely combatted by the conservative chiefs. For the reasons given in Para. 4, I favour the creation of forest reserves owned by the state, which (while providing for all the requirements of the local communities, which participate in their control, and share their profits) will add to the General Revenue, and thus decrease taxation . . . in view of the special circumstances in the two provinces to which I refer, and to their great forest wealth, I am not averse to the creation in them of one or two "Native Administration Forest Reserves" as an experimental measure . . . the Native Administration will undertake not merely their protection, but also their

management . . . it may be found necessary to apply some of these principles to some of the Reserves in the Northern Provinces.[40]

VII. Further Resistance in the Gold Coast, 1911-1916

Meanwhile, in the Gold Coast, the government had been faced with the almost entire collapse of their forest conservation plans. Between 1900 (the date of the Concessions Ordinance) and 1916, the Accra administration made a series of attempts to resurrect forest control legislation and to found a forest department. All of these failed ignominiously, so that, by 1916, the chiefs and their European timber-trading collaborators were left in effective control of the forest estate. The fact that, after 1916, the cocoa industry, with its associated agricultural migration and forest clearance, was becoming increasingly powerful, only set the seal on what was described in the Gold Coast Blue Book of 1923 as an "utterly useless" situation, as far as forest conservation was concerned.[41] Perhaps the single most humiliating decision forced on the government during this period was that which brought about the closure in 1917 of the Forest Department, which had been set up by Indian Forest Service staff in 1909. What were the historical roots of this fiasco, unrecorded in any other colony?

The ARPS had continued to oppose all legislation affecting forests, often assuming, wrongly and naively, that the economic interests of the chiefs were identical with those of the rural population as a whole. The forest issue had, in fact, become the political core, if not *raison d'etre*, of emergent Gold Coast nationalism, in a way in which it had never become in Nigeria. The rise to prominence of the ARPS and the forest movement as joint vehicles of nationalism was due, in part, to the abilities of Casely-Hayford as a charismatic leader, writer and lawyer. It was also due to the extraordinary "Magna Charta" statement made by Chamberlain, under some pressure, on the occasion of the ARPS deputation to London in 1898.[42] As it turned out, the forest issue lay largely dormant for a few years, until raised again by the introduction of a new Forest Ordinance in 1907. On paper, this measure prohibited the cutting of immature trees, but it was entirely ineffective. Then, in 1908, the Chief Conservator of Southern Nigeria, H. N. Thompson (earlier of the Indian Forest Service and previously, in 1880, a consultant to the Mauritius Government) visited the Gold Coast and recommended the introduction of the Southern Nigerian system. This gave rise to the introduction of yet another Forestry Bill. The ARPS was quickly goaded into action, one of its first actions being to telegraph the Colonial Office in protest, thus bypassing the local authorities. Suddenly appreciating the nature of the gathering political storm, the Conservator of Forests (in charge of a Department that was less than two years old) arrived in Cape Coast to try to convince the ARPS of his case. He was effectively ignored, while Casely-Hayford set about writing a major propaganda piece on the new Bill, entitled *Gold Coast Land Tenure and the Forest Bill.*[43]

Although the Forest Bill was passed in the Legislative Council in January 1911 it continued to run into opposition from the ARPS and the Head Chiefs of Accra and Osu. Casely-Hayford, meanwhile, prepared to lead another delegation to London. It was this plan which finally provoked the Colonial Office into despatching a Special Commissioner, H.C. Belfield, to report on the controversy. Belfield spent three months dutifully gathering evidence and holding enquiries at different centers, to which Casely-Hayford, the chiefs and the ARPS all made copious contributions. Even the "Lagos" option (that is, as in the 1902 Lagos Colony Ordinance), in which regulations would remain subject to a total chiefly veto, was rejected. Going even further for the opposition, Casely-Hayford and his colleagues specifically rejected the whole concept of "scientific forestry." Moreover they asserted, possibly in an attempt to avoid being seen as specifically anti-conservationist, that

> the principle of conserving forests is not unknown to the people of this country. The chiefs now and again set apart certain parts of the forest for the preservation of game, the collection of forest produce and as sacred groves. This has been done from time immemorial to the present day, so that, apart from the taking by the timber industry and the mining industry of timber for fuel, the forests would be in a state of good preservation.[44]

Belfield's own studies actually bore out the truth of this statement. It was only when the spread of the cocoa-farming industry was well under way that blame for substantial deforestation could really be attached to indigenous rather than European activity. Incidentally, it could be argued that the situation before about 1916 in the Gold Coast differed considerably from that found in the Lagos Colony, where deforestation was undoubtedly severe as well as largely indigenous in its dynamic. Furthermore, the evidence produced for the Belfield Commission was politically decisive. While the government in Accra still pressed for the 1911 Forest Bill to be implemented on the basis that "injury that is irreparable within any reasonable period is being done to the Gold Coast forests," the Colonial Office

itself took the quite different view that, "because land tenure questions are now under detailed consideration" the chiefs should simply be told "to stop felling trees indiscriminately."[45] In other words, the Colonial Office did not wish to pursue the matter further. The Accra government had thus, for the moment, entirely lost the support of Whitehall.

Between 1912 and 1917, when the Office of Conservator of Forests of the Gold Coast actually had to be abolished, no forest reserves were created at all in the colony, as the government did not possess the necessary statutory powers. To this extent Casely-Hayford, the chiefs and the ARPS had achieved their professed objective. Significantly, though, some prominent chiefs still expressed the need to protect forests, especially in the face of the rapid clearance which the cocoa industry was stimulating. In 1915 Chief Ofori Ata of Akim Abuakwa, for instance, was the first ruler to publish bye-laws controlling deforestation in his district. Such bye-laws, all passed at the initiative of the chiefs, prohibited cultivation of cocoa or food crops on all the outstanding hills in the district (thus, ironically, closely following the *dicta* of Moloney and the 1908 Thompson Report), and included a list of the forest trees that could not be felled without permission. The pattern established by 1915 never substantially altered in the Gold Coast itself, and the colonial authorities remained embarrassed until independence at their failure to carry out the kind of forest conservation objectives that were considered normal in India or Burma, for example. This position was neatly summed up by Major F. M. Oliphant in a report made to the Gold Coast government in 1934. The situation, Oliphant complained bitterly,

> appeared to be largely governed by the fact that the domestic and export trade is in the hands of Africans, the lack of organisation being such that the whole month might well have been spent in examining that position alone. On the question of supplies, I found that the measure of Government control over the forests was so small, destruction was proceeding so rapidly, and, for reasons given later in this report, both the present and future situation were so uncertain that no reliable opinion could be formed without a very searching enquiry and detailed inspection of forest areas.[46]

In Nigeria, by contrast, the colonial government was briefly able, during the period between 1919 and 1939, to establish a more draconian forest conservation policy, thus incurring considerable localized resistance, particularly from women opposing reserve policies jointly concluded by male chiefs and colonial administrators. After 1945, however, the situation was transformed by the influence of returning West African troops, many of them thirsty for political change. Thus, Nigerian Geological Survey staff during the early 1950s well knew that their researches and plans for conservation would only be tolerated in some districts; and they were forced to curtail their survey plans accordingly.[47]

VIII. Conclusion

By 1916, both in Nigeria and the Gold Coast, the conservation debate had come full circle. At least temporarily, indigenous interest-groups, with the aid of some unusual allies, had been successful in re-asserting control over forest landscapes which, still imbued with social and religious meaning, were now increasingly significant in an economic sense. This did not mean, of course, that the tension between new economic development pressures and traditional management methods were resolved. They had simply been displaced into a new dispensation of power, but one in which European conservation models had had to suffer a severe adaptation.

We believe that the environmental debate and struggles of the 1890-1916 period in West African history foreshadowed current concerns much more sharply than is generally appreciated. Specifically, then, in this article we can highlight the extent to which the practitioners of forest conservation, both African *and* European, chose to reject or were compelled to reject the colonial land management models which they had institutionally inherited or had thrust upon them, and which had earlier found favor in the Indian and Southern African colonial context. We can also trace the way in which colonial rulers were forced to select regionally adapted models of conservation that more truly reflected the weakness of the colonial state in West Africa, particularly as regards the relatively successful retainment of power by local chiefs and rulers *vis-a-vis* the state, in a context in which European settlement always remained a low priority. This pattern of adaptation was probably not limited to the Gold Coast and Nigeria, but we would need further detailed local research in the African context to come to such conclusions. In particular, we believe that we should seriously question the notion of a homogeneous kind of "colonial state" as far as the history of environmental policy was concerned. In fact, it seems that the differences between colonial state policies were very much

greater and more significant than the similarities. Even in India, where the forest department had long been considered by its harshest critics as a formidable oppressor of the people, it is now being established that there were enormous regional disparities in the way in which policies were actually adapted to real social conditions on the ground.[48] In colonial British and Francophone Africa, the disparities were almost certainly far greater. The way ahead, therefore, will be to construct much more detailed local environmental histories, both at government and village level, taking care to discard most preconceptions about colonial environmental policy along the way. At first this task will not be easy since, arguably, environmental history in Sub-Saharan Africa outside Nigeria and the bounds of the white settler states of South Africa, Southern Rhodesia, Tanganyika and Kenya is still very much in its infancy.

In much of South Asia and southern and eastern Africa it is probably true that the failure of the colonial state to heed indigenous valuations and uses of the environment, as well as the failure of the colonized population to effectively resist colonial land-use ambitions, meant that social pressures were stored up for what were eventually far more explosive political outcomes, of the kind that finally provoked the Mau-Mau rebellion in Kenya or the Naxalite revolts in post-independence India. In the course of such a storing-up of structural disadvantage, the possibility of the widespread application of indigenous knowledge and the chances of a conservationist local response to the impact of capital penetration were often largely obliterated. By contrast, the substantially different pattern which prevailed in some parts of southern Gold Coast and Nigeria set the scene, one might argue, for a more creative context for the development of indigenous land-use methods and tenures in the contemporary period. ∎

Reading Notes

1. *Acknowledgement*: The research for this essay was made possible by a grant from the Social Science Research Council, New York.

2. See for instance, R. H. Grove, "Colonial conservation, ecological hegemony and popular resistance; towards a global synthesis," in J. Mackenzie, ed., *Imperialism and the natural world* (Manchester, 1990), 15-51; and N. L. Peluso, "Co-ercing conservation? the politics of resource control," *Global Environmental Change*, June (1993), 21-42.

3. See for instance, P. Hill, Migrant Cocoa Farmers in Southern Ghana: a Study in Rural Capitalism (Cambridge, 1963).

4. On Moloney, see for instance, O. Omosini, "Alfred Moloney and his strategies for economic development

in Lagos Colony and hinterland, 1886-1891," *Journal of the Historical Society of Nigeria* 7(1975), 657-77.

5. For details, see W. E. F. Ward, *A History of the Gold Coast*, 2 vols (London, 1948).

6. The Basel missionaries were particularly active in promoting the spread of new varieties of seeds and plantation crops, introducing coffee and cocoa and founding the some of the first botanic gardens in the Gold Coast.

7. The Brafo is said to have been appointed by the God Bobiwisi of Winneba Hill, as a "deputy" in local matters, and was brought to Mankesim from Ashanti, where he had been pointed out by local priests. The deity thus had an importance over a very wide area of the Gold Coast at the time.

8. For details of the events summarized here, see Ward, *A History* . . .

9. Hill, *Migrant Cocoa Farmers*.

10. See for instance, R. H. Grove, "Conserving Eden: The European East India Companies and their environmental policies on St Helena, Mauritius and in Western India," *Comparative Studies in Society and History* 35 (1993), 318-51.

11. See for instance, R. H. Grove, Green Imperialism: Colonial Expansion, Tropical Island Edens and the Origins of Environmentalism, 1600-1860 (Cambridge, 1995).

12. On Hooker, see M. Allan, *The Hookers of Kew* (London, 1967).

13. He continued in this vein: "In Demerara the useful timber trees have all been removed from accessible regions, and no care and thought given to planting others; from Trinidad we have the same story; in New Zealand there is not now a good Kundi (Kauri) pine to be found near the coast; and I believe that the annals of almost every English colony would repeat the tale of willful wanton waste and improvidence. On the other hand in France, Prussia, Switzerland and Russia, the forests and waste lands are the subjects of devoted attention on the part of the government, and colleges, provided with a complete staff of accomplished professors, train youths of good birth and education to the duties of state foresters. Nor in the case of France is this law confined to the mother country. The Algerian forests are worked with scrupulous solicitude; and the collections of vegetable produce from the French colonies and New Caledonia etc. contain specimens which, though not falling technically under Class 87, abound in evidence of the forest products being all diligently explored'. See Allan, *The Hookers*, 12-13.

14. J. D. Hooker, "Forestry," *Journal of Applied Science*, 1, 1872, 221-223.

15. The result was compiled in P. R.O., Command Paper C. 1161 of 1875 (Forestry).

16. The full list was:-

 1. What are the kinds of timber trees produced in the country, and to what uses are they generally applied?

 2. Are the forests or lands producing trees owned by the government or private persons?

 3. What is the approximate extent of timber-producing forests or lands at the present time?

 4. Is this area increasing or diminishing?

 5. If diminishing, from what cause?

 6. Are any steps being taken for the prevention of waste or for replanting any area which has been cleared?

 7. What is the quantity of timber which might be fairly cut every year without permanent injury to the forests?

 8. What is the quantity actually cut every year?

 9. What is the proportion of home consumption and export?

 10. What have been the annual exports of each kind of timber during the last ten years; stating the proportions to each country, and the value of such exports?

 11. What are the reasons for or causes of the small exportations in comparison with the capability of production?

 12. (If it be so), what are the the causes of the small exportations in comparison with the capability of production?

 13. Have any observations been made or conclusions arrived at as to the climatic influence of forests or the effect of their clearance on rainfall, floods etc.?

 14. Forward any reports made by departments or societies, or any Acts of Legislature bearing on the subject [These two last points bear a strong resemblance to parts of a questionnaire sent out by the East India Company in 1847].

17. The responses were compiled by the Colonial Office in a Command Paper (No. 2197) in 1878.

18. H. Cleghorn, *The Forests and Gardens of South India* (Edinburgh, 1861); and G. P. Marsh, *Man and Nature* (New York, 1864).

19. Moloney, *Sketches*, 90.

20. *Ibid*.

21. See M. J. Schleiden, *Die Pflanzen und ihr Leben: Populare Vortrage* (Leipzig, 1848).

22. This would, in fact, have been an opinion expressed in the writings of John Croumbie Brown. The pioneering Colonial Botanist of the Cape colony. see J. C. Brown, *The hydrology of South Africa* (Edinburgh, 1875).

23. See for instance, O. Omosini, "The rubber export trade in Ibadan, 1893-1904," *Journal of the Historical Society of Nigeria* 10 1979, 21-42; and Toyin Falola, *The Political Economy of a Precolonial African State, c. 1830-1900* (Ile-Ife: University of Ife Press) 1984, chapter 5.

24. By "our Eastern allies," Moloney presumably meant the Government of India.

25. Moloney, *Sketches*, 4.

26. *Ibid.*, 3.

27. O. Omosini, "Background to the forestry legislation in Lagos colony and protectorate, 1897-1902," *Journal of the Historical Society of Nigeria* 7 (1975), 657-77.

28. F. E. R. Leigh and T. B. Dawodu, "Report on Nigerian Forests," 28 July 1897, PRO CO 879/65, No. 635, quoted in C. W. Newbury, *British Policy Towards West Africa: Select Documents, 1875-1914* (Oxford, 1971).

29. *Ibid.*

30. This section draws heavily on D. Kimble, *A political history of Ghana; the rise of Gold Coast nationalism, 1880-1963* (Oxford, 1963).

31. The society's opening public statement ran: 'Whereas in former times, all measures intended by the government for the whole Protectorate were brought before a meeting of the various Kings and Chiefs of the Protectorate convened for the purpose, and who in turn communicated them to the people of their respective districts by gong-gong. And Whereas this time-honored and effective custom has for some time been set aside and superseded by the Gazette And Whereas a very large majority of the population of the Gold Coast Protectorate are still unable to read And Whereas even the greater part of those able to read cannot well comprehend the meaning of the Bills passed from time to time by the government, the above society of which natives and residents alike can be members has been formed to discuss various Bills intended to be passed by the Government from time to time with a view to fully understanding the meaning purport object and effect thereof that every person may have the opportunity of understanding the same.

32. *Report upon the customs relating to the tenure of land on the Gold Coast*, (London, 1895).

33. *The Gold Coast Methodist Times*, 30 June 1897.

34. See for instance, E. O. Egboh, "Background to the forestry legislation in Lagos Colony and Protectorate, 1897-1902," *Journal of the Historical Society of Nigeria* 9 (1978), 45-69.

35. "The Forest Ordinance," *Lagos Standard*, 10 November 1897, in Egboh, "Background to . . .".

36. "The proposed Forest Ordinance," *Lagos Times*, 17 November 1897.

37. Colonial Office Minute, 8 February, 1898, Co147/121/314.

38. Colonial Office Minute, 8 Feb., 1898, Co147/121/314.

39. Thus he wrote in February 1900; 'At first I was under the impression that these forests were so considerable that the risk of exhaustion was of little moment compared with the direct benefit from the export trade. But it is now evident that this is not so and that an important natural asset is being rapidly used up. . . . the ultimate result will be for the land to become naked and dispossessed of its natural resources. It scarcely requires argument to show that such a state of affairs is eminently undesirable and would not be creditable to the British administration'; Kew Gardens to CO, dt 21 Feb 1900 PRO: CO879/65/635/146.

40. F. Lugard, *Political memoranda*, edited by A.H.M. Kirk-Greene, Frank Cass, London, 1970, pp 430-435.

41. Gold Coast Government, *Blue Book*. 1923.

42. Chamberlain had stated: "I think I can give you the assurance you wish . . . I am willing that, in all cases where natives are concerned, the native law shall remain and prevail . . . with regard to the devolution of land. And I am also willing that the Court which is to decide upon these questions should be a judicial court." *Report of the proceedings of the deputation*, Accra, 1898.

43. J. E. Casely-Hayford, *Gold Coast Land Tenure and the Forest Bill* (London, 1912).

44. *Ibid.*, 12.

45. Dispatch No. 747 of 30 Nov. 1912 from Harcourt to Bryan, Ghana National Archives.

46. F. M. Oliphant, *Report on the commercial possibilities and development of the forests of the Gold Coast* (Accra, 1934) 1.

47. See for instance, A. T. Grove, *Land use and soil conservation in parts of Onitsha and Owerri provinces.* (Zaria, 1951).

48. See for instance, M. Ragarajan, "Production, desiccation and forest management in the Central Provinces, 1850-1930," eds., in R. Grove, V. Damodaran and S. Sangwan, *Nature and the Orient: essays on the environmental history of South and Southeast Asia.* Oxford, 1995, 112-134. ∎

Endnotes

1. William Cronon, "The Uses of Environmental History," *Environmental History Review* 17/7 (1993): 19.

2. Ramachandra Guha, quoted in Alfred Crosby, "The Past and Present of Environmental History," *American Historical Review* 100/4 (1995): 1177–1189.

3. Jared Diamond, *Guns, Germs, and Steel: The Fates of Human Societies* (New York: W.W. Norton, 1997).

4. Alfred Crosby, 1186.

5. William Cronon, "The Uses of Environmental History," 19.

6. Walter Prescott Webb, *The Great Plains*, 1st Paperback ed. (Lincoln: University of Nebraska Press, 1981), 8.

7. John R. McNeill, "Observations on the Nature and Culture of Environmental History," *History and Theory* 42/4 Theme Issue 42: Environment and

History (2003): 5–43; Douglas R. Weiner, "A Death-Defying Attempt to Articulate a Coherent Definition of Environmental History," *Environmental History* 10/3 (2005): 404–420.

8. Roderick Nash, *Wilderness in the American Mind*, 4th ed. (New Haven: Yale University Press, 2001), xi.

9. Roderick Nash, "American Environmental History: A New Teaching Frontier," *Pacific Historical Review* 41/2 (1972): 362–365.

10. Donald Worster, *Nature's Economy: A History of Ecological Ideas* (Cambridge: Cambridge University Press, 1977); *Dust Bowl: The Southern Plains in the 1930s* (Oxford: Oxford University Press, 1979); *A Passion for Nature: The Life of John Muir* (Oxford: Oxford University Press, 2008).

11. Cronon, "Uses of Environmental History," 4–7.

12. Richard Grove, "Environmental History," in *New Perspectives on Historical Writing*, Peter Burke, ed. (University Park [PA]: Pennsylvania State University Press, 2001), 262.

13. Mark Cioc, Björn-Ola Lnnér, and Matt Osborn, "Environmental History Writing in Northern Europe," *Environmental History* 5/3 (2000): 396–406.

14. Colin Fisher, "Race and US Environmental History," in *A Companion to American Environmental History*, Douglas Cazaux Sackman, ed. (Oxford: Blackwell, 2010), 99–115.

15. Carolyn Merchant, "Shades of Darkness: Race and Environmental History," *Environmental History* 8/3 (2003): 380–394.

16. Carolyn Merchant, "Gender and Environmental History," *The Journal of American History* 76/4 (1990): 1121. See also her *Ecological Revolutions: Nature, Gender, and Science in New England* (Chapel Hill: University of North Carolina Press, 1989).

17. Donald Worster, "Worlds without Borders: The Internationalizing of Environmental History," *Environmental Review: ER* 6/2 Special Issue: Papers from the First International Conference on Environmental History (1982), 9.

18. Libby Robin and Tom Griffiths, "Environmental History History in Australasia," *Environment and History* 10/4 (2004): 439.

19. Alfred Crosby, *The Columbian Exchange: Biological and Cultural Consequences of 1492*, 30th Anniversary ed. (Westport [CT]: Praeger, 2003); Mike Davis, *Late Victorian Holocausts: El Niño Famines and the Making of the Third World* (London: Verso, 2001).

20. Richard Grove, *Green Imperialism: Colonial Expansion, Tropical Island Edens and the Origins of Environmentalism, 1600–1860* (Cambridge: Cambridge University Press, 1996).

21. Alfred Crosby, "Conquistador y Pestilencia: The First New World Pandemic and the Fall of the Great Indian Empires," *The Hispanic American Historical Review* 47/3 (1967): 321–337.

22. Andrew Kuech, "A Survey of World History Studies: Theory, Methodology, and Networks," *Middle Ground Journal* no. 4 (Spring 2012), accessed 31 August 2013, http://www2.css.edu/app/depts/his/historyjournal/index.cfm?cat=6&art=76; The World History Association, "What is World History," accessed 31 August 2013, http://www.thewha.org/world_history.php.

23. Edmund Burke III and Kenneth Pomeranz, eds., *The Environment and World History* (Berkeley: University of California Press, 2009).

24. John R. McNeill, *Something New Under the Sun: An Environmental History of the Twentieth-Century World* (New York: W.W. Norton, 2001).

25. Kenneth Pomeranz, *The Great Divergence: China, Europe, and the Making of the Modern World Economy* (Princeton [NJ]: Princeton University Press, 2000), 207.

26. Madhav Gadgil and Ramachandra Guha, *This Fissured Land: An Ecological History of India* (Berkeley: University of California Press, 1993).

27. Stephen Pyne, *The Ice: A Journey to Antarctica* (Iowa City: University of Iowa Press, 1986); an example of his recent interests may be found in *Vestal Fire: An Environmental History, Told Through Fire, of Europe and Europe's Encounter with the World* (Seattle: University of Washington Press, 1997).

28. Tom Standage, *History of the World in Six Glasses* (New York: Walker Publishing Company, 2006); Mark Kurlansky, *Salt: A World History* (New York: Penguin Books, 2003); Kurlansky, *Cod: A Biography of the Fish that Changed the World* (New York: Penguin Books, 1998).

29. Lise Sedrez, "Latin American Environmental History: A Shifting Old/New Field," in *The Environment and World History*, Edmund Burke III and Kenneth Pomeranz, eds. (Berkeley: University of California Press, 2009), 261–263.

30. William Beinart, "African History and Environmental History," *African Affairs* 99 (2000): 289–302, republished on H-Environment, accessed 31 August 2013, http://www.h-net.org/~environ/historiography/africaeh.htm.

31. James C. McCann, *Green Land, Brown Land, Black Land: An Environmental History of Africa, 1800-1900* (Portsmouth: Heinemann, 1999).

32. James C. McCann, Maize and Grace: *Africa's Encounter with a New World Crop, 1500–2000* (Cambridge [MA]: Harvard University Press, 2007).

33. Tamara Giles-Vernick, *Cutting the Vines of the Past: Environmental Histories of the Central African Rain Forest* (Charlottsville: University of Virginia Press, 2002).

34. Peter Thorsheim, *Inventing Pollution: Coal, Smoke, and Culture in Britain since 1800* (Athens [OH]: Ohio University Press, 2006).

35. Cioc, Linnér, and Osborn, 397–400.

36. Harriet Ritvo, "Discipline and Indiscipline," *Environmental History* 10/1 (2005): 75–76.

37. David Christian, *Maps of Time: An Introduction to Big History,* 2nd ed. (Berkeley: University of California Press, 2011).

38. This is a reference to a mini-big history by David Christian, *This Fleeting World: A Short History of Humanity* (Great Barrington [MA]: Berkshire Publishing Group, 2008).

39. United States Department of Agriculture, "Wheat," in *The Agricultural Outlook for 1931*, Prepared by the Staff of the Bureau of Agricultural Economics, Assisted by Representatives of the Agricultural Colleges and Extension Services and the Federal Farm Board, February 1931, (United States Department of Agriculture Miscellaneous Publication No. 108), 2–5. http://books.google.com/books?id=typRqWjokWoC& printsec=frontcover&source=gbs_ge_summary_r&cad =0#v=onepage&q&f=false, e-publication.

40. Richard Grove and Toyin Falola, "Chiefs, Boundaries and Sacred Woodlands: Early Nationalism and the Defeat of Colonial Conservationism in the Gold Coast and Nigeria, 1870-1916," *African Economic History* 24 (1996): 1–23.

CHAPTER 7

POST-STRUCTURALISM AND DECONSTRUCTION

CHAPTER OUTLINE

■ Modernism and Structuralism

■ Postmodernism

■ Post-Structuralism

■ Deconstruction

■ A Conclusion—Influences on the Profession

■ Thinking Like a Historian

"Gone too are the grand narratives that historicized the notion of social totality. Responding to the anti-reductionist logic of post-modernism means, therefore, thinking about new versions of the social, ones that require historians to be the inquisitors and perhaps the executioners of old valuations."

Patrick Joyce[1]

In the children's book *Frindle*, the young protagonist Nicholas Allen argues with his fifth-grade teacher over why words are the way they are. He embarks on a movement to change the system by renaming the word "pen" as a "frindle." It began as a joke, getting his friends to go into the local drugstore asking for a "frindle" until the clerk automatically reached for a pen when the word was used. Then it got serious. When the teacher commanded that he stop, he and his classmates refused. By the end of the novel, frindle was a word in the dictionary, Nicholas was a rich college student who earned money from a local businessman who invested in the word, and he learned, in a letter from his teacher that he was never allowed to open until then, the exact lesson of how words get into the dictionary. This children's story, beloved by third through fifth graders, gets right to the heart of the arguments post-structural scholars hope to make—that words, and the meanings they create, are arbitrary constructions.[2]

By now, you should have an understanding of the materialist conception of history, that is, a history that privileges the tangible world as the predominant mode of human experience and understanding. We are now going to shift gears and talk about another umbrella of history, an umbrella that generally privileges an **epistemological** approach to history—in other words, an approach that focuses on human perception and mental processes as the dominant mode of human understanding of the past. In this chapter, we discuss the emergence of the philosophical approaches known as post-structuralism and deconstruction, their roots in **linguistics** and **semiotics**, and their influence on the field of history. Once you read this chapter, you will discover, much like Nicholas Allen, that the things we often take to be static and fixed (words and ideas) are often only our perceptions that change over time and space.

MODERNISM AND STRUCTURALISM

Fernand de Saussure (1857–1913) was a linguist who taught at the *École Pratique des Hautes Études* in Paris. He also taught in Geneva from 1906 to 1911, and it was in Geneva that he developed a course in general linguistics. After his death, two of his students compiled his lectures and published the *Course in General Linguistics* because they were so influenced by his theories regarding the structure of language. In that course, Saussure put forth numerous ideas, including the idea that there is a science of language. In this way, Saussure's work was similar to the work of many scholars of the previous century who saw an objective scientific framework for scholarly work (see Chapter 2). Because he believed that science was formulaic, the structure of language is seen to be **synchronic** (ahistorical over time and place) rather than **diachronic** (changing over time in specific languages). That is, Saussure was not interested in the move, for example, from Old English to Middle English to Modern English, but rather was interested in the structure of language at any given moment. Accordingly, he believed that the study of the history of language (philology) was important, but it was not the only component of language. Two of his more complex ideas are that there is a relationship between language and individuals and that language makes meaning through difference. This meaning is achieved through a specific structure (i.e., a formula). Let's look at that structure in template form:

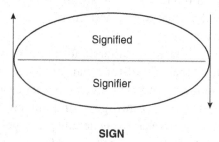

SIGN

This is what is known as a **dyad** (two-sided) formula of language. The **sign** is a union of a mental concept and a sound image or the combination of the **signifier** and **signified**. By way of example, after you read this sentence, try the following exercise: Close your eyes and think of a dog. You can visualize it in your mind and

you can say the word out loud. You can even sound it out: duh-aww-guh. The sign is the combination of all these events, events that happen nearly simultaneously but which nevertheless can be separated. Even if our *image* of a dog is different (e.g., Sayegh thinks of a beagle/terrier mix, and Altice thinks of a dalmation), we still have a basic understanding of what the sign is. But this bond, this union of mental imprint to sound and written image to create the sign, is not etched in stone. In other words, all signs are arbitrary. There is no naturalness to the word "dog," which has different names in other languages (chien, perro, hund, etc.). Recognizing this arbitrariness is key to getting at the structure of language.

In addition to recognizing arbitrariness of the sign/signifier/signified relation, Saussure also stated that language is a linear process—that is, there is a sequence to it. Words make sense in the structure of sentences with each word reliant on others to create meaning.[3] In other words, words make sense only through difference, which gives value/meaning to signifiers in a system. This difference is referred to as **negative value**, that is, defining something by that which it is not, resulting in signification or "meaning."

In Saussure's model there is a linear (what he refers to as a **syntagm**) relationship in language. It may differ between languages, but within language, there is a proper order for words that we as speakers determine is correct. For example, it makes sense to us to say "Look at the dog," but if we say "The dog at look" the meaning is lost. This is a result of the ways in which particular languages order words. Specific words also have certain value in the signification process, so we can exchange words with words of the same value and have the same signification (i.e., meaning). For example, "it was a cold, blustery day" can become "it was a chilly and windy day" very readily without distorting the meaning of the sentence. But it can only do this because we, as a community of speakers, have agreed to it. We have agreed that "blustery" is the equivalent to "windy." If we agreed that "flibberygibbery" was the equivalent to "windy," we could substitute the words thusly: "It was cold, flibberygibbery day." Ultimately, language is built on our agreement that words hold certain value. We can't say "cat" and mean "dog." The two values are completely different. We cannot say "car" and mean "child." We can say "kid" for child, "vehicle" for car, "golden retriever" for dog, or "kitty" for cat. Again, this gets back to negative value. We know a cat is not a dog, a car is not a tree, and so forth. Another way to think of this is to think of your closet. Language is like a closet where you pick out your clothes, but instead of picking out a shirt for the day, you are picking out letters and words that go together. Finally, according to Saussure, meaning is gathered through interaction with others, and therefore language is considered to be entirely a product of society.[4] Because he believed that language could be discovered through formulae, or structure, we get the name structuralism.

Another form of structuralism, and perhaps even more well known, emerged in the discipline of anthropology with the work of Claude Lévi-Strauss (1908–2009), who put forth an account of human societies based on the same kind of synchronic, formulaic system articulated by Saussure. Lévi-Strauss was educated at the Sorbonne, the University of Paris, and took a position in the academy by 1939. Perhaps Lévi-Strauss's most significant contribution to anthropology was his discovery that so-called primitive societies are guided by the same basic principles as so-called modern man—a quest for understanding the world around them. However, the difference between the modern man and the "Savage Mind" (which would become the title of his pathbreaking work) according to Lévi-Strauss is that the less-developed society insisted on order and meaning for everything—it had to become universal.[5] But the ways in which order is obtained are universal to humankind as every society relies on myth to establish some kind of structure. It helps them explain and order their world.

This realization on the part of Lévi-Strauss is a crucial indicator of his structuralism. Just as Saussure was not interested in the history of language, nor was Lévi-Strauss necessarily interested in the development of cultures. Through his friendship with the structural linguist Roman Jakobson, he found that structuralism enabled him to show how systems could be explained on their own terms. He created a formula for the role of myth in society that allowed him to take his notes of various societies at various levels of development and make sense of all of them. This approach put Lévi-Strauss at odds with much of the academic and intellectual community of Western Europe.

Saussure's model continued to be of importance into the twentieth century. In part, his insistence that language is fixed and stable became a straw man for scholars of post-structuralism. However, post-structuralism is only one of a few approaches to undermining the hegemony of modernity. In this section, we will examine postmodernism generally and then will move to exploring different manifestations of postmodern philosophy.

POSTMODERNISM

Postmodernism is a push away from the certainty of modernity. In many cases, one could argue that this push began within the modernist art movement of the late nineteenth and early twentieth century, with artists, musicians, and novelists toying with "unmeaning" in their works. Stream-of-consciousness became a technique of authors such as James Joyce or William Faulkner, trying to mimic through their works the meandering elements of thought patterns. Cubism, surrealism, Dadaism, were all art movements that contested the ability of art (or technologies such as photography) to mimic "reality," concentrating instead on the fleeting representations in our minds or the unconsciousness of the world of dreams. And in music, the work of Igor Stravinsky caused a riot in Paris in 1913 when he introduced *The Rite of Spring*—a work of such seeming discordant cacophony to its original listeners that meaning surely could not be found. However, just as many modern artists questioned meaning of their contemporary age, particularly after the violence and horrors of World War I, many others saw modernity as an end to irrational and backwards ideas. For these people, the "modern world" represented the culmination of Enlightenment ideals and would bring a better world.

The climate in which postmodern authors wrote suggested to them a necessity for throwing a wrench into the narratives of traditional Western philosophy. Those narratives were responsible for events such as World Wars I and II, the **Algerian War**, for May 1968, and for women's subordination. By drawing on semiotics and language, they could critique the **binary oppositions** established as "normal" in society and thereby reconstruct—in small increments at least—visions of the world that rejected the Enlightenment ideal. For all these scholars, discourse is at the center of their critiques, and consequently the nature of any fixed and stable text.

Postmodernists, like the artists who critiqued their world, disagreed with this assumption of an ever-improving world. Postmodernists generally reject the intelligibility of the modern world as well as the arrogant superiority of science from the early modern period forward. Specifically, postmodernists question the central role objectivity has taken in modern discourse (see Chapter 2) as a way to find a single, authoritarian "truth." Rather, truth is defined by people within their particular contexts, but cannot be universalized. There are various manifestations of postmodernism, but we will explore only two: post-structuralism and deconstruction.

The name most associated with this rejection of the **grand narrative** (or metanarrative) is Jean-François Lyotard (1924–1998). Lyotard was educated at the Sorbonne. During World War II, he served as a medical volunteer in the French Resistance. After the war, he spent some time as a teacher in Algeria, which consequently shaped his attitudes regarding the western grand narrative. So did his involvement in French political groups, particularly *Socialisme ou Barbarie*, a socialist revolutionary organization. By the middle of the 1960s, he rejected socialism and Marxism, though he remained committed to political activism, participating in the 1968 student movement. In *The Postmodern Condition,* he outlined a theory of the postmodern as a recognition that such stories (the triumph of the workers over the exploitive forces of capitalism, the triumph of reason over darkness) were problematic frameworks.[6] Instead, Lyotard asserted, we ought to focus on smaller narratives. The condition of the postmodern world is one in which the search for universals yields few, if any, positive results. In this way, a multiplicity of truths—or narratives—emerges.

POST-STRUCTURALISM

By now, you might be interested in language and its structure, in anthropology and human societies, or even postmodernism as a philosophy, but you might be a bit confused about its relation to history. Post-structural scholars and the historians influenced by this philosophy moved away from the study of material things to the study of language. One of the most important philosophers setting up that historiographic shift was Michel Foucault (pronounced Foo-coh).

Even though both Saussure and Lévi-Strauss critiqued certain frameworks of universalism, their systems for understanding human communities reinforce ideas of some universal truth "out there." Even with Saussure's recognition that signs have their meaning only through community agreement, there is an element of **essentialism** because those signs are fixed and in many respects get their meanings by that which they are not (negative value). Post-structuralists argue against such reductionism, and argue that meaning is not inherent or necessarily rational. In fact, meaning is embedded in instability. For post-structuralists, language is the force that creates and maintains the world (now, going back to the class struggle talked about in earlier chapters, you can see how this might trouble those who argue that there is some material base that upholds the intangible

elements of society). As a result, meaning exists only in a plurality (the multiplicity of ways in which language might create meaning) and loses its hegemonic position established by the modernists. Hence, we are back to the need to undermine the grand narratives of total history.

While there are many critical theorists, such as Jean-François Lyotard mentioned earlier, who work in the business of destabilizing the grand narrative, Foucault is the one most often associated with historians. In part this is because the body of Foucault's work resonates with the concerns historians have traditionally held of unraveling the power systems at work in post industrial revolution society. By using Foucault's roadmap of the "fissures" of society, historians have been able to articulate the **disjunctures** (i.e., paradigm shifts from one episteme to another) present in the transition from premodern to modern and consequently to problematize the very notion and understanding of modernity itself.

Foucault (1926–1984) held a very uneasy relationship both to structuralism and to post-structuralism. He was educated at the Sorbonne, part of the University of Paris, in the 1950s and he was trained in the ambience of existentialism and Marxism, though his specific fields of study were philosophy and psychology. In this book, we have covered Marxism, but only briefly touched upon existentialism. Like Marxism, existentialism is a very materialist philosophy as it presupposes that "existence precedes essence." That is, one's life meaning is not prior to experience—one must experience life and create meaning. This philosophy is embodied in the work of Albert Camus and Jean-Paul Sartre. So, during his formative intellectual development, these two theories were the most popular ways to critically examine the world.

Foucault entered into the larger critique of the grand narrative in a famous debate/discussion with the linguist/philosopher/political activist Noam Chomsky (1928–) in 1971. In this discussion sponsored by the International Philosophers' Project, Chomsky argued that there is a concept of justice aligned with the notion of freedom applicable across human societies. Chomsky was hardly a structuralist, however. His 1957 book *Syntactic Structures* represents his break away from structural linguistics, as he wrote about the differences between peoples' linguistic competence and their performance. In this debate, Foucault shows himself interested more in the fissures discussed above—moments of critical change from some moment in the past.[7]

Foucault occupies a special place in the hearts of historians—we either love him or we hate him, but we can no longer simply discount him. His work is too voluminous, his questions too multifaceted and "in the face" of our larger project of retelling the past that we must address it in some way. His early work (1960s) focused on histories of medicine. Later he produced *Discipline and Punish* (a study of the **gaze**, the power of observation to shape behavior, through the vehicle of the Panopticon and the prison) and *The History of Sexuality*, where he puts forth the concept of a science of sex as opening a whole new discourse for supposed defined deviants to maneuver. While it is impossible in a slim book to cover the corpus of Foucault's work, we can introduce some of the concepts that are infused throughout his work and which have the most currency for historians.

Discourse

Discourse is at the heart of Foucaultian analysis. If you go to a dictionary and look up the term, you are likely to come up with a definition that links it to conversation or talking. However, discourse is not just "talking." For Foucault, it is more than this. For Foucault and others, discourse is centered around a particular context in which statements, attitudes, and so on can have currency. Discourse is not language, but rather operates in and through language as well as other forms of communication. For Foucault, discourse enables the operations of power within a society by establishing specific norms by which individuals are characterized. Thus, discourses can be beliefs, value systems, professional verbiage, what have you, that permeate a society to such an extent that we naturalize them. Discourse, then, is a vehicle that drives social beliefs, power, and practices, and thus individuals within societies are limited by the discursive practices of any given age.

In other words, discourses are themselves structures that are historically specific and through which we are able to have conversations about an event, an item, an ideology.[8] An example is modern technology. Talking about things such as cell phones, 'droids, iPads, Wi-Fi, and so on makes sense because there is a discourse surrounding the particular technologies we use in the twenty-first century. Foucault's use of discourse is far more sophisticated, as he took it to create an analysis of the ways in which the intersections of things such as the confessional and nineteenth-century science enabled a particular way of thinking, talking, and exploring the world. There is a clear discourse in the medical profession, for example, (a way of thinking about the body, microbes, viruses, and so forth) as there is in any other professional organization. To understand this as "discourse," not simply "fact," we can compare this to other discourses about disease and medicine (say, that of the ancient Greeks or Asian discourses of medicine). While a modernist understanding of the difference between the ancient Greeks and modern medicine would simply say the Greeks' understanding of the body was tarnished by ignorance and superstition, and modern medicine has progressively improved our understanding, a Foucaultian analysis would emphasize each discrete medical "discourse," and ask how that discourse distributed knowledge/power through society. This discourse facilitates the process of defining, articulating, and finding meaning in ideas relevant to the discipline. As a consequence, Foucault suggests that there is nothing outside of the given discourses of a society (think here of our use of the word "flibberygibbery" for windy. It only makes sense if the community of speakers accepts it). In this way, he develops a theory of the relationship of language to power.

Normativity

Another major concept for Foucault is the concept of **normativity**. Foucault argued that the structural linguistic framework of negative value had been added on to culture, creating binary oppositions. Binary oppositions are problematic, because they create essential categories beyond which any differences cannot be overcome. An "us" versus "them." For Foucault, this binary is centered around normativity—that which integrates people into the **social body**.[9] The concept of the social body was built, in part, around Enlightenment ideas of the self, of "individual rights," and within those rights, the rights of people to obtain certain degrees of inclusion in society. Inclusion, however, requires exclusion. For example, even the moderate politicians of the 1840s pressed only for universal "male" suffrage—and most certainly this meant white male. The right to vote was not even thought to extend to women, and many activists worked very hard to argue against the inclusion of women. For example, many argued that there should be a "family wage" and as a result a "family vote." Women were inched out discursively from the workforce and the political force.

Normativity is imposed through disciplinary power, a power aimed at producing "docile bodies" ready to participate fully in the social body. To understand the concept of the social body, all you have to do is think of a human body. When one part does not work properly (say a broken leg or a malfunctioning kidney), the body is quite literally out of whack—it is not working to its fullest potential. If you apply this same logic to a particular society (or even subset of a society such as the military), the people within the society serve as parts of that larger body. Since all parts must work in tandem with each other, one part that is "broken" either needs to be excised or "fixed." Disciplinary power then takes the form of the school, the hospital, the prison, the madhouse, the military, to ensure the normativity of the social body.[10]

But normativity is not accomplished solely through disciplinary power for Foucault. Rather, there is a whole set of regulations regarding sex and populations, what Foucault calls "bio-power."[11] Foucault first introduces us to this concept regarding Malthusian economics—when overpopulation meant that population was now a problem, something to be contained. This gave the state certain "power over life." Bio-power leads people to take notice of things such as public health or personal hygiene. One is trained in the care of the self to manage everything from reproductive capacity to disease to death.

Binary oppositions were essential for creating the modern period of science, argues Foucault. Medicine and the social sciences are built around concepts of normal and deviant. If one defines oneself by what one is not (negative value), then if one is not "normal," then one is deviant (sick, perverted, criminal, mad, and so on). What this means is that a vast group of people was subject to frameworks that actively excluded them. This was accomplished through what Foucault calls "the gaze."

The Gaze

The **gaze** is simply the way in which "modern" society formed bureaucratic structures, such as the police, hospitals, educational structures, to establish a system of universal surveillance. Foucault best articulates the framework of the gaze with his analysis of the **Panopticon**. The Panopticon was the creation of British reformer Jeremy Bentham, who believed that prisons did no social good and did not adequately reform the prisoner. Part of the reason for the failure of the prison was its very structure. Bentham designed plans for a different kind of prison, one shaped as a circle, with the guard tower in the middle and all the cells on the outer limits of the circle. In this way, the guards would remain both seen and unseen. The prisoner, who would know that the gaze was always upon him (even though he could not see the guards in the tower), would find his "Morals reformed, health preserved, industry invigorated, instruction diffused, public burthens lightened, economy seated, as it were, upon a rock—the gordian knot of the Poor-Laws are not cut, but untied—all by a simple idea in Architecture."[12]

Foucault suggested that this material example of the utilitarian movement served as an example of society "since the Classical Age" (i.e., since the seventeenth century). While the gaze of the guard in the prison contributed to the normalization of the prisoner, and therefore to the future inclusion in the social body, various other gazes could ensure the same kind of normativity. The gaze of the doctor or psychiatrist, for example, could ensure that the hysteric woman, the homosexual man, or the "pervert" would be similarly reformed. This links back into the concept of normativity described earlier. These "constant, attentive, curious presences" were part of the operation of power that created a universal system of surveillance in bourgeois society.[13] Foucault suggests that the gaze could also be turned around, in that by naming that which is deviant, the now defined deviant has a power to name itself.[14]

Discourse, normativity, and the gaze all get to the heart of Foucault's concept of power itself. For Foucault, power is not top-down, enforced from on high, nor is it bottom up, willingly handed over by the populace. Rather, Foucault argues that power is omnipresent and what we normally perceive as power is simply what he calls "the terminal forms power takes." But power is the network of all relations, for Foucault, and nothing is outside of this power.[15]

DECONSTRUCTION

If you have ever watched *Iron Chef* or *Top Chef* on the Food Network, you have probably seen a deconstructed meal of some sort: a deconstructed chicken salad, deconstructed ice cream sundae. These are meals in which the whole is pieced out and the eater can savor all of the constituent elements. For example, a deconstructed ice cream sundae may look like this:

Ice Cream   Hot   Whipped   Chopped   Cherry
            Fudge   Cream   Nuts

Even *Top Chef* judge Tom Colicchio has begun to explain what deconstructed food means when answering a complaint by some chefs that "they don't do deconstructed food."[16]

This may seem like a flip way to approach the extraordinarily complex idea of philosophical deconstruction, but it does get to the root of the definition. French philosopher Hélène Cixous commented on the infusion of the term deconstruction in popular culture to the extent that the word lost its meaning, but in many ways, this is precisely the way to get a mass audience to understand the critical underpinnings of the philosophy. Simply put, the purpose of deconstruction is to reexamine the text, pull it apart, and locate competing meanings and truths through the language used in the text. The founder of deconstruction, Jacques Derrida (1930–2004), was an Algerian French scholar, trained at the *École Normale Supérieur* in Paris. His particular interests were to discount the structure of difference established in the Saussurean system by introducing an entirely new category of *différance*. If you recall earlier, Saussure posited a system in which the sign is the result of the unification of the signifier and the signified. For Derrida, this is impossible as they are always transforming, always in a state of flux. Specifically, Derrida argued that it was essential to move beyond the so-called scientific nature of linguistics as espoused by structuralism.

Like Foucault's, Derrida's work claims that "truth" or "the original" cannot be found, and therefore no formulaic model of a society or language can be satisfactory. Foucault critiques structuralism and shows his uneasy relationship to it in his work *The Order of Things*:

> There can be no commentary without the absolute precondition of the text [through language]' and inversely if the world is a network of marks and words, how else is one to speak of them but in the form of commentary? From the Classical Age, language is deployed within representation and in that duplication of itself hollows itself out. Henceforth, the primary text is effaced, and with it, the entire, inexhaustible foundation of the words whose mute being was inscribed in things; all that remains is representation, unfolding in the verbal signs that manifest it, and hence becoming discourse.[17]

Likewise, Derrida has famously stated that "there is nothing outside the text."[18] In other words, deconstruction for Derrida is a way to read texts and pull apart their stated meanings to address contradictory meanings. In this way, Derrida would play with words in a text and how those words take on simultaneous meanings of contradiction. One of his last series of lectures focused on the issue of hospitality and the ways in which the host must be violated in order to serve the function of host. So while at the same time as being in a position of power (the person whose home/office/workplace/country we visit), the host is also in a position of subjection (he must open himself for inspection—as Derrida says, the guest may peruse all the books on your shelf). So Derrida concludes, is the host truly a host? Or a stranger on whom hospitality has been imposed?[19] If we use the deconstructed food example earlier, we would see something like the following:

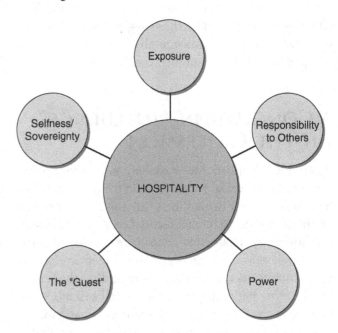

In *Of Grammatology* (originally published in 1967) and elsewhere, Derrida put forth the idea of **différence/différance** (this is not difference, as we would say in English). Différance (dif-er-ahnce) was built from rereading Saussure's *Course in General Linguistics* and locating the connections that Saussure unconsciously made between spoken and written language. While spoken language was the focus of Saussure's work, written language also played a pivotal role in establishing meaning. Derrida plays off of Saussure's idea of difference and shows Saussure's problems very literally on the written page. Both are pronounced exactly the same way but can only be truly distinguished through the written word. We can only know the meaning of that word in context—thus the meaning is "deferred" until the entire syntagm (how we understand language) is constructed. Derrida takes his syntagmatic discussion of the traces that each syntagm holds to entire texts and argues that they bear traces of other texts whether we consciously recognize them or not. Derrida finds practical application of this idea through deconstruction. Deconstructing a text enables the implied binary oppositions and privileged component of that binary to be laid bare, thus also laying bare the power structures upheld in Western philosophy. Deconstruction, then, can be a powerful tool for redressing social grievances. The close reading of the text is necessary to see the echoes of other texts in what is both said and unsaid. By laying bare the constituent parts, any claim to a hierarchical or hegemonic control is undermined. And as stated earlier, the Iron Chefs' "deconstructed" dishes suggest this, as the dish is understood in a fundamentally different way as its components are taken on their own terms.

A CONCLUSION—INFLUENCES ON THE PROFESSION

Postmodern philosophies have had tremendous influence on the historical profession. On the one hand, they have served as strawman for a rallying cry to toughen up the discipline, to remain focused on so-called proper methodology. Historians who have employed poststructural or deconstructive analyses in their works have faced numerous critques for "disregarding the real."[20] On the other hand, they have also served as a model for looking at the past through different lenses and for exploring the constructs various societies have created at different historical moments. Some scholars who have self-identified as postmodernists question whether we still live in a postmodern world or whether we need some equivalent of a post postmodern. Regardless, the project of the unmediated subject is at odds with this sense. For many scholars, the postmodern project is very problematic. Some claim that by critiquing the grand narrative in favor of a multiplicity of narratives, postmodernists in fact uphold the very framework they seek to undermine. Other scholars argue that to abandon the concept of modernity is nothing more than a "nonsense experiment."[21] Jürgen Habermas (1929–) is a leading scholar of the **Frankfurt School**, a philosopher

interested in the constructions of modernity such as public space and civic institutions. For him, postmodernism could be problematic because its claims could be used against them by neoconservatives looking for a pretense for their own claims.[22]

For still other scholars, postmodernism in whatever form it takes does not go far enough. As we will see in the next few chapters, postmodernism has provided a model for historians to rethink the tools of their trade but does not address the specific experiences of minority groups. The question for these scholars is simply this: How can one embrace postmodernism when one has not even finished the experience of modernity?

The question may remain in some minds: "what does this have to do with history?" The answer is easy for those who accept theory's position within historical thinking. It is important to recognize that Foucault's work, like most work in critical theory, is not constrained by one discipline, but is profoundly, inherently interdisciplinary. This can be disconcerting for historians used to the traditional "grand narrative." How can someone who writes about deviant *psychological* behavior have any relevance to history? There is, believe it or not, a rather large subfield called "psychohistory" that explores psychological issues in history.

Michel Foucault postulated numerous ways to rethink and resituate the past that destabilize our preconceived concepts of boundaries and "change over time." His *History of Sexuality*, volume 1 clearly articulates how we can use his particular concepts of "the gaze," "power," and the "repressive hypothesis" to better understand the particular society that existed in nineteenth-century Europe. He states that some call it "bourgeois society"; whatever we choose to call it, he argues, there were mechanisms the bourgeoisie put in place to assert their own positions—a hygienic world that controlled populations—and consequently established an empire at the *fin de siècle*.[23] In other words, the intersection of a certain kind of discourse (scientific—that lent itself to a kind of "truth is out there" phenomenon) with economic development put in motion a society radically different from the one preceding it (*Classical Age*). Historians have taken Foucault's theories as methods for their own examination of the past—the field increasingly explored the past on its own terms and not in some teleological fashion. Historians can thank Foucault in large part for this remapping of the past. In addition, ideas of self-discipline and the gaze—of being conscious that we are always under surveillance even in the confines of our own privacy—shape how we interact with others and how we develop policies.

An excellent example of Foucault's ideas of power, discipline, normativity, and the gaze can be found in Michael Ignatieff's *A Just Measure of Pain: The Penitentiary in the Industrial Revolution, 1750–1850*.[24] In this monograph, Ignatieff argues that from the mid-eighteenth century, prisons transformed from institutions that focused on disciplining the body to those that disciplined the mind instead. He further argues that the penitentiary represented a failure of liberal reformers who hoped to change not only the prisoners' attitudes but also the very institution of the penitentiary itself (such as Bentham's visualization of the Panopticon). Thus, like Foucault's work, Ignatieff's monograph explores the institutionalization and internalization of particular power structures at work in a particular society, and in so doing, plays upon the triad of discourse (reformers' language), normativity (criminals versus the populace), and the gaze (the Panopticon and the hope for prison reform).

In the end, we study Foucault because to not study Foucault is to ignore some of the basic foundational components of cultural history. If we are to truly understand the cultural umbrella, if we are to be responsible historians, we need to accept post-structuralism as transformative in our perceptions of the problems of modernity, the problems of the whiggish interpretation of the past, the problems of the terminal ends of power arguing that they are power itself. We need at least to be conscious of philosophies that posit radical transformation both of society and the historical method if we are going to be able to articulate and defend our own methodological positions.

THINKING LIKE A HISTORIAN

The primary source for this chapter comes from The Ordinary's Accounts from Newgate Prison. The Ordinary was a chaplain at London's Newgate Prison whose job was in part to record the final testaments of convicted criminals prior to their execution.

- Can you use some of the conceptual terms from this chapter to explain this legal record? Which terms, and how might you use them?

- What purpose might this account serve for the English public? Is there a moral tone to the transcription? Or something else?

- The Ordinary was tasked with taking down the final words and testaments of the condemned, but the Ordinary in this source seems to dialogue with the prisoners. How might this dialogue be used to explain normativity and deviance? Can you pull examples from the text?

- As a historian, how would you introduce this primary source to a larger audience?

- Finally, think about how you might use this source if you were looking at this source from another theoretical lens. Can those lenses overlap with what you learned in this chapter? How?

The secondary source by David Gaimster is clearly influenced by Foucault's theories. As a piece of museum history, the article's main focus is on the development of museum censorship of ancient art deemed too provocative for public consumption. As you read the article, look for the ways that Gaimster uses concepts such as normativity, binary oppositions, or the gaze. An additional task is to see how the article crosses theoretical boundaries by exploring gender and sex.

- What kinds of conceptual frameworks discussed in this chapter can you spot in the article, and how are those frameworks employed?

- Why did ancient art become so controversial? What period did this controversy begin?

- What kinds of binary oppositions (or normative frameworks) can we understand of Victorian society based on their sequestration (and other censorship) of some of this art?

- According to Gaimster, presentism was at work among the Victorians, where they read into the ancient world their own sensibilities that may not necessarily have reflected ancient attitudes. Provide one or two examples and explain how they can be interpreted historically with a post-structural lens.

- According to Gaimster, how does the Witt Collection at the British Museum reflect nineteenth-century Britons' ambivalent relationship to their ancient heritage?

Ordinary's Account, 19th July 1700

R. Wykes, Ordinary.[25] *Lonodn* [sic]. *Printed for E. Mallet, at the Hat and Hawk in Bride-lane.*

The Confessions, Behaviour, and Dying Speeches of Gerhardt Dromelius, Michael Van Bergen and Catherine Truerniet, Condemn'd for the Murder of Mr. Oliver Norris, and Executed by Harts-horn Brewhouse in East-Smithfield, on Friday the 19th of July, 1700.

These three Persons, being all of them Dutch, had the favour of Ministers of their own Nation to Instruct and Prepare them for another World, Ministers who made it their Business, together with the Ordinary, to perswade them to a Confession of the Crime for which they suffer'd, and of their other Wickedness that provok'd Heaven to punish them in this Exemplary manner.

GErhardt [sic] Dromelius accordingly gave the following Account of the barbarous Murder. That he himself committed it, and that his Master and Mistress were wholly ignorant of the Matter. The manner thus, That (being Drawer of the House,) his Master observing the unhappy Gentleman resolv'd to go home, laid his Commands upon him to conduct the said Gentleman to his Inn near Aldgate; that no sooner were they out of his Masters Doors, but the said Gentleman took the opportunity to ease himself in an adjacent broken Building; that whilst they were there the Gentleman gave him very angry Language, and attempted to draw his Sword upon him, that this made him close with him, and having got him down he wrested his Sword out of his Hand, and gave him several Wounds with it; that whilst the unfortunate Gentleman was in this Condition, and groaning for Life, he heard the Watchman coming on, and dreading a discovery, he drew his Knife and cut the Gentleman's Throat, that so there might be an end of his Groans and his own Fears. This is the substance of the Story as related by him in the English Tongue (for he cou'd speak English so as to be understood) and this engaged me to represent the improbability of the Story in several Particulars, as First, That it was not likely a naked Man, as he was, shou'd venture upon a Gentleman that draws his Sword upon him, when he had both room enough to run away, and it was no disgrace for him so to do, the Gentleman so drawing, being, as he knew he was, overcome with Liquor. Secondly, That tho' he shou'd be so Fool-hardy to close with him notwithstanding it was highly improbable they shou'd tumble together as he himself acknowledged and not dawb their Cloths with Dirt, that Night particularly having been very Rainy, and Thirdly, That if the Murder had been committed by him alone, near the place where the Body was found, there must have been a very great quantity of Blood, not only on the Cloths but on the Ground, and Fourthly, That the Wounds he had given him with his own Sword, being at first given, while his Cloths were on, it must follow by a necessary Consequence, that there must be several little holes in those Cloths, the contrary

whereof is apparent. To all which he answer'd. That he did close with him, magre all the disadvantage, but cou'd assign no reason besides his own Madness and the Devils Temptation. That their Clothes might be dirty tho' not observ'd. That there was a considerable quantity of Blood near the place where the Body was found, and that there wou'd have been more had not he tore the Gentleman's Shirt and put it into the bleeding Wounds; and in fine, that there might be small holes in the Clothes, tho' not taken notice of; Answers, so improbable, the first, and so contrary to Truth, the others, 'That' almost forc'd me to lay before him the hainousness of Murder, especially in his Case, as it was attended by an obstinacy peculiar to himself. For 'him to affirm that to be done by his own, which' cou'd not well be done without two or three pair 'of Hands; what cou'd he propose to himself from 'such a Humour? It cou'd be of no use to his Master and Mistress, when the Circumstances of the Fact 'were so fully prov'd upon them, and they die for it; 'and certainly if there be a hotter place in Hell for 'one more than another, it must be for such a Person, who durst obstinately deny the Truth, and venture his own Damnation upon it—Discourse that had this effect upon him, to fetch Tears from his Eyes, and Groans from his Heart, but no alteration in his Story. I then charged him with another Villainy, even blacker than the Murder it self, if possible, and that was an endeavour to murder the Gentleman's Reputation after he had taken away his Life; for he had industriously spread abroad the Gentleman's attempt to commit Sodomy with him, which was, as he said, the only cause why he fought and slew him; upon which he declared publickly, the Gentleman attempted no such thing, 'twas pure contrivance in him to make his Guilt appear less odious and abominable in the sight of the World, I then ask'd, who put him upon writing that Paper wherein this was contain'd? he protested, as in the presence of Almighty God, it was his own Act and Deed. I then observ'd, that tho' this might be true, yet since he acknowledg'd he had spoken falsely in that, there was great probability he had also spoken falsely in the main Point, and he wou'd do well to consider before too late, and confess that and all his other Sins. This made him particularly to bewail his Intimacies with his Mistress, and to wish likewise that he had a longer time to Consider.

Michael Van Bergen, Condemn'd for the same Murder, could not express himself intelligibly in English, but in Latin. He absolutely denied that the Murder was committed either in his House, or that he knew any thing of it. I put him in mind, that he with his Drawer was seen to come from the Common-shore, where the dead Body lay, betwixt 2 and 3 a Clock that Morning; that he also denied. I then took leave to observe, that he might possibly be there, after his Man had told him of the Murder, being willing, as I suppos'd, to hide the Body, and so conceal the Murder; but this neither could bring him to a Confession, not but that he owned, the Drawer inform'd him, as he lay in his Bed, immediately after the Fact was done, that he had Wounded the Gentleman, and that he did therefore assist him in his Escape upon such a supposal; but when he came to understand this Gentleman was really Murder'd, he declared this with great Confidence, that he then gave Money to persue the Murderer, that he might be made an Example and pay Blood for Blood. Upon this I could not but enquire, where those Persons were, to whom he gave the Money for that purpose? That it was most necessary to have produc'd such Persons, if such there were, and that since such did not appear, it gave a strong Presumption, there had been no such thing done; and that therefore, instead of making his Case better, it render'd it worse. I told him farther, that for my part, I could not conceive why he persisted in his Ignorance of the perpetrated Murder, when the World was satisfied he was Guilty, and he knew he must Die for it, and afterwards undergo the Judgment of that God, who certainly knew the Truth, and would Judge him accordingly. That not to Confess before his Death was no Demonstration of his Innocence, for no doubt but many Guilty Wretches, had taken the same Course in the like Circumstances; and that therefore it behov'd him to Consider, and Confess, before he precluded himself all Hopes of Mercy in the other and better World. This wrought him into Passion and Disdain, and made him ask, whether I would have him confess more than he knew? I reply'd by no means, but it was my Duty doubtless, if I had any value for Souls in his unhappy Condition to lay before them the necessity of Confessing their Guilt, lest their denying it at their Deaths, should oblige the Holy Jesus to deny them at his Judgment. I beseech'd him therefore to Consider, and Confess that and all his other Wickedness; to which he answer'd, he had never done any thing that touch'd his Honour; Your Honour said I, What is the Honour of a sinful Creature? Have you done any thing that has reflected on the Honour of God? That to be sure you have done, and that's what you are to Confess and Bewail; to which I cou'd obtain no other reply than a Discontent, in which he cou'd find no Words, and which indeed shew'd him very uneasie under the Dispensation of a Wife and Holy Providence.

Katherine Truerniet, so her Name was, having never been Married to Van Bergen, with whom she did Cohabit as his Wife : Being Examin'd about this Murder, for which with the others she was Condemn'd; she protested with all the Solemnity imaginable, that it was not committed in their House, nor did she know of it, till after it was done. Then indeed, she confest, that the Drawer came up Stairs, into the Room where she and Van Bergen lay, and declared in the Presence of them both, he had Murder'd the Gentleman. This she said, engag'd her to run for the Hamper, to put the Bloody clothes in, and to farther the Drawer's Escape. A Confession how far soever from Truth, yet gave me occasion to observe to her in the first place, that Van Bergen and she heard the News at the very same time, and for him, he affirmed, that the Drawer spoke only of the Gentleman's being Wounded, whereas she declared, that he spoke of the Gentleman's being Killed. 2dly That by her own Confession, she was guily [sic] of concealing the Murder, knowing the Person who was the Murderer, and at the same time assisting him in his Escape. To which she answered, That for the first her Husband, (as she call'd him) being at that time betwixt sleep and wake, might mistake Wounded for Killed, and for the Second, she did no more than what is customary in Holland. But whether these two Answers were satisfactory, will quickly appear, by considering 1st. That the very Noise of Murder to a Person so nearly concern'd, as Van Bergen was, must needs rouze him quickly out of his Sleep, and make him distinctly hear what was said. And 2dly. That a Topical Custom, if it be one, ought not to stand in competition with the Law of Nature, which obliges every Man to persue him, whom he knows to be a Murderer, and to bring him to condign Punishment. And thus much I remark'd to her, and at the same time charg'd her with the other matters Swore against her at her Tryal. She denied all, but the Business of the Coach and the Hamper; for the one, she said, she did it out of kindness to the Gentleman, for the other, she thought she might give it to the Drawer, it being really none of theirs, but his. I then urged upon her the necessity of Confessing all her other Sins that had justly brought this temporal Judgment upon her. I remark'd the great Wickedness of Co-habiting with a Man without the sacred Tie of Marriage. I took notice of the Intimacy and Familiarities that were said to pass between her and the Drawer, as well as the Master. I laid before her in the last place, a Scheme of those Vices the World charged upon her. For the First she made some scruple about Confession, that being in her Judgment to be made unto God, and not unto Man; but when I had shewn her, that where the Crimes are of a publick Nature, or had given publick Scandal, or where we are challenged with them as our Act and Deed, there we are to confess and deny not; because such a Denial at the Hour of Death, speaks such Persons Guilty of final Impenitence. This made her lament with Tears, her Cohabiting without Marriage, tho' she asserted at the same time, that it was long of her Parents, who would not permit her to Marry him. This made her also not dare to deny absolutely, her Intimat with the Drawer, tho' she fain wou'd have past it over. But for those other Lewdnesses the World generally reports of her; she denied them as she should answer for it at the dreadful Tribunal. I bid her once more to remember, that she was now upon the Brink of Eternity, and that as we cou'd not deny her the means of Salvation, the Blessed Sacrament, upon her desire of it, so she was to take an especial care, that her Confession be true, and her Repentance sincere, that so the receiving of the Sacrament might not prove her Damnation. She seem'd to acquiesce in this, and we must leave the Truth of born to God who judges Righteously.

On Friday the 19th of July, Michael Van Bergen, Katherine Truerniet, and Gerhardt Dromelius, were convey'd to the Place of Execution, where they behav'd themselves with that Meekness and Devotion as became Dying People; Praying unto God, and begging the Prayers of their own Country Ministers, the Ordinary and the rest of the Ministers that were with them. Gerhardt Dromelius being ask'd about the Barbarous Murder for which he suffer'd, persisted in the same Confession as before, and with that turn'd unto the People, and beg'd of them To take Example by him, and avoid Uncleanness, and all wicked Courses, especially violent. Passion, which had brought him to this untimely end. Katherine Truerniet and Michael Van Bergen, were prest severally to Confess the Crime for which they suffer'd Death, but there was no moving them to such an Acknowledgment, tho' they were told it was Swore against them, that he for his part, was seen to come from the Common-shore that very Morning, and that there was some Blood found behind their Door, it was all one, for they wou'd Confess no more, than that they knew of it after it was done. The Woman seem'd to be concern'd for her Reputation after Death; I desir'd her rather to be concern'd for her Soul, for that was the only valuable Consideration, to a Person in her Circumstances. The Man seem'd to be under a Dejection of Spirit, but upon Advice it was the Will of God he should thus suffer for his Wickedness, he took Courage, and gave him the Glory. After suitable Discourses, a Penitential Psalm and Fervent Prayers, their Souls were committed unto God. ■

Sex & Sensibility At the British Museum

David Gaimster[26] reveals the origins and contents of the BM's Secretum, a hidden repository of artefacts deemed pornographic and unfit for public gaze by Victorian curators.

SINCE THE INTRODUCTION of the printing press at the end of the Middle Ages with its ability to replicate the visual image, the dividing line between art and obscenity has been constantly changing. Today we are surrounded by the sexual image, on television, in magazines, on video and on our home PCs. Pornography is becoming an increasingly accepted part of British popular culture and remains the only business that consistently turns a profit on the net. But the political and moral dilemma between access to sexual culture and its regulation has a long heritage in Britain going back to the decades before the drafting of the first obscenity legislation in the mid-nineteenth century.

If museums are a physical metaphor for the way in which the present sees the past, then their collections reflect the cultural and moral attitudes of successive generations of curators in both their choice of artefacts and in the strategies used to classify them. Perhaps it is here that we can best trace the origins of public delicacy towards the erotic and the development of the strict division between art and obscenity. The British Museum 'Secretum' or 'secret museum', founded officially in 1865 in the wake of the Obscene Publications Act (1857), forms a unique laboratory in which to study changing public sensitivities, in particular to the sexual customs of the ancient, Classical and medieval worlds and to the new cultures being encountered through the growth of Empire. Fresh investigation of the Secretum provides a new chronology for the evolution of pornography as a distinct cultural category. The collection presents a historical context for the development of modern manners, and its study helps inform the current political debate.

The classification of antiquity on moral, as opposed to strictly scholarly, grounds can be traced back to early archaeological discoveries at Pompeii and Herculaneum, two flourishing Roman towns in the vicinity of Naples obliterated when Vesuvius erupted in AD 79. When excavations initiated by the Bourbon King Charles of the Two Sicilies in the mid-eighteenth century revealed streets, houses and shops in near-perfect preservation, they provided a snapshot of everyday life in the Roman Empire. But almost as soon as the excavations began, the field notebooks record with ill-concealed embarrassment the discovery of more and more 'obscene items': amulets, lamps, murals and reliefs depicting sex, explicit and often in the style of cari-cature. At first the objects were shown openly to Grand Tour visitors in the Museum Herculanense in Portici. One casualty of the finds was the myth of the austere moral grandeur of the Romans. In 1795 we read for the first time of the existence in the Herculaneum Museum of a room, number XVIII, the first 'secret museum', reserved for 'ob-scene' antiquities which could only be visited by those in possession of a special permit. With its star exhibit, a marble statue of Pan making love to a she-goat, the room represented a new taxonomy for the study of antiquity, that of the 'archaeological obscenity', one that was to be perpetuated across Europe for almost two hundred years.

In February 1819, the heir to the Neapolitan throne, the future Francesco I (1825–30), visited the museum, by then transfered to the Palazzo degli Studi, with his wife and daughter. He suggested that 'it would be a good idea to withdraw all the obscene objects, of whatever mate-rial they may be made, to a private room.' To this room, at first prosaically named the 'Cabinet of Obscene Objects' and in 1823 more coyly the 'Reserved Cabinet', only those people of mature years and sound morals would be ad-mitted. According to a contemporary guidebook, when the collection was first installed it contained 202 'abomi-nable monuments to human licentiousness'. Restricting access inevitably helped to promote the collection. In 1822 only twenty requests for visits were made; two years later these had increased to 300. By 1861, after decades of uncer-tainty, the Museo Borbonico, transformed as the National Museum of Naples, became a central feature of Garib-aldi's Neapolitan cultural policy and provided the writer Alexandre Dumas, as director, with a short introduction to the museum world. Libertarian zeal drove the immedi-ate publication in 1866 of a catalogue of the 'Pornographic Collection', as it was called, compiled by Giuseppe Fiorelli. Despite obvious discomfort in the vocabulary used to de-scribe the artefacts, with its over-reliance on obfuscatory Latin terms, the catalogue's arrangement forms the first nineteenth-century attempt at scientific classification of sexual material culture: the first experiment in the formali-sation of the 'secret museum' as a curatorial concept. The term 'pornography' leapt into English usage as a direct result: Webster's Dictionary of 1864 defined it as 'licen-tious painting employed to decorate the walls of rooms sacred to bacchanalian orgies, examples of which exist in Pompeii.'

Although the nineteenth century invented pornogra-phy, it did not invent the obscene. If sex was to be regarded as something separate from the rest of human experience,

then it was Christianity that effected that divorce, the very act of judgement creating and perpetuating the category of the profane. From the time of Augustine of Hippo (d. AD 430) the Church sought to police sex by private confession and public censure. From the sixteenth-century, sex and the print medium proved a powerful combination, and in the atmosphere of Reformation Europe a potentially subver-sive one. The Roman Catholic Church embarked on a pol-icy of actively destroying prints with erotic scenes, many of which had an explicit satirical dimension. It is this con-text which has produced one of the earliest survivals of the censored image.

The case revolves around a notorious set of sixteen drawings of couples in various sexual positions which were created by the young Italian master Giulio Romano in the early 1520s. Known as 'modi' (the positions), the drawings —a kind of good-sex guide—were first circu-lated privately and then made into engravings by the copyist Marcantonio Raimondi, for public distribution. The Catholic Church responded by judging the images obscene and threw the engraver into jail. Modelled in part on Classical sources, Giulio's drawings represent an early rediscovery of ancient erotic art and became a model for erotica throughout the sixteenth century, legitimised partly by their mythological reference. However, in the in-creasingly censorious atmosphere of the nineteenth cen-tury few examples of the engravings survived. Today only nine fragments of the sixteen original prints are preserved in the Department of Prints and Drawings at the British Museum. Acquired in 1830, the single sheet mounted with the heavily doctored fragments can be traced back to a private English sale of 1812. Looking closely it is possible to see that the censor has laboriously cut out the genitals leaving only heads and flailing limbs, enough to indicate vigorous sexual coupling. In spite of this the fragments were considered too vulgar by the Museum for catalogu-ing with the general collection and were kept in a separate folio in the Departmental Keeper's office. Only recently, after 150 years, has the folio been reunited with the rest of the collections. The explicitness made possible by the detail of the copperplate engraving helps to explain their suppression. The engravings represent some of the earliest examples of pornography as it would be recognised today. Their almost recreational imagery and medium of repro-duction, the print, are entirely modern in concept.

The sensibilities involved in the segregation of the modi engraving's prefigure the rationale behind the cre-ation of a 'Secretum' or 'secret museum' of artefacts in the Department of Antiquities during the early nineteenth century. The Secretum remained in the Department of British and Mediaeval Antiquities following the first subdivision of antiquities departments in 1861 and was transferred during the 1960s to the newly created Department of Medieval and Later Antiquities, where the residue of the collection is now housed. The 'Secretum' register indicates that some antiquities from the ancient Egyptian, Near Eastern and Classical civilisations were segregated from the run of the collections on the basis of their obscene nature as early as the late 1830s, with many more joining them during the 1840s and 50s. Many derive from collections donated by some of the foremost antiquaries of the day including Sir William Hamilton (husband of Nelson's Lady Hamilton), formerly Envoy Extraordinary to the Court of Naples, who donated votive phalluses made of wax from churches in Isernia, near Naples, and Richard Payne Knight, author of *A Discourse on the Worship of Priapus and its Connection with the Mystic Theology of the Ancients*.

The book, a study of customs and artefacts relating to the Roman fertility god, Priapus, was privately printed in London in 1865 by John Camden Ilotton, a publisher of pornography. Ironically, the British Museum, beneficiary of Payne Knight's collecting activities, responded with hostility to the book. Edward Hawkins, Keeper of the Department of Antiquities from 1826 to 1860, represented the official curatorial view and his reaction provides an insight into the evolving moralistic climate in which the Secretum was created:

> Of this work it is impossible to speak in terms of reprobation sufficiently strong: it is a work too gross to mention: and it is quite impossible to quote the indignant but too descriptive language of the critics in their severe but just remarks upon this disgusting production ...

A further highlight of the early years of the collection is the Joseph Nollekens (d. 1823) small-scale terracotta version of Pan copulating with a goat after the myth, which was done from memory by the sculptor having seen the Herculaneum marble original preserved in the Naples Museum during the 1760s. The object belonged at one time to Charles Townley (1737–1805), collector of classical sculpture and one of the chief benefactors to the British Museum during the late eighteenth century. Irrespective of cultural context, artefacts were being segregated on account of their peculiar subject matter in the manner of the 'secret collection' in the Naples Museum. The same approach was applied to the classification of printed books, which were already being assembled into the Private Case of the British Museum Library.

But it was in 1865 that the Museum 'Secretum' took on its official status with the donation by Mr George Witt of 434 diverse objects described as 'Symbols of the Early Worship of Mankind'. It is this collection of antiquities, and its subsequent fate that illustrates more than any other the growing anxieties of Victorian curators in relation to artefacts of an erotic nature. George Witt was born in Norfolk in 1803 or 1804 and entered Leiden University in 1828 to study medicine, graduating in 1830. On his return to England he took up an appointment at the Bedford County Infirmary, soon afterwards becoming Physician to that institution. In 1834 he was elected a Fellow of the Royal Society and Mayor of Bedford. His obituary in the *Bedford Mercury* some years later observes: 'Doctor Witt was at one time as familiar to our town and county as a household word.' In 1849 Witt emigrated to Australia and practised in Sydney for several years before dropping medicine altogether to become a banker. Having amassed a considerable fortune he returned to England in 1854 to take up residence at Prince's Terrace, off Hyde Park. His wealth enabled him to indulge in his taste for collecting antiquities, and it is said that he used to hold Sunday morning lectures on his collection of phallic artefacts. An illness in 1865 forced him to consider the fate of his collection, however, and he wrote to Anthony Panizzi, the Director of the British Museum:

> Dear Sir,
> During my late severe illness it was a source of much regret to me that I had not made such a disposition of my Collection of 'Symbols of the Early Worship of Mankind', as, combined with its due preservation, would have enabled me in some measure to have superintended its arrangement. In accordance with this feeling I now propose to present my Collection to the British Museum, with the hope that some small room may be appointed for its reception in which may also be deposited and arranged the important specimens, already in the vaults of the Museum—and elsewhere, which are illustrative of the same subject.

The Museum's Trustees, perhaps surprisingly, accepted the gift. Although divorced from their cultural context, the artefacts were of sufficient archaeological merit to justify acquisition. Of particular note is the scope of the collection, which covers all the principal ancient and Classical cultures as well as the medieval and Renaissance worlds and contemporary cultures from the colonial sphere. Key objects include Greek Figure vases, Egyptian sculpture, Roman terracottas and bronzes, Indian temple reliefs, medieval pilgrim badges, the insignia of eighteenth-century secret societies, watercolours of early discoveries from the ancient and Classical worlds. Of particular interest are the nine leather-bound scrapbooks arranged loosely by culture: Grecian, Etruscan, Roman; Persian, Egyptian; Indian, Tibetan, Chinese, Japanese; aborignial [*sic*] American; and modern European. Compiled over many years, they contain sketches, watercolours, pioneer photographs and descriptions of objects held in both public and private collections. Most intriguing is the correspondence with fellow collectors of phallic objects from Britain and Europe who sent Witt descriptions of further finds. Witt was clearly the centre of an international nexus of collectors of antique erotica. Like him they were all gentlemen of means and taste who would have considered themselves capable of responding in a detached, scholarly way to the subject matter. Looking through the scrapbooks, however, one can sense a certain erotic tension which is more difficult to interpret. Among the engravings of Roman bronzes and pottery lamps are eighteenth-century sketches of copulating couples, nineteenth-century Japanese colour porn cards, a Victorian reproduction of a medieval chastity-belt, early photographs of nudes in classical poses (including scantily clad females engaged in gladiatorial combat) and a Victorian cartoon showing a version of the Ages of Man which would today qualify as paedophile in character. In this shadowy area, where archaeology and the erotic meet, lies the key to Witt's motivation for collecting.

Witt's interest in the antique was almost entirely phallocentric, his thesis being that all pre-Christian cultures across the globe shared a common religious heritage in their worship of fertility gods and goddesses. This interest is reflected in his research library which accompanied the collection to the Museum. Personally monogrammed books include *Des Divinites Generatrices ou du Culte du Phallus*, published in Paris in 1805, Payne Knight's *Discourse*, (London, 1865), a catalogue of the Secret Cabinet of the Naples Museum (Paris, 1857) and M. Felix Lajard's book on the *Cult, Symbols and Attributes of Venus* (Paris, 1837). Entwined with Witt's obsession was a desire for scholarly recognition for his area of research. To mark the acceptance of his collection Witt presented to the Museum a pamphlet, published by himself, entitled *Catalogue of a Collection Illustrative of Phallic Worship* in 1866. What could be more respectable than official acceptance by the British Museum?

The Witt collection reveals a degree of the trauma experienced by Victorians in their encounter with the antique and cultures from the further reaches of the British Empire.

The Classical world was regarded as a model for nineteenth-century European civilisation, its architecture and art a blueprint of decency, taste and cultural aspiration. Its empires were a historical reference and motivation for imperial expansion. The British Museum and other metropolitan public buildings were based on strictly Classical conventions of style and proportion. What then of the discovery at the Vesuvian cities that private life in the Greek and Roman world was also a very public experience? Just as we are today, the citizens of Pompeii were surrounded by images of sex, on tavern signs, street corners and in the domestic interior. As the Classical art scholar John R. Clarke has noted, 'Here was a world before Christianity, before the Puritan ethic, before the association of shame and guilt with sexual acts.' Revealing their own prejudices, the early excavators reasoned that the erotic murals and artefacts could only derive from brothels. The finds confirmed the realisation—already clear from the literary sources—that the antique world was characterised by a quite different social and moral code from that of nineteenth-century Europe with its increasing onus on privacy and manners. Similar problems afflicted imperial Britain's encounter with the indigenous cultures of its colonies in India and the Far East. Here, in its monumental religious art, particularly its temple reliefs, heaven was depicted as a highly sexualised place, whereas the Victorian celestial vision—with its strong Judeo-Christian legacy—was entirely chaste in character. The only strategy, therefore, was to suppress the past, hide away the artefacts which might be misunderstood by all but the most educated of intellect who could be trusted to respond appropriately. This was, essentially, the rationale for the secret museum.

Following the line of the recently passed Obscene Publications Act, the formal foundation of the Secretum in 1865 enshrined a new code for cultural consumption: that what gentlemen chose to look at was a matter of taste, but that there must be regulations to control the circulation of images or erotic objects among the more vulnerable sections of society. The division along gender lines in particular belies more deep-seated fears held by the British (male) establishment, namely a quasi-Darwinian view that if women or children were exposed to pornography, and even to the sexual material culture of the past, it might provoke an imbalance in the relationships between men and women and hence a breakdown in the social order. Female sexual pleasure threatened not only the security of marriage and legitimacy, but also the security of men themselves and their own identity. Victorian Britain, it must be remembered, read Edward Gibbon's *Decline and*

Fall of the Roman Empire (1776–88) as a cautionary tale. It contained the equation that sexual excess equals general degeneracy which leads invariably to economic and social collapse. Class prejudice formed a further layer of anxiety. The first obscenity laws were part inspired by fear of the reaction of the working masses to cheap pornography. The 'casual' nature of the sex lives of the poor was already the object of a moral crusade by Victorian reformists. If archaeological discoveries or ethnographic collecting did contain an erotic element, then best to suppress it from those who would be incapable of understanding it. This paternalistic view involved removing artefacts from their original contexts and grouping them under the new and artificial heading of the 'obscene'. Ironically, it is this curatorial strategy of compartmentalisation that survived almost intact until the latter part of the twentieth century.

It was not until the inter-war period that attitudes in the British Museum became more liberal, and in 1939 the Trustees were informed that part of Witt's 'phallic and allied antiquities and works relating to primitive mysteries' were partially dispersed. Nevertheless, a considerable amount of the original donation remained in the Secretum, and in 1948 the Keeper ruled that anyone wishing to consult the collection was required to submit a formal application to the director of the Museum. The same year an outside scholar applied for a photographic copy of the register of the collection. His request was regarded as so sensitive that he was asked to state 'his qualifications for the study of the catalogue, the use he proposed to make of the photostats, and the arrangements made for the disposal thereof at his death'. Although there was further dispersal from the Secretum before the Second World War, new objects continued to be added. The last items were deposited in 1953. These were a group of animal membrane condoms, tied at the open end with silk ribbons, which can be dated by their original paper wrapper to the late eighteenth-early nineteenth centuries. They were discovered hidden in the pages of a book in the British Library, a 1783 *Guide to Health, Beauty, Riches and Honour*. Following the more permissive 1960s further Egyptian, Greek, Roman and Oriental material was dispersed.

Today around half of Witt's 1865 gift of 434 objects and around 100 of the 700 or so items of the pre-1865 Secretum remain together in the Department of Medieval and Later Antiquities. Despite the modern view that obscenity is not a scholarly category but a moral one, and that the continued orphaning of these artefacts from their host cultures can only diminish their research value, there is growing realisation that the collection is of greater value

today as a time capsule of Victorian collecting interest in sexual material culture. It is not intended to break up the Secretum any further.

The challenge remains, however, to explain the context in which these objects were made and appreciated in the past. Explication forms the motivation behind the BM's purchase in 1999 of the Warren Cup, a Roman silver drinking vessel decorated with scenes of homosexual love-making, probably made during the reign of Nero (AD 54-68). Had the Museum purchased the cup when it came up for sale in the 1950s, when homosexuality was still illegal in Britain, it would almost certainly have caused an outcry. Today, in contrast, the new acquisition stands in the centre of the Wolfson Gallery of Roman Antiquities (Room 70).

The cup, along with other objects and murals showing similar scenes, enables us to see, as opposed to read about, the dramatisation of sexual conventions and transgressions from the Hellenistic period onwards. Its acquisition and prominent position in the Museum galleries highlights the contrast in the response of previous generations to the erotic artefact. Today the emphasis is on illuminating the social and mental context for the representation of sex in antiquity. For the Victorians this was not an option. The Secretum is a product of its time, place and culture. It is a historical artefact in its own right, but also serves as a warning to future generations of historians against imposing their own contemporary prejudices on the material culture of the past. ∎

Endnotes

1. Patrick Joyce, "History and Post-Modernism I," *Past and Present* No. 133 (November 1991): 208–209.

2. Andrew Clements, *Frindle* (New York: Simon & Schuster, 1996).

3. Ferdinand de Saussure, *Course in General Linguistics* (Chicago: Open Court Publishing, 1983), 86, 126–127.

4. Paul Cobley and Litza Jansz, *Introducing Semiotics* (London: Icon Books, 1997), 15.

5. Claude Lévi-Strauss, *Myth and Meaning* (London: Routledge and Kegan Paul, 1978), 6.

6. Simon Choat, *Marx through Post-Structuralism: Lyotard, Derrida, Foucault, Deleuze* (New York: Continuum Press, 2010).

7. "Human Nature: Justice versus Power: Noam Chomsky Debates with Michel Foucault, 1971," *Chomsky.info: the Noam Chomsky Website*, last accessed September 7, 2013, http://www.chomsky.info/debates/1971xxxx.htm.

8. An excellent discussion of discourse is in Joan W. Scott, "Deconstructing Equality-Versus-Difference: Or, the Uses of Poststructuralist Theory for Feminism," in *Theorizing Feminism: Parallel Trends in the Humanities and Social Sciences*, 2nd ed., Anne C. Herrmann and Abigail J. Stewart, eds. (Boulder, CO: Westview Press, 2001), 256.

9. Michel Foucault, *The History of Sexuality: An Introduction, Volume 1* (New York: Vintage Books, 1990), 77–80.

10. Michel Foucault, *Discipline and Punish: The Birth of the Prison* (New York: Pantheon Books, 1978).

11. Michel Foucault, *The History of Sexuality: An Introduction, Volume 1*, 25, 140.

12. Jeremy Bentham, *Panopticon, or the Inspection House, &c. &c.* (London, 1791), 139–140.

13. Michel Foucault, *The History of Sexuality: An Introduction, Volume 1*, 41–47.

14. Foucault, *The History of Sexuality: An Introduction, Volume 1*, 101.

15. Foucault, *The History of Sexuality: An Introduction, Volume 1*, 92–95.

16. Tom Colicchio, "Deconstruction Junction, What's Your Function?" BravoTV.com: *Top Chef*, posted September 23, 2009, http://www.bravotv.com/top-chef/blogs/tom-colicchio/deconstruction-junction-what-s-your-function.

17. Michel Foucault, *The Order of Things: An Archaeology of the Human Sciences* (New York: Vintage Books, 1970), 79.

18. Jacques Derrida, *Of Grammatology*, trans. Gayatri Chakravorty Spivak (Baltimore: Johns Hopkins University Press, 1997), 158. For a Derrida's explanation of difference/différance discussed in this section, please refer to Jacques Derrida, "Différance," in *Margins of Philosophy*, trans. Alan Bass (Chicago: University of Chicago Press, 1982), 1–27.

19. Jacques Derrida, "Hospitality," Lectures at University of California, Irvine, Spring 1996; See also his *Of Hospitality* (Stanford: Stanford University Press, 2000) based on his lectures given both at Paris and Irvine in early 1996.

20. Lawrence Stone, "Notes: History and Postmodernism," *Past and Present* No. 131 (1991): 217–218.

21. Jürgen Habermas, "Modernity versus Postmodernity," trans. Seyla Ben-Habib, *New German Critique* No. 22 Special Issue on Modernism (Winter 1981), 10.

22. Habermas, "Modernity versus Postmodernity," 13–14.

23. Foucault, *The History of Sexuality: An Introduction, Volume 1*, 69.

24. Michael Ignatieff, *A Just Measure of Pain: The Penitentiary in the Industrial Revolution, 1750–1850* (New York: Pantheon Books, 1978).

25. Old Bailey Proceedings Online (www.oldbaileyonline.org, version 7.0, 03 July 2013), Ordinary of Newgate's Account, July 1700 (OA17000719).

26. David Gaimster, "Sex and Sensibility at the British Museum," *History Today* 50/9 (2000): 10–15.

CHAPTER 8

CULTURAL HISTORY

CHAPTER OUTLINE

■ Interdisciplinary Origins

■ Early Historical Studies of Culture

■ The 'Linguistic Turn'

■ Defining the History of Culture—
  Some Conclusions

■ Thinking Like a Historian

"Culture is a particular way of life which expresses certain meanings and values not only in art and learning, but also in institutions and ordinary behavior."

Raymond Williams[1]

Cultural history has very deep historical and interdisciplinary roots. As you could probably discern from earlier chapters, there are elements of culture in even the most material of histories. Because it finds influence in many different approaches and yet is also its own field, cultural history, as a fully articulated historical theory is often difficult to define, in part because the very notion of culture is, in the words of E.P. Thompson, "clumpish."[2] Before we explore cultural history on its own terms, we need to explain its long lineage by revisiting some points we have explored earlier in this text, namely, postmodernism, the New Left, and the *Annales* School. First, however, we will discuss some of the roots of cultural history outside the discipline.

INTERDISCIPLINARY ORIGINS

Cultural history borrows from anthropology, linguistics, and the New Historicist movement in literary theory. Its anthropological influence stems from the field of cultural anthropology, popularized by Clifford Geertz (1926–2006), Marshall Sahlins (b. 1930), and Pierre Bourdieu (1930–2002). Geertz, a World War II veteran with a Ph.D. from Harvard, was very early interested in understanding the meanings behind local customs and traditions in various cultures. From early in his career, Geertz disagreed with Claude Lévi-Strauss in the ways in which anthropologists examine culture. As you read in Chapter 7, Lévi-Strauss, as a structuralist, was not interested in change over time with cultures, but rather in the system of cultures themselves. Geertz, however, was interested in the social processes that enabled cultural systems to operate. In *The Interpretation of Cultures*, Geertz lays out a framework for exploring meaning within societies. He explores the difference between "thick" and "thin" description as the difference between reporting an action and reporting the meaning of the action. Using the example of the wink, Geertz explains that to truly understand a culture, you must move beyond the surface. Only then can you truly describe a culture and its values. There is a difference, he argues, between merely describing the physical action of the wink (thin description) and explaining the meaning behind it such as a parody, a knowing statement to another, or merely an unintended tick (**thick description**). The structuralist system does not facilitate this deep level of understanding.[3] This method is put into practice in his work on the Balinese cockfight, an ethnography meant as a means to get inside the culture of Bali while at the same time providing explanation of cultural practices.[4] The cockfight, argues Geertz, can be read as a metaphor for human relations, a symbol of human psychology, and a microcosm of everyday life. Through the study of leisure, we can better understand a culture. For Geertz, we can generalize from the specific, that is, we can take his method of thick description and its practical application in the Balinese cockfight and apply it to other cultures and other cultural institutions. Baseball in America, cricket in India, soccer in Brazil—sport and leisure can provide the anthropologist a window into a society. While the specific meanings cannot be generalizable outside a particular culture, as one must be inside culture to partake in its larger meaning, the methods of obtaining that meaning are universal. Thus, the Balinese cockfight's internal dynamic is a reference point of experience for Balinese men. According to Geertz, "culture of a people is an ensemble of texts" and therefore "in the cockfight . . . the Balinese forms and discovers his temperament and his society's temper at the same time. Or more exactly, he forms and discovers a particular facet of them."[5]

For his part, the prominent American anthropologist Marshall Sahlins began his career as a structuralist, or at least trained in the ambience of structuralism. Sahlins graduated from Columbia in 1954 and serves as professor emeritus at the University of Chicago. His work very specifically explores the intersection of cultural practices and historical development, challenging Marxist models of economic society used to explain premodern cultures. His individual work centered on Pacific societies such as Fiji, but it is his masterful monograph *Culture and Practical Reason* (1976) that established the view that human culture shapes human perception and consequently experiences. This hypothesis has had profound implications for historical thought. Sahlins argues that

we must recognize a certain relativity to human cultural experiences, and imposing a sameness to the varieties of rational thought present in human communities at different stages of development in different places and times merely reinforces a Eurocentric belief. Further, *Culture and Practical Reason* sets forth difficulties with maintaining a materialist outlook—specifically in the dual forms of Marxism and Structuralism—arguing that "cultures are meaningful orders of persons and things" and "since these orders are systemic, they cannot be free inventions of the mind."[6] In the book, Sahlins details the distinctions between materialism and culture and argues in favor of a more nuanced understanding of materialism. Symbols, according to Sahlins, are central to anthropological study. In creating the distinction between materialism and culture, Sahlins did not ignore the existence of material elements in society. Rather, he examined that these material productions (what Marx referred to as modes of production if you recall from Chapter 3) are produced in fundamentally different ways depending on one's contextual position. So material production proceeds from cultural—and thus produces another concept—that of "use-value." Once we get to the point of use-value, we can explore material goods and possessions in ways that unpack larger social meanings. According to Sahlins, no material thing, no tangible item, has or can have meaning outside of human culture. Humans give things their meanings. The example provided by Sahlins is the role of pants and skirts as distinctly male and female commodities. There is no natural essence of pants that make them a strictly male domain. Society dictated that the pants were signified as masculine articles.[7] Sahlins, then, takes Marxist assumptions of bourgeois society and argues that it has its own fields of cultural production.

Pierre Bourdieu was an interdisciplinary scholar. Born into a French upwardly mobile working-class family, he studied philosophy and entered the teaching profession. In 1955, he was conscripted into the French army, and despite his political opposition, he was stationed in Algeria in the midst of the Algerian war. After his required tenure in the military was over and he returned to France, he continued teaching, but turned instead to the "harder" social sciences—anthropology and sociology. For most of his career, he was a sociology professor at *Collège de France* and then director of the *Centre de Sociologie*. Bourdieu's work represents a synthesis in critical theory, using the combined methods of sociology and anthropology. His influence on the field of anthropology was such that he received the Huxley Medal from the Royal Anthropological Institute in 2001. In his work, Bourdieu articulated a disdain for the binary oppositions that are often set up in various disciplines (such as between the macro and the micro).

Bourdieu's longstanding work on **habitus** and cultural capital have been central influences on cultural history, just as Sahlins' work on culturally infused material structures and Geertz's work on thick description. Taken from ancient texts, *habitus* is a concept that underwent much revision in Bourdieu's work. In its most distilled form, *habitus* reflects the kinds of behaviors, attitudes, and posturings that we often consider to be natural affectations but are in fact cultural constructions. So, everything that makes up a person—mannerisms, speech inflection, what have you—constitutes *habitus* and therefore, according to Bourdieu, is only meaningful within a community of actors, much like Geertz's wink or Sahlins' pants.

This is not to say that Bourdieu neglected the material world. In fact, Bourdieu worked to reconcile the cultural framework of society with the material structures surrounding it. *Habitus* stems from Bourdieu's other major concept of cultural production and cultural capital. While there is a cultural production to *habitus*, the resulting **cultural capital** has very material consequences for people in societies. One obtains cultural capital through involvement in the arts and other "extracurricular" activities. Like economic capital, cultural capital is a form of wealth that one can accumulate and spend. Those who lack material resources—that is, members of the working class—have less access to such extracurricular opportunities and therefore acquire less cultural capital, resulting in less ability to be socially mobile. In this way, according to Bourdieu, the "ruling class" maintains a monopoly on its educational and ultimately economic and political institutions while maintaining a guise of equal access.[8]

A second major influence on cultural history is linguistics and language. In Chapter 7, you read about post-structuralism and deconstruction and the ways in which they worked to complicate the binary oppositions inherent in the Saussurean system. This system emphasized a science or an "objectivity" of sorts found in language. For structuralists, there was no relativity but an underlying structure even in languages from different language groups.

Many scholars believed that this kind of totalizing narrative was problematic and felt the need to move beyond structuralism and its connections to modernity. Postmodernists rejected the comprehensiveness of structuralism in part by seeking not the meaning, but a plurality of meanings. This philosophy quickly became popular within the field of literary criticism and ultimately cultural history as a field of study. We discuss this influence in more detail when we examine the linguistic turn later in the chapter.

A third major influence on cultural history was the New Historicism movement in literary theory. Led by Stephen Greenblatt, the New Historicists combined the study of texts with historical explanation. While literary scholars in the early part of the twentieth century also looked at historical context, the "new" historicists examined this context and the text with the influence of both cultural Marxism and post-structuralism. In particular, New Historicists examine the specific context of a work with the full knowledge that even with the context the text may not be wholly transparent. Greenblatt's work on the Renaissance, for example, explores the interrelationship between the historical actors and the literature of the period. Though New Historicism has been critiqued both within and without literary theory (particularly by historians) for too readily accepting the reality of literary **tropes**, the field nevertheless reawakened scholars to the importance of context in literature. Further, it reawakened many historians to the importance of literature and art as valid primary sources.

EARLY HISTORICAL STUDIES OF CULTURE

But there are plenty of influences within the discipline of history, too. When you read about the *Annales* School, you learned about the fourth generation, a group that focused on *mentalités*. This was a very conscious move away from the big history of the second generation and the number crunching of the third generation. *Mentalités* was a process through which historians could explore the attitudes, values, and beliefs of a particular society in the past. As you read in Chapter 4, the fourth generation took a snippet of the many ideas from Marc Bloch and Lucien Febvre and focused on it. While Bloch and Febvre wanted to find a snapshot of society to create a "total history," their stories remained committed to larger social structures and little space was left for *mentalités*. The fourth generation, then, led by Roger Chartier and Jacques Revel, focused on representation. Chartier's work is explored more fully in Chapter 4 in relation to the fourth generation of the *Annales* School. Clearly, these historical theories cross boundaries and are not hermetically sealed within one particular school of thought.

Just previous to the rise of the fourth generation of the *Annales*, many historians of the New Left saw the importance of culture in explaining the social relations of people of the past. Historians such as Eric Hobsbawm and E.P. Thompson (discussed in Chapters 3 and 5) routinely infused their histories of class struggle with the attitudes of their historical subjects. When you read about the New Left, we explored some of the movement toward less material ways of thinking about Marx and exploitive relations. The focus on history from below, for example, was a move to explore a group within society on its own terms. In Chapter 5, we discussed the works of early Frankfurt School scholar Theodore Adorno and how his work energized a generation of new scholars in the 1960s. While Adorno and his intellectual partner Max Horkheimer explored culture as interconnected with social control and mass media, a contemporary colleague, Walter Benjamin (1892–1940), put forth a very different hypothesis. In his masterful essay "Art in the Age of Mechanical Reproduction," Benjamin conceded that art could certainly be used and manipulated. However, he also argued that mechanical reproduction, by disrupting the control of high art, created a more democratic relationship to art. Because the "masses" could now consume art in ways they could not with museums, high art declined and popular culture rose. Writing in the 1920s and 1930s, at the height of Nazi and Fascist control of the media in Germany and Italy, Benjamin put forth a philosophy of popular culture that was truly revolutionary in its possibilities.[9]

As evidence of this turn to culture with the emergence of the New Left, scholars such as Raymond Williams, Richard Hoggart, and E.P. Thompson helped to found the Birmingham Centre for Contemporary Cultural Studies (CCCS) in 1963, with Hoggart serving as its first director. The Centre remained popular with students but was forcefully closed and redirected to social sciences by the administration in 2002, citing administrative "restructuring." During its tenure, however, CCCS became known more generally as the "Birmingham School"—a school of thought that emphasized a combination of popular culture, media studies, and sociology. While there are debates about whether the phrase "cultural studies" was founded at Birmingham, the fact remains that the Centre did much to popularize this course of study. The Birmingham School, combined with the ideas from the Frankfurt School and Walter Benjamin, both influenced and emanated from the New Lefts of the 1960s. The Birmingham School's founders were already well versed in cultural analysis by 1963. You read extensively about E.P. Thompson earlier. But the other scholars, even though not historians, did much to influence the trajectory of cultural history.

While a tremendous influence on cultural studies, the Birmingham School and "cultural studies" more generally has faced some critiques among historians, notably because it is assumed that "cultural studies all too often simply reverses the plus and minus signs in the name of transgression and subversion." That is, cultural studies is said to not work through issues of binary oppositions, but seemingly remains content only to claim that "all the ills of the world are blamed on modernity and Eurocentrism." In addition, the Birmingham School is often lumped with nonhistorical literary traditions and their emphasis on postmodernism.[10] However, both of these claims are imprecise as you will see in the work of the three primary leaders of cultural studies—Raymond Williams, Richard Hoggart, and Stuart Hall. Each of these scholars sought to explain the past on its own terms, not explain a progression from past to present.

Richard Hoggart was born into a working-class family in Leeds in North England, was orphaned at a very young age, and raised by a strict grandmother. He managed to secure a scholarship to university in Leeds and was sometimes known as "that scholarship boy," a phrase he said was designed to bully him for not having wealth or status.[11] Like so many others of his generation, he fought in World War II, serving in North Africa until the year after the war ended. When he returned, he finished school and began working in adult education. Hoggart's influence began with his 1957 classic *The Uses of Literacy*. In that monograph, Hoggart bemoaned the loss of class identity into an increasingly homogeneous consumer culture. Looking at popular consumer products—magazines in particular—Hoggart traced the transformation in post–World War II society to a consumer culture that transcended—or rather effaced—class. Like Marcuse, Hoggart argued that this shift undermined both local and class identities in favor of the uniformity of information. Mass culture created a faceless consumer no longer aware of its own meaning. The working class, Hoggart further argued, wanted more in terms of education and culture than was being offered but was taught to neglect its own interests in favor of this new consumer world.[12]

A second leader of the Birmingham School is Raymond Williams (1921–1988). You read about Williams' working-class background in Chapter 5, and this background heavily informed his scholarly interests. Born in Wales, the son of a railroad worker eventually went to Cambridge University, joined the Communist Party, and dropped out of college to join the Allied fight against Hitler in World War II. After the war, he returned to Cambridge, began teaching adult education, and started his writing career. Later in life, he returned to Wales as a Welsh nationalist. Throughout his life, Williams infused his narratives of popular culture with a sophisticated understanding of social relations. He coined the term **cultural materialism** in the early 1970s as a reference to his use of cultural analysis blended with Marxist analysis. According to one of Williams' students, the literary scholar Terry Eagleton, Williams' cultural materialism, "was a way of bringing an unashamedly materialist analysis to bear on that realm of social existence—'culture'—which was thought by conventional criticism to be the very antithesis of the material."[13]

Raymond Williams explored cultural materialism in part through the use of the concepts of dominant culture, emergent culture, and residual culture. Williams used the terms "emergent" and "residual" to speak of what he termed "oppositional cultures" to the dominant. Simply put, an emergent culture is one that adopts meanings and values different from and sometimes antithetical to the dominant culture, whereas the residual cultures and values are an echo of "some previous social formation."[14] The residual culture, no longer dominant, is often described as *passé* or perhaps old fashioned, but it still has a life within the current culture. These two cultures then, both outside of the main, compete with each other and put pressure on the dominant culture—that "central system of practices, meanings, and values."[15] In this way, Williams took the Gramscian notion of hegemony and injected it into the heart of social life—hegemony according to Williams is not simply overt power, but culture that is "organized and lived." Williams provides a new interpretation of the Marxist construct of base/superstructure and argues that culture is central, in part because we cannot look at "the base" as a fixed stable entity, but rather as a process. And as it is a process, we cannot simply look at the superstructure as a fixed complement that is merely acted upon by the base. It too can be seen as a process. So Williams moved away

from older, totalizing narratives that emphasized a teleology. Writing from this Marxian perspective clearly influenced by Antonio Gramsci and contemporaneous to Herbert Marcuse, Williams, like postmodernists writing at roughly the same time, critiques the framing of a fixed principle to better understand not just the literature he was trained to study, but social relations themselves.

Even earlier, Williams had begun to critique the assumption that culture somehow rested on the foundation of a politico-economic base. In his pathbreaking and highly personal 1958 essay "Culture is Ordinary," Williams talked about his life in Wales, his new world at Cambridge, and the quotidian forces at work in his thoughts:

> Culture is ordinary; that is the first fact. Every human society has its own shape, its own purposes, its own meanings. The making of a society is the finding of common meanings and directions . . . The questions I ask about our culture are questions about our general and common purposes, yet also questions about deep personal meanings. Culture is ordinary, in every society, in every mind.[16]

Stuart Hall (1932–) was the second director of the CCCS. Before taking this position, he served as the founding editor of *New Left Review*. Born in the Caribbean to a middle-class family, Hall moved to the United Kingdom while still a student as a Rhodes scholar. Once in England, he established a number of intellectual partnerships and friendships, including his longstanding relationships with Hoggart and Williams. In his position as editor of *New Left Review*, he opened the conversation regarding immigration and race relations, as immigration increasingly faced numerous restrictive laws in the 1960s.[17] When he moved to Birmingham to work with Hoggart, they tried to create a new kind of interdisciplinary framework and were literally marginalized by the institution (as they were housed in a series of portable structures through the 1960s, well away from the halls of specific disciplines). During that time, Hall states, "It was never a question of which disciplines would contribute to the development of this field, but of how one could decenter or destabilize a series of interdisciplinary fields. We had to respect and engage with the paradigms and traditions of knowledge and of empirical and concrete work in each of these disciplinary areas in order to construct what we called cultural studies or cultural theory."[18] And this required taking the kinds of intellectual risks that dared other disciplines to be something more than they were.

Hall's work focuses much attention, like Hoggart's, on mass media. But he has also done quite important work on youth culture and racial identity. Like Williams, he argues that culture cannot be divorced from society. In a recent interview, talking about his family life, he said that his personal narrative "is one of the reasons I have never been able to write about or think about the individual separate from society. The individual is always living some larger narrative whether he or she likes it or not."[19] For Hall, central to the work of cultural studies is the ability to navigate both mass media and visual culture. Specifically, he is interested in the construction and maintenance of subcultures, and how they are examined through the lens of the mass media. He explores this toggling between two realms in his edited volume *Resistance through Rituals*, a series of histories of subculture in Britain through an explanation of youth culture from the 1950s through the 1980s. In defining youth culture, Hall borrows from Thompson and states that "culture is the way, the forms, in which groups 'handle' the raw material of their social and material existence, and which includes the 'maps of meaning' which make things intelligible to its members."[20]

THE 'LINGUISTIC TURN'

The focus on language and cultural representation in context combined with the interdisciplinarity of historical works is known as "the **linguistic turn**." According to Stuart Hall, "Questions of culture and cultural change lay at the very heart of social life and could not be refused, that the issues of language were central to the understanding of the national culture and that any serious scholar must be engaged in the question of the nature of language and what it is saying."[21]

As with many other influences on cultural history, the linguistic turn began outside the field—in philosophy to be precise. It has a deep lineage into the nineteenth century as Richard Rorty, author of the 1967 book *The Linguistic Turn* notes. The linguistic turn is also often defined in dense philosophical terms and linked specifically to scholars such as Derrida.[22] But for historians, the linguistic turn has a very practical application. Yes, along with philosophy, linguistics, and literary theory, history as a field saw a new focus on language and cultural representation. However, for the most part, historians saw this turn toward language as a way

to understand the meanings imparted by people of the past, not as a primary determinant of the reality of the past. In other words, while influenced by the postmodern scholars discussed in Chapter 7, historians (for the most part) did not believe that "there is nothing outside the text." Historians who embraced the linguistic turn accomplished a turn toward the recognition that sources are not transparent windows into the past and that, like anthropologists, they need to jump into the culture under observation. As Lynn Hunt stated, "Historians do not have to ally themselves single-mindedly with either Clifford Geertz or Pierre Bourdieu, with either Northrop Frye or Jacques Derrida."[23]

As German historian Kathleen Canning has argued, the "linguistic turn" has become something of a catch-all for anything that even moderately critiques purely empirical or materialist history. Canning continues by stating that most historians note the linguistic turn in terms of the influence of Foucault, Derrida, and/or Lacan.[24] This reference to other disciplines, especially those rooted in literary theory, has raised alarm bells among more traditional historians. A very famous exchange between more "traditional" historians and historians influenced by the linguistic turn occurred in the journal *Past and Present* in the early 1990s. In that exchange, acclaimed social historian Lawrence Stone exclaimed that there were three threats to the discipline of history—New Historicism, linguistics, and cultural anthropology (which, by the way, we discussed earlier as having profound influence on cultural history)—which brought the discipline "seriously into question."[25] This provoked a response from two historians, Patrick Joyce and Catriona Kelly, that the linguistic turn did not neglect "the real," but rather, like postmodernism, hoped to throw into doubt grand narratives but not, "advocating the sort of over-assimilative relativism criticized by" others.[26]

Stone's argument made it seem as if the "linguistic turn" was something brand new in the 1990s, but as you may have noted in earlier chapters, language, how people describe themselves, began to inch into materialist thought early in the 1960s. In fact, as discussed in Chapter 7, poststructural theory itself built on already extant frameworks. And as discussed earlier, cultural studies had been at work challenging particular disciplinary structures by focusing on marginal characters in marginal spaces since the early 1960s.

One early historian interested in this linguistic turn was Gareth Stedman Jones (1942–). Stedman Jones received his D.Phil from Oxford and is currently Professor of Political Science and History at Cambridge University. From 1964 to 1981, he was an editor of *New Left Review* and was a founder of *History Workshop Journal*, a journal aimed at a popular audience and devoted to the discussion of history and its methods. Stedman Jones was trained in the Marxist intellectual tradition, but early on, he began having concerns about it. As early as 1974, Stedman Jones explored the shifting language embedded in class relations, and how workers adopted the language and discourse of the bourgeoisie. Exploring working-class politics, Stedman Jones argued that the central point of reference, however, should be the centrality of language. In a complex study of working-class life as seen through housing, marriage, charity, and music hall melodramas, Stedman Jones makes the case that the working class was impervious to any calls to change it from the outside (by middle-class reformers). To understand this cultural insularity, Stedman Jones argues that the two different worlds of middle-class reformer and working-class man must be studied relationally. This emphasis on relations and comparisons moves beyond older ideas of "history from below."[27]

Another major scholar of early cultural history is Lynn Hunt (1945–). A French historian, Hunt also writes about how theory operates in historical practice, in particular the cultural history of the French Revolution. Trained at Stanford, Hunt has taught in France, Beijing, Berkeley, and Los Angeles. Her work on the revolutionary politics of late eighteenth-century France infused the traditional stories of the French Revolution with an approach that took the *mentalités* of the period seriously. One of the goals of her early work on the French Revolution was to challenge the stodgy, top-down analysis or the rigid class analysis so characteristic of older histories. In *Politics, Culture, and Class in the French Revolution*, Hunt redefined the political to examine the intersection between seemingly political goals—change in the structural makeup of the French State—and cultural goals—the lives of the people who envisaged such change. To underscore the cultural framework of this politics, Hunt began with an examination of political clubs that catered to a predominantly urban population, then expanded her analysis to the structures of everyday life (to borrow a phrase from Braudel)—costumes and holidays, among other things. Together, these things facilitated a new political culture that differed remarkably from the beginning to the end of the 1790s.[28]

Finally, a historian who took an extreme micro-history approach to *mentalités* and culture was Carlo Ginzburg (1939–). In *The Cheese and the Worms*, Ginzburg plumbs the detailed records of the Inquisition courts to discover the life and beliefs of Menocchio, a sixteenth-century Italian miller who held some rather heretical beliefs. But for Ginzburg, that is merely a jumping-off point, as he connects the lives of those who testified in favor of, and against, Menocchio, to invoke the social relationships in which the miller expounded his ideas. Finally, Ginzburg provides in-depth reading of heretical literature of the era as he attempts to trace the complex nature of Menocchio's cosmology (which included a belief that, unlike biblical stories of creation, the world had actually been formed as a large mass, like cheese, that had been aerated by angels that took the form of worms, thus the title of the book). Not finding any such stories in the heretical literature of the day, Ginzburg argued that Menocchio's story of Genesis was likely the residue of a lost set of folk beliefs, a common culture that the Inquisition aimed to crush. Ginzburg readily accepts that an alternate reading of the sources could be that Menocchio was unhinged and his ideas idiosyncratic. But the possibility of bringing techniques of historical investigation to bear on an individual, and along the way hinting at a lost world of thought, is tantalizing.[29]

Defining the History of Culture—Some Conclusions

A key element of cultural history is that there is no "objective" knowledge—it is all mediated. If there is no objective knowledge, then texts are not transparent and there is no unmediated truth. We cannot take documents at face value. We need to understand the conditions under which they were written. In addition, cultural history as a field does not accept that economics is the foundation (base) on which all else is built. According to Lynn Hunt, culture is not subordinate to economics, but rather economic and social relations are themselves cultural practices—they are not "objective," "material" reality.[30]

Cultural historians have learned to search for alternative sources of evidence. Much of this work concerns the problematic of tackling meaning and popular culture—that is, what can we draw about how the past actually worked and lived on its own terms. This is very much a development influenced by the fourth generation of *Annalistes* and the study of *mentalités*. As stated earlier, cultural historians have long been accused of neglecting the "real," and cultural studies has been at the heart of the issue from the 1960s.[31] However, they are not suggesting that the other umbrella—that of materialism—does not exist at all. Cultural historians suggest that the social world must be understood in relationship to cultural production. That is very different from saying it does not exist at all.

Cultural history has become very widespread throughout the globe. There have been major cultural histories of societies on every continent. While much of the intellectual influence cited in this chapter is European, the methods of cultural historians to grapple with language, texts, and meanings are fairly universal. One excellent example is Michael Dutton's *Streetlife China*, which explores the structure of life in contemporary China from images of Mao Zedong (father of Communist China) to descriptions of Chinese streetlife and urban hooliganism. He describes Mao as now having contested and multiple meanings for the Chinese: "Mao as sage in a resurgent peasant messianic phase; Mao as 1950s leader bringing stability and offering an exemplary alternative to the chaos of economic reform; Mao as young rebel hero standing against authority in a similar fashion to the young Chinese punk rock heroes of today."[32] And he traces this multiplicity of meanings of numerous Chinese icons throughout urban subculture. Brazilian historian Bryan McCann also explores popular culture in his *Hello, Hello Brazil*.[33] In this monograph, McCann explores the complex relationship between music and political development from the 1930s through 1950s. McCann's study interlaces a story of the rise of popular music and mass media with constructions of national identity. Specifically, McCann explores the emergence of fan clubs as sites for identity formation. And for Africanists, numerous histories exploring non-elites and societal values have emerged over the last few decades. One interesting example is Neil Kodesh's *Beyond the Royal Gaze: Clanship and Public Healing in Buganda*, which explores contestation over material resources in the region just north of Lake Victoria from the sixteenth through nineteenth centuries. Focused on people who were not elites, Kodesh's study emphasizes the multiple voices involved in the production of knowledge—specifically, public health knowledge—in eastern Africa and how power was negotiated between center and periphery (or between royalty and clan healers).[34]

A final note on cultural history's own influence. As stated at the outset of this chapter, cultural history is both its own field of historical inquiry, but also a "parent" field of sorts for scholars who take the influences both of poststructuralism and cultural history to embark on more critical and focused studies of the past. Our last two chapters—Chapters 9 and 10—show the ways in which cultural history offers numerous opportunities, but not totalizing answers. In other words, as far as cultural history goes in terms of disrupting the hegemonic, grand narratives of Western civilization, there is much about it that remains locked in dominant power frameworks. As you will discover in reading the next two chapters, there is even more depth to historical studies, a depth that combines a variety of frameworks and methodologies.

THINKING LIKE A HISTORIAN

The primary source you are assigned for this chapter was published in the United States just after the Civil War during the period known as Reconstruction. It was meant as a political critique. Using the methods of the cultural historian, explore the following questions:

- What, supposedly, is the image critiquing?
- How do the themes in the image represent a particular sociocultural context in the United States?
- How can we, as historians, make sense of this period using this image?
- How would you incorporate some of the defining traits of cultural history to explain this image to a contemporary audience that might at first be appalled by its message?

The secondary reading that follows is Robert Darnton's "The Great Cat Massacre," one of the most popular pedagogical tools for learning about how the methods of the cultural historian can be put into practice. A past president of the American Historical Association, Darnton has been a leader in French cultural history. In this very short excerpt, Darnton details a story with several layers. Specifically, Darnton wants to tackle not just culture, but popular culture. The question for Darnton was how to get at popular culture without direct evidence. Can a child's nursery rhyme, a poem, or a cultural myth seriously be a historical primary source? How does Darnton incorporate this kind of evidence into his analysis of labor relations in eighteenth-century France? In the reading excerpt, see where Darnton includes material evidence and why it is significant to his story. Also pinpoint the specific interdisciplinary influences on his work.

- Where does he maintain an allegiance to a materialist tradition? Does he cite population statistics, wages, or other kinds of demographic trends?
- What were the kinds of myths and folklores present in eighteenth-century France, and how did these myths enable the apprentices to embark on their strategy of getting back at their master?
- What is the role of the print culture in this story?
- Why, according to Darnton, could there be no outright complaint to the "bourgeois"?

"The Reconstruction Policy of Congress, as Illustrated in California"[35]

THE RECONSTRUCTION POLICY OF CONGRESS, As illustrated in California.

The Great Cat Massacre

Robert Darnton[36]

In the Paris of the 1730s a group of printing apprentices tortured and ritually killed all the cats they could find— including the pet of their master's wife. Why did this violent ritual cause them so much amusement? And what light does the story throw on the culture and society of eighteenth-century France?

THE FUNNIEST THING THAT EVER happened in the printing shop of Jacques Vincent, according to a worker who witnessed it, was a riotous massacre of cats. The worker, Nicolas Contat, told the story in an account of his apprenticeship in the shop, rue Saint-Séverin, Paris, during the late 1730s. Life as an apprentice was hard, he explained. There were two of them: Jerome, the somewhat fictionalised version of Contat himself, and Léveillé. They slept in a filthy freezing room, rose before dawn, ran errands all day while dodging insults from the journeymen and abuse from the master, and received nothing but slops to eat. They found the food especially galling. Instead of dining at the master's table, they had to eat scraps from his plate in the kitchen. Worse still, the cook secretly sold the leftovers and gave the boys cat food–old, rotten bits of meat that they could not stomach and so passed on to the cats, who refused it.

This last injustice brought Contat to the theme of cats. They occupied a special place in his narrative and in the household of the rue Saint-Séverin. The master's wife adored them, especially *la grise* (the grey), her favourite. A passion for cats seemed to have swept through the printing trade, at least at the level of the masters, or *bourgeois* as the workers called them. One *bourgeois* kept twenty-five cats. He had their portraits painted and fed them on roast fowl. Meanwhile, the apprentices were trying to cope with a profusion of alley cats who also thrived in the printing district and made the boys' lives miserable. The cats howled all night on the roof over the apprentices' dingy bedroom, making it impossible to get a full night's sleep. As Jerome and Léveillé had to stagger out of bed at four or five in the morning to open the gate for the earliest arrivals among the journeymen, they began the day in a state of exhaustion while the *bougeois* slept late. The master did not even work with the men, just as he did not eat with them. He let the foreman run the shop and rarely appeared in it, except to vent his violent temper, usually at the expense of the apprentices.

This article is an extract from *The Great Cat Massacre and Other Episodes in French Cultural History* by Robert Darnton, published by Allen Lane (£14.95).

One night the boys resolved to right this inequitable state of affairs. Léveillé, who had an extraordinary talent for mimickry, crawled along the roof until he reached a section near the master's bedroom, and then he took to howling and meowing so horribly that the *bourgeois* and his wife did not sleep a wink. After several nights of this treatment, they decided they were being bewitched. But instead of calling the *curé*—the master was exceptionally devout and the mistress exceptionally attached to her confessor—they commanded the apprentices to get rid of the cats. The mistress gave the order, enjoining the boys above all to avoid frightening her *grise*.

Gleefully Jerome and Léveillé set to work, aided by the journeymen. Armed with broomhandles, bars of the press, and other tools of their trade, they went after every cat they could find, beginning with *la grise*. Léveillé smashed its spine with an iron bar and Jerome finished it off. Then they stashed it in a gutter while the journeymen drove the other cats across the rooftops, bludgeoning every one within reach and trapping those who tried to escape in strategically placed sacks. They dumped sack-loads of half-dead cats in the courtyard. Then the entire workshop gathered round and staged a mock trial, complete with guards, confessor, and a public executioner. After pronouncing the animals guilty and administering last rites, they strung them up on an improvised gallows. Roused by gales of laughter, the mistress arrived. She let out a shriek as soon as she saw a bloody cat dangling from a noose. Then she realised it might be *la grise*. Certainly not, the men assured her: they had too much respect for the house to do such a thing. At this point the master appeared. He flew into a rage at the general stoppage of work, though his wife tried to explain that they were threatened by a more serious kind of insubordination. Then master and mistress withdrew, leaving the men delirious with 'joy', 'disorder', and 'laughter'.

The laughter did not end there. Léveillé re-enacted the entire scene in mime at least twenty times during subsequent days when the printers wanted to knock off for some hilarity. Burlesque re-enactments of incidents in the life of the shop, known as *copies* in printers' slang, provided a major form of entertainment for the men. The idea was to humiliate someone in the shop by satirising his peculiarities. A successful *copie* would make the butt of the joke fume with rage—*prendre la chèvre* (take the goat) in the shop slang—while his mates razzed him with 'rough music'. They would run their composing sticks across the tops of the type cases, beat their mallets against the chases, pound on cupboards, and bleat like goats. The bleating (*bais* in the slang) stood for the humiliation heaped on the victims, as in English when someone gets your goat. Contat emphasised that Léveillé produced the funniest *copies* anyone had ever known and elicited the great choruses of rough music. The whole episode, cat massacre compounded by *copies*, stood out as the most hilarious experience in Jerome's entire career.

Yet it strikes the modern reader as unfunny, if not down right repulsive. Where is the humour in a group of grown men bleating like goats and banging with their tools while an adolescent re-enacts the ritual slaughter of a defenceless animal? Our own inability to get the joke is an indication of the distance that separates us from the workers of pre-industrial Europe. The perception of that distance may serve as the starting point of an investigation, for anthropologists have found that the best points of entry in an attempt to penetrate an alien culture can be those where it seems to be most opaque. When you realise that you are not getting something—a joke, a proverb, a ceremony that is particularly meaningful to the natives, you can see where to grasp a foreign system of meaning in order to unravel it. By getting the joke of the great cat massacre, it may be possible to 'get' a basic ingredient of artisanal culture under the Old Regime.

The first explanation that probably would occur to most readers of Contat's story is that the cat massacre served as an oblique attack on the master and his wife. Contat set the event in the context of remarks about the disparity between the lot of workers and the *bourgeois*—a matter of the basic elements in life: work, food, and sleep. The injustice seemed especially flagrant in the case of the apprentices, who were treated like animals while the animals were promoted over their heads to the position the boys should have occupied, the place at the master's table. Although the apprentices seem most abused, the text makes it clear that the killing of the cats expressed a hatred for the *bourgeois* that had spread among all the workers:

'The masters love cats; consequently [the workers] hate them.' After master-minding the massacre, Léveillé became the hero of the shop, because 'all workers are in league against the masters. It is enough to speak badly of them [the masters] to be esteemed by the whole assembly of typographers'.

Historians have tended to treat the era of artisanal manufacturing as an idyllic period before the onset of industrialisation. Some even portray the workshop as a kind of extended family in which master and journeymen laboured at the same tasks, ate at the same table, and sometimes slept under the same roof. Had anything happened to poison the atmosphere of the printing shops in Paris by 1740?

During the second half of the seventeenth century, the large printing houses, backed by the government, eliminated most of the smaller shops, and an oligarchy of masters seized control of the industry. At the same time, the situation of the journeymen deteriorated. Although estimates vary and statistics cannot be trusted, it seems that their number remained stable: approximately 335 in 1666, 339 in 1701, and 340 in 1721. Meanwhile the number of masters declined by more than half, from eighty-three to thirty-six, the limit fixed by an edict of 1686. That meant fewer shops with larger work forces, as one can see from statistics on the density of presses: in 1644 Paris had seventy-five printing shops with a total of 180 presses; in 1701 it had fifty-one shops with 195 presses. This trend made it virtually impossible for journeymen to rise into the ranks of the masters. About the only way for a worker to get ahead in the craft was to marry a master's widow, for masterships had become hereditary privileges, passed on from husband to wife and from father to son.

The journeymen also felt threatened from below because the masters tended increasingly to hire *alloués*, or underqualified printers, who had not undergone the apprenticeship that made a journeyman eligible, in principle, to advance to a mastership. The *alloués* were merely a source of cheap labour, excluded from the upper ranks of the trade and fixed, in their inferior status, by an edict of 1723. Their degradation stood out in their name: they were *à louer* (for hire), not *compagnons* (journeymen) of the master. They personified the tendency of labour to become a commodity instead of a partnership. Thus Contat served his apprenticeship and wrote his memoirs when times were hard for journeymen printers, when the men in the shop in the rue Saint-Séverin stood in danger of being cut off from the top of the trade and swamped from the bottom.

Contat himself believed that at one time journeymen and masters lived together as members of a happy family. He began his description of Jerome's apprenticeship by invoking a golden age when printing was first invented and printers lived as free and equal members of a 'republic', governed by its own laws and traditions in a spirit of fraternal 'union and friendship'. He claimed that the republic still survived in the form of the *chapelle* or workers' association in each shop. But the government had broken up general associations; the ranks had been thinned by *alloués*; the journeymen had been excluded from masterships; and the masters had withdrawn into a separate world of *haute cuisine* and *grasses matinées*. The master in the rue Saint-Séverin ate different food, kept different hours, and talked a different language. His wife and daughters dallied with worldly *abbés*. They kept pets. Clearly, the *bourgeois* belonged to a different subculture—one which meant above all that he did not work. In introducing his account of the cat massacre, Contat made explicit the contrast between the worlds of worker and master that ran throughout the narrative: 'Workers, apprentices, everyone works. Only the masters and mistresses enjoy the sweetness of sleep. That makes Jerome and Léveillé resentful. They resolve not to be the only wretched ones. They want their master and mistress as associates (*associés*)'. That is, the boys wanted to restore a mythical past when masters and men worked in friendly association. They also may have had in mind the more recent extinction of the smaller printing shops. So they killed the cats.

But why cats? And why was the killing so funny? Those questions take us beyond the consideration of early modern labour relations and into the obscure subject of popular ceremonies and symbolism.

Folklorists have made historians familiar with the ceremonial cycles that marked off the calendar year for early modern man. The most important of these was the cycle of carnival and Lent, a period of revelry followed by a period of abstinence. During carnival the common people suspended the normal rules of behaviour and ceremoniously reversed the social order or turned it upside down in riotous procession. Carnival was a time for cutting up by youth groups, particularly apprentices, who organised themselves in 'abbeys' ruled by a mock abbot or king and who staged charivaris or burlesque processions with rough music in order to humiliate cuckolds, husbands who had been beaten by their wives, brides who had married below their age group, or someone else who personified the infringement of traditional norms. Carnival was high season for hilarity, sexuality, and youth run riot—a time when young people tested social boundaries by limited outbursts of deviance, before being reassimilated in the world of order, submission, and Lentine seriousness. It came to an end on Shrove Tuesday or Mardi Gras, when a straw mannequin, King Carnival or Caramantran, was given a ritual trial and execution. Cats played an important part in some charivaris. In Burgundy, the crowd incorporated cat torture into its rough music. While mocking a cuckold or some other victim, the youths passed around a cat, tearing its fur to make it howl. *Faire le chat*, they called it. The Germans called charivaris *Katzenmusik*, a term that may have been derived from the howls of tortured cats.

Cats also figured in the cycle of Saint John the Baptist, which took place on June 24th, at the time of the summer solstice. Crowds made bonfires, jumped over them, danced around them, and threw into them objects with magical power, hoping to avoid disaster and obtain good fortune during the rest of the year. A favourite object was cats—cats tied up in bags, cats suspended from ropes, or cats burned at the stake. Parisians like to incinerate cats by the sackful, while the Courimauds (*cour à miaud* or cat chasers) of Saint Chamond preferred to chase a flaming cat through the streets. In parts of Burgundy and Lorraine they danced around a kind of burning maypole with a cat tied to it. In the Metz region they burned a dozen cats at a time in a basket on top of a bonfire. The ceremony took place with a great pomp in Metz itself, until it was abolished in 1765. The town dignitaries arrived in procession at the Place du Grand-Saulcy, lit the pyre, and a ring of riflemen from the garrison fired off volleys while the cats disappeared screaming in the flames. Although the practice varied from place to place, the ingredients were everywhere the same: a *feu de joie* (bonfire), cats, and an aura of hilarious witch-hunting.

But why was it that cats figured so prominently in these ceremonies? It should be said at the outset that there is an indefinable *je ne sais quoi* about cats, a mysterious something that has fascinated mankind since the time of the ancient Egyptians. One can sense a quasi-human intelligence behind a cat's eyes. One can mistake a cat's howl at night for a human scream, torn from some deep, visceral part of man's animal nature. Cats appealed to poets like Baudelaire and painters like Manet, who wanted to express the humanity in animals along with the animality of men—and especially of women.

This ambiguous ontological position, a straddling of conceptual categories, gives certain animals—pigs, dogs and cassowaries as well as cats—in certain cultures an occult power associated with the taboo. That is why Jews do not eat pigs, according to Mary Douglas, and why Englishmen can insult one another by saying 'son-of-a-bitch', rather than 'son-of-a-cow', according to Edmund Leach. Certain animals are good for swearing, just as they are 'good for thinking' in Lévi-Strauss's famous formula. I would add that others—cats in particular—are good for staging ceremonies. They have ritual value. You cannot made [make] a charivari with a cow. You do it with cats: you decide to *faire le chat*, to make *Katzenmusik*.

The torture of animals, especially cats, was a popular amusement throughout early modern Europe. You have only to look at Hogarth's *Stages of Cruelty* to see its importance, and once you start looking you see people torturing animals everywhere. Cat killings provided a common theme in literature, from *Don Quixote* in early seventeenth-century Spain to *Germinal* in late nineteenth-century France. Far from being a sadistic fantasy on the part of a few half-crazed authors, the literary versions of cruelty to animals expressed a deep current of popular culture, as Mikhail Bakhtin has shown in his study of Rabelais. All sorts of ethnographic reports confirm that view. On the *dimanche des brandons* in Semur, for example, children used to attach cats to poles and roast them over bonfires. In the *jeu du chat* at the *Fête-Dieu* in Aix-en-Provence, they threw cats high in the air and smashed them on the ground. They used expressions like 'patient as a cat whose claws are being pulled out' or 'patient as a cat whose paws are being grilled'. The English were just as cruel. During the Reformation in London, a Protestant crowd shaved a cat to look like a priest, dressed it in a mock vestments, and hanged it on the gallows at Cheapside. It would be possible to string out many other examples, but the point should be clear: there was nothing unusual about the ritual killing of cats. On the contrary, when Jerome and his fellow workers tried and hanged all the cats they could find in the rue Saint-Séverin, they drew on a common element in their culture. But what significance did that culture attribute to cats?

First and foremost, cats suggested witchcraft. To cross one at night in virtually any corner of France was to risk running into the devil or one of his agents or a witch abroad on an evil errand. White cats could be as satanic as the black, in the daytime as well as at night. In a typical encounter, a peasant woman of Bigorre met a pretty white house cat which had strayed in the fields. She carried it back to the village in her apron, and just as they came to the house of a woman suspected of witchcraft, the cat jumped out, saying 'Merci, Jeanne'. Witches transformed themselves into cats in order to cast spells on their victims. Sometimes, especially on Mardi Gras, they gathered for hideous sabbaths at night. They howled, fought, and copulated horribly under the direction of the devil, himself in the form of a huge tomcat. To protect youself from sorcery by cats there was one, classic remedy: maim it. Cut its tail, clip its ears, smash one of its legs, tear or burn its fur, and you would break its malevolent power. A maimed cat could not attend a sabbath or wander abroad to cast spells. Peasants frequently cudgelled cats who crossed their paths at night and discovered the next day that bruises had appeared on women believed to be witches—or so it was said in the lore of their village. Villagers also told stories of farmers who found strange cats in barns and broke their limbs to save the cattle. Invariably

a broken limb would appear on a suspicious woman the following morning.

Cats possessed occult power independently of their association with witchcraft and devilry. They could prevent the bread from rising if they entered bakeries in Anjou. They could spoil the catch if they crossed the path of fishermen in Brittany. If buried alive in Béarn, they could clear a field of weeds. They figured as staple ingredients in all kinds of folk medicine aside from witches' brews. To recover from a bad fall, you sucked the blood out of a freshly amputed tail of a tomcat. To cure yourself from pneumonia, you drank blood from a cat's ear in red wine. To get over colic, you mixed your wine with cat excrement. You could even make yourself invisible, at least in Brittany, by eating the brain of a newly killed cat, provided it was still hot.

There was a specific field for the exercise of cat power: the household and particulary [*sic*] the person of the master or mistress of the house. Folktales like 'Puss in Boots' emphasised the identification of master and cat, and so did superstitions such as the practice of tying a black ribbon around the neck of a cat whose mistress had died. To kill a cat was to bring misfortune upon its owner or its house. If a cat left a house or stopped jumping on the sickbed of its master or mistress, the person was likely to die. But a cat lying on the bed of a dying man might be the devil, waiting to carry his soul off to hell. According to a sixteenth-century tale, a girl from Quintin sold her soul to the devil in exchange for some pretty clothes. When she died, the pallbearers could not lift her coffin; they opened the lid, and a black cat jumped out. Cats could harm a house. They often smothered babies. They understood gossip and would repeat it out of doors. But their power could be contained or turned to your advantage if you followed the right procedures, such as greasing their paws with butter or maiming them when they first arrived. To protect a new house, Frenchmen enclosed live cats within its walls—a very old rite, judging from cat skeletons that have been exhumed from the walls of medieval buildings.

Finally, the power of cats was concentrated on the most intimate aspect of domestic life: sex. *Le chat, la chatte, le minet* mean the same thing in French slang as 'pussy' does in English, and they have served as obscenities for centuries. French folklore attaches special importance to the cat as a sexual metaphor or metonym. As far back as the fifteenth century, the petting of cats was recommended for success in courting women. Proverbial wisdom identified women with cats: 'He who takes good care of cats will have a pretty wife.' If a man loved cats, he would love women; and vice versa: 'As he loves his cat, he loves his wife', went another proverb. If he did not care for his wife, you could say of him, 'He has other cats to whip'. A woman who wanted to get a man should avoid treading on a cat's tail. She might postpone marriage for a year—or for seven years in Quimper and for as many years as the cat meowed in parts of the Loire Valley. Cats connoted fertility and female sexuality everywhere. Girls were commonly said to be 'in love by a cat'; and if they became pregnant, they had 'let the cat go to the cheese'. Eating cats could bring on pregnancy in itself. Girls who consumed them in stews gave birth to kittens in several folktales. Cats could even make diseased apple trees bear fruit, if buried in the correct manner in upper Brittany.

It was an easy jump from the sexuality of women to the cuckolding of men. Caterwauling could come from a satanic orgy, but it might just as well be toms howling defiance at each other when their mates were in heat. They did not call as cats, however. They issued challenges in their masters' names, along with sexual taunts about their mistresses: 'Reno! Francois!' 'Où allez-vous?'—'Voir la femme à vous.'—'Voir la femme à moi! Rouah!' (Where are you going?—To see your wife.—To see my wife! Ha!) Then the toms would fly at each other like the cats of Kilkenny, and their sabbath would end in a massacre. The dialogue differed according to the imaginations of the listeners and the onomatopoetic power of their dialect, but it usually emphasised predatory sexuality. 'At night all cats are grey', went the proverb, and the gloss in an eighteenth-century proverb collection made the sexual hint explicit: 'That is to say that all women are beautiful enough at night'. Enough for what? Seduction, rape, and murder echoed in the air when the cats howled at night in early modern France. Cat calls summoned up *Katzenmusik*, for charivaris often took the form of howling under a cuckold's window on the eve of Mardi Gras, the favourite time for cat sabbaths.

Witchcraft, orgy, cuckoldry, charivari, and massacre, the men of the Old Regime could hear a great deal in the wail of a cat. What the men in the rue Saint-Séverin actually heard is impossible to say. One can only assert that cats bore enormous symbolic weight in the folklore of France and that the lore was rich, ancient, and widespread enough to have penetrated the printing shop. In order to determine whether the printers actually drew on the ceremonial and symbolic themes available to them, it is necessary to take another look at Contat's text.

The text made the theme of sorcery explicit from the beginning. Jerome and Léveillé could not sleep because

'some bedevilled cats make a sabbath all night long'. After Léveillé added his cat calls to the general caterwauling, 'the whole neighbourhood is alarmed. It is decided that the cats must be agents of someone casting a spell'. The master and mistress considered summoning the *curé* to exorcise the place. In deciding instead to commission the cat hunt, they fell back on the classic remedy for witchcraft: maiming. The *bourgeois*—a superstitious, priest-ridden fool—took the whole business seriously. To the apprentices it was a joke. Léveillé in particular functioned as a joker, a mock 'sorcerer' staging a fake 'sabbath', according to the terms chosen by Contat. Not only did the apprentices exploit their master's superstition in order to run riot at his expense, but they also turned their rioting against their mistress. By bludgeoning her familiar, *la grise*, they in effect accused her of being the witch. The double joke would not be lost on anyone who could read the traditional language of gesture.

The theme of charivari provided an additional dimension to the fun. Although it never says so explicitly, the text indicates that the mistress was having an affair with her priest, a 'lascivious youth', who had memorised obscene passages from the classics of pornography—Aretino and *L'Academie des dames*—and quoted them to her, while her husband droned on about his favourite subjects, money and religion. During a lavish dinner with the family, the priest defended the thesis 'that it is a feat of wit to cuckold one's husband and that cuckolding it not a vice'. Later, he and the wife spent the night together in a country house. They fit perfectly into the typical triangle of printing shops: a doddering old master, a middle-aged mistress, and her youthful lover. The intrigue cast the master in the role of a stock comic figure: the cuckold. So the revelry of the workers took the form of a charivari. The apprentices managed it, operating within the liminal area where novitiates traditionally mocked their superiors, and the journeymen responded to their antics in the traditional way, with rough music. A riotous, festival atmosphere runs through the whole episode, which Contat described as a *fête*: Léveillé and his comrade Jerome preside over the *fête*', he wrote, as if they were kings of a carnival and the cat bashing corresponded to the torturing of cats on Mardi Gras or the *fête* of Saint John the Baptist.

As in many Mardi Gras, the carnival ended in a mock trial and execution. The burlesque legalism came naturally to the printers because they staged their own mock trials every year at the *fête* of Saint Martin, when the chapel squared accounts with its boss and succeeded spectacularly in getting his goat. The chapel could not condemn him explicitly without moving into open insubordination and risking dismissal. So the workers tried the *bourgeois* in absentia, using a symbol that would let their meaning show through without being explicit enough to justify retaliation. They tried and hanged the cats. It would be going too far to hang *la grise* under the master's nose after being ordered to spare it; but they made the favourite pet of the house their first victim, and in doing so they knew they were attacking the house itself, in accordance with the traditions of cat lore. When the mistress accused them of killing *la grise*, they replied with mock deference that 'nobody would be capable of such an outrage and that they have too much respect for that house'. By executing the cats with such elaborate ceremony, they condemned the house and declared the *bourgeois* guilty— guilty of overworking and underfeeding his apprentices, guilty of living in luxury while his journeymen did all the work, guilty of withdrawing from the shop and swamping it with *alloués* instead of labouring and eating with the men, as masters were said to have done a generation or two earlier, or in the primitive 'republic' that existed at the beginning of the printing industry. The guilt extended from the boss to the house to the whole system. Perhaps in trying, confessing, and hanging a collection of half-dead cats, the workers meant to ridicule the entire legal and social order.

They certainly felt debased and had accumulated enough resentment to explode in an orgy of killing. A half-century later, the artisans of Paris would run riot in a similar manner, combining indiscriminate slaughter with improvised popular tribunals. It would be absurd to view the cat massacre as a dress rehearsal for the September massacres of the French Revolution, but the earlier outburst of violence did suggest a popular rebellion, though it remained restricted to the level of symbolism.

The only version of the cat massacre available to us was put into writing, long after the fact, by Nicolas Contat. He selected details, ordered events, and framed the story in such a way as to bring out what was meaningful for him. But he derived his notions of meaning from his culture just as naturally as he drew in air from the atmosphere around him. And he wrote down what he had helped to enact with his mates. The subjective character of the writing does not vitiate its collective frame of reference, even though the written account must be thin compared with the action it describes. The workers' mode of expression was a kind of popular theatre. It involved pantomime, rough music, and a dramatic 'theatre of violence' improvised in the work place, in the street,

and on the rooftops. It included a play within a play, because Léveillé re-enacted the whole farce several times as *copies* in the shop. In fact, the original massacre involved the burlesquing of other ceremonies, such as trials and charivaris. So Contat wrote about a burlesque of a burlesque, and in reading it one should make allowances for the refraction of cultural forms across genres and over time.

Those allowances made, it seems clear that the workers found the massacres fun because it gave them a way to turn the tables on the *bourgeois*. By goading him with cat calls, they provoked him to authorise the massacre of cats, then they used the massacre to put him symbolically on trial for unjust management of the shop. They also used it as a witch hunt, which provided an excuse to kill his wife's familiar and to insinuate that she herself was the witch. Finally, they transformed it into a charivari, which served as a means to insult her sexually while mocking him as a cuckold. The *bourgeois* made an excellent butt of the joke. Not only did he become the victim of a procedure he himself had set in motion, he did not understand how badly he had been had. The men had subjected his wife to symbolic aggression of the most intimate kind, but he did not get it. He was too thick-headed, a classic cuckold. The printers ridiculed him in splendid Boccaccian style and got off scot-free.

The joke worked so well because the workers played so skillfully with a repertory of ceremonies and symbols. Cats suited their purposes perfectly. By smashing the spine of *la grise* they called the master's wife a witch and a slut, while at the same time making the master into a cuckold and a fool. It was a metonymic insult, delivered by actions, not words, and it struck home because cats occupied a soft spot in the *bourgeois* way of life. Keeping pets was as alien to the workers as torturing animals was to the *bourgeois*. Trapped between incompatible sensitivities, the cats had the worst of both worlds.

The workers also punned with ceremonies. They made a roundup of cats into a witch hunt, a festival, a charivari, a mock trial, and a dirty joke. Then they redid the whole thing in pantomime. Whenever they got tired of working, they transformed the shop into a theatre and produced *cópies*— their kind of copy, not the authors'. Shop theatre and ritual puning suited the traditions of their craft. Although printers made books, they did not use written words to convey their meaning. They used gestures, drawing on the culture of their craft to inscribe statements in the air.

Insubstantial as it may seem today, this joking was a risky business in the eighteenth century. The risk was part of the joke, as in many forms of humour, which toy with violence and tease repressed passions. The workers pushed their symbolic horseplay to the brink of reification, the point at which the killing of cats would turn into an open rebellion. They played on ambiguities, using symbols that would hide their full meaning while letting enough of it show through to make a fool of the *bourgeois* without giving him a pretext to fire them. They tweaked his nose and prevented him from protesting against it. To pull off such a feat required great dexterity. It showed that workers could manipulate symbols in their idiom as effectively as poets did in print.

The boundaries within which this jesting had to be contained suggest the limits to working-class militancy under the Old Regime. The printers identified with their craft rather than their class. Although they organised in chapels, staged strikes, and sometimes forced up wages, they remained subordinate to the *bourgeois*. The master hired and fired men as casually as he ordered paper, and he turned them out into the road when he sniffed insubordination. So until the onset of proletarianisation in the late nineteenth century, they generally kept their protests on a symbolic level. A *copie*, like a carnival, helped to let off steam; but it also produced laughter, a vital ingredient in the early artisanal culture and one that has been lost in labour history. By seeing the way a joke worked in the horseplay of a printing shop two centuries ago, we may be able to recapture that missing element—laughter, sheer laughter, the thigh-slapping, rib-cracking Rabelaisian kind, rather than the Voltarian smirk with which we are familiar. ■

Endnotes

1. Raymond Williams, *The Long Revolution* (New York: Harper & Row, 1966), 57.

2. E.P. Thompson, "Introduction: Custom and Culture," in his *Customs in Common* (New York: New Press, 1992), 13.

3. Clifford Geertz, "Thick Description: Towards an Interpretation of Culture," in his *The Interpretation of Cultures: Selected Essays* (New York: Basic Books, 1973), 6, 7.

4. Clifford Geertz, "Deep Play: Notes on the Balinese Cockfight," *Daedalus* 101/1 Myth, Symbol, and Culture (Winter 1972): 1–37.

5. Geertz, "Deep Play: Notes on the Balinese Cockfight," 29, 28.

6. Marshall Sahlins, *Culture and Practical Reason* (Chicago: University of Chicago Press, 1976), x.

7. *Ibid.*, 169, 185.

8. Pierre Bourdieu, *The Logic of Practice*, trans. Richard Nice (Stanford: Stanford University Press, 1990), 54–57, 124–125. See also, "The Forms of Capital," in *Handbook of Theory and Research for the Sociology of Education*, ed. John G. Richardson (New York: Greenwood, 1986), 241–258.

9. Walter Benjamin, "Art in the Age of Mechanical Reproduction," in *Illuminations: Essays and Reflections* edited and with an Introduction by Hannah Arendt, Trans. Harry Zohn (New York: Schocken Books, 1968), 217–251.

10. John Czaplicka, Andreas Huyssen, and Anson Rabinbach, "Introduction: Cultural History and Cultural Studies: Reflections on a Symposium," *New German Critique* No. 65, Cultural History/Cultural Studies (1995): 5.

11. Richard Hoggart, *BBC—Desert Island Discs—Castaway: Richard Hoggart, Presented by Kelly Young*, radio broadcast (London: The British Broadcasting Corporation, Sunday, October 15, 1995), last accessed September 7, 2013, http://www.bbc.co.uk/radio4/features/desert-island-discs/castaway/d6a86f6d.

12. Richard Hoggart, *The Uses of Literacy: Aspects of Working-Class Life with Special References to Publications and Entertainments* (London: Chatto and Windus, 1957).

13. Terry Eagleton, *Literary Theory: An Introduction* (Minneapolis: University of Minnesota Press, 2008), 198–199.

14. Raymond Williams, "Base and Superstructure in Marxist Cultural Theory," in *Culture and Materialism: Selected Essays* (London: Verso, 1980), 40–41.

15. Williams, "Base and Superstructure in Marxist Cultural Theory," 38.

16. Raymond Williams, "Culture is Ordinary," in *The Everyday Life Reader*, ed. Ben Highmore (London: Routledge, 2002), 93.

17. Tim Adams, "Cultural Hallmark," *The Guardian Online*, posted 22 September 2007, http://www.guardian.co.uk/society/2007/sep/23/communities.politicsphilosophyandsociety. On immigration policy, see Randall Hansen's *Citizenship and Immigration in Postwar Britain: The Institutional Origins of a Multicultural Nation* (Oxford: Oxford University Press, 2000).

18. Stuart Hall, "The Emergence of Cultural Studies and the Crisis in the Humanities," *October* 53, The Humanities as Social Technology (1990): 16.

19. Adams, "Cultural Hallmark."

20. Stuart Hall and Tony Jefferson, eds., *Resistance through Rituals: Youth Subcultures in Post-War Britain* (New York: HarperCollins Academic, 1991), 10.

21. Stuart Hall, "The Emergence of Cultural Studies and the Crisis in the Humanities," 14.

22. "The Linguistic Turn," in David Macey, *The Penguin Dictionary of Critical Theory* (New York: Penguin Reference, 2000), 231.

23. Lynn Hunt, "Introduction: History, Culture, Text," in *The New Cultural History*, ed. Lynn Hunt (Berkeley, University of California Press, 1992), 16.

24. Kathleen Canning, "Feminist History after the Linguistic Turn: Historicizing Discourse and Experience," *Signs* 19/2 (1994): 368–404.

25. Lawrence Stone, "Notes: History and Postmodernism," *Past and Present* No. 131 (May 1991), 217.

26. Patrick Joyce and Catriona Kelly, "History and Postmodernism," *Past and Present* No. 133 (November 1991): 208–210.

27. Gareth Stedman Jones, "Working-Class Culture and Working-Class Politics in London, 1870–1900: Notes on the Remaking of a Working Class," *Journal of Social History* 7/4 (1974): 460–508.

28. Lynn Hunt, *Politics, Culture, and Class in the French Revolution* (Berkeley, University of California Press, 1984).

29. Carlo Ginzburg, *The Cheese and the Worms: The Cosmos of a Sixteenth-Century Miller* (Baltimore: The Johns Hopkins University Press, 1992).

30. Hunt, "Introduction: History, Culture, Text," 16.

31. Stuart Hall, "Emergence of Cultural Studies and the Crisis in the Humanities," 13–14.

32. Michael Dutton, *Streetlife China* (Cambridge: Cambridge Modern History Series, 1999), 5.

33. Bryan McCann, *Hello, Hello Brazil: Popular Music in the Making of Modern Brazil* (Durham [NC]: Duke University Press, 2004).

34. Neil Kodesh, *Beyond the Royal Gaze: Clanship and Public Healing in Buganda* (Charlottesville: University of Virginia Press, 2010).

35. "The Reconstruction Policy of Congress, as Illustrated in California," *The Library of Congress*, last accessed September 7, 2013, http://www.loc.gov/pictures/item/2008661701/.

36. Robert Darnton, "The Great Cat Massacre, 1730," *History Today* 34 (1984): 7–15.

CHAPTER 9

FEMINIST AND GENDER HISTORY

CHAPTER OUTLINE

■ Feminism—A Political Movement

■ From Women's History to
Feminist History

■ Gender Theory and History

■ Queer Theory

■ Conclusion

■ Thinking Like a Historian

"What I hope my readers will do is not so much learn the precise origins of the feminist tradition, but see the varieties of ways of being a woman and the varieties of ideas people have had about why the relations between the sexes were wrong and how they could be changed."

Natalie Zemon Davis[1]

Have you ever read a novel set in the past or watched an old television show and wondered about the ways men and women related to each other or the choices that were available to women? For example, have you ever found yourself watching an episode of *I Love Lucy*, a popular 1950s sitcom? If you have, you know that black-and-white television aside, it was an extraordinarily funny show. Hilarious, in fact. But what made it so funny? The centerpiece of the show was the tension between Lucy and Ricky, specifically surrounding Lucy's constant bid to be more than a housewife—to work in Ricky's show at the Tropicana, to be in one of his films when they went to Hollywood, or simply to be famous. One of the most famous episodes is "Job Switching," where Lucy and Ricky place a bet about whose job is tougher. They drag their neighbors Fred and Ethel Mertz into the fray only to discover that housework is meant for women, and being "out to work" is meant for men. But other episodes deal with this sense of control over the household as well. An equally incisive critique of familial relations takes place in the episode "Lucy's Schedule." Ricky wants a promotion, but the owner of the club questions whether Ricky can run a nightclub if he cannot keep Lucy in check. Ricky then puts Lucy on a strict schedule that she follows until the club owner's wife arrives questioning why Lucy is undermining womankind. The three women (Lucy, the owner's wife, and Ethel) then cook up a scheme to undermine the schedule and restore balance. There is a moment of rebellion against male management and control in this episode, but at the same time, the balance restored is that the home is entirely the woman's realm, while the public space is the man's.

As you read in Chapter 8, popular culture, such as television or film, is an excellent way to get at a basic understanding of social relations, in this case relations between men and women. Popular culture also amplifies these relations, sometimes through caricature, but in ways that have a ring of truth, and the historian can use popular culture as a primary source to uncover attitudes and meanings of relations between the sexes. However, analyzing popular culture is not the only way to explore historical relations between the sexes or the historical position of women. It is simply one of many methods. Unfortunately, for a good portion of the twentieth century, critical histories of women and sexual relations were largely absent in the discipline. This chapter explores that absence, the emergence of women's and feminist history over the twentieth century, and will deal specifically with the frustrations scholars of the history of women have faced when showing that women, like men, are historical actors. To explore this issue, we must first talk about feminism as a political movement.

FEMINISM—A POLITICAL MOVEMENT

When we talk about feminist history, we need to explore a long trajectory of concern about women's issues moving up to the modern period. The feminist movement itself is relatively recent (we can place the "**first wave**" of modern feminism sometime in the nineteenth century with fights over suffrage), but that does not mean that women or men concerned with women's issues were complacent objects of governmental or societal formation. Quite the contrary, if we were to take a quick tour of global history, we would be able to find numerous accounts of women—and not only high-ranking women—who fought against the institutions that oppressed them or who were complicit in the making of oppressive social conditions.

In the ancient world alone, there are numerous accounts of women's active involvement. Hatshepsut, for example, moved against gendered constructions in ancient Egypt and ruled as Pharaoh in her own right—that is, instead of acting as queen or queen regent, she ruled as a man and started one of the most intensive building projects of ancient Egypt. Another example is Boudicca, the first-century Iceni queen in what is now East Anglia in England, who fought against Roman

power, and her struggle could be read in very feminist terms. After she was flogged and her daughters raped by the Romans, she launched an initially successful revolt. Other women throughout history have been shown to point out—if not fight like Boudicca—the inequality between the sexes. Ban Zhao was a Han historian writing in the second century CE. In "Lessons for Women" she matter-of-factly stated the subordinate position to which women were born: Boys are coddled and loved, girls are given potsherds (pieces of broken ceramic) to occupy their childhood. While Ban Zhao's own experience did not mirror her subjects (she was an educated woman writing in the Emperor's court), nevertheless, her work points out the general attitudes of her time toward women.[2] The Trung sisters of Vietnam fought against Chinese assimilation policies in the peninsula during the first century CE and have become important symbols of resistance for the Vietnamese.

Despite all of these examples about women's agency, it is crucial not to represent feminism in an ahistorical or a whiggish manner. In particular, historians must be careful to avoid stories of origins, trying to trace the modern women's movement to a specific point in the distant past and say "see, there is the first feminist." This is problematic and does a disservice to the multiple kinds of inequalities women faced across time and space. While a general understanding of patriarchal culture can help us to understand the kinds of struggles women faced in past societies, we cannot generalize from specific instances about women's *universal* struggles. As the early-modern historian Natalie Zemon Davis said in the opening quote for this chapter, women encountered and dealt with inequality differently depending on their historical context.[3]

The first known use of the word "**feminism**" as a political position is with the work of social utopian Charles Fourier who wanted to create an emancipatory society (see Chapter 3). While there are elements in the collected works of Marx and Engels that suggest a need for women's emancipation (e.g., their call for the dissolution of the bourgeois family in the *Manifesto*), their body of work was far more concerned with the structure of capitalism as an institution. In the nineteenth century, a variety of women's/feminist groups emerged throughout the globe. Notably, the United States saw the founding of a suffrage movement combined with temperance (as heavy drinking was said to negatively impact marital relations) and, prior to the Civil War, abolition. Led by Elizabeth Cady Stanton and, later, Susan B. Anthony, their conference at Seneca Falls, New York was intended to demand women's suffrage and better include women in the political process. In England at roughly the same time, women were involved in the Chartist movement, also striving for temperance and the right to vote, and meeting with unhappy results.[4] In China, from the turn of the twentieth century through the 1920s, women were very active politically, from the short-lived self-strengthening movement of the mid-nineteenth century through the May Fourth Movement of the 1920s. Previous to the 1911 revolution that established a republic in China, much of women's politics centered on footbinding as a symptom of China's regressive policies. Footbinding quite literally crippled a woman's ability to participate in meaningful social activity. With the bound foot, a woman could only hobble along, generally confined to the family compound.

In Western Europe, women continued to struggle for the right to vote (the franchise, or suffrage), arguing that the Enlightenment concepts of the social contract and natural rights extended to all, regardless of sex. It was only after World War I that women in Western Europe systematically earned the right to vote, though in some cases earlier (Finland in 1906) and others much later (France during World War II and Switzerland only in 1971).

But the right to vote did not remove deeply and historically institutionalized inequalities. This continued stratification of the sexes led to the **second wave** of feminism—the turning to social issues and fighting for such things as rights to divorce, reproductive rights, and workplace equality among many other things. The two pathbreaking works of the second wave of feminism were Simone de Beauvoir's *The Second Sex* (1949) and Betty Friedan's *The Feminine Mystique* (1963). De Beauvoir's (1908–1986) analysis focused on the historic subordination of women and challenged that position. While women and men had different reproductive capacities, these mere biological differences should not become a hindrance—as it had been—to women's complete equality. In other words, male-ordered society (**patriarchy**) created a system that imposed social frameworks on sexual difference. De Beauvoir argued men and women are the same species, but it was these social forces that created the female as "**other**" in face of the male "**subject**."[5] This claim was truly revolutionary.

Friedan's (1921–2006) *The Feminine Mystique* was equally revolutionary and was very much influenced by de Beauvoir's work. Arguing that American women were uniformly unhappy because they were denied an identity beyond "housewife," the book aroused anger from many sides, but also a consciousness on the part of many of its readers. Friedan argued that the role of housewife and mother was socially constructed for women by male advertising men and was designed to suggest that women's "natural" place was the realm of domesticity. She called this construction the "Feminine Mystique," a phrase that plays into the male suggestion that women were happy and natural in their domestic roles and advertisements and television shows ought to represent that framework. She concluded her book by making the case that women could be fulfilled and gain a sense of identity through education and meaningful careers.

Both of these works are credited with spurring the activism of the second wave of feminism—again, moving beyond the quest for legal recognition (through citizenship and the right to vote or own property). Betty Friedan contributed to this phase by helping to found the National Organization for Women (1967), which helped to fight for affirmative action laws for women such as Title IX that prevents discrimination in federally funded education programs. Simone de Beauvoir resisted labeling herself as a feminist for many years, but was active in the French women's movement in the 1970s, and was part of a campaign by French female celebrities to push for female reproductive rights.

The list of influential twentieth-century feminists could go on: Erica Jong, an American novelist whose first work *Fear of Flying* (1973) outlines a path for "contemporary womanhood" free of the shackles of sexual inhibition; Australian polemicist Germaine Greer (b. 1939) who argued for full women's liberation as Western civilization demoralized women's sexual identity; and Gloria Steinem, who cofounded *Ms.* Magazine in 1972 and its subsequent Foundation for Women.

FROM WOMEN'S HISTORY TO FEMINIST HISTORY

Previous to the mid-twentieth century, there had been several important histories of women, particularly women and work in England, but with few exceptions, these works tended to emphasize either women in power (such as Queen Elizabeth I or Eleanor of Aquitaine) or women existing in some kind of fictional golden age. Alice Clark's *Working Life of Women in the Seventeenth Century*, for example, emphasized a story of women as happy helpmeets to husbands before the Industrial Age disrupted traditional work and labor activities. However, a systematic attempt to examine women's lived experiences did not emerge until feminism met history.

There are numerous historical, historiographical, and theoretical roots to feminist history. For example, at least one American historian suggests that the methodology of "total history" from the *Annales* School inspired feminist history because of its influence on the masses of history. Susan Mosher Stuard stood against the bulk of Continental historians who critiqued what was described as the male chauvinism of the *Annales* School.[6] Stuard claims that the *Annales* School held the seeds of feminist history and many scholars, men and women, provided important frameworks for pushing the *Annales* School to be more mindful of relations between the sexes historically. Whatever its conceptual leaps, Stuard's article reminds historians that despite the seeming limitations of writing historical agency endemic in its first three generations, the *Annales* School was multifaceted enough to encourage writing from numerous frameworks. More often, however, feminist scholars are said to have found their footing partly in the wake of the rise of the New Left, both in Europe and in the United States. While women were not completely ignored in histories before the New Left, nor were they completely ignored in the New Social History, their stories were not given importance generally. After all, how many women were rulers of societies? How many were leaders of unionization? Women's histories continued to be relegated to second-class status, just as women active in the progressive political movements saw themselves assuming traditional "female" occupations even while they fought to change society for the better. Historian Sheila Rowbotham explained it this way:

> We were given a space, even though it was a slightly contained space. But in the student movement there was no space at all because only the people with very loud voices were able to get into it. Some women had small children and the men were always at meetings. Influenced by the American New Left, by France and Germany, we began to talk about all these things in our own lives and experience.[7]

According to Rowbotham, women had been "hidden from history," and it was imperative to rewrite them into the historical record. In addition, Linda Gordon stated that women had trouble working within the confines of the New Social History because of its inherent

problems in studying the family in relation to outside forces. She stated that "it reifies and hypostasizes the unit as if the family was a thing in itself instead of a set of complicated social relations among people."[8] Thus, influenced by feminist sociology and troubled by continuing the New Left history, feminist scholars rewrote history with a new set of lenses. So feminist history itself emerged in response to larger political movements and the ways in which women's subordination remained an issue, even in seemingly progressive circles.

To ensure that women's stories were seen as central, first those stories needed to be told—women had to be written into history. According to Catherine Hall, this first task was especially challenging as a result of male domination of the historical profession.[9] Feminist historians began by exploring women's work in all its forms, both at home and in the workplace. In a further complement to social history, feminist history explored women's everyday lives, but in early forms focused on "what forms of struggle they had engaged in, what battles they had won and what they had lost, how men had managed to maintain their power over women for so long."[10] In this regard, feminist historians specifically were interested in women as active agents in their own history.

But feminist history, with its concern about oppression, is also very much about changing the future. Feminist historians are firmly committed to changing the world in which they live, but to do that, they believe you need to understand how the world came to be what it is. To accomplish this, feminist historians established basic methodologies. First, they listened to silences in the primary sources and asked why those silences existed and where women fit into these stories. In other words, women who had been "hidden from history" were now "becoming visible."[11] Second, feminist scholars explored oppression, as it is crucial to understanding why there was an attempt to silence women's voices both in the past and in the past history of them. The silences in histories exist because there had been a notion that somehow women were unimportant because they did not operate in the public milieu. A famous story is relayed by Louise Tilly about her work: "A crusty old historian of the [French] Revolution rose during the question period and inquired, in his own eastern twang, 'Now that I know that women were participants in the Revolution, *what difference does it make?*'"[12] The "crusty old historians" read history through particular lenses that gave only a cursory glance at, if not outright rejected, women's histories. Feminist scholars, as Tilly eloquently points out, insisted that we need to focus on how it came to be that women were segregated at so many points and in so many places in history, *and* how the "so what?" attitude became so entrenched in the historical profession.

One of the first ways of conceptualizing this problem of oppression was through the notion of **patriarchy**, which became a central analytical category as feminists in the 1970s worked in their own contexts to challenge male power and assert equality. Defined simply, patriarchy draws on three main elements: rule by male authority, inheritance that is patrilineal, and emphasis on women's subordination. Its etymology, or word history, comes from the Latin *pater*, or father. The head of the family was known as the patriarch, and it is a common assumption that the first societies used the model of the family as a model of the state. As a feminist concept, patriarchy has a long lineage. At the turn of the twentieth century, the author Virginia Woolf as well as women involved in the Fabian movement in Britain explored patriarchy in relation to contemporary society.[13] By the 1960s, feminist theorists such as Kate Millet used the term specifically to critique the system of male domination over women. Historians, too, have examined patriarchy, placing it in larger historical context. In her book *The Creation of Patriarchy*, Gerda Lerner draws on the same traditions as Millet and layers the history of the institutionalization of male-controlled society over the more traditional textbook story of Western civilization. This male control was not a biological imperative, but rather a desire of social organization imposed on the two sexes and therefore ensuring an unequal power relation. By beginning her story with the organization of what we commonly define as the emergence of civilization, Lerner effectively historicizes the concept while also undermining claims of biological essence.

Early feminist histories emphasized this subordination of women in the past combined with Marxist frameworks to explore women's roles in class terms. Women's oppression was tied to reproductive capacity and to the balance of class relations. While Marxist feminism was particularly strong among sociologists and economists, many historians writing from a Marxist tradition gradually included feminist methodologies. These methodologies enabled them to explore the "relationship between the subordination of women and the organization of various modes of production."[14] One early example of a Marxist feminist approach is Jane Humphries' work on the nineteenth-century British working class.

In her work, Humphries argued that to the contrary of traditional Marxist philosophy, the fabric of the union of the working class actually facilitated class struggle. That is, rather than serving to produce more workers, or to reproduce capital through their **labor power**, the working-class family worked in and for itself. This storyline complements other stories of the insularity of the working class, such as that discussed by Gareth Stedman Jones (see Chapter 8).[15] Thus, Marxist feminism was not simply Marxism as usual with an infusion of women, but rather represented a synthesis of methodologies.

This synthesis, however, became a very uneasy relationship as the 1970s progressed. Feminist scholars questioned the continued dependence on Marxist theory as a useful analysis for women's particular experiences. In "The Unhappy Marriage of Marxism and Feminism," Heidi Hartmann argued that attempts by feminist scholars to integrate Marxism into feminist study resulted in the subordination of issues relevant to feminists. Marxist ideas of class and class struggle predominated and women's voices continued to be lost. Hartmann argued that feminists must continue to find ways to fight against the subordination of women inherent in the capitalist system that do not rely on Marxist structure because Marxist philosophy "give[s] no clues about why *women* are subordinate to men inside and outside the family and why it is not the other way around."[16] Further, she argues that because patriarchy as a concept reinforces hierarchies both among men and between men and women, and becomes further embedded in capitalist structures, "the struggle against capital and patriarchy cannot be successful if the study and practice of the issues of feminism are given up."[17]

Feminist historians, like feminist theorists, looked to other frameworks beyond the capitalist explanation—after all, women had been exploited previous to the rise of capitalism as an economic theory. Some of the great social histories of this period complicated the story of women's relationship to capitalism and put forth stories of women's agency. Christine Stansell's *City of Women*, for example, is a social history of women navigating the streets of nineteenth-century New York City. Rather than relying on the older trope of women's subordination or sexual oppression, Stansell instead explored the variety of working women in New York who "in the ebb and flow of large oppressions and small freedoms . . . traced out unforeseen possibilities for their sex."[18] Even women bound by traditional patriarchal structures could carve out a community with other women to limit the undisputed exercise of male power structures within the family, namely domestic violence.

In addition, many American feminist historians complicated the already complicated story of feminist history, making the argument that varieties of women's experiences also included women of color, not just cross class stories. To this end, Nell Irvin Painter discussed African-American women's experiences in the postbellum period and Vicki Ruiz wrote about Mexican cannery women in twentieth-century California.

In fact, the two main frameworks for feminist history in the 1970s and 1980s were labor history and the concept of separate spheres. Women's labor history, in which historians used the motif of history from below to write in the histories of women, proliferated in the period after 1968. The second framework for a long time was the construct of separate spheres that historians used to explore bourgeois women and the domestic realm. Also referred to as the "cult of domesticity," this history examined the historic roles of women and men as defined as public and private. Led by Barbara Welter and Nancy Cott, the use of domesticity as a historical framework explored the private roles of American women, particularly in the period of the early republic. Later, Linda Kerber would expand on this treatment in her conceptualization of "Republican Motherhood," a model of motherhood during the Early Republic wherein mothers, as special protectors of the next generation, taught children values of patriotism.[19] The study of bourgeois separate spheres also filled the historiography of France and Britain.[20]

Gender Theory and History

Another way that feminist scholars transformed the ways in which they explored the relationship between sex and power was through the introduction of **gender** as a category of analysis. In a seminal articulation of the use of gender for historians, the French historian Joan Scott argued that we need to radically shift our understanding of sexual oppression by exploring that oppression as a cultural construction. For Scott, feminist scholars, such as those described earlier in the chapter, had explored exploitation ahistorically. Instead, historians need to look at the ways in which different cultures over time defined sex roles. To do that requires the separation of **sex** from gender. Sex is based on biological function; that is, one is biologically male or female based on reproductive function. This biological function, however, does not determine identity.

Scott put forth the idea of gender as a mechanism for better understanding historical exploitation of women. Unlike sex, which refers specifically to biological function, gender refers to culturally defined norms of behavior between the two sexes. So for Scott, relations between the two are defined partly on physiology (reproductive capacity), but mostly on culture. There are "proper" roles for each of the sexes based on mere biological difference. These proper roles are often referred to as "masculine" and "feminine" behaviors. Further, these roles are historical, shifting both over time and space. In other words, gender roles are not stagnant, but differ depending on where you are in time and where you are in the world. While the history of separate spheres had earlier explored proper roles of the sexes, it did not address the historical specificity of those roles.

Gender as opposed to sex is a study of power and power relations. Whereas earlier scholarly feminism focused on oppression of women, it did not necessarily explore the meanings of shifts in power over time. Gender history, as Scott points out, drew much from the linguistic turn, but also from post-structuralism itself. Michel Foucault's theoretical discussions of binary oppositions and the omnipresence of power created an analytic framework for scholars interested in exploring these conditions historically. As a consequence, many feminists who rejected Marxist feminism and materialist feminism saw deconstruction and post-structuralism as areas wherein they could explore the textual, discursive framework of power relations between men and women. Language became a crucial ingredient for post-structural feminists. One of the most influential of these critical theorists remains Judith Butler (b. 1956). A professor of comparative literature, Butler has written numerous works examining power, gender, and sexuality. In *The Psychic Life of Power*, she argues that one of the problematic elements of Foucault's work is that resistance is simply an effect of the power it opposes. As a consequence, if nothing is outside of power, then resistance merely replicates the power structures. But then Butler turns Foucault around arguing that if he could argue that "a sign could be taken up, used for purposes counter to those for which it was designed, then he understood that even the most noxious terms could be owned, that the most injurious interpellations could also be the site of radical reoccupation and resignification."[21] In other words, through the lens of post-structuralism, gender can be used to destabilize fixed identities of norms of behavior imposed on sex. Even before this, however, Butler critiqued traditional feminist frameworks because they serve to reify conceptions of essential male and female characteristics—a concept known as **essentialism**. Her most well-known work, *Gender Trouble: Feminism and the Subversion of Identity*, works to break the barriers between biology of sex, the culture of gender, and the experience of sexuality. These works move far beyond the early feminism that basically accepted the categories of male and female as fixed, thereby focusing on the historical subordination of women as a group. With *Gender Trouble*, Butler articulated a new way of conceptualizing the relations between the sexes and how historians might understand identity formation of peoples of the past.

In a book coedited by Scott and Butler, Butler argued that the postmodern project can actually help the ultimate goal of feminism as the deconstruction of texts—literary and real—will aid in the process of "denaturaliz[ing] the terms" and therefore create contested sites. In other words, for Butler, the fixed subject—or identity (sex, gender, what have you)—sets up its own failure for working with the same structures as male-dominated society. For her part, Joan Scott also showed the value of deconstruction for feminists. Postmodernism's use of language, discourse, difference, and deconstruction provides significant analytic theories for feminism. Specifically, Scott argued that postmodernism could aid in "accounting not only for continuities but also for change over time."[22] Scott further argued that understanding the role of change over time can help historians break away from "uncritically accepting a gendered category" to examine meanings of these categories historically—over time and space.[23]

Butler's appropriation of Foucaultian discourse is matched by a more general hesitancy among feminists to approach Foucault. While influenced by poststructuralism, many feminist scholars remained rather distrustful of Foucault. Biddy Martin, for example, argued that postmodernism, in particular Foucault's ideas of power and subversion, provides very useful models for critiquing essential categories (search for *the* self or *the* nature of woman, and so forth). However, they also run the risk of losing sight of the very material structures that inform women's historical subordination—like patriarchy, for example. In other words, postmodernism is a good resource, but like Marxism, can lead to an unhappy relationship between itself and feminism.[24]

Working to combine the ontological with the epistemological is Elspeth Probyn in her work *Sexing the Self: Gendered Positions in Cultural Studies*. Her work is a crucial theory for historians wishing to remain within the materialist tradition. According to Probyn, we cannot just accept new definitions of the "feminine" used by postmodernists and male feminists. By doing that, we would accept "Woman" as a static category of imagination—remaining de Beauvoir's "other" pivoted against the normative "reality" of male. Further, she argues that "theorists" and "critics" are not academics cut off from the rest of social reality, but are deeply absorbed in some aspect of social reality—gender, race, class—and are speaking of the "lived experience" of that group. As such, her work is a very important reevaluation of the role of the critique and the role of experiences. For Probyn, experience is useful, in fact, necessary, despite attacks by deconstructionists, and can be a site wherein radical change is invoked.[25]

If we go back to the story of Boudicca, we can read her story in terms of gender. Told from a Roman (i.e., Tacitean) perspective, the people involved in the revolt were alien—feminine and fanatical. However, from a British standpoint, readily available in *The Annals*, the revolt was a revolt of vengeance for personal and political disrespect. Tacitus records her position thusly: "Boudicea, with her daughters before her in a chariot, went up to tribe after tribe, protesting that it was indeed usual for Britons to fight under the leadership of women. 'But now,' she said, 'it is not as a woman descended from noble ancestry, but as one of the people that I am avenging lost freedom, my scourged body, the outraged chastity of my daughters … If you weigh well the strength of the armies, and the causes of the war, you will see that in this battle you must conquer or die. This is a woman's resolve; as for men, they may live and be slaves.' " Thus, Boudicca's rebellion, though ultimately quashed by the Roman legionaries under Suetonius, was subversive in the way that it undermined Roman patriarchal structures—structures inherent in Roman conceptions of *pietas* and virtue (political), both of which were central to republican and imperial development.[26]

Gender history, then, explores the historical relationship between men and women and their social roles. By focusing more specifically on the social construction of roles for the sexes, gender history moves beyond the first manifestation of feminist history and takes feminist history beyond materialism. Anna Clark's work on Chartism in *The Struggle for the Breeches: Gender and the Making of the British Working Class* reflects both the influence of the linguistic turn and gender in writing about working-class lives. In this monograph, Clark explores the ways in which women's activism was used not only for political support by male Chartists, but also how it was used against women, constructing a very limited definition of class that firmly excluded women. Men used the middle-class rhetoric of separate spheres to argue that they were being denied their "manhood" and effectively excluded women from the struggle for working-class political rights. These exclusionary tactics would haunt working-class women as families could not subsist on one wage, and women's jobs, now confined to piecework, brought in considerably less than their previous work in factories.[27]

Gender constructions have also been used to examine the differences in women's participation in various revolutionary movements across the globe over the twentieth century. These historians of revolution argue that only through exploring women's constructed roles in society can historians (and outsiders to the revolutions) understand the choices women have made. For example, the West draws on the radical tradition of the French Revolution and the unsuccessful attempts by women such as Olympes De Gouges to obtain full participatory rights with men as the vanguard of women's revolutionary struggles, but as Mary Ann Tétrault, Valentine Moghadam, and others have shown, this expectation of women's roles based on the French case is as problematic as expecting all revolutions to be the same kind of "modern" revolutions generally. We need to realize that not only do women "experience revolution and its outcomes differently from men," as evidenced in De Gouges' experience (claiming the same rights as men and facing the guillotine for her claims), but also that women in different parts of the world draw on their own lived experience to define revolution from their own contexts, not in a larger, static, and ahistorical claim of "sisterhood." According to Sita Ranchod-Nillson, for example, "rural African women had their own agendas that were rooted in the rapid reconfiguration of gender relations that had taken place during the relatively brief colonial period."[28]

QUEER THEORY

If gender as a category of analysis is meant to call attention to the problems of binary oppositions and the essentialism those binaries invoke, **queer theory** works to destabilize it entirely. As discussed in Chapter 7, the concept of normativity draws necessary binaries of self versus other or normal versus deviant (among many other binaries). Queer theory expands on gender theory by questioning the existence of fixed sexual identity. As such, queer theory is distinct from gay and lesbian history, which focuses necessarily on identity politics, and is often quite critical of it. According to Annamarie Jagose, "Queer, then, is an identity category that has no interest in consolidating or even stabilising itself. It maintains its critique of identity-focused movements by understanding that even the formation of its own coalitional and negotiated constituencies may well result in exclusionary and reifying effects far in excess of those intended."[29]

The pioneer of queer theory is undeniably Eve Sedgwick (1950–2009), a straight woman who pushed the boundaries not just of gender theory but also of gay and lesbian studies. Born in Ohio and raised in Maryland, Sedgwick earned a BA in English at Cornell and then went to Yale where she earned her Ph.D. A prolific writer, her best-known work is *Epistemology of the Closet* published in 1990. Influenced by Foucault's later work, particularly his introductory volume to *The History of Sexuality*, Sedgwick argues the impossibility and untenable situation of being in the closet. According to Sedgwick, the construction of identities of heterosexual and homosexual serves only to reify perceived binary oppositions, oppositions that enforce difference and otherness. Queer theory, in essence, is the uncategorization of sexuality. Moreover, as a theory, it argues against the immediate framing of our own sexual behaviors implicit in the naming of sexual identity.

An example of both gender and queer theory is Matt Houlbrook's *Queer London*, a monograph about London's mid-twentieth-century gay community. While the periodization of the book ends in 1957, the year of the Wolfenden report and the move to legalization of gay activities, Houlbrook argues that his monograph is far from a celebratory history, as the very factors that enabled inclusion for gay men resulted in exclusionary tactics of those same men to weed out undesirable, unrespectable homosexuals. What Houlbrook does here is to challenge the very stability of fixed norms of sexuality across the board. Houlbrook's work, however, is very distinctly *not* feminist. As he says in his introduction, it is a book about men, not women. Thus, queer theory, like gender, builds from earlier strands of feminist theory, but often leaves the politics of feminism behind in favor of a more globalized, disruptured politics of identity.[30]

On the one hand, gender and queer theory have done much to explore the ways in which sexual relations are not "natural," but built on very specific social constructions that vary over time and space. In this way, the project of feminist history has expanded to explore, as Joan Scott stated, the ways in which norms of behavior are imposed on sexed bodies and how concepts such as patriarchy have become so embedded across societies. On the other hand, some have argued that later generations of gender theory and queer theory have lost the strength of critique embedded in earlier feminist history. Nevertheless, queer theory and gender theory, as feminism before them are committed to creating a more tolerant world by historicizing the ways in which intolerance has been culturally constructed.

CONCLUSION

This chapter, like all that preceded it, only scratched the surface of the varieties of feminist theory that have influenced historical writing over the last century focusing, as it does, predominantly on the Western feminist tradition and its relationship to historiography. Even within these space constraints, however, this chapter has explored a multiplicity of theoretical approaches to sex and sexuality that has broadened the scope of historical studies. Drawn to write new histories as a consequence of their own life experiences, feminist historians have provided the field not only with new methodologies and ways of reading/exploring documents, but also with vibrant accounts of the past.

Even with the move to more expanded gender analysis (LGBT analysis, for example) and queer theory that abandoned notions of the politics of feminism embedded in earlier historiography, feminism as a historical method—and indeed a political movement itself—remains a central category of analysis. Recently, there have been calls to return to a more materialist analysis, particularly in world and transnational history. Heidi Tinsman, for example, argued for "an alternative feminist materialist analysis." Tinsman used her work on Chile's fruit-growing regions to explain how women are exploited while at the same time increase their political agency. In other words, historians can combine the study of gender analysis with more traditional economic analysis to provide a more nuanced history of the roles of men and women.[31] About a decade later, Tinsman partnered with Ulrike Strasser to further explore how gender might be usefully employed in transnational history. In "It's a Man's World?" they use the case study of Latin America to argue the need to move beyond the either/or of the culture of sexuality or the materialism of global economics. Taking issue with a trajectory of world history that suggests that cultural histories of sexuality and gender could not intersect with world economic history, they opted for a different framework of transnational studies that suggests that "world history and histories of gender and sexuality converge naturally" around the concept of masculinity.[32]

Beyond rethinking materialism, however, feminist historians have argued that with all that is happening in the contemporary world surrounding women's rights, it is essential to get back to basics. In a recent article, Merry Wiesner-Hanks made the serious statement that even when we talk about representation and social construction, there are very real consequences for very real women and other subjected groups:

> I also want to add a final, more cautionary note. Individuals might very well understand themselves to be beyond a national identity or beyond a binarized notion of sexual identity, or even beyond gender. It is important to recognize, however, that national identities are not simply discursive categories but very real, as are gender and sexual identities also. Just as it produces national identities, the state continues to produce sexual and gender identities, often at its borders when it lets in or does not let in individuals whom it identifies as a certain type, thus barring them from full participation in a new globalized world.[33]

The old adage that sticks and stones may break bones but names can never hurt simply does not ring true. Names have very material consequences on women's lives and have affected legislation from personal property disputes, to employment concerns, to control over reproductive rights. While feminist history and its later variations have shed light on historical oppression of women, it is clear that there is still much work to be done.

THINKING LIKE A HISTORIAN

For this chapter, we would like you to go back to Chapter 5's excerpt, "Mrs. Walter Pinkus." Then, we had you read the document as social history inspired by the New Left. Now, we would like you to reexamine the source using a different (this time feminist or gendered) lens. As you reread the source, ask the following:

- How does Mrs. Pinkus weave her life story with her experiences as a woman?

- In looking at the story through the lens of gender as opposed to class, how does the interpretation differ?
- Were any of her occupations gendered and if so, how?
- What was her relationship with her husband like, and how does her relationship connect with traditional views of family life and gender roles?
- How might you use Mrs. Walter Pinkus' story in a history of twentieth-century women? Provide one or two examples.

The secondary reading for this chapter is by noted South Asian feminist historian Tanika Sarkar, whose work includes analysis of women's rights within Hinduism. As you read the article, consider the following:

- How does Sarkar historicize women's positions in India? How does she relate women's rights to law, politics, religion, and social trends?
- Find examples of and explain how Sarkar's discussion of "waves" of women's movements relates to concepts explained in this chapter.
- Is this a materialist history, a cultural history, or something in between? Explain by examining her methods and source material.
- How does Sarkar use gender history in this article? What theoretical traditions within feminist and gender history does she draw on?

Re-Read Mrs. Walter Pinkus from Chapter 5

Women in South Asia

The Raj and After[34]

Tanika Sarkar examines the evolving position of women in India before 1947 and since independence.

The fiftieth year of Indian independence lends itself to various kinds of stocktaking. It seems almost natural that the history of modern Indian women should be an essential part of this exercise, so when and why did the condition of women become an index to measure the nation's progress?

The nineteenth century started with extensive and anxious debates about the state of gender relations in Indian traditions. The new print culture, journalism and other forms of vernacular prose took up discussions about 'private' family matters and 'intimate' subjects concerning women and the household: suttee or widow immolation, age and forms of marriage, the possibility of divorce, of widow remarriage, education and male polygamy and so

on. Social and religious reform associations spent a great deal of time arguing about such matters. Later, with the deepening of popular anti-colonial protest, the possibility of womens' participation in this widened the area of discussion still further.

All this was very new. Not only were the issues of debate unprecedented, so was the amount of talk expended on them. Prior to this gender relations were frozen in sacred laws and in custom. If they were challenged it was within the context of everyday acts of defiance by women, in their secret transgressions, protest masked as sorrowful dirges and tales indicating a sense of the unfairness of the world. Now a qualitative leap was made away from these oblique expressions to a more open interrogation— not only by women, but also by men of liberal reformist persuasion.

The change has been explained in terms of an exposure to a liberal Western education that taught middle-class Indians to question the subjection of women. However, recent interpretations have been more critical of the gender perspective of these liberal reformers, attributing the changes to a desire to emulate Victorian moral codes and aping a bourgeois form of companionate marriage.

The first to question patriarchal traditions came from modern, dissident religious sects—the Brahmo Samaj, the Prarthana Samaj and later, the Arya Samaj. It is argued that their dissent isolated and excluded these reformers from larger networks of kinship and neighbourhood ties. In terrible personal loneliness, they turned to their core family group for social sustenance: wives and daughters suddenly emerged as crucial figures in their lives and this, in turn, brought their problems into focus.

Inspired by an acute sense of the deep social malaise of the country, there was little the reformers could actually hope to change. Their upper-caste, middle-class social moorings prevented a critical engagement with issues of peasant or caste exploitation and before the formation of nationalist associations in the late nineteenth century, there was an unwillingness to reflect on the colonial condition. Given these constraints, and the fact that Indian élites were excluded from administrative and entrepreneurial initiatives, there was little else that they could try to achieve.

The very fact of political subjection, which came to be regarded as a state of humiliation, raised sensitivity to wider issues of domination and subordination. How could it be recommended for one group of people and questioned for another? The subjection of women at home was immediately thrown into the spotlight. Recommended by the highest religious authorities, what had passed as unquestionable prescription suddenly lost its force.

Early women writers—from Kailashbashini Debi in Bengal in the 1860s, to Tarabai Shinde and Pandite Ramabai from Maharashtra in the 1880s—were already identifying the distribution of power in intimate human relationships in gender-political terms. The same vocabulary was often used to describe the subjection of the country as it was the subjection of women.

Since the late eighteenth century, British rule had exempted the domain of personal laws from state intervention, unless customary or scriptural sanction could be cited as a reason for change. Three important historical developments followed from this. First, the domestic sphere, governed by the personal laws, and a site of relative autonomy, became the last bastion of a vanished freedom, as well as the possible site of an emergent nation. Secondly, law as a domain of self activism led to a widespread involvement with the processes of legal change. The spread of print culture enabled a continuous interaction among various social groups on the everyday lives of ordinary folk. In the Telegu speaking areas of Madras, reformers relied on vernacular journalism to campaign on widow remarriage, in sharp contrast to Tamil speaking areas where reformist campaigns were moderate and dependent on English. As a result of the debates, gender norms were detached from the realm of sacred prescription or commonsense, and their ideological basis was made transparent.

Thirdly, legality now clashed with religious prescription in unprecedented ways. Suttee—hitherto a universally accepted sign of womanly virtue—was now legally classified as a crime. Widow remarriage—previously castigated by all pious Hindus as an entirely illegitimate desire—was now made legal. Not that the laws actually transformed partiarchal [sic] practices and prejudices. Iswarchandra Vidyasagar, the chief campaigner for remarriage, died a disappointed man. He often had to bribe men to marry widows and quite a few deserted their wives later. The number of remarried widows remained negligible. The Widow Remarriage Association at Rajamundry under Viresalingam Pantulu achieved a total of forty remarriages in the Telegu speaking areas of the south between 1881 and 1919. Yet the laws opened up a faultline, a tension, between what was becoming illicit practice and what was now legally permissible. Moreover, arguments replaced the unquestioned acceptance of what defined a 'good' woman. In 1870, Vishnu Shastri Pandit initiated a famous debate at Poona, the stronghold of Braham orthodoxy, on the

question of remarriage. It went on for ten days. Reformers were defeated, but they had forced the orthodoxy to engage in debate.

Up until the late nineteenth century, there was a powerful customary belief that educated women were destined to be spinsters. Reformist endeavours strained against this. Starting with Calcutta, Bombay and Madras, they were able to make some education available for middle-class girls. This was done in the teeth of orthodox resistance. In colonial India, male claims to power depended very largely on their intellectual achievements, since most other forms of 'manly' and masterful enterprise were closed to them. Educated women, therefore, posed a threat to the very basis of masculinity. Orthodox reactions often took in the form of satirical imaginings of emasculated, effeminate men and masculinised women on top.

The content of women's education tended to be moderate and geared to home management—a fact which has to be separated from the actual social consequences of the act of learning. The pressure for education at least, from women in reformist, élite families was, therefore, persistent. The first girl graduates from Calcutta University received their degrees decades ahead of British women.

Reformers could not always achieve new legislation, however. Malabari's campaign for raising the age of marriage was truncated into a highly modified age of consent. Agitations against polygamy did not produce any legal deterrents. The new laws never really acquired the power and influence that religious prescriptions had enjoyed. Nor were they grounded in a strong or coherent notion of equality or individual rights. Their significance, then, was not so much the creation of a new order as questioning existing practice and rattling the bars. Once suttee, absence of education, remarriage of widows, non-consensual, indissoluble, early marriage for girls were reinterpreted as signs of great oppression, the Hindu home and the family were recast as primary sites for the practice of oppression. So the discussions extended beyond their specific objectives and made porous the divide between the private and the public spheres.

The Petition against the Abolition of Suttee of 1829 had claimed:

Hindu widows perform of their own accord and pleasure and for the benefit of their husbands' souls and for their own the sacrifice of self immolation called suttee.

Later, the 1856 Bill to remove all legal obstacles to the marriage of Hindu widows stated:

In the case of the widow who is of full age or whose marriage has been consummated, her own consent shall be sufficient to constitute, her remarriage lawful.

The two statements came from two very different positions, one from the orthodox view that defended suttee, and the second from a reformist bill, legalising widow remarriage. Yet both refer to the woman's own consent, pleasure and will as the ultimate arbiter in the decisions. No doubt, the inference is purely strategic, consent meaning something far less than informed and adult assent. But, it was a sign of the new times that the words were used at all on the basis of internal imperative, rather than as a purely externalised prescription. In the case of the Age of Consent controversy of 1891, after a girl of ten died in Calcutta having been raped by her husband, the language of willed consent clashed too obviously with the Hindu revivalist imperative of justifying a state of non-interference and status quo in the Hindu patriarchal order. As a result, in the last decades of the nineteenth century revivalists moved away from the domain of personal laws altogether. Swami Vivekananda gathered around a group of male ascetics who would try to rejuvenate Hindu society through philanthropic service.

In Punjab and in the United Provinces, the revivalist. Vedas-based Arya Samaj of Swami Dayanand marked out a different trajectory. This group introduced quite drastic changes in conventional domestic practices: widow remarriage, an end to child marriage and male polygamy and the introduction of education for women. However, whereas earlier liberal reformers had advocated remarriage by normalising the sexual desires of child widows, Dayanand advised it in the interests of a better growth rate for the community. A widow was permitted only to remarry a widower, and the marriage, had to be terminated after procreation. The women was to be educated solely for more disciplined child-rearing. Each change denied individual rights and further provoked the woman to the demographic and pedagogic purposes of an authoritarian community.

It is true that reformers, generally, functioned within a middle-class, upper-caste orbit. Few would support the Act of 1891, curtailing working hours in factories for women and children. There was little concern for the problems that tribal women faced over the encroachments of a modern market economy. Large-scale industrial production severed the earlier links between the household and production and the woman's role therein.

With the commercialisation of agriculture and the emergence of an upwardly mobile peasantry, peasant women were pulled out of farm labour in the interests of social respectability and confined to the household where their labour inputs were relatively invisible. In the new factories, there were practically no government regulations to ensure living wages, security of jobs and welfare facilities. In the tea plantations there was reckless economic and sexual exploitation of coolie women. These developments occasionally produced flashes of concerned, investigative journalistic exposure, but, otherwise, received little systematic attention. Education was largely confined to affluent, upper-caste urban families.

However, the limited reforms had some influence beyond the upper social level. There had been a long-term percolation of Brahmanical orthodoxy among upwardly-mobile low castes. Suttee, for instance, had become fairly common among several low castes in Bengal, even though the custom was meant for upper-caste widows. A prohibition against widow remarriage and the spread of infant marriage had become prevalent among castes whose custom did not prescribe such practices. Reforms that encouraged widow remarriage, womens' education and a higher age of marriage, gradually emerged as alternative ways of acquiring social respectability. It is interesting that low-caste reformers like Jotirao Phule in western India, knitted up the oppression against high-caste women with the exploitation of low castes to indicate the scope of Brahmanical disciplines.

Much of the nineteenth-century legal and educational reforms were restricted within the Hindu community. Modern education was a domain that even Muslim men entered rather late, after substantial resistance from the orthodoxy. Sayyid Ahmad Khan, who fought a hard battle to legitimise Western education and science, believed that women needed to be shielded from Western innovation like schooling. However, a consensus developed later in the century that women could be given an education befitting to their sex at home. Nadhir Ahmad wrote several best-selling Urdu novels popularising a new ideal for the élite woman: instead of following the typically feminine preoccupations of a leisured class, secluded education at home would turn her into a pious, responsible housewife.

While such literature reflected new patriarchal needs in an embourgeoised household, it also found enormous resonance among women readers. Accessible, fictionalised Urdu satisfied a thirst for reading matter that was at once interesting as well as serious. The narrative of home-based achievements through education created a hopeful blueprint for women whose status so far had depended only on kinship connections. While the new novels did not expand the boundaries of domestic confinement, they conveyed, nonetheless, a sense of self-worth by underlining women's importance both to home and society. They were also sensitive to the problems of seclusion.

Following upon his *Mirat al ars* and its sequels that appeared from the 1870s, and partly as a reaction to their relatively non-denominational and open nature, Maulana Ashraf Ali Thanawi came up with novels within the same format but with a different set of values. His *Bihishti Zewar* (1905) attempted a thoroughgoing Islamicisation of women who shared a lot of female custom with Hindu women. It was also careful to shore up the domestic confines that were now troubled by demands for schools for girls. In 1906, in the face of opposition from the local Urdu press, Begum Abdullah and the Begum of Bhopal had managed to open a girls' school at Aligarh.

While formal education for Muslim girls came late in the day, and legal reforms had to wait until the first few decades of the twentieth century, a different kind of battle over womens' rights was going on in the Anglo-Indian lawcourts throughout the nineteenth century. This laid the basis for the Shariati Act of the 1930s. The British Government was formally committed to privileging Quranic and Shariati regulation over customary norms and practices. The policy provided for larger property entitlements. Widows, for instance, could claim and win the restoration of the full amount of the *mehr* (the sum promised to the bride at the time of the marriage) which customarily was rarely given to her. Despite problems of deposition of evidence in court by women in Purdah, we find them tenaciously fighting out disputes in law-courts.

The reforms had created great interest in domestic issues and women were the privileged authorities on the subject. The first generations of middle-class women graduates, doctors and teachers were seen as saviours of their sex. Their achievements were celebrated less in terms of economic independence as for proving the innate intellectual abilities of women.

Gradually women began to organise public institutions for reform: mostly, schools and widows' homes. Pandita Ramabai founded the Sharda Sadan at Poona for widows to educate and train them as teachers, doctors and nurses. Sister Subbalakshmi established a school for high-caste widows in Madras.

In the early years of the twentieth century, Begum Rokeya Sakhawat Hussein founded a chain of schools. She also wrote biting satire on the nature of religious sanction for patriarchal double standards. Subbalakshmi and Ramabai had converted to Christianity, although Ramabai's relations with her church were very tense; Rokeya was suspected of Christian leanings. All three were bitterly criticised by the custodians of their respective religious communities.

From public institutions for reform and welfare, women leaders had moved into the corridors of mainstream political activism by the second decade of the twentieth century. Associations like Womens' Indian Association, the National Council of Women in India and the All India Womens' Conference campaigned for suffrage, marriage reform, participation in municipal and legislative politics. The language of reform did not directly challenge the public/private divide, nor did it unambiguously speak about equality. Public activism of a few, however, strained against the domestic confines of most. Also, at a time of worsening Hindu-Muslim relations throughout the country, these associations represented all religious communities and advanced issues that concerned women across religious divides.

There has been considerable debate about whether the militant political activism that the Gandhian Congress offered to women empowered them in the long run. Gandhi himself espoused the ideology of separate spheres for men and women, although he was critical of specific abuses like women's seclusion. The urgent pressures of anti-colonial protest made it difficult, in any case, to focus adequately on an agenda of social reform. In practice, however, Gandhi opened up forms of political activism to all women. During the Civil Disobedience movement, peasant women became 'dictators' of underground Congress units at village level while Marwari women from deeply conservative families joined street demonstrations, picketed shops and courted arrest. The principle of non-violence saw to it that women's political activism would not appear as too radically transgressive an act.

The deployment of familial images and kinship terms that described the nationalist community as a family, helped women to inhabit the political domain more easily. Bi Amman, the mother of the Ali brothers, could address mass meetings of men whom she called her sons, during the Khilafat movement, reaching a stage when she could publicly unveil herself. The forms of political activism breached the boundaries of feminine domesticity irretrievably. Ordinary housewives transgressed ritual taboo by going to prison, joining street demonstrations, and facing police violence. In this vein, nationalism also created immensely widened networks of female solidarity. The active and creative political struggles of women created some of the authentic sources for Indian democracy, and disseminated a highly informed political understanding despite widespread illiteracy and poverty.

The mass movements of the Left openly repudiated the ideology of separate spheres. Women from tribal and poor peasant milieus joined enormously risky peasant armed struggles. Yet in spite of this they were excluded from decision-making processes, and thrust back into old roles after the collapse of the movements. In working-class movements, women workers joined strikes and demonstrations, and middle-class women trade unionists worked in the slums. Yet, specific problems of women workers were routinely placed at the bottom of general charters of demands and working-class women, for all their militancy, would be absent from union leadership.

When independence came, the liberal premises of Indian nationalism were embodied in the secular-democratic constitution which recognised all adult Indian women as fully-fledged citizens of the country. At the same time, a very different logic of state-sponsored patriarchy unfolded when Hindu women, abducted into Pakistani territory during the riots, were collected by state agencies and returned to their families without their consent being solicited. The tension between a formal commitment to equality and deeply ingrained patriarchal traditions in the organs of the state have remained constant. In the early 1950s, a series of laws modified Hindu marriage, divorce, inheritance and maintenance rights. Though they outraged conservative Hindu opinion, radicals and women politicians felt them to be far too moderate. The state does not interfere in the laws of the religious minorities which remain the preserve of orthodox community leaders.

A new wave in women's movements was evident from the 1970s, in the wake of radical class struggles in the late 1960s and 70s where women had participated on a wide scale, but on somewhat unequal terms. Autonomous organisations developed along with a strengthening of womens' groups within mainstream Left parties. Their radicalism has forced the state to embark upon a spate of fresh legislation, especially concerning rape and dowry.

However, women's radicalism has produced an orthodox backlash that legislative activity failed to contain. Suttee was spectacularly celebrated at Deorala in 1987 when a teenaged widow was publicly burnt to death, with the criminal instigators released by court order this year. Bhanwari Debi, a poor low-caste woman was gang-raped at Bhateri village in Rajasthan for trying to prevent infant marriage among high-caste landlords. The police brutally humiliated her when she approached them. Law, justice and the police remain deeply implicated in the most unambiguous forms of patriarchal controls.

The recent growth of religious fundamentalism and violent Hindu majoritarianism seeks to compel women to submit to the discipline of community custodians. Majoritarian violence puts a difficult choice before Muslim women since Muslim fundamentalism uses the image of an endangered minority community to reinforce its rule, and opposes reform of divorce and maintenance regulations. The Hindutva movement, which has so far insulated its women from active politics, now offers them leading roles within violent attacks on Muslims.

The New Right divides and separates women into communities, and gender-based commonalities are sought to be undermined. This comes at a most opportune moment for the current phase in Indian capitalism when structural adjustment programmes, with their inflationary plans and their cuts into extremely meagre welfare spending, have created immense hardships for poorer women. The sectorisation of women and the constant presence of communal violence may sap women's resistance to upper-caste and ruling-class control over the labour force, trade union rights and the bodies of low-caste, peasant, tribal and working-class women.

Have we moved ahead at all, or are we running round in circles, rooted to the same spot? There is no easy answer. The widening mobilisation of élite women for prestigious management and bureaucratic jobs must be set against the increasing vulnerability of large masses of women as employment becomes rare or informal and casual, and as prices continue to rise, cutting into their limited share of domestic resources.

Indian women still live with murders related to dowry demands, suttee, rape—especially of low-caste and labouring women—female infanticide and foeticide. Female mortality is much higher and literacy rates are considerably lower in India than they are in sub-Saharan Africa. The real measure of change lies, perhaps, more in the domain of political activism: the capacity for protest, the understanding and the world view that sustain the protests and the collectivities that enable and embody them. ■

For Further Reading

1. J. Krishnamurty (ed), *Women in Colonial India* (Oxford University Press, 1989); Gail Minault, *The Extended Family: Women and Political Participation in India and Pakistan* (Chanakya Publications, Delhi, 1981); Sangari and Vaid (eds), *Recasting Women: Essays in Colonial History* (Kali for Women, Delhi, 1989); Zoye Hasan (ed): *Forging Identities. Gender, Communities and the State* (Kali for

Women, Delhi, 1994); Tanika Sarkar and Vrashi Butalia (eds), *Women and the Hindu Right* (Zed Press, 1995).

2. Tanika Sarkar is Senior Lecturer in History, St Stephen's College, University of Delhi and the author of *Bengal 1928–34: The Politics of Protest* (Oxford University Press, 1987). ∎

Endnotes

1. Natalie Zemon Davis, interviewed by Rob Harding and Judy Coffin, in *Visions of History: Interviews*, eds. Henry Abelove, Betsy Blackmar, Peter Dimock, and Jonathan Schneer (New York: Pantheon Books, 1983), 116.

2. Tacitus *Annals* Book XIV, accessed April 21, 2012, http://classics.mit.edu/Tacitus/annals.10.xiv.html; Ban Zhao, "Lessons for Women," in Nancy Lee Swann, *Pan Chao, Foremost Woman Scholar of China, First Century A.D.: Background, Ancestry, Life and Writings of the Most Celebrated Chinese Woman of Letters* (New York: The Century Company, 1932), 82–86, http://hdl.handle.net/2027/heb.04225.0001.001.

3. Natalie Zemon Davis, in *Visions of History: Interviews*, 116.

4. Anna Clark, "The Rhetoric of Chartist Domesticity: Gender, Language and Class in the 1830s and 1840s," *Journal of British Studies* 31 (1992): 62–88.

5. Simone de Beauvoir, *The Second Sex*, Reprint (New York: Vintage Press, 2010).

6. Susan Mosher Stuard, "The Annales School and Feminist History: Opening Dialogue with the American Stepchild," *Signs* 7/1 (Autumn 1981): 139.

7. Sheila Rowbotham, interviewed by Dina Copelman, in *Visions of History: Interviews*, eds. Henry Abelove, Betsy Blackmar, Peter Dimock, and Jonathan Schneer (New York: Pantheon Books, 1983), 54.

8. Linda Gordon, interviewed by Carol Lasser, in *Visions of History: Interviews*, eds. Henry Abelove, Betsy Blackmar, Peter Dimock, and Jonathan Schneer (New York: Pantheon Books, 1983), 83.

9. Catherine Hall, *White, Male and Middle Class: Explorations in Feminism and History* (New York: Routledge, 1992), 5.

10. *Ibid.*, 8.

11. This sentence takes its inspiration from two important works of feminist history, Sheila Rowbotham's *Hidden from History: 300 Years of Women's Oppression and the Fight Against It* (London: Pluto Press, 1973) and Renate Bridenthal's *Becoming Visible: Women in European History*, 3rd ed. (Boston: Houghton Mifflin, 1998).

12. Louise Tilly, "Gender, Women's History, and Social History," *Social Science History* 13/4 (Winter 1989): 439.

13. Veronica Beechey, "On Patriarchy," *Feminist Review* no. 3 (1979): 66.

14. *Ibid.*, 66.

15. Jane Humphries, "The Working Class Family, Women's Liberation, and Class Struggle: The Case of Nineteenth-Century British History," *Review of Radical Political Economics* 9/3 (October 1977): 25–41; also Humphries, "Work, Class Struggle, and the Persistence of the Working-Class Family," *Cambridge Journal of Economics* 1 (1977): 241–258.

16. Heidi Hartmann, "The Unhappy Marriage of Marxism and Feminism: Toward a More Progressive Union," *Capital and Class* 3/2 (Summer 1979): 8 (emphasis hers).

17. *Ibid.*, 24.

18. Christine Stansell, *City of Women: Sex and Class in New York, 1789-1860* (New York: Alfred A. Knopf, 1986), 221.

19. Nancy Isenberg, "Second Thoughts on Gender and Women's History," *American Studies* 36/1 (1995): 93–103.

20. Bonnie Smith, *Ladies of the Leisure Class: The Bourgeoises of Northern France in the Nineteenth Century* (Princeton: Princeton University Press, 1981); Leonore Davidoff and Catherine Hall, *Family Fortunes: Men and Women of the English Middle Class, 1780-1850* (Chicago: University of Chicago Press, 1987).

21. Judith Butler, *The Psychic Life of Power* (Stanford: Stanford University Press, 1997), 98–104.

22. Joan Scott, "Deconstructing Equality-Versus Difference, or, The Uses of Poststructuralist Theory for Feminism," *Theorizing Feminism: Parallel Trends in the Humanities and Social Sciences*, 2nd ed. eds., Anne C. Hermann and Abigail J. Stewart (Boulder [CO]: Westview Press, 2001), 254.

23. *Ibid.*, 265–266.

24. Biddy Martin, "Feminism, Criticism, and Foucault," *New German Critique* 27, Women Writers and Critics (1982): 3–30.

25. Elspeth Probyn, *Sexing the Self: Gendered Positions in Cultural Studies* (London: Routledge, 1993), 56, 57, 22–31.

26. Tacitus, *Annals* Book 14, http://classics.mit.edu/Tacitus/annals.10.xiv.html; Michael Roberts, "The Revolt of Boudicca (Tacitus, Annals 14.29-39) and the Assertion of *Libertas* in Neronian Rome," *The American Journal of Philology* 109/1 (Spring 1988): 118–132.

27. Anna Clark, *The Struggle for the Breeches: Gender and the Making of the British Working Class* (Berkeley: University of California Press, 1995).

28. Mary Ann Tétrault, "Introduction," and Sita Ranchod-Nilsson, " 'This, too, is a Way of Fighting': Rural Women's Participation in Zimbabwe's Liberation War," in *Women and Revolution in Africa, Asia, and the New World*, ed. Mary Ann Tétrault (Columbia [SC]: University of South Carolina Press, 1994), 20, 64.

29. Annamarie Jagose, "Queer Theory," *Australian Humanities Review* no. 4 (December 1996), http://www.australianhumanitiesreview.org/archive/Issue-Dec-1996/jagose.html.

30. Matt Houlbrook, *Queer London: Perils and Pleasures in the Sexual Metropolis, 1918-1957* (Chicago: University of Chicago Press, 2005)

31. Heidi Tinsman, "Reviving Feminist Materialism: Gender and Neoliberalism in Pinochet's Chile," *Signs* 26/1 (Autumn 2000): 147.

32. Ulrike Strasser and Heidi Tinsman, "It's a Man's World? World History Meets the History of Masculinity, in Latin American Studies, For Instance," *Journal of World History* 21/1 (2010): 77.

33. Merry Wiesner-Hanks, "Crossing Borders in Transnational Gender History," *Journal of Global History* 6 (2011): 378.

34. Tanika Sarkar, "Women in South Asia: The Raj and After," *History Today* 47/9 (September 1997): 54–59.

CHAPTER 10

SUBALTERN STUDIES, POSTCOLONIAL THEORY, AND THE HISTORY OF RACE AND NATION

CHAPTER OUTLINE

■ Europe and the New Imperialism

■ Postcolonial Theory

■ Subaltern Studies

■ Theories and Histories of Race and Nation

■ Conclusion

■ Thinking Like a Historian

"Subaltern Studies obtains its force as postcolonial criticism from a catachrestic combination of Marxism, poststructuralism, Gramsci and Foucault, the modern West and India, archival research and textual criticism."

Gyan Prakash[1]

By now, if you have read this book from the beginning, you should have a strong sense of the various critiques of Whiggish history and the consequent move away from histories of elites. This last chapter, focused on race, takes many elements of theories you have encountered to better understand histories of formerly colonized peoples or the history of race relations. Histories of race and empire, like nearly every other theory we have encountered in this text, are reliant on a number of different theoretical traditions and approaches. In addition to the specific theorists that we explore in this chapter, we refer back to earlier chapters you have read, particularly Chapter 8, but also Chapter 5. In this chapter, we explore interrelated yet also very distinct theories, sometimes hotly debated among their practitioners in terms of value for histories of race and nation. Clearly, there is a relation between Subaltern Studies and postcolonial history, but they are not necessarily mutually inclusive, as you shall read later in the chapter. As you can see by our opening quote, scholars from within this tradition very much see their own work as an "odd mix" of traditions. Before we explore these theories, however, we provide a quick overview of European imperialism and the process of decolonization to provide a basic foundational knowledge of the historical contexts surrounding these scholarly debates.

EUROPE AND THE NEW IMPERIALISM

European colonization can be said to encompass two very distinct periods. The first period lasted roughly from 1450 to 1800 and the second period from 1850 to post-World War II. While there are many similarities between these moments of European dominance over the rest of the world, they do have some marked differences. The first age of colonization was defined by Europe's mercantilist framework, and as a result was marked by competition for the world's resources and souls. It was the period of navigational improvements and the consequent "opening of the ocean" where Europeans were no longer confined to hugging the African coast afraid of getting lost at sea. Through a better understanding of the winds of the Atlantic and the realization that the world's landmass was much larger than previously imagined, Europeans established an imperial legacy, one that decimated the indigenous populations of the Americas and destroyed long-lived cultures.

The second age of colonization occurred during the period of the triumph of science. In an earlier chapter, we discussed Charles Darwin, Herbert Spencer, and social Darwinism. These ideas helped Europeans explain the world and provide meaning for the world around them. **Scientific racism**, as it is now known, served as a vehicle for Europeans to pursue imperialist policies that moved beyond the quest for resources. Certainly, the desire for raw materials to bring to the home country (known as **economic extraction**) still existed, with Europeans creating a monopoly economy in Africa for rubber (for tires and other commodities), ivory (for trinkets and piano keys), and gold and diamonds (luxury items), but the justification for the brutality toward indigenous populations centered on very "modern" notions of science as well as Enlightenment ideals of rights to pursue property. As you read in Chapter 2, any society that remained migratory was said to have no understanding of permanent possession of the soil, and therefore no real concept of how to be a true nation.[2] The second wave of imperialism also had two distinct imperial frameworks—the settler colony and the administrative colony. In an administrative colony, the European country sent administrators to govern a region, but those administrators held government positions and could be recalled at any time, as with any government position. The settler colony, much like the early British colonies in what would become the United States, also had an administrative component, but administration was conducted predominantly by emigrants—those who left the home country to settle permanently. Settler colonies, such as those in Rhodesia (modern-day Zimbabwe), Kenya, or Algeria, often established entrenched policies of apartheid.

The task of removing imperial possessions—or **decolonization**—began seriously after World War II when many colonial regions made the case that they had fought for their "mother country" in two major conflicts but had received nothing in return. Further, the colonial powers themselves, namely Britain and France, simply lacked the economic power to maintain vast holdings. This process began in 1945 with the change in status of many colonized areas and continued through 1997 with the British formally leaving Hong Kong after its long residence since the Opium Wars of the mid-nineteenth century.

POSTCOLONIAL THEORY

In its simplest definition, **postcolonial** refers to the moment after decolonization is complete. However, while countries such as India may have achieved independence, there were still residues of empire in the language as well as in the architecture and infrastructure built during the colonial period. As a consequence, many scholars from former colonies began to use the term "postcolonial" as a way to think about the fact that empire never really left even if the seat of government did. This residue of empire has been described by some as "a more dangerous cancer" than imperialism itself.[3] Therefore early studies of race and nation explored the ways in which this infrastructure and language remained, serving as a ghost of the past exploitation of local societies. This residue—or echo—of empire was very early conceptualized by Frantz Fanon in the 1950s. Fanon (1925–1961) was born in a middle-class family in French Martinique, and he moved to France to study psychiatry. While his family's economic standing provided him certain privileges at home, he quickly learned how embedded racism was in colonial society when he left for college in France. When he was assigned to work in an Algerian hospital in 1953, he witnessed firsthand the psychological destructiveness of colonial struggle.

Even before postmodern critics such as Lyotard, Derrida, or Foucault wrote about dismantling the universal structures of modernity, scholars such as Frantz Fanon argued that white, male Europe disregarded stories of other groups, in particular, the story of independence. In a speech given at the Congress of Black African Authors in 1959, Fanon argued that critics of the modern nation-state and of national culture seem to forget that for the vast majority of people on the earth, the process of making the nation was not yet complete:

> National claims, it is here and there stated, are a phase that humanity has left behind. It is the day of great concerted actions, and retarded nationalists ought in consequence to set their mistakes aright.

We, however, consider that the mistake, which may have very serious consequences, lies in wishing to skip the national period. If culture is the expression of national consciousness, I will not hesitate to affirm that in the case with which we are dealing it is the national consciousness which is the most elaborate form of culture.[4]

In this passage, Fanon's concept of the necessity of national culture is at odds with Europe's increasing sense of internationalism. At the time of his speech, France was among the leaders of Europe trying to institute a European common market in an attempt at strengthening unity among Europeans. Fanon, long before cultural historians, but fairly contemporaneous with Hoggart or Williams, argued for the unifying elements of shared traditions, and Europeans cannot simply disregard them because they believe the world has moved on. For Fanon, those shared traditions emerged in national discourse.

In addition to his commentary on national structure, Fanon was among the first to theorize the nature of violent colonial struggle, and his work has been of tremendous importance to postcolonial scholars. *Wretched of the Earth* argued that violent struggle is warranted when all other attempts at securing freedom have failed.[5] Moreover, unlike any commentator since Marx, Fanon argued that only the landless and dispossessed—those with their backs against the wall, the "wretched" of the book's title—could ever be the true agents of revolutionary change. No industrial working class, no vanguard of the proletariat, just the down and out in their most raw and unmediated form. Published the year of his death, *Wretched of the Earth* remains a classic discussion of the liberation movements of colonial peoples.

However, Fanon's most famous work remains his first publication *Black Skin, White Masks* (1952), a polemic against the inherent racism of colonialism. Widely regarded as the foundation for Postcolonial Studies, the book talks about the psychological effects of colonialism on colonized people in terms of shifting their attitudes toward their own biological skin color. According to Fanon, not only do people of color speak differently among themselves than they do with others, but they also speak differently with those who have been to the **métropole** than with those who have not. Blacks have internalized their own oppression and sense of oppression resulting in this duality of discourse. For Fanon, what is required is raising of consciousness of one's identity in relation to global politics rather than buying into a false hierarchy of race.[6]

Fanon's influence can be clearly seen in the 1990s. As Fanon did with the European idea of the nation-state, postcolonial scholars argued that modernity has not exhausted its currency, and just because the first world rejected modernism does not mean it can be so easily tossed aside for the rest of the world.[7] Postcolonial scholars thus have a very uneasy relationship with postmodernism's critique of the grand narrative. In particular, they argue that the critique itself is Eurocentric, disregarding many independence movements and struggles by colonized regions, as Fanon's discussion of nationalism contends. Dipesh Chakrabarty's "Postcoloniality and the Artifice of History: Who Speaks for 'Indian' Pasts?" very directly states some of the problem: It is easy for scholars in the West to write histories of their nations or groups of people within the nation without so much as a casual thought to colonized or formerly colonized peoples, but this is an impossibility for anyone who has been subject to colonialism.[8]

While Fanon's work has a deep cultural memory for postcolonial scholars, the first theoretical work of modern postcolonial theory probably belongs to Edward Said (pronounced Sie-eed, 1935–2004) and his seminal work *Orientalism* (1978). Said was born in a Palestinian Christian family that migrated to Egypt in 1948 after the division of the area following the founding of Israel. Educated at boarding schools in the United States, he attended Princeton University for his BA and Harvard University for his graduate degrees before taking a faculty position at Columbia University in 1963. Said was a lifetime supporter of Palestinian statehood, but while critical of US foreign policy, he was equally critical of Palestinian intransigency. He was a self-described secular scholar critical of the use of religious images for political purposes. He died from complications of leukemia in 2003.

Orientalism was Said's second major work and his most profound. In this book, he explored the concept of Otherness and how the West imagined its relationship to the East—what it called "the Orient"—in binary frameworks. Us versus them, Occident versus Orient, modern versus premodern, self versus other. Like Simone de Beauvoir, Michel Foucault, and Jacques Derrida, Said argued that the construction of these binaries enabled the West to imagine an exotic, effeminate, distinctly unmodern Orient—a world so different that a chasm exists, "beyond which all difference is insurmountable." And like de Beauvoir, Derrida, and Foucault, Said recognizes that these binaries are socially constructed, not based on essential differences. It is, rather simply, the West's imagination of the rest of the world. Because the "East" is so far removed, Western intellectuals and politicians justified colonization because their imagination suggested an inherent Western superiority.[9]

Further, this system of representation is designed to deny the Orient its own history. Indeed, in being named it loses control to the West and is subject to its hegemony, denied its own history, language, and culture unmediated by Western intrusion. This is the brilliance of the monograph as it sets up a theoretical foundation for scholars to reimagine the Orient and reclaim it. The representation also occurs within prescribed geographic boundaries. In other words, people inhabit these spaces, so the representation of the Orient also operates in an ontological space and there are material consequences of this construction. The policies built on the Orientalist foundation may have no basis in reality but are built on cultural fictions that consequently negatively impact living, breathing people.

In addition to Fanon's concept of internalization and Said's concept of Orientalism, Homi Bhabha's construct of **hybridity** has tremendously influenced postcolonial theory and history even while being the subject of much debate within the field. Born in India in 1950, Bhabha went to school in Mumbai and at Oxford in the United Kingdom studying English literature. He has spent his professional career at a number of universities in both the United Kingdom and the United States and is currently the director of the Humanities Center at Harvard University.

Bhabha builds from Said's work in examining how the West constantly reshapes the Other, but his most well-known conceptualization is hybridity. When the so-called "other" (colonial migrants) comes into contact with the imperial "self" (i.e., moves to the "mother country"), the migrant inhabits a space in between two worlds, neither here, nor there. This is a space in which the differences—both real and imagined—between self and other come into conflict. It is what Bhabha calls a third space—or liminal space. This space is a place of power according to Bhabha, as it can serve the potential of undermining the strict categories of race or nation by accepting the hybrid voice.[10] This hybrid voice offers the best possibility for understanding contemporary culture.

It is in this context that **diaspora** becomes central to postcolonial theory. A diaspora is any group of peoples dispersed from their homeland. It is through the diaspora that the very notion of hybridity can exist. And it

is also through diaspora that historians can understand the complex ways in which cultures blend, producing new mixtures. According to Bill Ashcroft, "the diasporic writer [or musician or filmmaker] provides the prospect of a fluidity of identity."[11] In other words, it is possible to retain your home identity even when you plant new roots halfway around the world. And this can be a good thing.

Bhabha's influences touch on a key element of the migrant in the métropole. By way of example, the London-based author Salman Rushdie borrowed playfully from the *Star Wars* films to announce that the "Empire Writes Back." Clearly, the empire for Rushdie means something fundamentally different from George Lucas' film, as he refers to the colonized peoples and their intellectual interactions with and in the métropole. In a monograph by the same name, authors Bill Ashcroft, Gareth Griffiths, and Helen Tiffin explore a long legacy of conflicted meanings of hybridity to argue that postcolonialism's strength lies in the ways it can offer a comparative methodology and worldview through the lens of hybridity.[12]

Another concept related to hybridity is **creoleness**. Like hybridity, creoleness demands an identity different from the "other" of the migrant or the sameness of the home country. Proponents of creoleness, primarily located in literary studies, suggest that identity in the modern, postcolonial world cannot be narrowed down to a single, unified factor, but rather exists as a multiplicity of self-perceptions. Hence, creole and creoleness advocate a multicultural identity—a mixing of a number of things.[13] This differs slightly from hybridity in that hybridity suggests that the mixing of two cultures produces a completely new identity (the same way hybrid plants are produced), whereas creoleness asserts more of an interaction, or conglomeration of identities, sometimes described as a "kaleidoscopic totality."[14]

Chris Mullard, English commentator and one-time director of the Notting Hill Carnival, discussed this sense of dual identity in his 1970s semiautobiographical work, *Black Britain*. In this self-reflection piece, Mullard described his realization of his blackness when he moved to London from elsewhere in Britain. This early work reflected the kinds of identity articulated by Fanon, but his later discussion of race in urban London is suggestive of the kaleidoscopic identity of creoleness. As the director of the Notting Hill Carnival in the first decade of the twenty-first century, Mullard was adamant about articulating London as "a global, multicultural city" inextricably linked to a larger "multicultural Britain."[15]

Both creoleness and hybridity have their supporters and detractors. If as Bhabha argues, like the early Derrida, that if nothing exists outside of representation, how can there truly be a break from the representation of the West, now matter how uncertain of itself it may be? For example, Aijaz Ahmad suggests that Bhabha's cultural critique of hybridity neglects significant elements such as class and gender.[16] In addition, it has been critiqued for its "apparent failure to take into account the material status of the operation of power."[17]

SUBALTERN STUDIES

Just as feminist scholars found their relationship to Marxism to be an "unhappy marriage," **subaltern** scholars were disappointed in "traditional" histories of empire, specifically what became known as the Cambridge School's interpretation of history and subsequent Marxist responses to it.[18] This is not to say that empire was not discussed nor that there were no histories of countries outside the West. Marxism, supposedly the champion of the underclasses, the proletariat of the world, simply was not theoretically sophisticated enough to deal with issues of race, caste, or religion in any substantive way primarily because of the Eurocentrism embedded in its foundation. It is in this context that **Subaltern Studies** emerged as one of the most incisive critiques of colonialism in the late twentieth century. Begun as a series of journal articles written in collaboration with Oxford University, Australian National University, and Jawarhalal Nehru University, Subaltern Studies became a way for scholars from South Asia to look at their society in critical ways and to examine historically this exploitation on their own terms. Writing against the Cambridge school, which tended to be a Western-focused institutional history of imperialism and neglected the stories of the nonelites and the indigenous populations, Subaltern Studies offered an opportunity, much like social history, to provide a history from the bottom rail. The founder of Subaltern Studies, Ranajit Guha, began his historical career examining peasant communities in northern India. Born in Barasal, India in 1922, Guha migrated to Europe in the 1960s and is considered one of the leading thinkers both of Subaltern Studies and postcolonialism. His early work on Colonial Bengal anticipated Subaltern Studies in its focus on peasant insurgency in the highlands. His later work, particularly a series of lectures in the 1980s, questioned the continued Western progressivist history of empire and examines the relation between time, memory, and historiography.[19]

The institutional aspect of the Cambridge School emphasized official governmental records, in part arguing that it was the only way to write a history of empire. Guha and his fellow subalternists argued that reliance on these records had only produced traditional top-down narratives and therefore simply reaffirmed the West's idea that the colonized rarely spoke for itself—especially the lower echelons of society. The Subaltern Studies Collective argued that, in fact, you *can* capture the voice of the colonized, even with seeming silences. Ranajit Guha described this process as reading history "against the grain."[20] Imagine feeling a piece of velvet. If you stroke the cloth in one direction, it is very soft, but if you stroke it the other way (against the grain of the cloth), it feels very rough. It is the same cloth, but it provides a different sense perception. We can do the same thing with historical records. We can take an official record, such as a Foreign Office report or a court record of the kind favored by the Cambridge School, and read it against the grain. It is the same source, we are just approaching it in a different way. As with the bolt of velvet—it is the exact same material—nothing has changed except the way we read it.

The early years of the Subaltern Studies History Collective reawakened Indian historiography and focused on a form of history from below championed by early New Left scholars. Begun as a distinctly historical enterprise focused on South Asian history, the methodology of Subaltern Studies expanded into other national histories. As the field grew, many members of the collective were influenced by postcolonial theory (and literary studies), including Gyan Prakash, who wrote a defense of the integration of the two approaches in *The American Historical Review*.[21] Other scholars, such as Gayatri Chakravorty Spivak (b. 1942), retained their commitment to Subaltern Studies while expanding its boundaries to include a more global focus or other theoretical traditions, such as feminism.[22] Among the founders of Subaltern Studies, Spivak has emerged as one of the leading postcolonial feminists. Along with other feminists, namely Sara Suleri, Spivak has complicated the postcolonial narrative. In "Can the Subaltern Speak?" Spivak critiques postcolonial theory, particularly because it simply reinforced a male and privileged perception of the world.[23] In addition, she argues that by naming itself in relation to Western power, the subaltern reinforced a subjected status. Spivak's work also reflects her interdisciplinary. A deconstructive scholar, she has translated Jacques Derrida's *Of Grammatology*; a feminist, she has written about women's roles in the state and the ways in which women are actively excluded from politics; and finally as a global scholar, she has begun to focus on transnational cultural studies.[24] Spivak is an incredibly diverse scholar, sometimes describing her work as interdisciplinary, other times rejecting the term. She most often describes herself as a disciplinary rule breaker, for which her critics chide her for lack of commitment to any one philosophy.

Very recently, subaltern scholars have begun thinking about the profession after Subaltern Studies. Partha Chatterjee suggests that the original project "has run its course" but has left an indelible mark on the ways in which historians view the study of race and nation. Chatterjee suggests that in its wake, Subaltern Studies has created a more diverse and vibrant scholarship to address questions relevant to a twenty-first century world, specifically for scholars outside of South Asia.[25] Regardless of the debates within the field of Subaltern Studies about its directions, it is clear that it has had profound influence on other histories, particularly the appropriation of the history from below motif to recover histories of minority and/or subjected groups within particular national histories. Subaltern Studies has been used by national historians intent on capturing the voices of historically subjected groups previously lost to history. Daniel Nugent, for example, talked about the difficulty of using Guha's dictum to listen to the silences in relation to rural Mexican politics. Despite concerns over the "perennially indeterminate outcome,"[26] Nugent's work drew parallels to the ways in which Ranajit Guha first discussed peasant uprisings in Northeast India to peasant insurgency in Latin America, speculating that, indeed, the methodology could be useful for studying peasant communities globally. The Subaltern Studies' working model provided a framework for Nugent and others to write their histories of the underclasses. By focusing on everyday politics of everyday people, historians can successfully employ the subaltern model originally established specifically for South Asian historiography. At about the same time as Daniel Nugent began his work on peasant insurgency in Mexico, Florencia Mallon examined the usefulness of Subaltern Studies as a lens through which to view Latin American history.[27] For Mallon, despite the strengths of the subaltern project, the best course of action for Latin Americanists is to find a middle ground between the original subaltern framework and more deconstruction-inspired postcolonial works.

THEORIES AND HISTORIES OF RACE AND NATION

Both Subaltern Studies and postcolonial theory have created possibilities not only for histories of empire, but also for more sophisticated analyses of national histories. In particular, they have complicated the European narrative of the homogeneous nation. The concept of a single identifying national characteristic is eloquently discussed in Benedict Anderson's *Imagined Communities*. In this monograph, Anderson (b. 1936) describes the ways in which people construct cultural as well as geographic boundaries to create what we understand as the modern nation-state. Since a state's identity is no longer attributed to allegiance to a monarch in the modern period, language, culture, and race can help fill in the gaps. Anderson, a scholar of Southeast Asia, is considered one of the leading scholars of the origins of the modern nation-state. Again, people have studied the history of the nation-state previous to Anderson, but he problematized the Enlightenment idea of subjecthood connected to a self-conscious nationalism. The brother of Marxist historian Perry Anderson, Benedict Anderson connects the modern nation-state to new technology that facilitates the development and growth of localized identities as expressed in vernacular language that becomes more unifying and hegemonic. Therefore, the nation-state brings together previously diverse populations into a geographic wholeness. For Anderson, neither Marxism nor liberal theory has provided a satisfactory understanding of the nation, in particular the fact that "nation-ness, as well as nationalism, are cultural artefacts of a particular kind."[28]

In the early twentieth century, W.E.B. Dubois (1868–1963) discussed the ways in which the white working class in the United States was encouraged to work against its own economic self-interest through the cultural separation of race. This cultural separation ensured that the working class would be split and therefore could not effectively operate as a *class*. Later in the twentieth century, labor historians would call this a "split-labor phenomenon" in which one part of a class would be subject to false consciousness, thereby creating a hierarchy within a class that ought to be unified by its economic interests, effectively destroying substantive working-class agitation. The result of this economic separation within a class was a cultural divide.

Born in a small, predominantly white town in rural Massachusetts, Dubois attended college at Fisk

University in Tennessee and received his Ph.D. in history from Harvard University in 1895. He took a teaching position at Atlanta University, and with his writings became what we now consider to be the first scholar of American Black life. Over time, his writings became more radical, from first arguing for inclusion and an end of segregation through knowledge (indeed, Dubois is one of the founders of the National Association for the Advancement of Colored Peoples) to outright agitation. After being persecuted by the United States Government during the witch hunts of the 1950s for his participation in the Communist Party, Dubois moved to Ghana and renounced his American citizenship, dying a year later.

Despite (or perhaps because of) the contentiousness of his life's work and biography, Dubois' histories have provided a theoretical foundation for scholars studying race. Not only influential for black cultural studies, his work also provides a way of looking at the construction of national identity. Specifically, his theory of **double consciousness** in his *Souls of Black Folk* (1903) argues that African Americans are trapped in two identities as Americans. Life in America, according to Dubois,

> Yields him no true self-consciousness, but only lets him see himself through the revelation of the other world . . . One ever feels his twoness,—An American, a Negro; two souls, two thoughts, two unreconciled strivings; two warring ideals in one dark body, whose dogged strength alone keeps it from being torn asunder.[29]

From Dubois to Anderson, Subaltern Studies to postcolonial studies, historians have a wealth of theoretical framework before them in which to explore how race has been historically and discursively constructed in particular circumstances. Among historians of the United States, David Roediger stands out for his willingness to explore the personal history of his own whiteness in *The Wages of Whiteness*. The monograph itself details the ways in which different classes in the Antebellum United States consolidated and constructed a distinctly white identity not only through laws, but also through cultural productions of things such as minstrelsy. Roediger's work combined labor history, Marxism, and emergent race studies to examine the racial politics of nineteenth-century America through the lens of whiteness.

So the histories of race and nation, particularly in the United States, are in many ways histories that recognize that identity politics must also include whiteness. This draws on ideas we have discussed in earlier chapters, notably that to understand binary oppositions (of whatever kind), we must problematize it and explore identity relationally—this is very much a cultural-history motif.[30] To ignore that whiteness is a constructed category by which particular groups of people impose meaning on other groups, is to normalize these binaries, and therefore to reinforce power relations. It is a form of essentialism. Like gender in feminist studies, this was a revolutionary turn for literary and historical scholars as well as social commentators. How can we possibly overcome racial barriers if society sees only nonwhite identity formation as the problem to address? This concept of race and nation, like hybridity and creoleness, moves away from early twentieth-century ideas of **négritude**. First postulated in the Caribbean in the 1930s, négritude was an Afro-Caribbean philosophy that declared that black culture was good in and of itself and need not request any accommodation with a dominant political culture. According to Fanon, négritude matured and gained theoretical legitimacy with the writings of Aimé Césaire, whose works much influenced Fanon. Roediger's work and the theoretical framework underpinning it suggested that studying blackness was double pronged. On the one hand, it provided a much-needed discourse for identity formation for a group so long denied its own sense of self. On the other hand, taken only on its own terms, it merely reinforced essentialist categories of race, and therefore the power structures that created them in the first place.

Since Roediger's monograph was published in the late 1980s, a series of histories regarding whiteness has emerged, particularly in US history. For example, in *Whiteness of a Different Color: European Immigrants and the Alchemy of Race*, Matthew Frye Jacobson explores the ways in which nativist discourses operated in nineteenth-century America. According to Jacobson, these discourses incorporated European immigrants into a homogeneous category of new Americans to help Anglo-Americans fight against a savage "other."[31] In *Popular Culture in the Age of White Flight: Fear and Fantasy in Suburban Los Angeles*, Eric Avila examines the ethnic mixing of early twentieth-century Los Angeles and the ways in which the post-World War II construction of the city's infrastructure and its periphery served to segregate these races and ensure as little cultural interaction between groups as possible. In other words, it created a white (or at least whitewashed) city. In *Satchmo Blows Up the World: Jazz Ambassadors Play the Cold War*,

Penny von Eschen examines how race was used as a cultural weapon during the Cold War. The monograph uncovers a world in which jazz musicians were used to prop up a false world of racial harmony in the United States even as these same musicians were actively excluded from many activities in the United States itself.[32]

In European history, we can see the emergence of similar motifs of nationhood. For example, the work of Paul Gilroy examines British and American contemporary history within the larger frameworks of hybridity, subaltern criticism, and national identity. According to Gilroy, we cannot understand the dynamics of an interracial, postimperial society without understanding the ways in which the black migrant inhabits two realms. In *The Black Atlantic*, for example, he argues for a new conceptualization of blackness, one that takes into account the multiplicity of identities forced on Africans. Arguing, in part, that "you can't go home again" and using the example of the nineteenth-century African-American traveller Martin Robison Delaney who took a trip to Africa but saw no one culturally like himself, Gilroy used the concept of hybridity to make an argument about the emergence of a new diasporic identity for blacks spanning the Atlantic.[33]

A sociologist by training, Gilroy is distinctly concerned with the contemporary racial climate and how it is historically and culturally constructed. In *"There Ain't No Black in the Union Jack,"* he examines how the imagination of nationhood in Great Britain is underscored by a sense of homogeneity. Further, Gilroy distinguishes between the biology of skin color and the culture of race, noting that there are not essential cultural characteristics of race, but, like we discussed with regard to gender and culture, these characteristics change over time and place.[34] Gilroy also details the ways in which the rhetoric of whiteness was used by political leaders. Specifically, he examines the "Rivers of Blood Speech" by Conservative politician Enoch Powell in the 1970s. In this speech, Powell used a metaphor of a prim old white lady to describe a once happy, content, white Britain being denigrated by black hooligans. Black migrants could never be British argued Powell because of their inherent differences—differences that could never bridge the chasm of cultural difference.[35] As you can see, a number of different ideas, from Bhabha, to Said, to Fanon, to Guha can be found in historical accounts.

In addition to Gilroy, other British scholars have examined race and the British nation (as opposed to empire). In particular, Stuart Hall (discussed in Chapter 8) has written about the politics of identity and argued that we must understand that identity is both discursively constructed and historical."[36] In "Dark Strangers in our Midst," Chris Waters examines increasing hysteria by Britons in the mid-twentieth century regarding supposed (and much exaggerated) immigration numbers. This hysteria emerged almost immediately following World War II and culminated in the passage of the Commonwealth Immigrants Act designed to limit migration to Great Britain. Randall Hansen has explored whiteness from a policy/legislative framework. By examining a series of acts and other legislation designed to limit immigration, Hansen also details the ways in which people from Britain's Commonwealth—those given citizenship by virtue of being part of empire or former empire from the 1920s on—were parsed by race and actively excluded from entry. His work culminates with a discussion of the "BOC" or British Overseas Citizen—a citizen of Britain with British rights—except the right of entry to the mother country itself. These works, both social and cultural histories, have benefitted from, even if not directly influenced by, the wealth of analysis by those studying postcoloniality and Subaltern Studies.[37]

Taking the history of race and nation a bit further is the New Imperial History, a methodology that works to incorporate narratives of the colonized as well as constructs of sexuality into the larger national narrative. New Imperialists argue that race, gender, and class must be integrated into histories both of the center and the periphery. Arguing that national culture cannot really be understood outside the framework of imperial constructs, New Imperialists have created a rich historical narrative that challenges the story of the imperial center as the sole locus of national identity. For example, historians Kathleen Wilson and Philippa Levine both have injected a gendered analysis to the study of race and nation. Wilson is an eighteenth-century historian who examines the construct of Britishness along the borderlands. Her work details the ways in which performance generally and theatre specifically worked to inscribe an Englishness to the character of those serving abroad by recharacterizing the frontier as a British possession. Arguing that "new imperialism" actually reflects "critical imperial studies," her work explores the ways in which women were depicted both as the moral hope for representing Britishness but also as materially unfit for spreading that national character on their own.[38] For her part, Philippa Levine's work on empire globalizes the nation in the same ways as Wilson's work, making the case that gendered analysis is central to understanding the ways in which Britain constructed empire from the eighteenth through the twentieth centuries. In "What's British about Gender and Empire," Levine examines the ways in which exceptionalism predominated the British construction of imperial identity, focused intentionally on proper masculine and feminine imperial roles. In this article, Levine argues that women and colonized peoples were defined by socially constructed gendered or racial characteristics in ways that white men avoided for themselves. White women often appropriated these gendered frameworks themselves to mark themselves as British. Gender, then, is a central vehicle to understanding the history of race and nation and the construction of British stories of whiteness.[39]

French history, too, has a version of whiteness. Todd Shepard's *The Invention of Decolonization* explores how the end of the French Empire in Algeria profoundly affected *France's* self-identity. Because France viewed Algeria *as* France since the 1830s, the nation was forced to redefine itself both geographically and culturally after 1962, resulting in vast suppression of citizenship and identity. For example, French politicians in Algeria no longer had representation at home. More insidious, however, was that Algerians living in France lost their formal citizenship. Rearticulating a postcolonial "Frenchness" meant imposing a homogeneity through the politics of exclusion. Muslims, stripped of their French citizenship, were now classified as refugees and forced to reapply as foreigners if they wanted to reclaim French status. Combined with the story of the BOC for postcolonial Britain, the story of the refugee, or *harki*, reflected an attempt by the government to turn to whiteness as an element of national identity.[40]

Outside the European and US frameworks, historians have used the frameworks of postcolonial studies to reclaim their own histories. As mentioned earlier, Latin Americanists, in particular, have written histories that complicated the already complex racial hierarchies of the region. For example, Irene Silverblatt examined the ways in which Incas turned Indians in Colonial Peru used their newly imposed identities to reclaim their own pasts. It was a way for the Indians to fight against the Spaniards by co-opting Spanish language and institutions and declare their own "Indianism."[41] For African studies, scholars have examined the ways in which postcolonial theory might be used to undermine the binary inherent in the "first world"/"third world" divide. Pal Ahluwalia, for example, challenges not only this divide,

but also the construct of négritude. Though it does reconstruct the binaries of whiteness/blackness, Ahluwalia argues, like Fanon decades earlier, that négritude provided a path of resistance against colonialism for Africans. More important, Ahluwalia argues that postcolonial theory is essential in fighting against the tired trope of Africa as a "dark" continent unable to lift itself to the modern world.[42] All of these works represent the kinds of directions and projects Chatterjee alludes to in his adieu to Subaltern Studies.

CONCLUSION

As we discussed in previous chapters, an "us" (the nation) denounces "them." But even when scholars attempt to write a history of their nation, there can be problems. According to Dipesh Chakrabarty, "to think the modern or the nation-state was to think a history whose theoretical subject was Europe."[43] Thus postcolonial studies, Subaltern Studies, and various theories of race and nation problematize this politics of exclusion even while recognizing its unifying power.

The history of race, as you have read, is profoundly interdisciplinary and intertheoretical. With a lineage stretching back to nineteenth-century America with the work of W.E.B. Dubois, the history of race has become a truly global history, influenced by the ideas of the residues of empire with Postcolonial Studies and reading history against the grain with the Subaltern Studies Collective. The resultant histories have transformed the ways in which historians think not only about the nation, but also about culture and identity. We have come a long way from the nineteenth-century Whiggish histories you encountered in Chapter 2. Indeed, the scholars who were part of these key historical approaches have urged historians not to rely on static notions, but rather, in a manner reminiscent of E.P. Thompson's claim that you cannot keep theory locked in a drawer, to build and conceptualize new projects about issues of relevance to the twenty-first century.

THINKING LIKE A HISTORIAN

The primary source for this chapter was published in the British magazine, *The New Statesman*, in 1971. A "patrial" was a person in the British Commonwealth who had a legal right to claim British domicile. That legal right shifted drastically from 1948 (British Nationality Act) to the Commonwealth Immigrants Acts of the 1960s and 1970s such that many Commonwealth citizens were denied admission to Britain. The referenced characters are Reginald Maudling (the law enforcement officer in the cartoon) who in his position as Home Secretary worked to tighten immigration laws, requiring five years of work and police registration before earning the right to permanently settle in Britain. The man in the background is a reference to Enoch Powell's platform of repatriation for all immigrants. If you were a postcolonial scholar, what might you draw on to unpack the meaning of this political cartoon?

- What is being depicted in the cartoon? That is, what do you see? What does "White Commonwealth" represent?

- How would a scholar such as Said, Fanon, Bhabha, or Gilroy respond to the document? Is it possible that despite different methods, there are areas in which these scholars might come together intellectually?

- In other words, what ideas raised in this chapter (négritude, hybridity, diaspora, otherness, etc.) could you use to explain this larger social meaning?

- What do images provide as sources that traditional texts do not? Explain how you might use political cartoons to explain a particular historical moment.

The secondary reading for this chapter is a classic work of Subaltern Studies by one of the members of the Subaltern Studies Group. Written in 1975, the article operates within a larger context of what has come to be known as the Bangladesh Liberation War (1971) that created a permanent political separation between the already geographically split Pakistan and East Pakistan. In reading the article, ask the following questions:

- What is Chatterjee's argument?

- How does this article introduce the concept of the nation-state discussed in the chapter, and how does he differentiate a nineteenth-century set of nationalisms from newer forms of nationalism that include colonized and postcolonized regions? How does his subsequent discussion of long-term processes in identity formation in the subcontinent, particularly Bengal, reframe the concept of the nation?

- How might his use of political documents reflect the process of "reading against the grain"?

- Explain the relations you may draw between this work and the theories raised in earlier chapters.

- This article was written in 1975, just after the early 1970s war to split East Pakistan from Pakistan and create its own country. How do you imagine later postcolonial scholars might complicate or change this history?

Homecoming: Sour Note from an Ungrateful Patrial[44]

Bengal: Rise and Growth of a Nationality

Partha Chatterjee[45]

THIS ARTICLE deals with certain issues pertaining to the national question in India in relation to political-economic developments in Bengal before 1947. I begin by introducing certain concepts and a framework of analysis without an elaborate theoretical discussion.[1] The nation-state was built in western Europe in the era of capitalism. In its historical archetype, it emerged out of feudalism in the course of a national movement led by a rising bourgeoisie and culminating in the bourgeois revolution. It was a movement which reflected the demands of a bourgeois class seeking to assume control of state power as well as of the home market, both defined territorially. In fact, a national movement, insofar as it is a bourgeois movement, has as its objective the creation of a sovereign nation state.

This political movement is necessarily armed with a political ideology—a nationalism, which identifies its supporters and its opponents. It is this range of support which defines the nation, that is those on whose behalf the bourgeoisie claims to lead the struggle. Hence, the specific identification of a nation by its proponents is dependent entirely upon the nature and strength of the class which leads a national movement, its expected sources of support, its opponents and the specific historical context within which the struggle has to be carried on.

There are two distinct paths of capitalist development and industrial revolution in the archetypal bourgeois nation-states. In one, capitalism develops on the basis of small units of industrial production and the abolition of rent as the predominant mode of extraction of the surplus from agriculture. As in England, Holland and Switzerland, there is only a minimal need for state intervention in the sphere of production; the state thus assumes an apparent position of neutrality in regard to all issues of conflict arising out of the development of capitalist relations of production. The second way of development followed by the later capitalist nations such as Germany or Japan proceeds on the basis of positive state initiative in production so as to carry the economy forward towards the path of industrial revolution.

In the first way, the capture of state power by the bourgeoisie is followed by its attempt to extend its hegemony over all structures of society, including its ideological-cultural superstructure. It does this by separating the two realms of the state and civil society (gesèllschaft). It declares all distinctions of birth, rank, language, race or religion, to be non-political distinctions; it declares the state to be neutral with respect to such distinctions.[2] At the same time: the bourgeoisie, through the various civil social institutions (family, cultural associations, communications media, and particularly the educational system which, in bourgeois society becomes the most influential part of the ideological state apparatus) seeks to diffuse its own individualistic world-view over the rest of society: an individualistic world-view which, again, seeks to de-emphasize cultural distinctions within society. In the second way of capitalism, because of direct participation of the state in the system of production, the bourgeoisie is unable to achieve this separation between the state and civil society.

Driving Forces

In either case, however, the bourgeoisie seeks to create a cultural homogeneity within the nation-state. In the first way, this is achieved by the diffusion and legitimization of the new "rationalist" ideology of the liberal democratic state; in the second way, the bourgeoisie has necessarily to depend upon the older ideological structures of a cultural community historically developed since precapitalist times.

This community (gemeinschaft), already possessing a distinct and common cultural identity in the precapitalist era, we will call a nationality. This cultural identity of a nationality contains elements such as a distinct language, a distinct literary and aesthetic tradition, perhaps a distinct material culture (reflected in, for instance, food habits, clothing and festivals) perhaps certain common religious practices at the level of folk culture. It is possible, but not strictly necessary, that in the course of development of such a nationality a unified feudal state or an organized religious tradition served to consolidate the culture of the community but once created, it is necessary that these cultural foundations be strong enough to survive the collapse of such a feudal state or organized religion.[3]

In its classical form, the nationalism which accompanied first-way capitalism initially grew out of one nationality (say, the English). Later, depending upon the economic-political strength of the bourgeoisie and its corresponding ideological sway over the people, that is, its hegemony over civil society, the concept of the nation could include other nationalities (such as the Welsh, the Scottish or the Irish) since the new rational-liberal ideology could afford to dispense with the older ideological notions of cultural communities. For second-way capitalist countries (such as Germany or Japan), the weakness of the bourgeoisie meant a corresponding weakness of the rational-liberal ideology and reliance upon concepts of nationality, "national traditions" and, "national spirit". The nation here had to be defined very exclusively in terms of a nationality. Consequently, it was virtually impossible for second-way capitalist countries to be "multinational".

Nationalisms upto the later nineteenth century generally fall into the classical archetype described above. With the age of competitive capitalist imperialism and the incorporation of virtually the entire world into the sphere of the capitalist world economy, there grew up nationalisms of a different genre altogether. The crucial concept here is that of the uneven development of capitalism.

'Third World' Nationalism

When there is perceptible uneven development within the political boundaries of a nation-state, including its dependencies, and the lines of division between the developed and backward regions, or more precisely, peoples, (it is not necessarily true that uneven development is always perceived in terms of geographical areas) are perceived along the lines of division between the ethno-cultural communities of nationality, there is the growth of separatist national movements. It is important to note the difference between this kind of nationalism which arises out of a perception of uneven development within the realm of capitalism, and the earlier kind of nationalism which represented the first consolidation of bourgeois nation-states out of feudalism.[4]

It is also important to emphasize that the crucial concept in analyzing twentieth-century nationalism, in countries of the so-called third world, is the uneven development of capitalism. It is not necessarily true that all nationalisms in these countries are primarily antithetical to imperialism. There are three tendencies to be considered here. In the first place, because of uneven development, the leading class, that is, the bourgeoisie of the backward nationality is necessarily weak. In most colonial situations in fact, it is the indigenous big traders and the uppermost layers of the professional classes dependent upon the colonial system who start the national movement in order to secure better terms of trade or employment. The fact that the leading class is weak and to a large extent dependent upon the imperial power or, in a larger sense, the world capitalist economy, explains the various compromises this class will make with the imperial powers abroad as well as with feudalism at home.

Secondly, a colonized country very often consisted more than one clearly identifiable nationality. Now, because of their imperial connections the economic and political interests of the first nationalists usually ranged throughout the territorial span of the entire country generating a nationalism which was "multinational". However, with the spread of nationalist consciousness among wider strata of the population, the inevitable lopsidedness of colonial economic development in large-sized dependencies could well create an awareness of uneven development even within the peoples of the colonized country. This would give rise to separatist nationalism aimed not so much against the foreign imperialist, but against the allegedly more advanced ethno-cultural community in the colony as expressed in the demand for Pakistan.

Thirdly, even after the victory of a separatist nationalism and the creation of a sovereign nation-state, the persistence or growth of uneven development in a multinational situation could produce a new separatist nationalism, with clearly identifiable oppressing and oppressed nationalities even without the objective foundations of imperialism within the nation-state, as exemplified by Bangladesh.

It should be realized that this framework is designed only to analyze and *explain* national movements. The question of identifying progressive or regressive tendencies in such nationalisms, and the corresponding question of deciding which movements are worthy of support from the standpoint of the capture of state power by the oppressed classes require an entirely different set of criteria and a different mode of analysis.

Nationalities Take Shape It is between the eighth and the fourteenth centuries that one notices the development of the different nationalities in different regions of the Indian subcontinent. Niharranjan Ray identifies these as distinct "cultural-ecological zones" and, doubtless keeping in mind his basic perspective of a single Indian "nation", describes this development of distinct cultural communities as "regionalism".[5] However, he gives sufficient indication as to the elements constituting the cultural distinctness of these "regions" for us to be able to relate this phenomenon to our concept of precapitalist nationalities. First the collapse of the Gupta empire was followed by the establishment of several ruling dynasties whose visions of political and military power rarely transcended their limited regional boundaries. Secondly, from the eighth century onwards the hitherto common denominator of Indian art is replaced, in varying degrees in various regions, by what is termed local or regional schools of art.

Thirdly, by the twelfth century there is the development of mutually distinguishable scripts (proto-Nagari, proto-Bengali, proto-Gujarati and others) and by the fifteenth century the scripts of our modern northern and western Indian languages are all but fully evolved. By the fourteenth century, nearly all modern Indian languages had been formed and had started producing creative literatures of their own. In fact, there was by this time distinctly regional traditions of artistic and literary aesthetics: ". . . from about the fourteenth century, India's cultural endeavours have been in the main centred round the regional languages and literatures, not round Sanskrit or Persian except in isolated cases. . ."[6] Finally, there even grew up distinct patterns of caste and kinship organizations in each of these ecological-cultural areas characterized by its own regional language.

Bengali Cultural Community

The development of the Bengali nationality, too, occurs roughly in this period. Notwithstanding the divisive pulls of independent feudal lords and chieftains characteristic of all feudal political structures, the definite political consolidation of the region under several independent dynasties—a process growing steadily under the Pala-Sena dynasties to reach full proportions under the independent sultans—certainly aided the consolidation of the people of Bengal as a distinct cultural community. The Bengali language and literature, with its own distinct aesthetic ideals and traditions greatly influenced by the spread of Gauriya Vaishnavism, constituted the basic cultural medium. Alongside there also grew up a distinctive Bengali tradition in art and architecture. Finally, the community also came to possess a distinct set of social institutions: its local pattern of caste structure, its own rituals and code of social conduct embodied in its own laws of inheritance.

What is important to note in this early phase of the history of the Bengali people is the fact that whereas the basic character of the society was obviously agricultural, for a period of about four centuries Bengali merchants carried on a flourishing sea trade. The conquest of the eastern seas by the Arabs in the eighth century, however, led to a precipitate decline in this trade. In consequence, there was a clearly discernible fall in the political power and social standing of the mercantile community in Bengal. "In the fifth and sixth centuries we find one class enjoying as a matter of course the support of the state, namely the artisans, bankers and traders. We know that they were the chief producers of wealth; consequently, it was only natural that the state should support them.[7] From the eighth century onwards, however, the situation is completely changed.

It is an indubitable fact that from the eighth century onwards Bengal did not have any significant role in the external sea trade of India, and although there was some dominance in internal trade, the merchants and traders did not on this account continue to enjoy their earlier influence and authority over state and society. From the eighth century Bengali society is increasingly forced to depend upon its agriculture, and it is the agriculturists who come in o the forefront of social life. At the same time, the power of the trading and mercantile classes is largely reduced.[8]

With the establishment in the sixth and seventh centuries of a feudal structure based on ownership of land and the spread of Brahminism and its associated ideology and culture,

the relations of the state were strengthened with two classes—one the different strata of landowners, the other the majority of the *literati* i. e., the Brahmins. . . With the decline of manufacturing, trade and commerce in the eighth century these ties of mutual interest between the state and the landowning classes were further strengthened. . . Though the Pala and Chandra dynasties were Buddhist . . . the Brahmins were a powerful force in both these states. In the realm of the Sena-Varmana dynasties their power and authority increased further, and the alliance between feudalism and Brahminism was firmly established.[9]

Classes In 19th Century Bengal   This phenomenon of the absence among the Bengali people of a wealthy mercantile and trading community was something which continued right up to the period of British domination and conquest. Throughout the Mughal period, the most prominent figures in the inland trade of Bengal, as well as those connected with the overseas trade from ports like Sonargaon or Saptagram, were Punjabis or Gujaratis. The wealthiest bankers were also from northern and western India.

With the expansion of the European trade, however, one section of the artisans of Bengal did achieve a measure of prosperity: those who manufactured commodities which were in demand in the new European markets, particularly textiles. In the eighteenth century, there grew up prosperous manufacturing centres around the British, French or Dutch residencies in different parts of Bengal. By the second decade of the nineteenth century, however, a process of massive deindustrialization had started, and by the end of the century, its effects were far more destructive than in any other part of India.

Consequently, the potentialities for the growth of a Bengali capitalist class, which were virtually non-existent before the European connection because of the absence of a wealthy traditional mercantile community of any significant size, received its death-blow with the complete ruination of the traditional artisan class.

At the same time, the management of the agrarian system of Bengal and the series of legislations imposed upon it by the British, undoubtedly with the basic motive of establishing a profitable and secure source of revenue, strengthened the bases of a proliferating class of landed gentry with an almost uniquely unproductive orientation. This was the core of an expanding class of the famous Bengali *bhadralok*, about whose clannishness, quarrelsomeness, cunning, pettiness and other sundry vices so much is being written today by historians and sociologists. The point, however, is not that they were a "traditional elite" who had "modernized" and thereby adapted themselves to a new system of power and patronage. As a class, they were entirely the product of the process of colonial development.*Compradore* when the chief business of the English was to export commodities out of Bengal, these were the people who had played only a secondary role under the system of the Company's monopoly trade, and with all avenues for alternative investment closed, they directed their newly acquired wealth to the purchase of land. 'After the declaration of free trade, and a brief period of some productive investment of native capital in the 1830s, the entire direction of English trade was reversed: while the Indian manufacturing industry was destroyed, the home market was now flooded with British manufactures, and the subordinate position of a 'dependent bourgeoisie' was perpetuated.

Landowning Rentiers

The landed proprietors of the early nineteenth century were big zamindars with enormous estates. Many of them had residences in the city of Calcutta. By the middle of the century, however, began a process of distinct differentiation within the class of landed proprietors. Throughout the latter half of the nineteenth century, we notice the almost infinite subdivision and diffusion of the landed interest in Bengal. In 1882 there came to exist as many as 110,456 estates in Bengal, of which only 0.41 per cent were larger than 20,000 acres, 11.1 per cent ranged from 500 to 20,000 acres, while as much as 88.4 per cent of the estates were smaller than 500 acres.[10] One reason for this was the splitting of estates through inheritance. But this was not all. Throughout the nineteenth century and well into the twentieth, there occurred the subdivision and diffusion of the proprietory interest in land. Just one scrap of data will indicate this trend: between the Bengal census figures of 1921 and 1931, one notices that the number of landlords and rent-receivers increased by as much as 62 per cent while that of cultivating owners or tenants decreased by 34 per cent.[11] And it must be mentioned here that the 1931 figures exclude from the category of rent-receivers those who are rentiers only as a "subsidiary occupation".

Indeed, the situation was such that as the prices of agricultural commodities increased steadily throughout the latter half of the nineteenth century and the first decades of the twentieth, and as commercial crops, particularly jute, were introduced on a major scale, there occurred a sizable gap between the fixed revenue payable by the zamindar to the treasury and the value of the rent which could be efficiently extracted from the actual cultivator. This gap served as the basis of assets into which flowed the savings of the Bengali "middle class," people with small amounts of capital acquired through inheritance, dowry, profits from petty trade or commerce, or savings from professional incomes. Left with no other profitable means for investing this capital, they bought intermediary rights in land which guaranteed a small but nevertheless secure rent income. Hence the much discussed phenomenon of subinfeudation, which in some districts like Bakarganj reached the amazing scale of 15 or 16 distinct levels of intermediary rights between the zamindar and the *raiyat*.

From the last decades of the nineteenth century, provincial politics in Bengal was dominated by this class of intermediate proprietors in land. The Indian Association was set up in 1876 to voice the interests of precisely this class. This was also the stratum of society from which came the early generation of successful professionals in law, journalism, teaching and the civil service. In their role as rentiers, their interests were territorially provincial and ideologically conservative. They were concerned with the legal protection of their proprietory rights for which they had to influence the course of provincial legislation on agrarian matters. The Indian Association, for instance, was one of the principal organizations representing this interest of the non-agriculturist and non-cultivating proprietors and tenants.[12]

Intermediate Proprietors

In their role as professionals, however, they had developed a range of interest which was all-India in scope: as members of the legal profession or the civil service or as teachers they would envisage as their province the law courts, the administrative machinery or the growing educational system all over the country. In this role, therefore, they could associate with similar professionals from Bombay or Madras or Allahabad in an all-India forum such as the Indian National Congress.[13]

In terms of the economy, this leading class in Bengal lived entirely on "revenue"; only the distribution of the surplus concerned them, they had no role in its creation. The rift between the older zamindars and the intermediate proprietors-cum-professionals was a differentiation within the same class of landowning rentiers. There was, however, another dynamic trend in the agrarian economy of Bengal which came to have a major influence upon Bengal's politics in the twentieth century. We have noted earlier the process of subinfeudation of the landed interest in the nineteenth century. This was not, however, a process restricted only to intermediary rights of proprietorship above the legally recognized raiyat. As long as there was a sizable difference between the rent payable by the raiyat to his superior landlord and the rent which could be extracted from an under-tenant (whatever be the legal status of this tenancy, increasingly this became a system of sharecropping), there was every incentive for the raiyat to lease out his holdings rather than have them cultivated by hired labour. This was particularly true for those raiyats who held tenurial rights where the rent was fixed by law. This process of constant proliferation of tiers of rent-receivers above the actual cultivator was made economically viable by the fact of an abject scarcity of land in relation to the abundance of labour having no other means of livelihood except agriculture. There was the additional factor of the active policy of the British-owned industries of the Calcutta region to recruit labour from Bihar or the United Provinces in order to keep down wages and prevent the growth of trade unions led by local politicians. This prevented any possible outlet for the surplus labour in Bengal's agricultural sector. Consequently it became more lucrative for this richer section of the peasantry to dissociate itself from actual cultivation and turn to moneylending and grain trade.

Notwithstanding innumerable proclamations of concern for the cultivator, from both official as well as "national" forums of opinion, no amount of tenancy legislation could stop this process of the gradual transfer of land to the non-cultivating owner. The crucial malady lay in the unwillingness of all vested interests to define the occupancy raiyat in terms of his role in cultivation. Such were the stakes which the lowest rungs of the Bengali middle class had developed in subinfeudation and rent income. Consequently, controversy hinged merely around the length of time a piece of land is occupied continuously that would give the raiyat rights against eviction or increase of rent. No one was prepared to tie occupancy rights to actual cultivation.

Jotdars

Unlike the intermediary proprietor, however, the basis of the economic interests of this rich peasant turned non-cultivating landlord-cum-usurer (the most common term for this class in Bengal, despite several local variations in meaning and nomenclature, is *jotdar*) was not in the main a legal right of proprietorship. His economic gains depended far more on his social standing in the village, on the innumerable extra-legal ties of dominance and bondage with his sharecroppers and debtors, on the potential threats of eviction, or even of sheer terror, with which he could exact far more than the agreed share of the produce or charge exorbitant rates of interest, all entirely outside the pale of the law. His chief interest was, in other words, political power in its most fundamental sense, at the village level.

Certain superstructural developments must now be tied up here. To analyze the history of development, and isolate the major elements of the ideology of the Bengali middle class is, in the limited space available here, extremely difficult. The task has been complicated by historians who, by characterizing this class as an "elite group", have sought to emphasize the determining role of the attitudes and social behaviour of this group to the exclusion of more basic structural features of the economy and society. It needs to be repeated once again that as a class this so-called "elite" group was entirely a product of the conditions imposed under colonialism. The system of land tenure, combined with the disincentive to the entry of domestic savings into native industrial enterprises and the destruction of indigenous manufacturing, created the basic economic structure from which emerged a class of rent-receivers totally divorced from, and entirely uninterested in, the conditions of social production. Added to this were the new opportunities opened up to precisely this class of people by the expansion of the judicial, administrative and educational apparatus of the country. The fact that higher education, in the English language and solely as a means of entry into a white collar job or a profession, remained confined largely to the same group of people only replicated in the cultural sphere the enormous distance of this group from the sphere of social production.

This entire complex of economic and cultural forces, producing a class enjoying pre-eminent authority over society and polity yet dissociated from its productive system, centred around the metropolitan life of Calcutta. The political structure of British India gave Calcutta a rather unique position in the political life of the province. The formal representative institutions did not even touch the vast mass of the rural population and all major forums of "national" opinion in Calcutta were dominated by representatives of this class. Consequently, it is not surprising that they could claim to exercise political leadership over the entire province without being able, and indeed without finding it necessary, to give a corresponding lead to the production economy.

Muddled Political Inadequacy

The crucial point is that whereas they were a "middle" class in the sense that their control over society was incomplete and their class ambitions unfulfilled, yet there was really no class above them in the structure of Bengali society: in ordinal terms, they were not "middle" at all. The traditional nobility had been demolished by the cumulative effects of British consquest and the new agrarian system imposed under conditions of colonialism. In its place there grew up this "middle" class which did not have to oust anybody in order to become the leading spokesmen on behalf of their countrymen. They became leaders almost by default. As a consequence, quite unlike the political role of the middle class in the growth of the national states in Europe, they could not define an enemy within their society. Everybody from the zamindar down to the office clerk with a petty tenure in the village was soaked into this amorphous gel. The leaders, therefore, necessarily lacked that clear vision of class goals on which basis they could draw up a programme for a national alliance. While the genuineness of their nationalist feelings against their imperial rulers was unquestioned, they could never combine this role as national leaders with a purposeful programme for leadership over the economy and society.

This explains the total atrophy of objectives and hopeless muddle of forms revealed in the *Swadeshi* movement after 1905. Sumit Sarkar has now given us an excellent account of the period,[14] and there is no need to repeat the story. Here again, there is no question that the Bengali bhadralok were sincerely agitated over what they considered to be an arbitrary division of "the Bengali nation". Yet the insensitivity of the leaders, zealously enforcing the boycott of British goods, towards the problem of providing alternative means of livelihood to petty traders or cheap substitutes to consumers, the rather farcical attempts at starting swadeshi industries, their complete failure on the Hindu-Muslim question, the growing trend towards individual terrorism completely divorced from any programme of mass mobilization or action, all these were indicative of the inadequacies of this class in providing the leadership necessary for creating a genuine national alliance of all classes oppressed by imperialism.

Into the 20th Century Mass Movement There are thus three distinct political levels which become relevant to a study of Bengal's politics in the twentieth century. One was the village level, where the leading class consisted of the richer sections of the raiyat peasantry whose primary concern was with political power at the local level. The second level was provincial, dominated by a "middle class" nationalism in political sentiments but uninformed by any positive role in the production economy. And finally there was the question of Bengal's participation in the larger Indian national movement, where the early generation of Bengali nationalists had played a major part as representatives of the upper stratum of English-educated professionals. Consequently, a characterization of Indian politics in this period in terms of "locality, province and nation" does encapsulate this differentiated structure of the national movement.[15]

With the advent of mass politics in the 1920s, this constellation of class forces occupied the centre of the political stage in Bengal. Mass participation in the national movement, although widespread in several scattered localities all over the province, was particularly intense and sustained in the districts of south-western Bengal. For every major movement, Midnapore in particular was always recognized in official circles as "one of the worst affected districts in India". In the initial phase of mass mobilization and organization for purposes of these movements in rural areas, the lead was generally taken by the more prosperous sections of the peasantry. For them the objective was to establish a position of leadership and social command over the village. They were agitated by the increasing tax burden on villagers. They were also vocal in their grievances against zamindars who would try to enhance rents without performing any of their duties regarding the improvement of the conditions of cultivation or of village life in general. They resented the arrogance of petty government officials visiting the village. When these people took up the task of mobilizing the mass of the villagers in support of the national movement, they were not (and it is important to note this) acting in their individual roles in order to grab their individual shares of the crumbs of patronage distributed by the government in the locality. Wherever these rural movements became intense and subtained, their leaders—the upper and middle peasantry—were acting to realize very clear class demands.

This becomes evident from a study of the Union Board boycott movements carried out in several areas.[16] The decision in 1919 to create Union Boards in the countryside was, in fact, an official recognition of the growing importance of the class of upper peasantry turned non-cultivating landowner-cum-graindealer-cum-usurer. The Union Boards were designed to serve the double purpose of creating a new reservoir of patronage to be distributed to these people aspiring to political power in the locality, as well as to widen the net of administrative control to interior villages beyond the police station towns. Yet it so happened that in several areas of the province it was precisely the upper peasantry which led the movement to boycott the Union Boards. Their decision to spurn the offer of government patronage, and their success in rallying the lower ranks of the peasantry behind them in their efforts to resist further administrative penetration into the countryside and the accompanying burden of increased taxation, were both results of a clear perception of their class ambitions.

Stir in the Countryside

The Salt Campaign of 1930 and the Civil Disobedience Movement broadened the mass base of the national movement in the countryside. An organized move to stop payment of government taxes was likely to be popular everywhere. Particularly in the coastal areas of Midnapore, the issue of salt manufacture was not merely an act of symbolic defiance of authority but a matter concerning the satisfaction of one's daily consumption needs, affecting the poorest sharecropper or labourer. In the subdivisions of Contai and Tamluk it was the salt movement which drew large sections of the poorest strata of the population into the organized national movement. Besides, the widespread organization of the spinning and weaving industry in cottages created for a large section of the poor people in the villages an economic stake in the movement. In areas within this region of Bengal where the burden of zamindari rent was particularly oppressive, such as in Hooghly or Bankura or parts of Midnapore, a mass no-tax campaign inevitably led to a no-rent movement against the bigger zamindars.

Indeed, a sustained mass movement comprising different strata of the peasantry develops a dynamic logic of its own. Once the political consciousness of the poorer sections of the peasantry is aroused, and they realize the potential strength of organized struggle, tensions within an alliance led by the richer peasantry become inevitable. In Midnapore, this took the form of a sharecroppers' agitation for a more equitable share of the produce, a lower rate of interest on grain loans, and the abolition of all illegal exactions. Some of the landlord elements were soon estranged from the movement; others took the initiative for a compromise solution in the interests of organizational unity. The growing self-confidence of the middle and small peasantry was clearly manifested in 1942 when the vacuum left by the imprisonment of the older leadership was filled in by a younger generation from a distinctly less prosperous background and a far more radical policy.

That these rural mass movements remained confined to their localities and could not be organized and integrated into a larger political challenge even at the provincial level was due fundamentally to the distorted social development we have described above.[17] The peasantry as a class is never capable of independently leading a national alliance. The underdeveloped state of market relations in the Bengal countryside made it impossible for even the richer peasantry to think independently in terms of provincial interests. The working class was miniscular in size, and in any case, as we have mentioned before, comprising a large section which did not regard Bengal as its home and which was not integrated to its political life. The task of uniting locality and province and drawing it into the mainstream of all-India politics could only have been performed by a "middle class". Yet, the nature of the middle class in Bengal made it hopelessly unsuited for this task.

Problems of Leadership

The immense gulf which separated the provincial leadership in Calcutta from the growing movements in the countryside can be illustrated to no end. I will mention a few of the more telling ones. An attempt in 1925-26 to create an alliance of district leaders involed in mass movements in order to challenge the entrenched Calcutta leadership was defeated. The move, led by Birendranath Sasmal, leader of the Midnapore movement, was ill-organized, hasty and tactless. But the entire Calcutta leadership— J M Sengupta, Subhaschandra Bose, the famous 'Big Five'— and both major terrorist organizations fought against it with all their strength. Sasmal was defeated and withdrew from the Congress. A complete lack of comprehension of the crucial elements in a successful national struggle was again reflected in the stand of the Congress-Swarajya party members during the debates on the Bengal Tenancy Act Amendment Bill in 1928. The divisons on virtually every clause and every amendment produced the curious picture of members of the Swarajya Party, the party of non-cooperation and uncompromising champions of complete independence, siding with the government in favour of the rights of intermediate proprietors and against those of undertenants and sharecroppers. Indeed, so glaring was this anomaly that during the discussion on a government proposal to allow a landlord to eject a raiyat "on the ground that he has used the land comprised in his holding in a manner which renders it unfit for the purposes of tenancy", Sir Abdur Rahim, himself no peasant leader, commented: "The majority of this Council in combination with the Swarajists, the most powerful party in the House, have already finished with the *bargadars*, the cultivators of land . . . This powerful combination, which it is not possible for those who have taken up the cause of the ryots to resist successfully, have now taken away the rights of the ryots."[18]

The most telling summing up of the priorities of provincial leadership is provided by a Secretary of the Bengal Provincial Congress Committee himself. Writing to the AICC in reply to repeated inquiries regarding the progress of the Civil Disobedience Movement in Bengal, he concluded a rather unconvincing report with the following sentence: "If we can now put a little more vigour into the movement as we hope to do as soon as we are relieved of the burden of the Corporation elections which come off on the 18th instant, we feel we shall be able . . . to stir up the masses all over the province into activity."[19]

On the plane of all-India politics, Bengal's position did indeed decline, once the political forms of the early nationalists finally fell through the trap-door of history. After the

1920s, the all-India Congress ceased to be just a gathering of the upper strata of professionals. The growing all-India bourgeoisie, which did have substantial investments in Bengal, however had no Bengali component. Even on this score, therefore, the nationalist leaders of Bengal had no sustaining interests which would lead them to formulate an economic programme.

Congress in Decline

Interestingly, Muslim leaders from the districts of eastern Bengal realized early enough where their constituency lay. We do not as yet have any systematic study of rural movements in East Bengal from the 1920s and the reasons for this difference in the nature of leadership can only be guessed. There was the fact that the Muslim section of the Bengali middle class was a later development; hence their rural roots had probably not been severed so thoroughly. Secondly, even within the world of middle-class ambitions in a colonial set-up, the Muslim intelligentsia carried a distinct perception of uneven development of the two religious groups. In eastern Bengal particularly, the fact of Hindu domination could be clearly identified in their disproportionate ownership of land. It did not, therefore, require a brilliant stroke of imaginative leadership for Muslim leaders of the eastern districts to connect even a slogan for "more education, more jobs" with a defence of the interests of the vast mass of Muslim peasantry. However, this awareness among Bengali Muslim politicians of the crucial importance of the agrarian question was ideologically limited by another distortion: they could only see its importance in relation to the Muslim question, where the principal enemy was Hindu dominance. They failed to link the whole question to the fact of imperialism. It is not surprising, therefore, to find the entire mass following of the Krishak Proja Party being transferred to the command of the Calcutta Muslim League coterie, which was an almost exact replica of the Bengal provincial Congress leadership.

It would be labouring the obvious to add after this that the national question was not solved in 1947. Perhaps there were differences in the extent to which the potentials for the productive regeneration of a national economy and polity were mobilized within the different nationalities of India: we know that the case of Gujarat was different from that of Bengal. In the absence of adequate knowledge of grassroots nationalism in other parts of India, it is difficult to answer this question satisfactorily. It is probably true that the depth and intensity of colonial exploitation made the distortions in Bengal's social development the most glaring, both in its economy and in ideology. However,

we know that the fundamental questions relating to the agrarian economy have not been solved anywhere in India today. We also know that the only genuinely all-India bourgeoisie has developed a monopoly character almost from its birth, and has numerous ties of dependence with world capitalism. Finally, there is ample evidence of the continuous growth since 1947 of the unproductive sector of the economy, and the mutually sustaining relations between this phenomenon and the populist stance adopted by the ruling classes.[20] It is not difficult to understand, then, that failing a major restructuring of the economy, based on a solution of the agrarian question, the enduring effects of an unsolved national question will remain with us. Indeed, an attempt at a more efficient and disciplined capitalism, under state bureaucratic protection, can only aggravate the fundamental problem, not solve it.

A modern historian of Bengal, commenting upon the decline of the Bengal Congress in Indian politics in the 1930s, has said, "The province which had inspired Indian nationalism was sacrificed for its sake. Imperialism devours its own children. Nationalism destroys its own parents." [21] Had this really been true, India would have been a different country today! ∎

Reading Notes

1. I have discussed the theoretical issues at length in a forthcoming article, "Analyzing Nationalism: Some Concepts and a Framework".

2. On this point, see Karl Marx, "On the Jewish Question" in Lloyd D Easton and Kurt H Guddat (Eds.) *Writings of the Young Marx on Philosophy and Society*, Doubleday, Garden City, N Y 1967, pp 216-48.

3. The existence from precapitalist times of this cultural community of nationality, as distinct from the bourgeois concept of "nation" was explicitly recognized by Engels in his three articles on Poland in the *Commonwealth* (March-May 1866): See Marx-Engels, *Werke*, Vol 16, Dietz Verlag, Berlin 1973, pp 153-63. Engels maintains this distinction implicitly in *The Peasant War in Germany*, where he talks of "the entire German people" while noting at the same time that "the low level of industry, commerce and agriculture ruled out any centralization of Germans into a *nation*". The distinction is quite explicit in his manuscript on the "Decay of Feudalism and Rise of National States", appended to *The Peasant War in Germany*, Progress Publishers, Moscow 1974, pp 178-88. See also, Roman Rosdolsky, "Worker and Fatherland: A Note on a Passage in the *Communist Manifesto*", *Science and Society* 29, 1965 pp 330-7. The distinction has also been made in connection with Chinese discussions on the national question in that country. See Chang Chih-i,

"A Discussion of the National Question in the Chinese Revolution and of Actual Nationalities Policy" in George Moseley (Ed.) *The Party and the National Question in China*, MIT Press, Cambridge, Mass. 1966, pp 29-159. Stalin unfortunately attributes to the "nation" all these characteristics which should properly apply only to the "nationality". This lands him in all sorts of conceptual difficulties when discussing the national question in eastern Europe: J V Stalin, "Marxism and the National Question", *Works*, Vol 2, Gana-Sahitya Prakash, Calcutta 1974, pp 194-215.

4. This, I believe, is the central point of the distinction between the "two ways of nationalism" made by Barun De in "Two Ways of Nationalism: Observations on the Relationship between Nationalism, Capitalism and Imperialism", *Essays in Honour of Niharranjan Ray* (forthcoming).

5. Niharranjan Ray, "The 'Medieval' Factor in Indian History", General Presidential Address, Patiala, 1967, pp 24-29; Ray, *Nationalism in India*, Aligarh Muslim University, Aligarh 1973, pp 28-33.

6. Ray, *Nationalism in India*, p 32.

7. Niharranjan Ray, *Bangalir Itihas, Adiparba* (in Bengali), abridged edition, Lekhak Samabay Samity, Calcutta 1967, p 173. My translation.

8. *Ibid.*, p 97.

9. *Ibid.*, pp 173-4.

10. B H Baden-Powell, cited in the "Memorandum by the Bengal Provincial Kisan Sabha," *Report of the Land Revenue Commission, Bengal*, Vol 6, Bengal Government Press, Alipore 1941, p 24.

11. *Ibid.*, p 28.

12. See in this connection the discussion on the Indian Association's memoranda on the Bengal Tenancy Bill of 1885 in Asok Sen, *Vidyasagar and His Elusive Milestones*, Chapter on "The Economic Problem", CSSSC, Calcutta 1975 (forthcoming).

13. For an occupational break-up of early Congressmen, see Bimanbehari Majumdar and Bhakat Prasad Mazumdar, *Congress and Congressmen in the Pre-Gandhian Era, 1885-1917*, Firma K L Mukhopadhyay, Calcutta 1967, pp 18-19.

14. Sumit Sarkar, *The Swadeshi Movement in Bengal, 1903-1908*, People's Publishing House, New Delhi 1973.

15. John Gallagher, Gordon Johnson and Anil Seal, *Locality, Province and Nation: Essays on Indian Politics, 1870-1940*, Cambridge University Press, 1973; particularly Seal, "Imperialism and Nationalism in India", pp 1-27.

16. The following observations on the national movement in Bengal are based on research currently being undertaken at the Centre for Studies in Social Sciences, Calcutta.

17. John Gallagher, in an essay concerning this period of Bengal's politics, suggests that it was the gradual democratization of various representative institutions after the First World War which gave "the enemies of privilege" the opportunity to wrest the control of local patronage "from the zamindars and their clients". His explication of these rural movements runs on these lines: "When the malcontents of the neighbourhood aligned themselves with the provincial and national campaigns which arose from time to time, they hoped to exploit these issues for their own causes". His zeal to establish this argument leads him to overlook the latent dynamic, and gloss over the more obvious ones, which represented the potential strength of a national alliance based upon a programme for the solution of the agrarian question. The point I have tried to make above is that there exists ample evidence to show that the upper and middle peasantry leading these sustained local movements were conscious of their class ambitions and were led by the logic of united struggle to realize that these class ambitions were inseparably linked with the fate of the entire production economy in rural areas, a solution that was being objectively thwarted by the presence of imperialism. But then, there is probably little use making this point with these new interpreters of Indian history, since "ideology", they believe, "provides a good tool for fine carving, but it does not make big buildings". See Gallagher, "Congress in Decline: Bengal 1930 to 1939", in Gallagher, Johnson and Seal, *op.cit.*, pp 269-325; also Seal's essay cited above.

18. *The Statesman*, 16 August 1928.

19. Letter from Harikumar Chakrabarty, Secretary BPCC, to Jawaharlal Nehru, President AICC, dated 15 March 1930, AICC Papers, File G-120/1930, Part II, Nehru Memorial Museum and Library, New Delhi.

20. Arup Mallik and Partha Chatterjee, "Bharatiya Ganatantra o Bourgeois Pratikria" (in Bengali), *Anya Artha*, No 8 (May 1975), pp 6-25.

21. Gallagher, *op.cit.* ∎

Endnotes

1. Gyan Prakash, "Subaltern Studies as Postcolonial Criticism," *The American Historical Review* 99/5 (1994): 1490.

2. Domingo Faustino Sarmiento, *Life in the Argentine Republic in the Days of the Gauchos* (New York: Collier, 1961).

3. Ngugi wa Thiong'O, quoted in Tejumola Olaniyan, "On 'Post-Colonial Discourse': An Introduction," *Callaloo* 16/4 On 'Post-Colonial Discourse': A Special Issue (Autumn 1993): 745.

4. Frantz Fanon, "Reciprocal Bases of National Culture and the Fight for Freedom," *Marxists Internet Archive*, accessed September 3, 2012, http://www.marxists.org

/subject/africa/fanon/national-culture.htm. It is also in *Norton Anthology of Theory and Criticism*, Vincent B. Leitch, ed. (New York: Norton, 2001).

5. Frantz Fanon, *Wretched of the Earth*, Preface by Jean-Paul Sartre, trans. Constance Farrington (New York: Grove Press, 1963).

6. Frantz Fanon, *Black Skin, White Masks*, A New Edition, Translated from the French by Richard Philcox with a Foreword by Kwame Anthony Appiah (New York: Grove Press, 2008), 205, 206.

7. Rey Chow, "Postmodern Automatons," in *Feminists Theorize the Political*, eds. Judith Butler and Joan W. Scott (New York: Routledge, 1992), 102, 103.

8. Dipesh Chakrabarty, "Postcoloniality and the Artifice of History: Who Speaks for 'Indian' Pasts?" *Representations* no. 37 (1992): 1–26.

9. Edward Said, *Orientalism* (New York: Random House, 1979), 1–28.

10. Homi Bhabha, *The Location of Culture* (New York: Routledge, 1994), 5, 53–56.

11. Bill Ashcroft, Gareth Griffiths, and Helen Tiffen, *The Empire Writes Back: Theory and Practice in Post-Colonial Literatures*, 2nd ed. (New York: Routledge, 2002), 218.

12. Ashcroft, Griffiths, and Tiffen, *The Empire Writes Back: Theory and Practice in Post-Colonial Literatures*, 35.

13. Jean Bernabé, Patrick Chamoiseau, Raphaël Confiant, and Mohamed B. Taleb Khyar, "In Praise of Creoleness," *Callaloo* 13/4 (Autumn 1990): 886–909.

14. *Ibid.*, 892.

15. Chris Mullard, *Black Britain* (London: Allen & Unwin, 1973); "Time to party: The whole of Britain needs the Notting Hill Carnival's celebration of cultural diversity" Saturday August 24, 2002 *The Guardian Unlimited*, http://arts.guardian.co.uk/nottinghillcarnival2002/story/0,,780006,00.html.

16. Aijaz Ahmad, "The Politics of Literary Postcoloniality," *Race and Class* 36/3 (1995): 1–20.

17. Ashcroft, Griffiths, and Tiffen, *The Empire Writes Back: Theory and Practice in Post-Colonial Literatures*, 206.

18. Gyan Prakash, "Subaltern Studies as Postcolonial Criticism," *American Historical Review* 99/5 (1994): 1476, 1477.

19. Dipesh Chakrabarty, "Guha, Ranajit," in *Encyclopedia of Historians and Historical Writing, Vol. 1* (Chicago: Fitzroy Dearborn Publishers, 1999), 494. See also, Ranajit Guha, "Not At Home in Empire," *Critical Inquiry* 23/3 Front Lines/Border Posts (Spring 1997): 482–493.

20. For a good introduction to Guha's methodology, refer to Gayatri Chakravorty Spivak's "Subaltern Studies: Deconstructing Historiography," in *Selected Subaltern Studies*, eds. Ranajit Guha and Gayatri Chakravorty Spivak, Foreword by Edward W. Said (Oxford: Oxford University Press, 1988), 3–32.

21. Gyan Prakash, "Subaltern Studies as Posctolonial Criticism," *The American Historical Review* 99/5 (1994): 1475–1490.

22. An excellent history and collection of these debates may be found in *Mapping Subaltern Studies and the Postcolonial*, Vinayak Chaturvedi, ed. (London: Verso, 2000).

23. Gayatri Chakravorty Spivak, "Can the Subaltern Speak?" in *Marxism and the Interpretation of Culture*, edited and with an Introduction by Cary Nelson and Lawrence Grossberg (Urbana: University of Illinois Press, 1988), 287, 271–314.

24. Gayatri Chakravorty Spivak, *A Critique of Postcolonial Reason: Toward a History of the Vanishing Present* (Cambridge [MA]: Harvard University Press, 1999) puts forth both a feminist and transnational argument.

25. Partha Chatterjee, "After Subaltern Studies," *Economic and Political Weekly* XLVII/No. 35 (September 01, 2012), http://www.epw.in/perspectives/after-subaltern-studies.html.

26. Daniel Nugent, *Rural Revolt in Mexico: U.S. Intervention and the Domain of Subaltern Politics*, Foreword by William C. Roseberry (Durham: Duke University Press, 1998), 17, 18.

27. Florencia Mallon, "The Promise and Dilemma of Subaltern Studies: Perspectives from Latin American History," *American Historical Review* 99/5 (1994): 1491–1515.

28. Benedict Anderson, *Imagined Communities: Reflections on the Origin and Spread of Nationalism*, Revised Edition (London: Verso, 1983), 4.

29. W.E.B. Dubois, *The Souls of Black Folk* (Rockville [MD]: ARC Manor, 2008), 12.

30. David Roediger discusses the history of whiteness studies in literary theory in *The Wages of Whiteness: Race and the Making of the American Working Class* (London: Verso, 1991), 6.

31. Matthew Frye Jacobson, *Whiteness of a Different Color: European Immigrants and the Alchemy of Race* (Harvard: Harvard University Press, 1998).

32. Eric Avila, *Popular Culture in the Age of White Flight: Fear and Fantasy in Suburban Los Angeles* (Berkeley:

University of California Press, 2006); Penny M. Von Eschen, *Satchmo Blows Up the World: Jazz Ambassadors Play the Cold War* (Cambridge [MA]: Harvard University Press, 2005).

33. Paul Gilroy, *The Black Atlantic: Modernity and Double Consciousness* (Cambridge [MA]: Harvard University Press, 1993), 23, 24.

34. Paul Gilroy, *"There Ain't No Black in the Union Jack": The Cultural Politics of Race and Nation* (Chicago: University of Chicago Press, 1987), 38, 39.

35. *Ibid.* There are many places online to read the full text of Powell's speech including "Enoch Powell's 'Rivers of Blood' speech," *The Telegraph Online*, posted November 6, 2007, last accessed September 2, 2012, http://www.telegraph.co.uk/comment/3643823/ Enoch-Powells-Rivers-of-Blood-speech.html.

36. Stuart Hall, "Introduction: Who Needs Identity," in *Questions of Cultural Identity*, eds. Stuart Hall and Paul du Gay (London: Sage Publications, 1996), 4.

37. Chris Waters, "'Dark Strangers' In Our Midst: Discourses of Race in Nation in Britain, 1947–1963," *Journal of British Studies* 36/2 (April 1997): 207–238; Randall Hansen, *Citizenship and Immigration in Post-War Britain: The Institutional Origins of a Multicultural Nation* (Oxford: Oxford University Press, 2000).

38. Kathleen, Wilson, "Old Imperialisms and New Imperial Histories: Rethinking the History of the Present," *Radical History Review* 95 (Spring 2006):

211–234; "Rowe's Fair Penitent as Global History: or, A Diversionary Voyage to New South Wales," *Eighteenth Century Studies* 41/2 (2008): 231–251.

39. Philippa Levine, "What's British About Gender and Empire? The Problem of Exceptionalism," *Comparative Studies of South Asia, Africa and the Middle East* 27/2 (2007): 273–282. See also *The British Empire: Sunrise to Sunset* (Harlow, UK: Pearson Education, 2007).

40. Todd Shepard, *The Invention of Decolonization: The Algerian War and the Remaking of France* (Ithaca [NY]: Cornell University Press, 2006).

41. Irene Silverblatt, "Becoming Indian in the Central Andes of Seventeenth-Century Peru," in *After Colonialism: Imperial Histories and Postcolonial Displacements*, Gyan Prakash, ed. (Princeton: Princeton University Press, 1995), 279–298.

42. Pal Ahluwalia, *Politics and Post-Colonial Theory: African Inflections* (London: Routledge, 2001).

43. Chakrabarty, "Postcoloniality and the Artifice of History: Who Speaks for 'Indian' Pasts?" 8.

44. Arthur Horner, "Homecoming: Sour note from an ungrateful patrial," *New Statesman*, 12 March 1971; The British Cartoon Archive, University of Kent, catalogue record AH0319 at <http://www.kent.ac.uk/cartoons/>

45. Partha Chatterjee, "Bengal: Rise and Growth of a Nationality," *Social Scientist* 4/1 The National Question in India Special Number (August 1975): 67–82.

GLOSSARY

Algerian war war from 1952 to 1962 between France and Algerian nationalists. The war was brutal and resulted in the French pullout of the region.

Alienation in Marxist terms, the ways in which human beings in capitalist society become separated from the direct products of their labor.

Annales School named after the journal created by Marc Bloch and Lucien Febvre, the *Annales* School is characterized by four generations of scholars who represent very different ideas of approaching history. From total history to the *longue durée*, to quantitative microhistory, to a cultural approach to history called *mentalités*, Annales scholars represent a French historical tradition that has had global impact for decades.

Annaliste a follower of any generation of the *Annales* School.

Base/Superstructure in early Marxist terms, the base was considered the economic foundation of social relations (which was the superstructure). If economics predetermined social relations (such as religion, government, etc.), it could be said that the base was the foundation on which other elements stood.

Beatniks 1950s and early 1960s, beatniks focused on free expression of ideas, including artistic expression, combined with a rejection of social norms.

Binary oppositions phrase used to describe the ways in which societies and cultures naturalize difference. Binaries are socially constructed and often serve as vehicles for imposing inequality. See "other."

Bourgeoisie simply, the middle class. More complexly, those in nineteenth-century industrial capitalist Europe who controlled the means of production.

Capital *Capital* is a book written by Karl Marx and Friedrich Engels. Capital also consists of the accumulated goods, money, and commodities that can be used for trade and/ or investment.

Caudillos "strong men." Men in South America in the nineteenth century, often mestizo, who held military and political control in their nations/regions.

Chartism a movement in England in the 1830s and 1840s pushing for greater political equality for workers, which included demands for the right to vote, the secret ballot, payment of salaries for members of Parliament, and yearly elections. Chartism failed by 1848, though the government did provide some concessions to workers.

Conjoncture part of Fernand Braudel's exploration of time that focused on a middle span of time, roughly 50–100 years. What we might commonly refer to as an "age."

Creoleness related to, but different from hybridity, creoleness is most often used in literary studies to suggest that postcolonial identity (whether in the former colonies or in the métropole among migrants) is best developed as a multiplicity of self-perceptions. Unlike négritude that emphasizes essential African qualities of diasporic communities, creoleness emphasizes the heterogeneity of cultures and languages.

Cultural capital explored by Pierre Bourdieu, cultural capital is the artistic, intellectual, or social wealth developed by individuals that can then be "spent." One accrues cultural capital through access to education and high culture. Bourdieu argued that it contributes to disparities within societies.

Cultural history history that focuses on the attitudes, values, and beliefs of historical subjects and does not privilege a material exteriority over social constructions.

Cultural materialism phrase coined by Raymond Williams to explain cultural analysis informed by material processes. Cultural materialism binds the base and superstructure together more firmly than presented by Marx and early Marxist scholars.

Decolonization the process of an imperial power removing itself from its colonial possession.

Deductive reasoning reasoning that is based on previous thought processes, or premises, rather than on observation or data.

Demography the study of people and populations.

Dependency Theory theory of society that argues that western, capitalist nations keep poorer nations in a state of dependence, unable to rise out of poverty. This relationship of dependence maintains the wealth of capitalist nations and leads to a perpetual state of underdevelopment for poorer nations.

Deskilling resulting from the simplified labor of industrialization, deskilling consists of the process of hiring workers at piece work resulting in inability to participate in entire process of a craft. Connected to proletarianization.

Diachronic changing over time; historical.

Diaspora any group of people dispersed from a homeland.

Dialectic though an ancient framework for understanding knowledge, modern notions of the dialectic begin with Immanuel Kant and G.W.F. Hegel. For historians, the work of Hegel and his discussion of truth obtained through struggle are central. The dialectical model, then, sees progress as a result of the reconciliation of two competing ideas (a thesis exists, struggles with an antithesis and ultimately produces a synthesis). This then becomes the new thesis until the end of history (in Hegelian terms, the Absolute Spirit) is obtained. This theory is an example of a teleological theory.

Difference/différance Derridean term emphasizing the interaction between written and spoken language in determining meaning.

Discourse used by Michel Foucault to develop a theory about the relationship of language to power; discourses are the beliefs, values, "truths" that permeate particular societies and that those societies accept as natural. Discourses themselves are historically specific.

Disjunctures Foucaultian term representing breaks between particular paradigms of any given time and place, periods Foucault calls "epistemes."

Double consciousness W.E.B. Dubois put forth the idea, speaking solely about US society, that African Americans were trapped in a dual identity, on the one hand of being an American, and on the other, of being black in a white society.

Dyad two-sided construct or formula; in this text, used in relation to linguistics.

Economic extraction the harvesting and refinement of raw materials; in this text it refers to the extraction from one area for the economic betterment of another area.

Economism see vulgar Marxism.

empiricism (empirical) views of the world based on observation and experiment.

Epistemological an approach to history that focuses on human perceptions and mental processes as the dominant mode for understanding the past.

Essentialism the declaration that certain physical, mental, or structural characteristics of a group of people are inherent or natural. Tends to reaffirm binary oppositions by imposing qualities onto a person ahistorically.

Eugenics a late nineteenth century philosophy arguing for the improvement of hereditary characteristics of humans. This often took the form of selective breeding, forced sterilization, or antipathy to birth control for certain classes of people.

Événementielle the immediate moment, or history of the event. Used by *Annales* School historians to distinguish between short-term causes of an event and more long-term causes.

Evolutionary socialism a form of socialism that worked to incorporate workers into society slowly through legislation. Contrary to revolutionary socialists who advocated an overthrow, or saw an inevitable decline of capitalism, evolutionary socialists saw capitalism itself as inevitable and worked within the system to improve the lot of workers.

Fabian a follower of a form of evolutionary socialism, predominantly in Great Britain, Fabians fought for inclusion of workers in the democratic process.

Feminism first articulated in the nineteenth century by utopian socialist Charles Fourier who wanted to improve the status of women. As a movement, feminism argues for the equality of women and men in society and politics.

First-wave feminism feminist movement begun in the nineteenth century and moving through the middle of the twentieth century focused on obtaining parliamentary rights for women.

Frankfurt School a school of thought originating in Frankfurt, Germany; the Frankfurt scholars were Marxian scholars who critiqued the entrapments of the modern world. As founders of a body of thought called critical theory, they espoused the importance of social agency and critiqued the economic determinism of other branches of Marxism.

Gaze Foucault used Bentham's framework of the Panopticon and applied it to psychological and medical science. For Foucault, the gaze is at once defining for the object of it (the inmate, the pervert, the child, etc.) as well as the person who is the subject (the gazer, so to speak—the prison guard, the psychiatrist, the parent/educator). Through the gaze, normativity is constructed.

Gender an analytical term that examines the social construction of so-called essential qualities imposed on the sexes. Scholars of gender argue that to understand gender norms, the construct of gender must be explored relationally. Often related the two sexes (male/female) to qualities (masculine/feminine).

Grand narrative (metanarrative) a grand narrative is a narrative, or story, that provides a comprehensive explanation of human experience. Examples of such totalizing narratives include the Enlightenment, which suggests that all humans are capable of rational thought and that society can move in a more rational, just direction; or Marxism, which provides an economic explanation for the human condition. Jean-François Lyotard critiqued the teleology implicit in the grand narrative in his *Postmodern Condition*.

Habitus explored by Pierre Bourdieu throughout his career, *habitus* is everything that makes up the person (attitudes, posturings, voice inflections, and so on). People within societies often take these mannerisms as being natural, but they are in fact socially constructed.

Hegemony Gramscian term noting all-encompassing, overarching power and control of one social group over another.

Historicism the belief that history can provide an effective explanatory model of the world.

Historiography the study of the arguments, methods, and approaches of historians over time and space.

Humanist human centered; concerned with the interests and welfare of humanity.

Hybridity based on the work of Homi Bhabha, hybridity refers to the third space between imperial and colonial migrant identity in which a new identity can be carved. Hybridity is of special importance in discussing diasporic communities.

Ideology A group of ideas, values, conceptual frameworks that reflects the beliefs of particular groups.

Inductive reasoning a form of reasoning that uses observed data to reach conclusions.

June Days an uprising by Parisian workers in 1848. Thousands of people were killed, injured, or exiled as a result of the uprising.

Labor power a Marxian phrase, labor power refers to the workers' capacity to engage in work that is subsequently sold (as wages) to the bourgeoisie. In industrial capitalism, "labor power" is a form of capital.

Linguistic turn in the field of history, the linguistic turn reflects the recognition that language can create meaning for societies. Historians of the linguistic turn also suggest that material processes are socially constructed, and also that language was one way to provide meaning about the past.

Linguistics the study of language, its history, and its structures.

Longue Durée Translated at "long term" or "long duration," this is Fernand Braudel's third component of time; it consists of large-scale, almost imperceptible shifts in structures.

Luddism Named after the mythical "Ned Ludd," luddism was a movement in early nineteenth-century Great Britain to break machinery to stop the incursion of industrial processes in the weaving industry. Often used in contemporary times to refer to someone who dislikes technological change.

Marxism theory that follows the philosophical principles of Karl Marx, notably, emphasis on the role of capital in society, the materialist conception of history, and the relationship of base/superstructure.

Means of production in Marxist terms, the means of production are all of the raw materials, resources, facilities, and labor power necessary for production.

Mentalités the structure of thought of a given society; worldview or value system of a society.

Mestizo South America; a person of mixed race, generally Spanish/Indigenous.

Métropole the imperial center, as opposed to the periphery. Often the capital city of empire.

Microhistory a type of history that provides a detailed study of one region, or even a town, over time.

Models in Braudelian terms, a model is a sample periodization or even conceptualization that the historian tests for accuracy. Using the metaphor of a floating/sinking ship, Braudel argued that models "work" as long as the ship (the concept or the period) "floats." Once it begins to sink, the model is closed.

Monograph a detailed, book-length study of a specific topic.

Negative value defining something by that which it is not. Negative value tends to reinforce binary oppositions.

Négritude postulated in the Caribbean in the 1930s, négritude is an identity movement that declared that black culture was good in and of itself and need not accommodate to the dominant political culture. Négritude, or "blackness," emphasizes shared African heritage of diasporic communities as a means to counteract colonial identities.

Neo-Marxism Marxist scholars who held that Marxist theory connects to historical practice rather than political realities. Neo-Marxists tend to de-emphasize ideas of teleology and revolution prevalent in earlier Marxist thought. The opposite of a vulgar Marxist.

New Europes any place outside Europe whose climatological conditions mirrored those of Europe and therefore enabling the easy transition of people and foodstuffs.

Normativity a Foucaultian term, normativity is part of the nineteenth-century shift in discourses. With the concept of normativity, culture establishes (defines) "normal" (or norms) within a society and medicalizes or otherwise places limits on all that falls outside of those defined norms (deviant).

Objectivity the concept that one can remove bias in observing and explaining events and phenomena.

Ontological a philosophical position that assumes that knowledge is gained through being, experience and existence. Ontology refers to a material exteriority (beingness). So, ontology is the study of what exists.

Other used by Simone de Beauvoir and Edward Said, and consequently employed in feminist and postcolonial research, otherness implies a difference so vast it cannot be known. Otherness as a structure reinforces binaries (man versus woman, white versus black, us versus them, self versus other).

Pacifism the act of resisting the concept of war or violence.

Panopticon designed by British reformer Jeremy Bentham in the late eighteenth century, the Panopticon was a circular prison with cells on the outside walls facing a guard post in the center. Bentham believed that this new structure of a prison would stimulate reform of the inmate as he internalized good behavior. Foucault used the construct of the Panopticon to examine the scientific discourse of the nineteenth century that claimed this "gaze" would have similar reforming (and consequently normalizing) effects in institutions beyond the prison.

Patriarchy a system rule by male authority with emphasis on women's subordination.

Phenomenology often defined simply as the study of things shown, phenomenology as a branch of philosophy is concerned with the ways in which we experience things. Related to ontology and epistemology.

Positivism theory of the world that states that knowledge is based on empirical processes and is therefore always objective and true.

Postcolonial at its most basic definition, postcolonial refers to the moment that decolonization is complete; in critical theory, postcolonial refers to a body of scholarship that approaches the study of newly independent states with a recognition that the residues or echoes of colonialism remain.

Postmodernism a variety of scholars are considered to be "postmodern," but perhaps the term is most synonymous with the French philosopher Jean-François Lyotard, who suggested that modernity as a construct carries with it certain ideals of "progress" and "certainty" that cannot be adequately justified. Postmodernism is interdisciplinary, encompassing art and architecture as well as philosophy and history.

Praxis in Marxist terminology, praxis is the practical application of human ideas, or more simply, putting theory into practice.

Presentism assumptions of the past based on knowledge of the present or present-day ideas.

Proletarianization in Marxist terms, proletarianization is the downward social movement of people as a result of industrial capitalism. As an example, small-scale weavers were "proletarianized" with the onset of the mechanical loom. As skill was no longer a necessary component to creating textiles (refer to deskilling and alienation), craftsmen found themselves pushed into the proletariat.

Proletariat the working class in industrial capitalism.

Queer theory building from but moving beyond gender, queer theory seeks to destabilize gender identity by questioning the existence of fixed sexual identity.

Scholasticism a method of investigation characteristic of medieval scholars by which the writer first sets up a problem in the form of a question and attempts to address that problem.

Scientific racism a form of racism developed in the nineteenth century that used modern science to justify social and political hierarchies based solely on race.

Second-wave feminism after gains of first-wave feminism (suffrage), second-wave feminists reacted to continued social inequalities and turned toward social issues such as rights to divorce, reproductive rights, or workplace equality.

Semiotics semiotics is the study of signs and symbols and their functions within societies.

Serf unfree workers who were tied to the land. In western Europe, through the fourteenth century; in central and eastern Europe, from the seventeenth through the nineteenth century.

Sex referring to reproductive capacity of males and females.

Sign the union of the signifier and signified, and therefore, the words as a whole that we know.

Signified the mental imprint of an idea or object.

Signifier the sound and written image of an idea or object.

Social body the concept that society and culture operate much like a human body. In Foucaultian terms, it refers all of the social structures comprising society.

Structures as conceptualized by Fernand Braudel, structures are constructs that appear never changing (or synchronous) because of their slow movement of change. Examples he provides are capitalism or imperialism.

Subaltern theorized first by Antonio Gramsci in the early twentieth century and then applied by the Subaltern Studies Working Group in the last third of the twentieth century, subaltern refers to the lower echelons of society. Gramsci referred to the working class as the subaltern classes; the Subaltern Studies Group referred to colonized people, particularly in South Asia.

Subaltern Studies represents a historiographic shift in South Asian studies, focusing not on the histories of the imperial center, but on the local histories of South Asia. Led by Ranajit Guha, who founded the Subaltern Studies Working Group, the approach represents an important component of postcolonial studies.

Subjective based on or influenced by personal feelings or positions. The opposite of objective.

Synchronic static and unchanging; ahistorical.

Syntagm in linguistics, a string of words ordered in a particular way. Syntagms differ in each language because of sentence syntax and placement of nouns and verbs.

Teleology a belief in final causes. In history, a teleological view assumes some direction to a final end.

Thick description concept first articulated by the cultural anthropologist Clifford Geertz, thick description works to examine the meaning behind particular actions within a society.

Total history (histoire totale) a type of history, popularized during the first and second generations of the *Annales* School; designed to create a history that was all-encompassing.

Trope any figurative allusion or use of figurative language to convey a point.

Vanguard vanguard was developed by Vladimir Lenin in relation to the direction of revolution in Russia. According to Lenin, a dedicated group of party leaders (or vanguard) was necessary to propel the country to revolution.

Vulgar Marxism use of Marxist analysis in a very simplified way that does not take into account historical complexities. Vulgar Marxists tend to be economic determinists. Sometimes referred to as economism.

FURTHER READING

The books and articles in this section are those we have found helpful not only in researching this book but also in teaching our respective courses. This list is not all encompassing. It is, however, a place to start if you are interested in reading more about the approaches discussed in this book or the theoretical works themselves. Please refer also to our footnotes for some additional reading material.

Chapters 1 & 2

Appleby, Joyce, Lynn Hunt, and Margaret Jacob. *Telling the Truth About History*. New York: Norton, 1995.

Bentley, Michael. *Modern Historiography: An Introduction*. London: Routledge, 1999.

Berger, Stefan et. al., eds. *Writing History: Theory and Practice*. Oxford: Oxford University Press/Arnold Publishers, 2003.

Breisach, Ernst. *Historiography: Ancient, Medieval, and Modern*. Chicago: University of Chicago Press, 1994.

Burke, Peter, ed. *New Perspectives on Historical Writing*. University Park, PA: Pennsylvania State University Press, 2001.

Carr, Edward Hallett. *What Is History?* New York: Knopf, 1962.

Evans, Richard J. *In Defense of History*. New York: W.W. Norton Company, 2000.

Gilderhus, Mark T. *History and Historians: A Historiographical Introduction*. 6th ed. Upper Saddle River, NJ: Prentice Hall, 2006.

Hunt, Lynn, ed. *The New Cultural History*. Berkeley: University of California Press, 1989.

Munslow, Alan. *The Routledge Companion to Historical Studies*. London: Routledge, 2000.

Novick, Peter. *That Noble Dream: The "Objectivity Question" and the American Historical Profession*. Cambridge: Cambridge University Press, 1988.

Tosh, John. *The Pursuit of History: Aims, Methods, and New Directions in the Study of Modern History*. New York: Longman, 1991.

Chapter 3

Abelove, Henry, Betsy Blackmar, Peter Dimock, and Jonathan Schneer. *Visions of History: Interviews*. New York: Pantheon Books, 1983.

Fleischer, Helmut. *Marxism and History*. London: Allen Lane Publishers, 1973.

Gramsci, Antonio. *Selections from the Prison Notebooks*. New York: International Publishers, 1971.

Heilbroner, Robert L. *The Worldly Philosophers: The Lives, Times and Ideas of the Great Economic Thinkers*. 7th ed. New York: Touchstone Press, 1999.

Hill, Christopher. *The English Revolution, 1640: An Essay*. London: Lawrence & Wishart, Ltd., 1955.

Hobsbawm, Eric J. *Industry and Empire: An Economic History of Britain, 1750 to the Present Day*. New York: Pantheon Books, 1968.

_____. *On History*. New York: New Press, 1997.

Soboul, Albert. *The Parisian Sans-Culottes and the French Revolution, 1793-4*. Oxford: Clarendon Press, 1964.

_____. *A Short History of the French Revolution, 1789-1799*. Translated by Geoffrey Symcox. Berkeley: University of California Press, 1977.

Tucker, Robert C., ed. *The Marx-Engels Reader*. New York: W.W. Norton, 1978.

Chapter 4

Bloch, Marc. *Feudal Society*. Translated by L.A. Manyon. Chicago: University of Chicago Press, 1961.

_____. *The Historian's Craft*. Introduction by Joseph R. Strayer. Translated by Peter Putnam. New York: Vintage Books, 1964.

Braudel, Fernand. *Civilization and Capitalism, 15th-18th Century: The Structures of Everyday Life*. Translated by Siân Reynolds. Berkeley: University of California Press, 1992.

_____. *The Mediterranean and the Mediterranean World in the Age of Philip II*. Translated by Siân Reynolds. New York: Harper & Row, 1972.

_____. *On History*. Translated by Sarah Matthews. Chicago: University of Chicago Press, 1982.

_____. "Personal Testimony." *Journal of Modern History* 44/4 (December 1972): 448–467.

Burguière, André. *The Annales School: An Intellectual History*. Translated from the French by Jane Marie Todd. Ithaca, NY: Cornell University Press, 2009.

Chartier, Roger. *The Cultural Origins of the French Revolution*. Translated by Lydia G. Cochrane. Durham, NC: Duke University Press, 1991.

Daileader, Philip and Philip Whalen, eds. *French Historians, 1900–2000: New Historical Writings in Twentieth-Century France*. Oxford, UK: Blackwell Publishing, 2010.

Goubert, Pierre. *The French Peasantry in the Seventeenth Century.* Translated by Ian Patterson. Cambridge: Cambridge University Press, 1986.

Hunt, Lynn. "French History in the Last Twenty Years: The Rise and Fall of the *Annales* Paradigm." *Journal of Contemporary History* 21 (1986): 209–224.

Le Roy Ladurie, Emmanuel. *Montaillou: The Promised Land of Error.* Translated by Barbara Bray. New York: G. Braziller, 1978.

_____. *The Peasants of Languedoc.* Translated and with an Introduction by John Day. Urbana, IL: University of Illinois Press, 1974.

Stoianovich, Traian. *French Historical Method: The Annales Paradigm.* Ithaca, NY: Cornell University Press, 1976.

Chapter 5

Adorno, Theodore and Rolf Tiederman. *History and Freedom: Lectures, 1964–1965.* New York: Polity Press, 2006.

Althusser, Louis. *For Marx.* London: Verso Press, 1969.

Calhoun, Craig, ed. *Habermas and the Public Sphere.* Cambridge, MA: MIT Press, 1993.

Frank, Andre Gunder. *Latin America: Underdevelopment or Revolution: Essays on the Development of Underdevelopment and the Immediate Enemy.* New York: Monthly Review Press, 1969.

_____. *ReOrient: Global Economy in the Asian Age.* Berkeley: University of California Press, 1998.

Gutman, Herbert. *Work, Culture, and Society in Industrializing America: Essays in American Working-Class and Social History.* New York: Knopf, 1978.

Habermas, Jürgen. *The Philosophical Discourse of Modernity: Twelve Lectures.* Translated by Frederick G. Lawrence. Cambridge, MA: MIT Press, 1987.

_____. *Theory and Practice.* Translated by John Viertel. Boston: Beacon Press, 1973.

Hall, Stuart. "Life and Times of the First New Left." *New Left Review* no. 61 (2010): 177–196.

Marcuse, Herbert. *Hegel's Ontology and the Theory of Historicity.* Translated by Seyla Benhabib. Cambridge, MA: MIT Press, 1987.

_____. *One Dimensional Man: Studies in the Ideology of Advanced Industrial Society.* Boston: Beacon Press, 1991.

Thompson, E. P. *Customs in Common: Studies in Traditional Popular Culture.* New York: The New Press, 1993.

_____. *The Making of the English Working Class.* New York: Pantheon Books, 1963.

_____. *The Poverty of Theory and Other Essays.* Monthly Review, 1980.

Wallerstein, Immanuel et. al., eds. *The Capitalist World-Economy: Essays.* Cambridge: Cambridge University Press, 1979.

_____. *Geopolitics and Geoculture: Essays on the Changing World-System.* Cambridge: Cambridge University Press, 1991.

Chapter 6

Anderson, David and Richard Grove, eds. *Conservation in Africa: People, Policies, and Practice.* Cambridge: Cambridge University Press, 1987.

Bentley, Jeremy. "Hemispheric Integration, 500-1500 C.E." *Journal of World History* 9/2 (1998): 237–254.

Burke III, Edmund and Kenneth Pomeranz, eds. *The Environment and World History.* Berkeley: University of California Press, 2009.

Christian, David. *Maps of Time: An Introduction to Big History.* Berkeley: University of California Press, 2004.

Crosby, Alfred. *Ecological Imperialism: The Biological Expansion of Europe, 900-1900.* Cambridge: Cambridge University Press, 1986.

_____. *The Columbian Exchange: Biological and Cultural Consequences of 1492.* Westport, CT: Greenwood Publishing, 1972.

Grove, Richard H. *Green Imperialism: Colonial Expansion, Tropical Island Edens and the Origin of Environmentalism, 1600-1860.* Cambridge: Cambridge University Press, 1996.

Hughes, Donald J. *What is Environmental History?* Cambridge, UK: Polity Press, 2006.

McNeill, John R. *Something New Under the Sun: An Environmental History of the Twentieth-Century World.* New York: W.W. Norton, 2001.

Pomeranz, Kenneth. *The Great Divergence: Europe, China and the Making of the Modern World Economy.* Princeton: Princeton University Press, 2000.

Chapter 7

Choat, Simon. *Marx Through Post-structuralism: Lyotard, Derrida, Foucault, Deleuze.* New York: Continuum Press, 2010.

Derrida, Jacques. *Writing and Difference.* Translated with An Introduction and Additional Notes by Alan Bass. Chicago: University of Chicago Press, 1978.

_____. *Of Grammatology.* Translated by Gayatri Chakravorty Spivak. Baltimore: Johns Hopkins University Press, 1997.

Foucault, Michel. *The Archaeology of Knowledge.* New York: Pantheon Books, 1972.

_____. *Discipline and Punish: The Birth of the Prison.* New York: Pantheon Books, 1977.

_____. *The History of Sexuality: Volume 1, An Introduction.* New York: Vintage, 1978.

_____. *The Order of Things: An Archaeology of the Human Sciences.* New York: Pantheon Books, 1971.

Lacan, Jacques. *Écrits: A Selection.* Translated by Bruce Fink. New York: Norton, 1977.

Lyotard, Jean-François. *The Postmodern Condition: A Report on Knowledge.* Translated by Geoff Bennington and Brian Massumi. Foreword by Fredric Jameson. Minneapolis: University of Minnesota Press, 1984.

Rabinow, Paul, ed. *The Foucault Reader*. New York: Random House, 1984.

Saussure, Ferdinand de. *Course in General Linguistics*. Translated by Albert Riedlinger. Chicago: Open Court Publishing, 1983.

Chapter 8

Benjamin, Walter. *Illuminations: Essays and Reflections*. Edited and with an Introduction by Hannah Arendt. Translated by Harry Zohn. New York: Schocken Books, 1968.

Bourdieu, Pierre. *Distinction: A Social Critique of the Judgment of Taste*. Translated and Edited by R. Nice. Stanford: Stanford University Press, 1990.

_____. *The Logic of Practice*. Stanford: Stanford University Press, 1992.

Certeau, Michel de. *The Practice of Everyday Life*. Translated by Steven F. Rendall. Berkeley: University of California Press, 1984.

Chartier, Roger. *Cultural History: Between Practices and Representations*. Ithaca, NY: Cornell University Press, 1988.

Davis, Natalie. *Fiction in the Archives: Pardon Tales and their Tellers in Sixteenth-Century France*. Stanford: Stanford University Press, 1989.

Geertz, Clifford. *The Interpretation of Cultures: Selected Essays*. New York: Basic Books, 1973.

Ginzburg, Carlo. *The Cheese and the Worms: The Cosmos of a Sixteenth-Century Miller*. New York: Penguin Books, 1982.

Hall, Stuart and Tony Jefferson, eds. *Resistance Through Rituals: Youth Subcultures in Post-War Britain*. New York: HarperCollins Academic, 1991.

Hoggart, Richard. *The Uses of Literacy: Changing Patterns in English Mass Culture*. Boston: Beacon Press, 1961.

Hunt, Lynn, ed., *The New Cultural History*. Berkeley: University of California Press, 1989.

Lévi-Strauss, Claude. *Myth and Meaning*. London: Routledge and Kegan Paul, 1978.

_____. *Structural Anthropology*. Translated by Claire Jacobson and Brooke Grundfest. New York: Basic Books, 1963.

_____. *The Savage Mind*. Chicago: University of Chicago Press, 1966.

Morley, David and Kuan-Hsing Chen, eds. *Stuart Hall: Critical Dialogues in Cultural Studies*. London: Routledge, 1996.

Ogborn, Miles. *Spaces of Modernity: London's Geographies, 1680-1780*. New York: The Guilford Press, 1998.

Sahlins, Marshall. *Culture and Practical Reason*. Chicago: University of Chicago Press, 1976.

Stedman Jones, Gareth. *Languages of Class: Studies in English Working Class History, 1832-1982*. Cambridge: Cambridge University Press, 1983.

Williams, Raymond. *Problems in Materialism and Culture*. London: NLB, 1980.

_____. *Marxism and Literature*. Oxford: Oxford University Press, 1977.

_____. *Culture and Materialism: Selected Essays*. London: Verso, 1980.

Chapter 9

Beauvoir, Simone de. *The Second Sex*. Translated and edited by H.M. Parshley. New York: Knopf, 1952.

Butler, Judith. *Bodies that Matter: On the Discursive Limits of Sex*. London: Routledge, 1993.

_____. *Psychic Life of Power: Theories in Subjection*. Stanford: Stanford University Press, 1997.

Chinchilla, Norma Stoltz. "Marxism, Feminism, and the Struggle for Democracy in Latin America." *Gender and Society* 5/3 (1991): 291–310.

Cott, Nancy. *The Bonds of Womanhood: "Woman's Sphere" in New England, 1780-1835*. New Haven, CT: Yale University Press, 1977.

Hartmann, Heidi. "The Unhappy Marriage of Marxism and Feminism: Towards a More Progressive Union." In A. Jaggar and P. Rothenberg, eds., *Feminist Frameworks*. 3rd ed. Boston: McGraw-Hill, 1993.

Hartmann, Heidi and Claire Goldberg Moses, eds. *U.S. Women in Struggle: A Feminist Studies Anthology*. Urbana: University of Illinois Press, 1995.

Houlbrook, Matt. *Queer London: Perils and Pleasures in the Sexual Metropolis 1918-1957*. Chicago: University of Chicago Press, 2005.

Probyn, Elspeth. *Sexing the Self: Gendered Positions in Cultural Studies*. London: Routledge, 1993.

Ryan, Mary. *Sex and Class in Women's History*. London: Routledge and Kegan Paul, 1983.

Scott, Joan Wallach. *Gender and the Politics of History*. New York: Columbia University Press, 1999.

Sedgwick, Eve Kosofsky. *Epistemology of the Closet*. Berkeley: University of California Press, 1990.

Tilly, Louise. "Gender, Women's History, and Social History." *Social Science History* 13/4 (Winter 1989): 439–462.

Chapter 10

Ahluwalia, Pal. *Politics and Postcolonial Theory: African Inflections*. London: Routledge, 2001.

Anderson, Benedict. *Imagined Communities: Reflections on the Origin and Spread of Nationalism*. London: Verso Press, 1991.

Ashcroft, Bill, Gareth Griffiths, and Helen Tiffen. *The Empire Writes Back: Theory and Practice in Post-Colonial Literatures*. 2nd ed. New York: Routledge, 2002.

Bhabha, Homi. *The Location of Culture*. New York: Routledge, 1994.

Chakrabarty, Dipesh. *Provincializing Europe: Postcolonial Thought and Historical Difference*. Princeton: Princeton University Press, 2001.

Chaturvedi, Vinayek. *Mapping Subaltern Studies and the Postcolonial.* London: Verso Press, 2000.

Fanon, Frantz. *Black Skin, White Masks.* A New Edition. Translated from the French by Richard Philcox. Foreword by Kwame Anthony Appiah. New York: Grove Press, 2008.

_____. *Wretched of the Earth.* Preface by Jean-Paul Sartre. Translated by Constance Farrington. New York: Grove Press, 1963.

Gilroy, Paul. *The Black Atlantic: Modernity and Double Consciousness.* Cambridge, MA: Harvard University Press, 1993.

_____. *"There Ain't No Black in the Union Jack": The Cultural Politics of Race and Nation.* Chicago: University of Chicago Press, 1991.

Guha, Ranajit, ed. *Subaltern Studies No. 1: Writings on South Asian History and Society.* Delhi: Oxford University Press, 1982.

_____. *Dominance Without Hegemony: History and Power in Colonial India.* Cambridge, MA: Harvard University Press, 1997.

_____. *Elementary Aspects of Peasant Insurgency in Colonial India.* Oxford: Oxford University Press, 1983.

Mallon, Florencia E. "The Promise and Dilemma of Subaltern Studies: Perspectives from Latin American History." *American Historical Review* 99/5 (1994): 1491–1515.

Prakash, Gyan. "Subaltern Studies as Postcolonial Criticism." *American Historical Review* 99/5 (1994): 1475–1490.

Said, Edward. *Orientalism.* New York: Random House, 1979.

Spivak, Gayatri, Chakravorty. *A Critique of Postcolonial Reason: Toward a History of the Vanishing Present.* Cambridge, MA: Harvard University Press, 1999.

INDEX

A

a priori/a posteriori, 14
Adorno, Theodore, 55, 56, 115
Ahluwalia, Pal, 153
Algerian War, 97, 113
alienation, 21, 50, 56, 86
Alltagsgeschichte, 52
Anderson, Benedict, 3, 150
Annales d'Histoire Economique et Sociale, 33, 34
Annales School, 6, 15, 33–47, 57, 58, 68, 72, 112, 114, 115, 132
Annalistes, 33, 35, 36, 37, 39, 118
Antarctica, 73
anthropology, influence on historical profession, 2, 15, 33, 69, 97, 98, 112, 113, 114, 117
Aquinas, Thomas, 9, 10

B

Bacon, Francis, 2, 8, 10, 11, 14, 15
Bali, in the work of Clifford Geertz, 113
Bancroft, George, 12, 13, 14, 15
Bangladesh Liberation War, 154
base/superstructure
    in Classical Marxism, 57, 116
    in the work of Raymond Williams, 116
Beard, Charles and Mary, 53
Beatniks, 54
Beauvoir, Simone de, 131, 135, 147
Becker, Carl, 15, 34
Benjamin, Walter, 115
Bentham, Jeremy, 100
Bermingham, Ann, 74
Bhabha, Homi, 148, 149, 152
Big History, 75, 114
binary oppositions, 97, 99, 100, 102, 103, 114, 115, 134, 136, 151
bio-power, 100
Birmingham School, 53, 115, 116
Black Skin, White Masks, 147
Blassingame, John, 3, 4
Bloch, Marc, 34–35, 36, 37, 38, 39, 40, 52, 114
borderlands, 72, 73, 74, 152
Bourdieu, Pierre, 112, 113, 114, 117
bourgeois revolution, 24, 25, 154
bourgeoisie, 20, 21, 22, 52, 53, 56, 102, 118, 154, 155, 156, 157, 162
Braudel, Fernand, 33, 34–37, 38, 39, 40, 41, 57, 68
British Museum, 106–110

British Nationality Act, 153
Brody, David, 54
Bryant, Jack, 26–27
Bunyan, John, 26, 27–31
Burke III, Edmund, 73
Butler, Judith, 134
Butterfield, Herbert, 15

C

Cambridge School, 149
Camus, Albert, 98
Capital, 20, 21
Carson, Rachel, 69, 71
caudillo, 13
Centre for Contemporary Cultural Studies (CCCS), 53, 115
Chakrabarty, Dipesh, 147, 153
Chaos Theory, 7
Charles X, 18
Chartier, Roger, 38–40, 114
Chartism, 18, 135
Chatterjee, Partha, 150, 154
Chinese Revolution, 17
Chomsky, Noam, 98
Christian, David, 75
Cicero, Marcus Tullius, 9, 10
Cixous, Hélène, 101
Clark, Alice, 131
Clark, Anna, 135
Clements, Andrew, 110. *See also Frindle*
Colicchio, Tom, 101
colonization, 47, 145, 146, 148
Columbian Exchange, 72, 73
Commons, John R., 54
Communist International (Comintern), 56
Comte, Auguste, 11, 14, 20
conjoncture, 36
Consensus history, 53, 54
Constitutional Charter (France), 18
Copernicus, Nicolas, 10
creoleness, 148, 149, 151
Critical Theory, 55, 102, 113
Cronon, William, 68, 70, 71
Crosby, Alfred, 69, 72, 73
Cubism, 97
cultural capital, 114

cultural materialism, 116
Culture and Practical Reason, 113
"Culture is Ordinary", 116
Cyborg Theory, 7

D
Dadaism, 97
Darnton, Robert, 119, 120, 121
Darwin, Charles, 11, 12, 22, 146
Davis, David Brion, 58
Davis, Mike, 25, 72
Davis, Natalie Zemon, 39, 129, 130
de Gouges, Olympes, 136
Dean, Warren, 73–74
decolonization, 145, 146, 153
deconstruction, 95–110, 114, 134, 135, 150
deductive reasoning, 9, 10
Deleuze, Gilles, 7
demography, 6
dependency theory, 57–58
Derrida, Jacques, 101, 147, 149
deskilling, 18
diachronic, 36, 37, 38, 96
dialectic, 19, 55
Diamond, Jared, 69
diaspora, 148, 154
difference/différance, in Derrida's work, 101
discourse, 3, 25, 54, 59, 79, 97, 99, 100, 101, 102, 103,
    104, 106, 108, 109, 118, 135, 147, 151
disjunctures, 98
Domesticity, Cult of, 134
double consciousness, 151
Dubois, W.E.B., 150, 153
Durkheim, Emile, 34, 35
Dutton, Michael, 119
dyad, 96

E
Eagleton, Terry, 116
École Pratique des Hautes Études, 37, 38, 96
economic extraction, 146
economism, 23
Empire Writes Back, 148
empirical, 2, 14, 116, 117
Engels, Friedrich, 17, 18
environmental history, 6, 34, 68–90
epistemology/epistemological, 6, 19, 70, 74, 95, 135, 136
essentialism, 98, 135, 136, 151
eugenics/eugenicist, 12
événementielle, 36
Evolutionary Socialism, 22
Existentialism, 98

F
Fanon, Franz, 146, 147, 148, 151, 153, 154
Febvre, Lucien, 34, 36, 39, 43, 114

Feminism, 130–131, 137
    1st Wave, 130
    2nd Wave, 131
Fernand Braudel Center for the Study of Economics,
    Historical Systems, and Civilizations, 40, 57
Feuerbach, Ludwig, 19, 20
Finney, Charles Grandison, 21
Fisher, Colin, 72
Foucault, Michel, 3, 98, 102, 134, 147
Fourier, Charles, 22, 130
Frank, Andre Gunder, 57
Frankfurt School, 55, 56, 57, 58, 102, 115
Friedan, Betty, 131
Frindle, 95. *See also* Clements, Andrew
Frontier Thesis, 69–70. *See also* Turner, Frederick Jackson
Fukuzawa, Yukichi, 14

G
Gadamer, Hans Georg, 7
Gadgil, Madhav, 73
Gaimster, David, 106
Galilei, Galileo, 10
gaze, 7, 34, 37, 44, 99, 100, 102, 103, 106, 119
Geertz, Clifford, 112, 113, 114, 117
Gender
    as distinct from sex, 103, 134
    as feminist theory, 135, 136
Genovese, Eugene, 59
German Communist League, 18
Giles-Vernick, Tamara, 74
Gilroy, Paul, 152
Ginzburg, Carlo, 39, 118
Glorious Revolution (Britain, 1688), 24, 27
Gorender, Jacob, 25
Goubert, Pierre, 38
Gramsci, Antonio, 56, 57, 58, 116, 145
grand narrative, 98, 102, 117, 147
Great Reform Act, 53
Greenblatt, Stephen, 114
Greer, Germaine, 131
Grove, Richard, 71, 72, 75
Guattari, Félix, 7
Guha, Ramachandra, 73
Guha, Ranajit, 149, 150
Gunnar, Myrdal, 4
Guthrie, Woody, 26
Gutman, Herbert, 55

H
Habermas, Jürgen, 102
Habib, Irfan, 25
habitus, 114
Hall, Catherine, 132
Hall, Stuart, 51, 52, 115, 116, 117, 152
Haraway, Donna, 7

harki, 153
Hartmann, Heidi, 133
Hayles, N. Katherine, 7. *See also* Chaos Theory
Hegel, G.W.F., 11, 19
hegemony, 54, 56, 57, 58, 59, 78, 97, 116, 148, 155
heliocentrism, 10
Herodotus, 8, 9
Hill, Christopher, 24, 25, 26, 27, 52
histoire immobile, 38
Histoire Totale (total history), 34–35
Historian's Craft, 14, 36
historical materialism, 5–6
historicism, 14, 114, 117
historiography, 1, 3, 24, 25, 26, 57, 73, 74, 134, 137, 149, 150
history from below, 6, 25, 52, 54, 58, 59, 60, 115, 118, 134, 149, 150
Hobsbawm, Eric, 17, 24, 25, 51, 52, 115
Hofstadter, Richard, 53
Hoggart, Richard, 52, 53, 115
Horkheimer, Max, 55
Horner, Arthur, 165
hospitality, as deconstruction, 101
Houlbrook, Matt, 136
humanism/humanist, 9
Hunt, Lynn, 117, 118
Hutton, William, 59, 61–65
hybridity, 148, 149, 151, 152, 154

I

I Love Lucy, 129
ideology, 12, 15, 22, 54, 56, 57, 59, 80–83, 99, 141, 142, 154, 155, 157, 159, 162
Ignatieff, Michael, 103
Imagined Communities, 150
imperialism, 12, 37, 145–146, 155, 156, 160, 162
Indianism, 153
inductive reasoning, 10
Institute for Social Research, 55
Iron Chef, 100, 102

J

Jacobson, Matthew Frye, 151
Jong, Erica, 131
Journal of Social History, 52
Joyce, Patrick, 95, 117
June Days (France), 19

K

Kelly, Catriona, 117
Khrushchev, Nikita, 25
Kurlansky, Mark, 73

L

labor power, 18, 20, 133
Labrousse, Ernest, 38, 43, 46
Lawrence Stone, 2, 117

Le Roy Ladurie, Emmanuel, 37–38, 40, 72
Lefebvre, Georges, 25
Lerner, Gerda, 133
Lévi-Strauss, Claude, 97, 98, 112
Levine, Philippa, 152, 153
liberal, 19
linguistic turn, 117–118, 134, 136
linguistics, 2, 95, 96, 98, 101, 114, 117
Linnaeus, Carl, 69
Lockridge, Kenneth, 40
longue durée, 36, 37, 38, 40, 41, 42, 58, 69–70, 75
Louis XVIII, 18
Luddites, 18
Lyotard, Jean-François, 98

M

Macaulay, Lord Thomas, 13, 15
Machiavelli, Niccolo, 10
Madonna, 5
Making of the English Working Class, 52, 53, 55
Mallon, Florencia, 150
manhood/masculinity, 18, 136, 137, 139
Manifesto of the Communist Party, 19, 20
Marcuse, Herbert, 56, 115, 116
Martin, Biddy, 135
Marx, Karl, 3, 11, 17–24, 52, 53, 56, 68, 113, 115, 130, 147
materialism, 5–6, 24, 113, 116, 119, 137
Maudling, Reginald, 154
McCann, Bryan, 119
McCann, James, 74
McCarthyism, 53, 54
McNeill, John R., 70, 71, 73
means of production, 20, 21
Medici, Cosimo de, 9
Mediterranean and the Mediterranean World in the Age of Philip II, The, 36, 37, 42, 69
Menocchio, 118. *See also* Ginzburg, Carlo
mentalités, 15, 34, 35, 36, 37, 38–40, 72, 114, 118
Merchant, Carolyn, 72
mestizo, 13
metanarrative, 98
métropole, 57, 58, 73, 147, 148
microhistory, 6, 34, 38, 39, 118
Millet, Kate, 133
mode of production, 20, 25, 57
models, 9, 13, 24, 26, 34, 37, 40, 53, 86, 90, 113, 135
Montgomery, David, 54, 55, 58
Moynihan Report, 55
Ms. Magazine, 131
Mullard, Chris, 148

N

Nash, Roderick, 70–72
National Organization for Women (NOW), 131
natural history, 69–71

Nazi-Soviet Non-Aggression Treaty, 53
negative value, 96, 98, 99, 100
négritude, 151, 153, 154
Neo-Marxism, 24
Neue Rheinische Zeitung, 17, 18
New Europes, 13
New Historicism, 114, 117
New Labor History, 54
New Left,
   in Britain, 51–53
   influences on, 58
   in the United States, 53–55
New Left Review, 25, 51, 116, 118
Newgate Prison, 103
normativity, 99–100, 103, 136
Novick, Peter, 8, 15
Nugent, Daniel, 150

O
objectivity, 8, 9, 14–16, 97, 114
Of Grammatology, 101, 149
Old Hegelians/Young Hegelians, 19, 20
ontology/ontological, 5, 15, 19, 24, 69, 70, 71, 74, 123, 135, 148
Ordinary's Account, 103–106
Orientalism, 147, 148
other(ness), 136, 147, 154
Owen, Robert, 22

P
pacifism, 51
Painter, Nell Irvin, 134
Panopticon, 99, 100, 103
patrial, 153, 154
patriarchy, 87, 131, 133, 135, 137, 142
Pearson, Karl, 12, 14
Perkin, Harold, 58
Perlman, Selig, 54, 55
Peterloo Massacre, 18
Petrarch, 10
phenomenology, 19
Philip II (Spain), 37
Phillips, U. B., 3, 4
Pilgrim's Progress, 26, 27–31
Pinkus, Mrs. Walter, 59–61, 137, 138
Pliny the Elder, 69
Pomeranz, Kenneth, 73
Poor Laws, 52, 100
Poor Theory, 7
positivism, 11
postcolonial, 6, 72, 146–154
postmodernism, 6, 15, 97–98, 102, 112, 115, 117, 135
poststructuralism, 70, 95–110, 114, 119, 134, 135
Powell, Enoch, 152, 154
power, in Foucault's works, 98, 99, 103, 134
Prakash, Gyan, 145, 149

praxis, 20
presentism, 15, 103
Probyn, Elspeth, 135
professionalization of history, 8–16
proletariat, 20, 22, 56, 147, 149
Pyne, Stephen, 73

Q
quantitative history, 34, 38
Queer Theory, 6, 136–137

R
Radical History Review, 52
Renaissance, 9, 10, 114
resignification, 134
Revolution of 1830 (France), 18
Rite of Spring, 97. *See also*, Stravinsky, Igor
"Rivers of Blood" Speech, 152
Roediger, David, 151
Rorty, Richard, 117
Rowbotham, Sheila, 132
Rushdie, Salman, 148
Russian Revolution, 17, 56

S
Sahlins, Marshall, 112, 113, 114
Said, Edward, 147, 148, 152, 154
Sarkar, Tanika, 138
Sarmiento, Domingo Faustino, 13, 14
Sartre, Jean-Paul, 98
Saussure, Fernand de, 96–98, 101
Savage Mind, 97
scholasticism, 9
Scientific Racism, 146
Scientific Revolution, 10, 11
Sedgwick, Eve, 136
Sedrez, Lise, 74
serf, 22, 35
semiotics, 95, 98
Shepard, Todd, 153
sign, 96, 101, 134
signifier/signified, 96, 101
Silverblatt, Irene, 153
Slavery, United States, historiography of, 3–4
Soboul, Albert, 25
social body, 99–100
Social History, 6, 34, 35, 40, 50–65, 132, 133, 137, 149
Socialism
   Fabian, 133
   Utopian, 22
Spivak, Gayatri Chakravorty, 149, 150
Stalin, Josef, 25
Stansell, Christine, 133
Stedman Jones, Gareth, 117–118, 133
Steinem, Gloria, 131

Stojanovich, Traian, 33
Stone, Lawrence, 2, 117
Strasser, Ulrike, 137
Stravinsky, Igor, 97. *See also Rite of Spring*
stream-of-consciousness, 97
structures, in Braudel's work, 37, 40
Stuard, Susan Mosher, 132
Student Nonviolent Coordinating Committee, 58
Styles, John, 59, 60, 61
Subaltern Studies, 145–163
subjective, 9, 15, 16, 126
suffrage, 18, 99, 130, 131, 141
Suleri, Sara, 149
Surrealism, 97
suttee (sati), 138, 139, 140, 142
synchronic, 36, 96, 97
syntagm, 96, 102

T
teleology/teleological, 10, 12, 19, 21, 23, 51, 52, 56, 102, 116
thick description, 113, 114
Thompson, E. P., 1, 2, 24, 50, 51–55, 58, 60, 63, 65, 112, 115, 117
Thorsheim, Peter, 74
Thucydides, 8–10
Tilly, Louise, 132
Tinsman, Heidi, 137
Title IX, 131
trope, 114, 133, 153
Turner, Frederick Jackson, 70, 71. *See also* Frontier Thesis

V
vanguard, 22, 136, 147
Voltaire, 10–11
vulgar Marxism, 23

W
Wallerstein, Immanuel, 57, 58
Watches and timepieces, 61–65
Webb, Sidney and Beatrice, 52
Webb, Walter Prescott, 70
wheat, 75–78
Whig/Tory, 13, 15
Whiggish history/Whiggism, 15, 145, 153
whiteness, as a category of historical analysis, 151–153
Wiesner-Hanks, Merry, 137
Williams, Raymond, 52, 53, 112, 115, 116, 117
Wilson, Kathleen, 152
Wisconsin School, 54
World History, 34, 47, 69, 72, 73, 75, 137
World History Association, 72
World Systems Theory, 57–58
Worster, Donald, 70–72
Wretched of the Earth, 147

Z
Zimbabwe, 146
Zinn, Howard, 25, 58
Žižek, Slavoj, 7